TRAILS GUIDE

TO

FRONT RANGE COLORADO

DENVER TO PIKES PEAK

Foreword by Governor Bill Owens

Edition 6.5 (Third Version of 6th Edition)

by

Zoltan Malocsay

Squeezy Press

With Digital Maps from Mike Henry's CD-Rom
Companion from Ghost Town Software

Printed in the United Stares of America

ISBN: 0-9629250-4-7

Cover Design by Phil Barber and Diane Russelavage

Cover photography by Andy de Naray (Crystal Reservoir) and Bill Bevington (Roxborough State Park)

Additional art by Marcia Phillips

First Edition published by the Pikes Peak Area Council of Governments in 1980 as the *Hiker's Guide to Trails in the Pikes Peak Region,* Second and Third Editions were called: *Hiker's Guide--Pikes Peak and South Park,* Century One Press. Fourth and Fifth Editions were called *Trails Guide To Pikes Peak Country with a Foreword by Governor Roy Romer*, Squeezy Press.

Published by Squeezy Press, Crystal Park, Manitou Springs, Colorado 80829

The majority of the black-and-white photos in this book are by Mike Henry and come from his CD-ROM companion (where they appear in color); most of the others are by the author, with two courtesy of the National Park Service, two from Jefferson County Open Space Parks, one from Mueller State Park, one from Andy de Naray, one from Sue Mischka and another from Dick Bratton.

Outdoor sports have inherent dangers and no guide can substitute for sound judgement. Good decision making is the responsibility of the individual. Do not trespass. Pack it in; pack it out. Take only photos; leave only tracks.

Foreword—A Message from Governor Bill Owens

Greetings:

Colorado is a glorious place to live and play. Just look around and you will see majestic peaks, clear streams and sparkling lakes, grassy meadows and remote forests, all belonging to the citizens of our state. Unlike some places in the world, the best scenery in Colorado belongs to you and your family. Too often we think of ourselves as "visitors" in these places, when in fact we are owners.

With a sense of ownership in our state's lands and waters comes a sense of pride. That pride urges us to protect and preserve those areas that we have set aside from necessary development, and urges us to keep those special places as we found them, so that future generations can enjoy them as we have.

As Governor I take great pride in the wealth of inexpensive recreation available to our citizens and to our guests from around the world. The more you experience the natural beauty of Colorado, the more you discover what a treasure we all have in our own backyards. Ours is not a land that disappoints.

Sincerely,

Bill Owens, Governor

Bill Owens
Governor

Why You Need This Guide

So we get to the trailhead and it's gone! Moved or closed? So we go to call, but the government phone number no longer works. When we get the new number, personnel has changed and nobody knows!

And so it goes. Trails open and close. Rules, routes, trailheads, parking, road directions, phone numbers, hours, fees and personnel change here and there, so we scramble to keep up. At least YOU get the benefit of hearing it all from us, instead of wasting your weekends finding out for yourselves.

Change is generally unwelcome in our wilderness. We practice Minimum Impact, erasing all signs of our passing through the woods, just to keep our beloved mountains unchanged, but change goes on anyway. For a generation now, we've labored with love to record, negotiate and advance positive change in our area. You get the benefit of that, but do you know who else benefits?

Everybody from government agencies to Search and Rescue uses this guide. The reason is simple: We've really been there, and we submit our work to the many authorities involved for approval.

Our last revision of the Sixth Edition probably should have been called the Seventh. Too late now, but since this is only an updated reprint of that second version, we don't want to trick old friends into thinking this is an entirely new edition. That's why we're calling it Edition 6.5. But as soon as we go to press, more changes are bound to occur. We keep trying.

Our maps are courtesy of Mike Henry of Ghost Town Software, publisher of the CD-Rom companion distributed by Squeezy Press.

Wait 'till you see how these CD maps print out in color on your PC! The CD puts us (and you) in total control, letting us all customize our printouts, even changing contour intervals. This is a digital, color map of a huge region that we can fly around like aliens, zooming down from a view 50 miles wide to only one mile wide, spying on the scenery by calling up color pictures of what it's like down there. And, of course, the CD also has road directions and trail descriptions, so you can print up just the pages you need. Still, I hope you'll continue to enjoy using the book as much as I enjoy updating it.

If you'd like to photocopy a few pages, rather than carrying the book, just show this page to the folks at the copy shop. So long as you're doing it just for your own peresonal use and not for publication or sale, it's okay by me and I grant you permission. But if you want to do this very often, it's actually cheaper to tear up the book and buy another. Hope you have fun!

—Zoltan, Your Guide to Public Real Estate

TABLE OF CONTENTS

TRAIL DESCRIPTIONS

*NOTE: DEER CREEK NEAR BAILEY IS NOT TO BE CON-
FUSED WITH JEFFCO'S DEER CREEK CANYON PARK*

This book is dedicated to Dolores the Wonder Wife

Happy 31st Anniversary!

ACKNOWLEDGMENTS

Many people, both in and out of government, helped to make this book so accurate, not as a favor to the author, but as a public service to all those who enjoy the trails of Front Range Colorado.

Federal Level—For the Pike National Forest: Steve Priest, Rick and Linda Ellsworth, Frank Landis, Sharon Kyhl, Jerry Davis, Neal Weirbach, Mike Sugaski, Dan Lovato, Tim Garcia and Dianna Barney. For the National Park Service: Jo Beckwith and Tim Schad. For the U.S. Air Force Academy: Mike Babler and Dana Green. For the Bureau of Land Management, John Nahomenuk.

State Level—Governor Bill Owens and Michelle Puhr. For the Division of Wildlife: Doug Krieger, Dave Clippinger, Trina Lynch, Mindy Gasaway, Greg Policky, Phil Goebel. For Parks and Recreation: John Geerdes, Greg Nootbar, Susan Smith, Terry Gimbel, Susan Trumble, Cheryl Galvin, Carolyn Bredenberg, Heather Poe, Brad Buckner and Parrish Watson.

County Level—For the El Paso County Health Dept., Dr. John Muth. El Paso County Parks: Ken Pals, Dr. Donna Scheeter. Jefferson County Open Space: Thea Rock, Bridgette Al-Bawab Special thanks go to the former staff of the Pikes Peak Area Council of Governments and former Executive Director Roland Gow.

City Level—Colorado Springs: Bill Stookey, Rick Severson, Paula Vickerman Vic Eklund; Denver Water: Bill Newberry. Denver Mountain Parks: Manitou Springs: Dan Wecks. Green Mountain Falls, Dick Bratton. Woodland Park: Sally Riley. Palmer Lake: Della Gins, Cindy Allen, Dale T. Smith.

Individuals—Very special thanks to Mike Henry of Ghost Town Software, whose maps and photos grace this book, and to Cover Designers Phil Barber and Diane Russelavage. Thanks also to the late Gary Kenyon, to Mike Porter of El Paso County Search and Rescue, William A. Fauver, Billy Jack Barrett, John Cappis, Dr. Frank Barry, Cindy Beggs, Robert Houdek, Ken Jordan, Randy Jacobs, Larry Leaveck, George Gibson, Brian Gravestock, Skye Ridley, Dan Cleveland, and two old friends who first showed us around the mountains, Monte and Terry Barrett. Bless you.

WHAT YOU SHOULD KNOW BEFORE YOU GO

Suppose someone knocked on your door and announced that your Uncle Samuel had just left you and your family well over a million acres of scenic mountain property: Wouldn't you immediately ask where it's located? And suppose you learned that it started almost at your back door, right on the outskirts of your city, and sprawled across a half dozen counties, a vast playground of majestic peaks, clear streams and fish-jumpin' lakes, grassy meadows and remote forests, all belonging to you and yours.

Wouldn't you want to go see it all, go explore it with your family?

Well, that's the glory of Colorado. The best real estate belongs to you and your family forever (so take care of it!) and it offers an exciting array of outdoor recreation. **But where can you go this weekend?** How do you get there, and what's it like? What can you do there and what do you need to take along? This book is designed to answer all those questions and more. And since this guide started as a government publication a generation ago, it continues to be the one reliable intergovernmental reference checked and used by all the many government agencies that have jurisdiction over your property.

And yes—we really do these trails—on mountain bikes, on foot, on horseback and, clumsily, on skis.

We cover a vast area southwest of Denver, beginning at its Denver gateway at Waterton Canyon, west across the summit of Mount Evans to Fairplay and Georgia Pass. It extends south beyond Pikes Peak to the Beaver Creek Wilderness and west to the Buffalo Peaks Wilderness, south of Fairplay. At its heart is the world famous Pike National Forest, but there is also a huge patchwork of many other public lands administered by federal, state, county and city governments. All this belongs to you!

It trails exist for your enjoyment, so the purpose of this book is to help you enjoy them as much as possible. **We'll try to show you all the little things that a walking, talking human guide would show you.** We'll show you where to camp and fish, the best places for mountain biking and cross-country skiing, great places to ride a horse or take the family for a hike. There is even wheelchair access in some areas. We'll give you precise road directions and trail descriptions, tell you a little about the plants and wildlife, about the history and geology, and we'll show you how to preserve and protect these delicate areas so that you and your family and friends can enjoy them—as they are—for generations to come.

This guide covers virtually all of the public trails that are marked and maintained and definitely legal. There are some trails that we could not mention because they have become so obscure that no written guide could lead you safely there. Others have trespass problems. Where ever private property is involved, legal work has been done to guarantee your right-of-way. If we tell you to ignore a particular sign, rest assured that the proper authorities agree. In fact, we give editorial control to many governmental agencies.

Rules differ greatly from area to area, so always check our guide before heading out. Trails that receive the heaviest use always have the most no-nos. But for those who wish to walk or ride a ways, the National Forest offers all of the freedoms and responsibilities of backcountry. In the most remote areas, the Forest Service offers virtually no facilities, only paths and a very few signs. **You are very much on your own. Outdoor recreation always involves an element of risk, and no guide can be a substitute for sound judgement. Your comfort and safety are your own responsibility.**

But there are other responsibilities also. The Forest Service could never clean up after all those who use the trails, so visitors themselves must watch over the land and protect it by careful use. We'll also show you the art of "minimum impact," how to enjoy the mountains without changing anything. But don't be afraid to do more than your share. If someone in your party is misbehaving, then clean up after them; they might catch on. And if you see other visitors abusing your forest, be cordial but don't be shy about correcting them. Many greenhorns just don't know any better or don't believe that anyone cares.

Right now there are only a few rules for those trails marked with a Forest Service trail number. You may not pick or dig up wildflowers or other plants, may not cut on living trees or plants, may not remove moss or take souvenirs. You are welcome to look and touch and take photographs, but you are asked to leave everything in its place, to treat the forest as a living museum.

Have Fun Mountain Biking

It is no disgrace to dismount and push your bike uphill, no matter what my wife says. You'll soon find a gentler stretch where you can pedal again. Downhill is a breeze, unless you find a place so steep that you have to have to walk it down. If you're really out of shape, a little preconditioning would be wise, but our guide includes many trails where the pedaling is easy. All trails are rated with the average citizen in mind. Just be very careful and you'll get stronger every trip.

Biking allows you to cover more distance than you could on foot, but this

also means that it will take you farther from your car, which brings up a safety point. Mountain biking is really more like hiking than many purists would like to think. You need most of the same gear—warm clothing, rain protection, food, drinking water, all the stuff that day hikers carry for comfort and safety. Going without is actually dangerous!

Don't use a backpack; it'll spoil your balance. Panniers tend to snag rocks and trees, but there are packs made to Velcro to a rack atop the back wheel. Rack packs solve those problems.

Even if you never fall down riding street bikes, you can expect to fall while riding mountain bikes, and since falls occur among rocks and stumps, if not downhill, no one should have to convince you to **wear a helmet.**

Some biking footwear is entirely too slick. When you dismount on a steep trail, you don't want your feet sliding out from under you. Your feet need tread just as your tires do.

The greatest danger to the sport itself is lack of sportsmanship. Bikes are banned in some areas and may be banned in more areas because of bikers speeding downhill, riding out of control, spooking horses, chasing hikers off trail, shortcutting switchbacks, rutting soft ground or tearing up tundra and marsh.

Always yield the right-of-way, even when it is inconvenient. This means that biking is not much fun wherever there are crowds of people because you end up walking the bike more than riding. There are lots of better places. That's what guidebooks are for. When we say someplace is popular, that means lots of people!

Pass with care. Sometimes people don't hear you coming, so let them know with a friendly greeting. If you wind up overtaking people, you often have to wait until there's a good place where they can let you by. In any case, hikers and horses have right-of-way. Be especially careful around horses; wait for a nod from the rider.

Safe speed depends on terrain. At one speed, you have enough control to stay on the trail, but that isn't good enough. You need to be able to stop, if you encounter the unexpected.

Lots of trails in our guides are open to bikes, but there are scattered exceptions, so be sure to check. Have fun!

Have Fun Hiking With Our Guide

There is an old song that talks about going "a-wandering with a knapsack on my back." Now *that* is the proper attitude! Just go a-wandering. Don't go on a forced march to see how much you can take. Fun is your chief goal.

Our guide offers every kind of trail, so **always plan an expedition around the**

weakest member of your party. Never take friends and loved ones on a hike that is so difficult that they will never want to go again.

And when you find yourself grunting uphill, stop and take a few deep breaths and look around. Try not to miss the far-off scenery or the close-up wonders around you. Then wander up to the next switchback and see how the view changes. Keep that up and you can wander for miles, having fun all the way, appreciating everything and growing stronger every time.

Always tell someone where you're going and when you expect to be back. Estimating hiking time is very tricky. As a rule of thumb, realize that many back-packers figure on making only one mile per hour packing uphill, but twice that on the downhill.

Dayhikers need to watch the time and start back with plenty of daylight. We recommend carrying a small disposable flashlight in case some delay should leave you in the dark, but we have a whole section on **What to Take Along--and Why.** A small item can make the difference between fun and misery, between safety and danger.

We've seen grown-ups fall flat on their faces because steep trails are lubricated with fine gravel. You need lug soles to bite down through that to grip the moun-tain. Modern light hikers come ready to wear. Buy a pair big enough to accommo-date two pairs of socks, a thick wool outer pair and a thin soft inner pair. That's still the best way to prevent blisters. Take the socks with you when you buy the boots and always use the same kinds. If the ensemble doesn't feel like heaven, keep on shopping.

You can prevent blisters by paying attention to your feet and stopping immedi-ately if you feel a hot spot. Put Moleskin on that spot soon enough and a blister won't form. If the blister has already formed, never put Moleskin directly on it. Instead, cut a hole in the Moleskin the same size as the blister. (Molefoam is better for this, being thicker.) That will keep your boot from rubbing the blister.

No joke: It is important to cut your toenails because your foot will scoot farther forward than you can imagine on a steep downhill, bumping the ends of your toenails so gently that you won't feel it, yet bruising the quick. Then your toe-nails turn blue and later may fall off!

No matter how great the weather seems, take along some warm clothes and a poncho to keep you dry. Read up on hypothermia, discussed later, because it is truly more deadly than bears.

And please never drink raw water from streams or spring pools. Read our sec-tion on water parasites before you scoff.

Pack the night before and be sure to get an early start with a good breakfast. With a little preparation, you can almost guarantee a great time

Have Fun Riding Horseback

If grunting up a mountain makes you stop and pant, ever consider a horse? They stop and pant, too, but Indians and mountain men found them pretty handy—and so will you. No need to own one. You can rent horses a number of places, even outside some parks. Check the yellow pages.

Indeed, visitors to our area should consider using local horses rather than bringing horses from lower altitudes because mounts have to be conditioned for the high country, just as people do. When going uphill, you have to stop frequently and rest your horse with the head pointing downhill to help circulation.

An anxious horse can expend so much energy in the first hour that it may never be able to recover for the rest of the day, so it is especially important to hold back for awhile. Horses allowed to travel at their own pace may collapse and die. Be especially careful above timberline, of course, where the air is thinnest. Some horses get frisky when they break out of the trees and want to run in the open. Above timberline, that could be deadly.

Never carry your wallet in your back pocket; they tend to squirm out of your hip pocket as you ride.

All the stuff that you would normally carry in a daypack is still necessary on a trailride, except that you've got saddlebags to carry it. But if you should need to reach for a poncho or a jacket, remember to stop and dismount so the horse won't spook. Speaking of which, the breath freshener called Tic Tacs come in a case that rattles just like a rattlesnake.

The average horse would just as soon go back to the trailer without you, so you really do need to keep your mount under control every second. Always be willing to have someone hold your horse while you make some adjustment. Never try to tie it by the reins. Don't give a strange horse the chance to slip away. Davy Crockett's diary has a story about following a loose horse day after day without being able to lay hands on it. The horse was simply going home!

Horse manure is no problem in backcountry, but very popular trails can turn into manure troughs, creating a nuisance for all those who hike or bike. So when you ride in popular areas, please dismount and move manure off the trail. That way its nutrients can do some good. Before now, this has never been a part of trail etiquette in these parts, but this comes with heavy use. Your consideration will be appreciated and may prevent future restrictions.

One other thing, authorities require that you use only certified weed-free feed in Wilderness Areas, but it's a good idea anywhere in backcountry.

We did some of our longest trails on horseback. It's a great way to see the mountains.

Have Fun Cross-Country Skiing

Imagine skiing without lift lines, without crowds, without lift tickets, without bumper-to-bumper traffic on the way home. No wonder cross-country skiing is such a fast growing sport!

Colorado has only two problems when it comes to cross-country skiing—too little snow and too much snow. Many areas are only skiable after major storms because our sunny weather soon melts it all away. And in higher country, the problem may be getting there. The Crags area, for example, offers wonderful tour skiing, but the road leading there is seldom plowed and creates a lot of business for tow truck operators. Lost Park is likewise a beautiful area, but the road has the same problem.

Which brings up the subject of emergency gear for your car and for your pack. Tour skiing is generally safer than downhill because you don't go as fast or fall as hard, but then again, there is no ski patrol on our trails, and **an accident in backcountry can turn into a survival situation.** It is most important that you don't go alone, that you tell someone where your party is headed, and that you take the food and clothing that dayhikers normally carry. See **What To Take Along—And Why**.

Have Fun Fishing Remote Areas

Imagine an airplane flying over a mountain peak, then diving over the other side, swooping down to a lake hidden in a glacier-gouged pocket. The airplane bombs the lake with catchable size trout, then flies out the valley.

That's your State Division of Wildlife making sure that Colorado fishermen have plenty to brag about. **Despite the impact of whirling disease in many areas, some waters featured in this book have just about all the fish they could possibly support!**

Our guide will show you all the hidden places that can only be reached by those who hike or ride. No roads go there All you need is a valid Colorado fishing license, some gear and an understanding of the rules.

Regulations have become a little more complicated in recent years because biologists are trying to fine-tune fishing to maximize each particular situation. So watch for changes in the literature provided with your license each year. The rules are meant to improve your fun in the long run.

Only poaching can ruin this effort. If you see a violation, try to make note of the vehicle description, license plate, direction of travel, clothing, anything possible, and call Operation Game Thief at 295-0164 in the Denver or 1-800-332-4155. You need not reveal your name or testify in court, but you may receive a reward. Even if you don't have enough information to catch them this time, a pattern of reports may lead to future arrests.

The DOW is spending $15,000,000 trying to eradicate whirling disease from hatcheries, but because the life cycle of the parasite also involves the bloodworm that burrows in mud, wild waters infected with the disease are pretty much stuck with it. Waters not already infected are only stocked with fish free of the disease, which means that some unaffected areas cannot receive the optimum stocking until the year 2001, when disease-free fish will be in good supply.

Yet biologists also worry that fishermen may accidentally spread spores to other areas. *They recommend that fishermen treat everything that touches the water with a 25% solution of chlorine bleach. Dip felt-soled waders in this solution. Spray it on waders and lures and even on fishing line. Your dog might turn green, so leave your dog at home next time. Even a dog might spread whirling.*

Whirling disease is not dangerous to people. **Raw fish can be contaminated with E-coli, the same fecal bacteria that is sometimes found in packing house meats, but** *no Colorado fish disease can be transmitted to people.*

When removing hooks, biologists now recommend that you handle fish with dry hands whenever possible; wet hands have to squeeze too hard to get a good grip. It's best to become practiced with a pair of surgical hemostats, which can pluck out a hook without your having to touch the fish at all.

Be careful about over-playing fish in warmer lake waters because a fish can die of exhaustion. If a fish appears weak, revive it by holding it gently and pushing it through the water, making figure eights so that water runs through the gills.

Non-motorized trails lead to many lakes, streams and beaver ponds, but don't ignore the many smaller streams where you can sneak up on brook trout. They can be a lot of fun, and the more you fish them, the better they do. Brookies grow to 22 inches in our area (honest), but tend to stunt themselves through overpopulation, so the state allows you ten extra brookies under eight inches.. Judging from the size I generally catch, I need plenty.

Our trail descriptions tell you about the kind of fishing there, the types of fish and other information that might be useful. But one caution: We've seen people hike in with a big tackle box, when all the gear they really needed could have fitted in pockets, and then start back early because they didn't bring a flashlight. So just when the fish started to bite at dusk, they were forced to leave. If you're going to be hiking at night, be sure to familiarize yourself with the trail in daylight. Night hiking is always risky. Bring extra batteries.

Don't miss out. The best trout we ever tasted was cooked within minutes of leaving the water, so if you've never experienced hike-in or bike-in fishing, you're missing a lot of what Colorado has to offer.

Have Fun Camping—For Free!

Camping is just like real estate—location, location, location—except the pricing is just backwards! *The very best locations are absolutely free,* **while you have to pay good money to camp in a crowded spot, where the ground is trampled to dust, where you breath smoke from other people's campfires, where you have to listen to people's music, their dogs, kids and squabbles, and where you can often find the restrooms with your nose. As a realtor, I personally think that's slum living.**

If that's what you like, there are lots of pay campgrounds, some on a reservation basis and some not, some for groups only—and you're reading the wrong book to find them all. Many tourists feel they need the convenience, the services (potable water, trash haul-out, etc.) and the knowledge that other folks are nearby. One change you'll notice is that concessionaires are becoming more common at these pay campgrounds, and because the FS simply cannot go around cleaning a lot of restrooms, any time you see a restroom in the future, you can pretty well bet there will be a fee involved.

But if you'd rather get away from it all, away from everybody, and take care of yourself, then you have just opened the right book!

Our area alone offers well over a million acres of *free* **camping on a first-come basis with no services. Get away from the crowds, the smoke, the dust, the noise, the dogs and children. With few exceptions, you may camp along any of the National Forest trails, but the Forest Service would like you to camp with ecology in mind. Again, your comfort and safety are strictly your own responsibility.**

The ideal location is a not on a busy trail, but back away from it on a quiet cul de sac, private, serene. You want a sunny location with a beautiful view, but not up so high that wind and lightning are a problem. Locating near water is great, but right next to water is both unecological and dangerous because of flash flood. One hundred to two hundred feet back is recommended, just as if you were building a house. Level ground is recommended, and ideally, it's nice to locate in a neighborhood that has good schools (of fish).

Just as in real estate, such spacious, elegant, secluded locations are generally reserved for those who are willing to travel a little farther to get there.

Because water attracts campers, people who want to avoid people find marvelous solitude by hauling enough water in their car so they can camp anywhere near any of the many forest access roads and spurs. Oddly enough, hauling all this water is called "dry camping."

Above timberline you will damage tundra by simply walking around—

and you become lightning bait!—so you'll never catch me camping above timberline. You'll find much more protection in the trees.

Cutting green boughs for bedding is illegal, it damages the forest and it makes a lumpy bed for your effort. Light foam pads will serve both you and the forest better. Trenching your tent may be necessary in other parts of the country, but Colorado *mountain* soil (decomposed granite) is so porous that water tends to sink straight down instead of gathering around your tent. Trenching makes ugly scars that encourage erosion. (Don't take our real estate references too far in this regard: Poor drainage and expansive foothill soils are the chief causes of structural problems in Colorado homes.)

All camp cleaning should be done with biodegradable soaps, but even biodegradable soap should never be used near streams or lakes. Nobody likes to drink your wash water.

If you use minimum impact camping skills, the Forest Service allows you to camp in one spot for two weeks at a time. But eventually, even minimum impact takes a toll, so after two weeks move to another area to give your old campsite a chance to recover. In return for this stewardship, you may camp all you want.

The point of all this is to enjoy the forest without leaving a mark, without changing the beauty you came to admire. If you do it right, you should be able to look back and see nothing but some bent grass where your tent was.

Building Campfires Safely

Indians had a saying that Indians build small fires and sit up close, but whitemen build big fires and sit way back. Guess who had the better idea?

Campfires are an outdoor tradition that may be going the way of the buffalo robe. They are becoming illegal in more and more areas and are banned in most areas when fire danger becomes high. They scar the land, encourage vandals to cut living trees, they burn up wood used for homes and food by wildlife—and sometimes they burn down the whole forest, just as they did at Buffalo Creek.

If you like to cook in backcountry, get used to carrying a lightweight backpacker stove. Once you have tried one on a wet and cold morning, you won't begrudge carrying the extra few ounces. They are clean, fast, efficient and they work when open fires won't. But most of all, they protect the forest, and that is why they are becoming required in more and more areas.

If you do make a fire, make it small. A small fire makes less smoke, and you won't have to strip the woods to keep it going. Pots are easier to handle on a little fire, and wind won't blow so many sparks from it. A small campfire is safer in case someone stumbles and falls, is much easier to put out and is much less likely to rekindle itself. **Large diameter wood is especially prone to reigniting after you think the fire is dead.** You'll also find that small fires are much easier to erase. You can hide all traces. No need to leave a fire ring. We've erased plenty.

All that said, **never make even the tiniest fire when fire danger is high. Remember that Smoky the Bear was named after a real bear cub orphaned by a forest fire.**

Trail Etiquette

A great many people can share a wilderness with a sense of privacy, if everyone shows a little consideration. Good manners are essential to the kindly and relaxed atmosphere that visitors are seeking. Try to keep your party from becoming a loud party. Loud radios and shouting are not appreciated by others.

If you are being overtaken by a faster group, move aside and let them pass. If you should meet horses on the trail, remember that they always have the right-of-way. When horses are come along, move off to the side, preferably downhill, and talk among yourselves in order to make sure that the horses know that you are there and won't be startled.

Never allow members of your party to roll or throw rocks from the trail. You cannot be certain that no one is below because well-mannered adventurers don't make much noise.

Never allow anyone in your party to short-cut down slopes whether barriers exist or not. It may not seem to do any harm at the time, but the first hard rainstorm will start making a gully out of your short-cut. Whenever you leave the trail for any reason, pick the gentlest route and tread carefully.

And please **pack out your garbage. Anything that you try to hide or bury will only be dug up by animals and scattered around,** so please carry out your garbage and as much of anyone else's garbage that you can. **Disposable diapers are no exception.** Animals dig them up and then rains wash them into streams.

Sanitation—How to Poop in the Woods

All nature requires is a little cooperation. Select an area at least 50 to 100 feet from any open water or spring. With your heel, scrape out a hole no deeper than several inches. That's because the first several inches—the biological layer—contains a system of disposers that will break down the waste. If you go deeper, you spoil this effect. If there is any sod, try to keep it intact and replace it after covering the hole with dirt. Sprinkle on some needles and such. Nature does the rest.

Taking Dogs Along

Division of Wildlife officers are legally empowered to shoot dogs chasing wildlife and to arrest their owners. Both civil and criminal penalties apply. And not having your dog on a leash can cost you $400 anywhere in Jefferson County, not just in the parks. Many owners mistakenly believe that having their pet "under voice control" excuses them from leash laws, but that will lead to a fine in some areas such as Palmer Park's watershed. These are a sample of the serious considerations involved in taking a dog to the woods.

You do have the right to take your dog with you on most of the trails in this book, but **everyone who enjoys this freedom is in danger of losing it because of problems caused by some dogs and their masters.** Dogs used to be allowed in the Florissant Fossil Beds, but they ran the elk, chased other critters and gobbled the ground-nesting birds, so now they are totally banned. There are a number of such places listed in our guide including Roxborough and Mueller (so always check) and the number is increasing.

Dog owners can help protect their freedoms by making sure that their pets don't become the cause of new regulations—and by encouraging others to be just as considerate. Indeed, when you enter a Wilderness Area, current regulations require that your dog be on a leash—period.

Don't fool yourself into believing that your pet cannot catch the critters it chases: Persistence pays.

When considering whether or not to take a dog along, a lot depends upon the personality of your pet, its training and your willingness to control it every second. So treat it like a member of the family. If you had a member of the family who threatened other visitors, picked fights with their dogs, went after horses and llamas, you might well leave such a brat at home next time.

And if your child pooped on the trail, you would stop and move it, so do the same for the four-legged member of your family. Seriously, it does the environment no good left on the trail. It creates a nuisance and resentment (and ultimately more regulations). But when moved off-trail, it becomes fertilizer.

Besides all this, keeping your dog strictly under control may prevent your trip from being ruined by an encounter with a porcupine, a skunk or something meaner that was only trying to hide from you both. Your consideration will help protect your dog and your right to take a dog onto trails

Meeting Cattle

Parts of the National Forest are leased to ranchers as pasture, so you are bound to meet cattle on some of our trails. Cattle rarely hassle people who know how to handle them, but bulls or cows with calves can be very protective, so don't assume that such powerful animals will always run away from you. Even a cow may charge if she feels that you are endangering her calf.

Cattle will usually be found directly in your path because it is really their path. In such areas, cattle make more trails than the Forest Service does, and you will have to navigate carefully. **The best thing to do is to keep your distance and hike quietly around them. If you climb high enough and keep enough distance, they will probably be too lazy to move, and you can pass them.**

Carrying a large stick may make you feel more secure, but you must be careful not to spook cattle. If you do, they will start off along the trail ahead of you. They will not be anxious to leave their trail or to climb uphill, so they will continue to block your way, stopping when you stop, moving when you move, and you could be left following in their dust for miles.

Don't assume that you can scatter them because cattle have a herding instinct that makes them tend to huddle together when frightened. And the rancher won't appreciate your running precious pounds off his cattle. So the best thing to do is leave them where you find them, and try to pass at a distance.

Meeting Mountain Lions and Bears

Colorado's wildlife boom means that mountain lions and bears are becoming more common, and since a teenage jogger was killed by a mountain lion in Idaho Springs in 1991, everyone should be aware—and be more careful. NOTE: advice about what to do—and not do—has changed! Many factors must come together to trigger a rare attack, so understanding those factors and changing the situation may help protect you. Determine what the animal is feeling and act accordingly.

If an animal is surprised and feels threatened, reduce the threat, but if an animal is really coming for you, be threatening and ready to fight.

Also called cougars or puma, mountain lions generally prowl at night and are often seen near dawn or dusk. They are generally shy and try to flee, so if you feel you have surprised one, that is no time to be threatening! Talk calmly to him and back away with your arms raised above your head to make yourself appear as big as possible (too big to eat). Don't make eye contact with a surprised animal, but don't turn your head. However, a different situation requires a different response.

If you encounter a mountain lion in daylight, he may be hungry. If he follows as you back away (very rare), square off and DO make eye contact. He will tend to freeze and reconsider when stared at. Don't try to bend down to pick up something to throw because you want to appear as big as possible. Keep your arms raised above your head, again to look big, and keep backing away to stretch the distance he feels he needs to make a charge. **Never, never run because running triggers their chase response.** Talk to him very firmly in a low-pitched voice as you go.

In the extremely unlikely event of attack, fight back as fiercely as you can and try to keep the cougar from getting behind you. They generally kill with a bite below the base of the skull.

There are no grizzlies reported in our area, but the black bear population seems to be on the rise. Bears try to avoid you, but if you should meet one, follow the same procedure outlined above.

Only 10% of a bear's diet is meat, so they are not as likely to be hunting something to kill. Sows with cubs can be especially dangerous, however. If you find a cub, chances are that mom is close by and will come back soon. A sow will be very protective of cubs and is far more likely to attack, if defending cubs, so try not to threaten her in any way. Don't make eye contact and back away, talking softly.

But there is another, *very rare* kind of attack that requires the opposite response. Bear follows you curiously. This is typically a young male and this may be a predatory stalk. If he meets no resistance, no thrown rock, no brandished stick, he'll keep pressing. If you lie down for this bear, you're lunch. Make eye contact, be huge, talk tough, back away. **Don't play dead: That only works for grizzlies. Never run. If attacked by a black bear, always fight back! If you are wearing a pack, keep it on. If you are knocked down, your pack offers good protection because the bear may damage it more than you.**

Always maintain a clean camp. If you pour grease on the ground, for example, take it a long way from camp. Don't sleep with food in your tent. Lock it in the trunk of your car or suspend it at least 10 feet off the ground on a wire or rope. Avoid cooking foods that give off strong odors and don't sleep in the clothes you wore cooking. Don't bury garbage. Pack it out or animals will dig it up.

Evidence indicates that bears may be more aggressive toward those wearing scented cosmetics, hair spray, deodorant, toward women during their menstrual period or—sorry—couples making love.

DOW authorities estimate that if you have been on a dozen hikes, a mountain lion or bear has sat and watched you go by! That may seem creepy, but it should be reassuring because the pattern is clear: They don't want to bother you. You are not really on the menu.

Meeting Motorcycles

Years ago we shunned trails open to motorcycles, but mountain biking showed us what we'd been missing! Now we're having a great time exploring more and more of them, on bikes, on foot, whatever. These are not opposing groups of users any more: We know folks who enjoy it all. Lighten up and enjoy this playground together.

One thing: Always yield to motorcycles, not as a courtesy (because right-of-way could be debatable) but as a safety issue. As a matter of fact, mountain bikers, hikers and horseriders can easily hear a motorcycle coming, but motorcyclists can't hear you coming at all. Motorcycles have the "right of weight" because they can't stop as fast or get off trail as fast, so just watch out for them. They come and go quickly and are soon gone.

Getting Lost With Map and Compass

We were two days deep in the Lost Creek Wilderness, correcting the old USGS topo map where no one then working for the Forest Service had ever been, when suddenly we came to a stream that was flowing the wrong direction! Woops!

So we backtracked, carefully exploring to see where we went wrong. As it turned out, we were on the right trail, but the government had it wrong on the map, which only goes to show that even the U.S. Geological Survey can get mixed up in the woods.

That should never have happened, of course, but **that's the problem with getting lost: It should never happen, but it does. Search and Rescue tells us that the most common error people make is believing—through ego—that it just can't happen to them. (By the way, Mike Porter, President of the El Paso Search and Rescue, tells us that all his Mission Coordinators carry and use our guide.)**

We corrected our map (the USGS never did correct theirs, not even in a subsequent update, even though we recommended that they should). So we're proud that are maps are more accurate than anyone else's, but even so, no guide can guarantee that you won't get lost. So it is best to learn how to protect yourself.

First of all, never strike out alone: If you should get hurt, it's handy having someone along who isn't hurt. Have a trip plan and stick to it! Someone should always know where you are going and when you expect to be back.

Search and Rescue suggests that you also leave a note in your car saying where you're going, when you expect to be back, and if you use our new CD-Rom you can even print out a duplicate of your customized map to leave in the car. They also suggest—no kidding—that you leave some smelly socks or other item of clothing in your car so they don't have to search your home for something to give their search dogs.

Your party must stay together! Don't let individuals race ahead or straggle behind or stray off on other routes, planning to meet up later. And never ignore your own backtrail. Keep turning and looking back so you know what the trail looks like in reverse. Follow your progress on the map and, if you think you've gone wrong, hug that trail and carefully backtrack. Continuing ahead could take you anywhere, and leaving the trail could take you nowhere!

You'll generally find it easy to keep your bearings by following your progress on our new maps. Especially important is keeping track of which drainage you are in: **Water is your best compass!** If you are hiking up a trail that follows a stream, you cannot change streams unless you climb over a ridge that leads to a whole new drainage. However, that mistake is easier to make higher up where one side of a bump may lead to one creek and the other side to a different creek, so be careful on such finger ridges.

A compass will not keep you from getting lost, especially if you don't know how to use it. Never strike out "as the crow flies," following a compass bearing. Stay on trail and backtrack. **If all else fails, listen to your wife.**

That's how you keep from getting lost, but suppose you get lost anyway. Suppose you have lost the trail entirely. **The first thing to do is sit down and think and relax.** There is a great temptation to panic, to run, so beware of that and try to remember that **your first job is to take good care of yourself. Virtually all people who get lost are eventually found, dead or alive, so the idea is to stay alive no matter how long you have to stay lost.**

But think for now. Which way did you come? Getting lost in the mountains isn't like being lost on the flats where you might wander anywhere. In the mountains your routes are restricted by the lay of the land. Trails tend to follow water or ridges or hillsides, so what kind of trail was it? By looking around and by using process of elimination, you may be able to discover which way you came simply because there aren't that many choices. But again, this only works if you are calm!

But suppose that doesn't work. Well, you have to make some cool and logical decisions. How much time do you have? Estimate how long it has been since you left camp and realize that it will take even longer to get back. If the weather is turning sour or nightfall is coming on, you may not be able to make it, so **use your precious daylight to prepare for night. Hole up somewhere in the most sheltered spot you can find. Collect firewood, but don't let your pack out of your sight: If you lose that pack, you're in much worse trouble. Build a tiny fire that won't use up all your firewood, the kind you can huddle over. Try to make yourself as safe and comfortable as possible.**

Never try to travel at night or in the rain or in fog. Sit it out. The wilderness SOS consists of three signals of any kind repeated at regular intervals, three flashes of a mirror or shiny knife, three shouts, three whistles. You can whistle longer than you can yell.

Now let's suppose that you are on a high lookout and still can't fathom which way to turn. In that case, **the best way to go is the safest way, for the only thing worse than being lost is being** *hurt* **and lost!** Never start down into a canyon or gorge because you may trap yourself. Instead, **follow the gentlest route, no matter which way it leads. You must be extra careful with yourself.**

Look for a stream. That's usually a route to civilization. The only exceptions here are the Lost Creek Wilderness, where Lost Creek disappears into box canyons, **and the Rampart Range,** where most roads are on ridges and where water drains down some very dangerous gulches. Be extra careful in those areas.

If you are injured and lost, try to make it to a clear area or for a high point of some kind where you can build a signal fire or use a signal mirror. Search and Rescue climbs to such places to look for those signals on surrounding high points. We have quite a section on What to Take Along and Why, so take the stuff. If Search and Rescue learns that someone is lost but has those essentials, they pretty well expect to find you alive instead of dead. For example, dayhikers must take a little flashlight along, even though they never expect to use it, because any kind of delay can leave you stranded overnight without it.

And it's also important to know a little about how Search and Rescue works. **Make sure your relatives don't hesitate to call Search and Rescue! Call 911 and ask for the Sheriff's Office. People hesitate because they believe there will be a big bill to pay. THERE IS NO BILL FROM SEARCH AND RESCUE!**

What you've heard about are big National Park situations, which does not apply to our area. Search and Rescue personnel are highly trained and dedicated volunteers who work through Sheriff's Departments.

Also be aware that Search and Rescue looks for clues more than just looking for the individual. That's why your CD-Rom map or notes in your car, etc. are so important. Then they lay down a grid and use some very sophisticated methods to go about their search in the most logical way. **And this brings up our final point: Having sat out the night, please don't get up and keep wandering! If you do that, you may just wander into an area they have already searched and, therefore, they might miss finding you!**

Again, remember that you will be found eventually, either alive or dead, so concentrate on staying alive, no matter how long you have to stay lost.

What Non-Hunters Should Know

All forest visitors should be aware of hunting season and should wear the same orange reflective clothing that hunters are required to wear. There is no such legal requirement for non-hunters, but the safety advantage is obvious. Non-hunters should also be aware of hunting regulations because the Division of Wildlife needs the vigilance of all visitors to protect wildlife from poachers. Colorado's Operation Game Thief even pays rewards. You do not have to reveal your name or testify in court. Just call 295-0164 in Denver or 1-800-332-4145 toll-free. Provide as much information as you can about the vehicle, direction of travel, clothing, any descriptive details. Anything might help.

Contrary to popular belief, putting food on the table is one of the least common motives for poaching. Poachers represent the same greed for thrills and profit that once nearly wiped out Colorado's wildlife. Here's how far we've come:

Early in this century, when Colorado Springs financier Spencer Penrose wanted to take a maharajah elk hunting, they planned to go to Wyoming because early settlers had virtually killed off Colorado's elk! Embarrassed about that, Penrose imported 55 elk from Yellowstone in 1915, the beginnings of the Pikes Peak herd. Today, thanks to generations of scientific game management—based on carefully regulated sport hunting—Colorado has huge and thriving populations of elk. All sorts of other wildlife have experienced similar booms, so today we see far more wildlife of all kinds.

For many, the idea that sport hunting could somehow *increase* wildlife populations seems absurd, but it works for the same reasons that ranching works. Every ranch works by harvesting excess males in order to leave more food for the very young and for those needed for breeding, and that's what the hunting license system is designed to do by designating which categories of animals will be taken in each area. And like a ranch, the profits from this harvest (license fees) are used to improve and acquire habitat and even buy food to help the herd survive the worst winter storms. The result is a healthier herd with far more young surviving in the spring. Despite the killing involved, this system is restoring Colorado's wildlife to levels not seen since pioneer days.

Certainly, you don't have to become a hunter to support this effort. By checking the wildlife donation box on your Colorado Income Tax Form or by making a direct donation to the DOW, you can help pay for managing non-game species, protecting endangered species and reintroducing species that Colorado lost, such as the peregrine falcon and the moose. The DOW does not use state taxes. It is sportsmen who pay for wildlife programs. Indeed, the DOW also pays for some of the trails, restrooms and parking lots used by non-sportsmen and has championed the cause of opening forbidden watershed areas to all of us.

What To Take Along–And Why

We're grateful to an elderly couple who save us a bad time. On our first visit to Devil's Head, we saw lots of people starting up the trail with nothing, just as if they were going to stroll out to a roadside overlook. The sign said it was only a little more than a mile, but an elderly couple in the parking lot gave us a warning: "That's a real hike," the old man said. "If you've got hiking stuff, take it along."

That proved to be wonderful advice! We saw visitors in sneakers and sandals slipping and sliding, but our lug soles gripped the mountain. That steep trail was sweaty work for awhile, so we were grateful to have our icy canteens. And then a cloud came over, so we were glad to have long trousers and warm shirts in our packs. When the wind blew, we had jackets to wear. Other visitors were shivering. Our lunch was the envy of everyone, and when it started to rain, we were snug in our ponchos, enjoying the storm that drove others off the mountain. Yet we could hardly feel smug about all this because we had nearly left everything in the car!

We hope to pass on that old man's advice so that you and yours can have a great time on these trails. **You don't want to lug a heavy load, but you do want to take along a few things than can make the difference between comfort and misery, between safety and danger.** So here's a list of handy items for day trips, plus another list of things to add for overnighters. Hikers, bikers, equestrians and cross-country skiers all need essentially the same gear to have fun in the woods.

What to Take Along on Day Trips:

Take drinking water (see Water Parasites for an explanation), lunch, rain protection (see Hypothermia), light long trousers (though you may start out in shorts in summer), a long-sleeved shirt, a jacket or vest, a bandanna to use as a washcloth or handkerchief or bandage or sling; Swiss army knife, wristwatch so you'll know when to start back, toilet paper, sunglasses, SPF-l5 or better sun lotion, lip balm with sunscreen (remember that sunlight has more dangerous UV the higher you go in the mountains), extra plastic bag for carrying out trash, a guide book or map, compass, a small (fresh) flashlight or headlamp in case you get caught on the trail after dark, plus a little whistle for signalling and an emergency kit.

Sports Medicine Specialist Dr. Frank Barry, MD, recommends the following emergency kit packed lightly in a freezer-size ZipLoc bag: For example, you don't need a bottle of pain-relieving ibuprofen, just a few tablets wrapped in foil or plastic. And things such as tweezers, scissors and a surgical blade that are usually mentioned in such kits may already exist on your Swiss army knife. But you should have: Moleskin for blisters (see Hiking), a lighter, tiny tube of Neo-sporin ointment, an antihistamine such as Benadryl for allergy or insect stings and bites, one 2x3 Telfa pad for any dry wound and a Duo-Derm for a wet wound (sealed), a size #4 tube elastic dressing (fits over and holds the other dressings, won't loosen with use and eliminates the need for tape), a new sealed bottle of water purification tablets just for emergencies when you can't boil anything; Imodium A-D caplets (anti-diarrhea) and an antacid. If you ever experience severe allergic reactions or asthma, an Epi-Pen (prescription) can save your life.

We generally carry a steel Sierra cup with instant soup mix in case of hypothermia. Building a tiny fire to make hot soup in that cup is also a pleasant way to sit out a storm. And in chilly seasons or at high altitude, a stocking cap and gloves are also snuggy.

What to Take Along Overnight:

Take everything listed for day trips, plus more food, a second flashlight (head-mounted lights leave both hands free), a second lighter, some biodegradable soap, a scouring pad, cook kit, tent, sleeping bag, foam pad and a bigger pack to carry it all.

Your pack must fit properly or it can hurt your back. A tent is necessary because rain generally comes with a windy storm. Fiber-filled sleeping bags are cheaper than down and have the advantage of drying out quickly if they get wet. Down is still the lightest and most compressible for the warmth provided, but if your down sleeping bag gets wet, you may as well start for home.

Food is the big limiting factor in a multi-day pack trip. Freeze dried food may not win prizes for taste, but the weight savings make it wonderful. For example, fruit dried to a crisp is much lighter than fruit dried to a leathery consistency.

The old rule of thumb was: The heavier your pack, the heavier your boots should be. The new lightweight hikers have changed that slightly. You need only look for a stiffer sole, which does weigh more, but not a lot more. See **Hiking**.

REAL DANGERS OF THE MOUNTAINS:

There are some real dangers in the mountains, but not the ones you might imagine. You have little to fear from wild animals, but you have more chance of being stricken by hypothermia, heat prostration, altitude sickness, water parasites, or even lightning.

For example, many visitors fear what used to be called "Rocky Mountain spotted fever," yet the State Health Department reports that Colorado averages only one case per year and that no deaths have resulted in recent years. Your chances of contracting this rare disease are much greater in flatland states, so in fairness to the Rockies, this disease is now being called "New World Tick Fever" or "Tickborne Typhus Fever."

The State Health Dept. believes that the public is safer knowing what they should really worry about. The point is to give you a realistic perspective so you may take proper precautions.

The Great Killer—Hypothermia

A reader once told me that our guidebook had seriously saved his life and he wasn't kidding. He was soaked to the skin, freezing, going into hypothermia, when he remembered all the great information we have about hypothermia. So he dug into his pack, pulled out our *Trails Guide* **and, well, he used it to start a fire! It was the only dry thing he had.**

Too many people don't realize that you can freeze to death in 50-degree weather, and that is why hypothermia has become such a common killer. Even worse, this condition affects the brain, so victims show poor judgement about saving themselves. In other words, it quickly makes you stupid.

Hypothermia—also called "exposure"—begins when the body starts losing more heat than it generates, and two things contribute to this: inadequate food and lack of warm, dry clothing. The explorer who skips breakfast or who eats lightly on the trail soon loses the nourishment that it takes to produce heat, and after that, even sweat can dampen clothing enough to begin the chilling process. **No blizzard is required. No mountains are required. You can run out of gas and get hypothermia waiting in your car for help.**

Warm sunny mornings fool many a greenhorn into believing that the Rockies are a paradise where all you need are a pair of sneakers and shorts and sunglasses, and that may be true for awhile, but rain showers occur often and suddenly, especially in summer. The weatherman may say that no storm systems are moving into the area, but the mountains create their own local weather, and the summer forecast will still read "Clear to partly cloudy with chance of isolated thunderstorms." And that is precisely what happens all too often--clear, then cloudy, then rainy, then clear again. And by then you're dead.

As heat radiates from hands and feet and elsewhere, the body tries to conserve warmth by concentrating circulation among the vital organs and by restricting circulation to the extremities, including the brain! Our victim may be shivering constantly, but may also insist that everything is all right. Coordination gets bad as well. When the shivers start coming in violent waves, the victim's thinking becomes even more confused, disoriented, apathetic. The victim may lose the sense or the will power to zip up a jacket, so you must watch your friends and yourself and be ready to help. Stupidity is a dangerous thing. Especially in the mountains

If you suspect that a friend is coming down with hypothermia, stop at once to change out of damp clothing and to eat. Make hot soup or cocoa, but do not let your friend out of your sight, even to answer a call from nature, because victims sometimes wander off into the bush and never come back.

Near the end, the victim may become even more convinced that everything is all right, for the shivering stops, though arms and legs feel strangely stiff. Coordination is so bad that victims often stumble and hurt themselves; sometimes they walk off cliffs or just keep plodding along until they faint. Without aid, they never wake up again.

All this may happen in as little as 30 minutes, though usually it takes longer, and recovery with hot soup and everything may take six or eight hours, so be prepared for a long wait.

Make the victim eat while changing out of wet clothing. If you have a sleeping bag along, prewarm it with someone else's body and have the victim climb in. Better yet, double up in the bag so the patient shares body heat with one or two healthy persons. You may actually rescue the rescuers this way, for other members of the party may be ready to come down with hypothermia as well.

Of course, dayhikers, mountain bikers, trailriders and tour skiers generally don't carry sleeping bags or much in the way of cooking gear, yet run the same risk of getting hypothermia, so prevention is the key. **You must stay warm and dry and well nourished, which means that you must take along the minimal day trip gear that we recommend, even if the weather seems warm and sunny when you start, even if members of your party complain.**

Water Parasites—Why You Must Not Drink From Streams!

Take it from somebody who learned the hard way:

No matter what you have read or heard, mountain water is not safe to drink without boiling or careful treatment. No matter how beautiful it looks, no matter how cold, no matter how high the altitude, no matter how remote,

no matter how far it tumbles, surface water often carries cysts that spread giardia, a single-celled parasite that attacks both people and animals worldwide.

Giardia infests the intestinal tract, causing diarrhea, gas, vomiting, loss of appetite and loss of weight. Symptoms may come and go, returning with greater strength later, and some people contract the disease but never show symptoms, thus becoming carriers. Your friend who says this ain't so is probably a carrier.

Other types of disease can also be contracted by drinking wild water, but giardia may be the most difficult to avoid because its cysts are so difficult to kill, and the State Heath Dept. warns that all surface water supplies must be suspected of containing giardia. If you must drink from streams, please try another planet.

For day trips, always carry water processed by municipal filtration plants. We fill plastic canteens about a quarter full, then freeze them overnight and top them off with sparkling water before starting out. The result is cold water that tastes as good as the streams. **But since it is not possible to carry enough safe water for longer trips, campers should boil water or use one of the new filter devices made for backpackers.** At present, filter devices yield fairly small amounts of water, offer no protection against any virus that might be present and recent studies studies show that some don't actually work as promised!

New studies also show that giardia is even harder to kill with chemicals than previously thought. Even the most disgusting concentrations don't always work, so **boiling is by far the best form of treatment** against bacteria, virus and giardia and surely produces the best tasting water. Boil, then chill. Tastes great.

Other critters may be harder to kill, but the latest studies show that **giardia cysts die in only one minute in water heated to only 176 degrees F.** Water boils at lower temperatures at higher altitudes, but UCCS Chemistry Prof. Cindy Beggs calculates that you would have to climb to 20,000 feet or more to make water boil at only 176F. **To be safe, health authorities recommend that you heat water to a rolling boil, however, and maintain that for several minutes.** (Guides who claim you should boil it for 20 minutes have never actually tried that: Any container backpackers use would boil dry in that time!) Then fill your canteen, cool it in a stream, and you have good tasting water.

Heat Prostration and Heat Stroke

Weakness, dizziness, cramps and rapid pulse are signs of heat prostration, and the victim who is not helped at this stage may faint with heat stroke. This can be fatal, so get the victim out of direct sunlight, give plenty of water and apply moist cloth to face and back of neck. You may prevent this from happening, however, by drinking plenty of water as you go and by adjusting clothing to the rapid changes of temperature.

Altitude Sickness

Hiking burns up so much oxygen that visitors from lower altitudes sometimes become ill from the thinner air at high altitude. Symptoms include headache, dizziness, weakness, poor appetite, nausea, impaired judgment and--in extreme cases--severe shortness of breath caused by pulmonary edema. The only real treatment is retreat to lower altitude. Do not hyperventilate: Short, shallow breathing can make you pass out.

Lightning

Trees split and charred by lightning mark almost every ridge, so let these remind you to watch the clouds overhead, especially as you cross ridges or wide meadows. You will never be entirely safe, but lightning usually strikes the highest point or peak, lone trees, cliff edges, caves high in cliffs or simply the largest object in a flat area. Obviously, pitching a tent above timberline is asking for it.

Retreat from high or open ground if a storm threatens and wait until it passes. If you find yourself trapped in an exposed area, crouch down with your poncho forming a tent around you and wait it out.

Rattlesnakes

The rattlesnake is the only poisonous snake naturally occurring in Colorado. Rattlers have been known to climb to timberline, but that is very rare. They are more often seen at lower altitudes (under 8,000 feet). Listen and watch for them, especially in the rocks and bluffs of the foothills. Roxborough State Park, Castlewood Canyon and the Air Force Academy are among the areas that report rattlers most often. Generally they try to get away, if they can, but they will fight if cornered or if they are protecting their young.

Health authorities no longer recommend tight bindings or cutting and sucking bites. Instead, wash the wound with soap and water or mild antiseptic, then wrap above the bite firmly with cloth, but do not cut off circulation. Immobilize the limb with a splint. Ice packs are recommended, though you aren't likely to have one. Watch for signs of shock while monitoring vital signs, and seek medical attention, which means get to civilization.

Rattler fangs make one or two puncture wounds. A bite that looks like a horseshoe is non-poisonous. The bull snake does a good imitation of a rattler, but they generally overact, being more aggressive, puffing their neck out and spitting or even barking. But they don't have rattles or poison.

Rare Problems

The State Health Dept. would like to remind all visitors to discuss your travel and outdoor experiences with doctors, if you should experience any puzzling symptoms. For example, vermin living under old cabins may transmit bubonic plague, the old Black Death, or another disease called Hantavirus, so never sleep in such places except as an emergency. For the same reason, don't try to hand-feed wildlife. Especially avoid any animal that behaves strangely because rabies is commonly found in wild animals. Hand-feeding birds is believed to be safer. (We show a picture of a hiker feeding a chipmunk, but it is not recommended because he might have had a flea.)

The most common tick fever usually produces a mild infection, but may be serious in small children, with acute headache, muscle ache and loss of energy. Tick-borne Relapsing Fever has similar symptoms, but may come back many times, if not properly treated. Lyme disease is serious but rare in Colorado. It is characterized by a donut or bullseye rash that develops around the bite days or weeks later.

Colorado does not have as many ticks or bugs of any kind as most other states and ticks are generally a springtime problem. The blooming of the columbine at any given altitude (sometime in June) generally signals the end of tick season. If you find one attached, health officials say you should remove it immediately by slowly and gently tugging until it gets too tired to hang on. The best tool is something like the edge of your driver's license. If you should get sick days or weeks later, remember to tell your doctor about the tick bite.

Again remember: If you should experience puzzling symptoms. always discuss your travel and outdoor experiences with doctors, If you should hear that a visiting friend or relative has gotten sick upon returning home, remind them of this advice. That may solve the mystery.

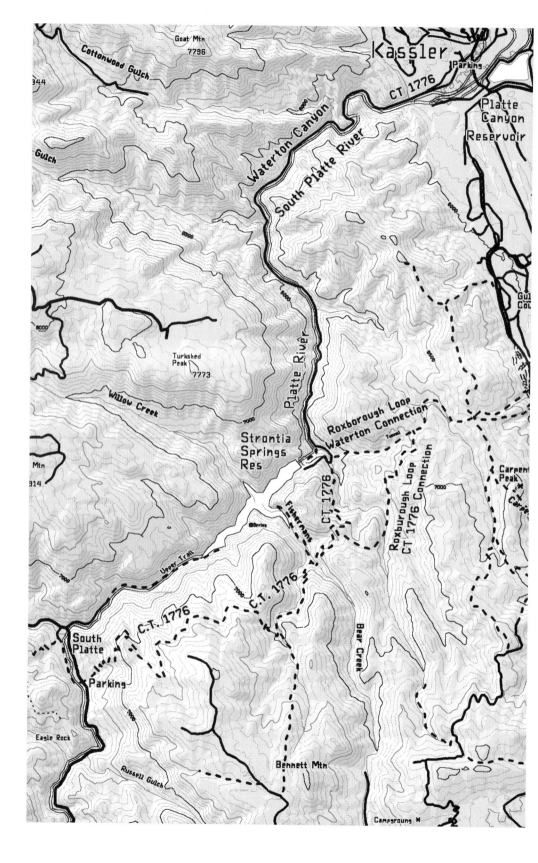

COLORADO TRAIL 1776
Denver to Georgia Pass

Cathedral Spires above the North Fork of the South Platte River

Segment One (From Denver's Waterton Canyon)
Through Segment Six (Georgia Pass)
Plus the Lost Creek Wilderness Bike Detour

Denver to Durango—469 miles!—the Colorado Trail 1776 is a continuous trail created by thousands of dedicated volunteers. This is not an old historic route, but since it was begun to commemorate Colorado's centennial and the nation's bicentennial, it has a new claim to history of its own.

Most people enjoy this trail by taking it in pieces, for it is cut by roads in many places, providing excellent access. For that reason, our descriptions will offer a lot of **road directions to help you enjoy the six segments that cross the region west of Denver dominated by Denver's closest National Forest.**

Beginning in Waterton Canyon just south of Denver, 1776 wanders 73.7 miles across the Pike National Forest before leaving our area at the

Continental Divide just above Georgia Pass. That's the only bite our guide can chew, but the entire route is described in an excellent book by Randy Jacobs, *The Colorado Trail.* We urge you to buy it because all proceeds from the Jacobs guide, plus the set of topographic maps which are sold separately, go to the non-profit Colorado Trail Foundation to help maintain and improve 1776.

Tragically, the fire of 1996 wrought many changes to both the landscape and the trail. Your first bridge had to be replaced due to fire-caused flooding, campgrounds were permanently closed, trailheads and parking had to be moved, and still the burn was so extensive that you must journey through much of it. **However, we have remapped and updated 1776 to reflect these changes, so this is 1776 updated for 1999.**

No other trail is so versatile. Many major trails connect with it, so you can design your own adventures. Mountain bikers now outnumber hikers and horse riders in many areas, and some sections are also very popular with cross-country skiers. **In the Pike National Forest, all of 1776 is open to bikes except for the Lost Creek Wilderness, so an alternate route has been created to skirt that area.** We describe this detour at the end of Segment Six.

The Colorado Trail Foundation will continue to need public support. You can help in several ways. You can volunteer to work on a trail crew; you can even adopt a section to maintain as your very own. You can contribute a tax-deductible donation to the Foundation, becoming a "Friend of the Colorado Trail," and you can buy the Jacobs book and maps. **Our own maps are based on the corrected CD-Rom companion to our guide produced by Ghost-Town Software.**

SEGMENT ONE—DENVER, FS #1776, 10 miles one way including 6.2-mile approach through Waterton Canyon; elevation gain 1,720 ft., loss 1,500 ft.; rated easy, then more difficult.

ROAD DIRECTIONS: From Denver take 1-25 South to Colorado 470, then west 12.5 miles to Colorado 126 (Wadsworth). Go south on Wadsworth 4.5 miles to its end just before the entrance to Martin Marietta. Turn left onto a side road and continue 0.3 miles, following signs to Waterton Canyon Recreation Area parking lot. From Colorado Springs, take 1-25 North past Castle Rock and take the Hwy. 85 exit to Sedalia. Go 5.8 miles past Sedalia and turn left (west) on Titan Road. After three miles this straight road turns left (south). Another 1.7 miles distant, turn right onto Waterton Road. Follow signs for another 2.4 miles to the parking lot.

Frontier explorers (and later the railroads) always followed water whenever they could. So trail builders could not have picked a more fitting gateway to the Rockies than Waterton Canyon at Denver's doorstep. Think of it this way: Colorado's major cities were all located where the Rockies finally give up their storehouse of snowmelt in currents of treasure to the plains.

Indeed, most of Denver's closest National Forest drains to the plains here at Waterton. Both forks of the South Platte River meet at the head of this gorge and flow down between these rock walls, interrupted only by Strontia Springs Dam, which you'll see just before reaching the 1776 singletrack trailhead. In 1820 the Long Expedition noticed this gateway, and in 1877 Territorial Governor John Evans built his Denver South Park and Pacific Railroad up this canyon.

Still, you can think about "the 1776 trailhead" two ways. Our measurements begin at the parking lot at the canyon's mouth because that is where you must leave your car and begin hiking or riding, but the Colorado Trail construction begins 6.2 miles higher up. That's why we speak of another trailhead higher up. Because of its segmented nature, CT 1776 has many many trailheads. Good thing. If it didn't, working people like you and me would never have time to see it.

Your exploration begins with a gentle journey up the canyon along a wide gravel service road that is closed to all but official vehicles. **This is a popular recreation trail in itself, a place where mountain bikers carry flyrods and where Denverites come to cross-country ski and snowshoe, but there are many special regulations. For example, no dogs, not even on a leash. That's because the north rim is a special bighorn habitat, off limits to people, and the bighorn come right down to the trails. No swimming or fireworks. Firearms and bows are permitted only during hunting season. Camping is not permitted until you climb into the National Forest on the CT 1776.**

Once you see the 243-foot dam, the road climbs more sharply. Just beyond a caretaker's house on your left is one of the trailheads for Roxborough Trail, here looking like a road. Less than half a mile later you find the CT 1776 trailwork with its official sign.

Now your singletrack begins with a series of switchbacks through dense Douglas fir, leading to a saddle where the second Roxborough Loop (south fork) joins your trail from the left. (Roxborough Loop is a triangle trail. See Roxborough State Park for special rules.)

Now your trail dips into the Bear Creek watershed (your last reliable water). Where it crosses the main creek (mile 8 from the parking lot), notice a fisherman's trail on your right leading down to Strontia Springs Reservoir. That's the old Deansbury sawmill road, leading to an inlet that is one of only two places where you can reach and fish Strontia, for this lake has a shoreline made of cliffs!

Next you cross a tributary called West Bear Creek and climb a mile to a point where 1776 shares its route with Motorcycle Trail #692. After another half a mile, you recross the tributary and leave the motorcycle trail, climbing to your right. The motorcycle trail crosses the CT once more about a half mile higher. At last you are traveling the side of the canyon itself with views of the lake and foothills. After

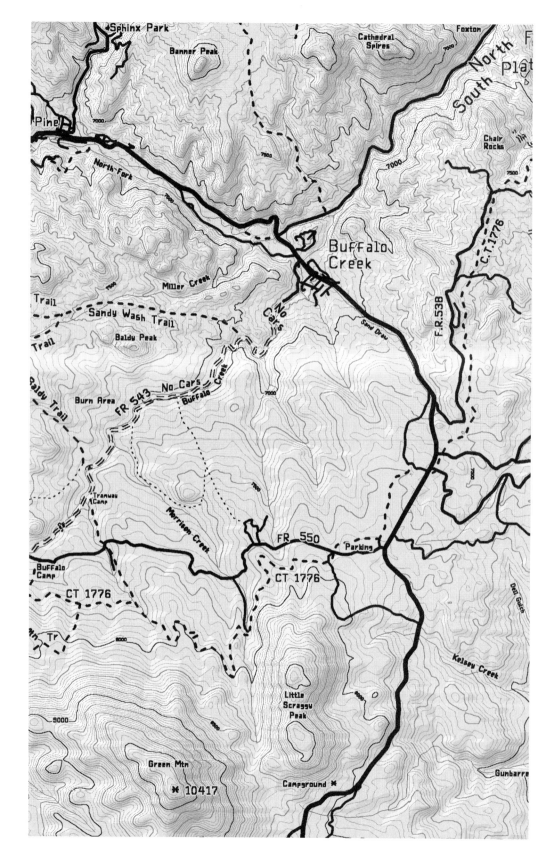

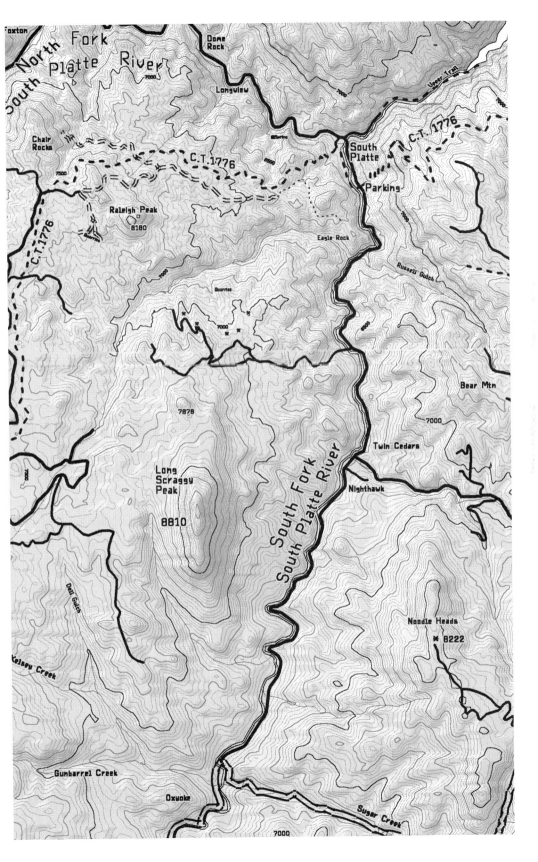

skirting a high valley, you begin switchbacking down to the river's other fork.

At the bottom you find the gravel portion of Highway 67 from Deckers, well south of the confluence of the North and South Platte River. Here mountain bikers, horses and hikers cross the South Fork via a very long and sturdy (and expensive) bridge constructed with funding contributed by the CT Foundation. This bridge is securely closed to motorized vehicles with heavy steel barricade-work. Across river, the trail heads upstream as a singletrack, then resumes the old route.

Non-motorized CT bridge across the South Fork

SEGMENT   TWO, FS# 1776, 9.4 miles one way, elevation gain 580 ft., loss 80ft.; rated difficult, then easy. Features a lesson in forest fire damage.

ROAD DIRECTIONS: No matter which way you go, you'll find some public roadside fishing along the rivers leading to South Platte townsite, but please respect private property. From Denver take Hwy. 285 south. Immediately south of Conifer, turn left on Foxton Road (County 97). Past Reynolds Park, turn left on County 96 and follow the North Fork downstream to South Platte. From Colorado Springs, take Hwy. 24 to Woodland Park, then right on 67. At Deckers, DON'T cross the bridge (to 126), but continue on 67, following the South Fork down-

**stream. Look for roadside parking and the new CT bridge that crosses
the South Fork well south of South Platte townsite and the confluence.**

Not much remains of the historic South Platte townsite except a boarded-up and vandalized hotel (this area did survive the fire of 1996), but in the old days a lot of trains passed this way. After crossing the CT bridge, your trail follows the river upstream toward the historic townsite. Be sure to water your horses and bring extra canteens because there is no more reliable water for the next 13 miles.

At first, it's all uphill. This is the segment that shows you the fire damage. Sometimes your trail follows the margin of the fire, and sometimes you're going through the charred area. Several miles from the river, you find a large granite outcrop from which you can see Pikes Peak, Devil's Head and the Platte Canyon. Watch your markers because the trail makes use of short sections of old roads before ducking back into the woods as a single track once more. Bikers, watch out for cactus beside the trail.

At mile 7.1 a short side trail used to lead uphill to Top of the World Campground, now gone. As its name suggests, that lofty campground once boasted a panoramic view, but in 1996 it was an inferno. Boy Scouts and other visitors fled to the river. No one was killed, but their cars burned so intensely that aluminum engine blocks melted down and ran away in rivulets. Now, even the access road FS# 538 has been closed.

Beyond this point, the CT becomes more gentle, rolling toward Hwy 126. Just as it reaches 126, it has been rerouted uphill along the right of way, for old the trailhead and its parking lot across the highway were closed due to fire. That used to be the end of Segment Two and may still be for bureaucratic and measurement purposes, but for anyone parking, the effective end is now the next trailhead uphill. The CT crosses two paved sideroads (Spring Creek Trail and Road), then immediately crosses 126 (be careful!) one mile below FS Road 550. Just out of sight of 126, it then resumes the old route, paralleling 126 though unburned timber to the Little Scraggy trailhead parking off 550 just to the northwest of its intersection with 126. You have now put the fireland behind you, because you cannot see any more of it from 1776 from here on, but it will remain a reminder to your grandchildren.

*SEGMENT THREE, 13.4 miles one way, elevation gain 1,320 ft., loss 600;
rated easy, then moderate.*

**ROAD DIRECTIONS, From Denver take Hwy. 285 32 miles south to Pine
Junction, then left on 126. From Colorado Springs, take Hwy. 24 West
to Woodland Park, then right on 67 to Deckers and left, crossing the
bridge to 126. The most popular parking area on 126 near Buffalo
Creek was closed due to fire. To find the expanded lot at Little**

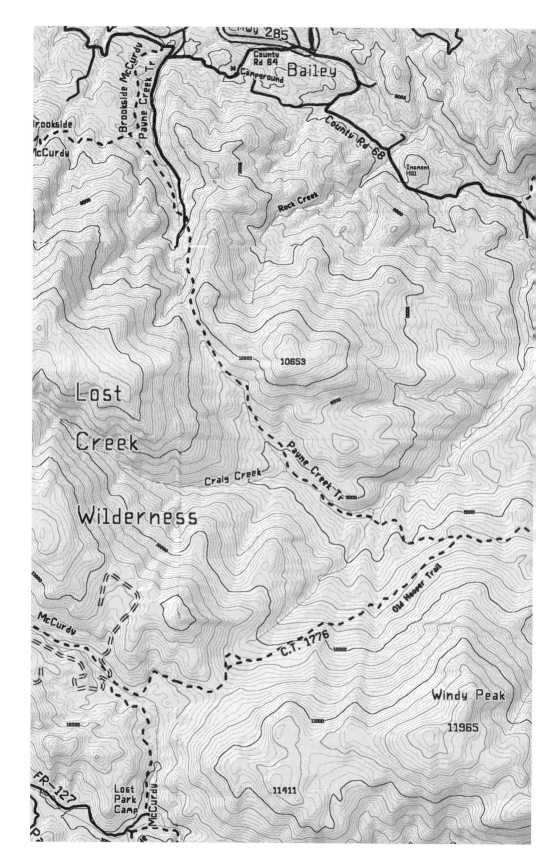

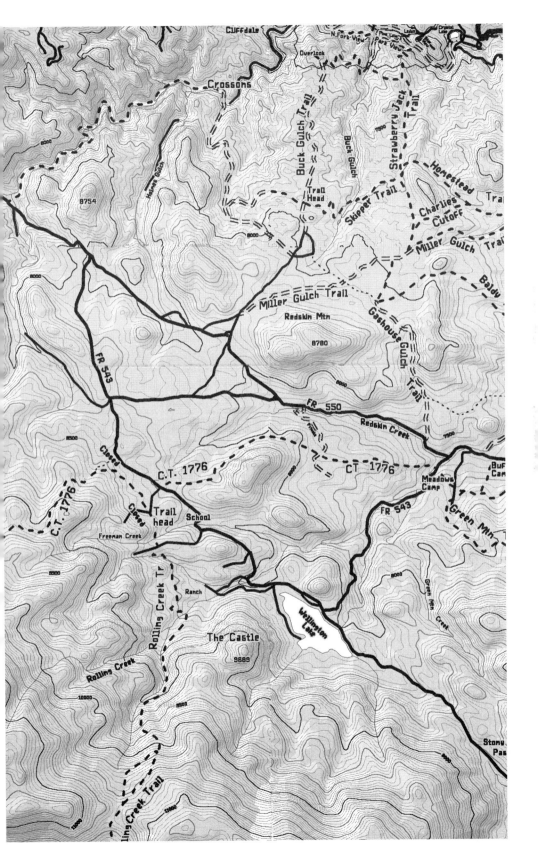

Scraggy Trailhead, turn west on FS-550, located 4.1 miles south of Buffalo Creek or 11.3 miles north of Deckers. This over-used lot is immediately on your right. Note: some maps seem to show the CT crossing 550 at this lot, but It actually crosses 550 half a mile farther west. This is only important because there is a false trail marked "closed to motor vehicles" near that location. Since Little Scraggy is often jammed with 70 cars, we advise you to try other parking farther along 550, especially the large newest one just to the right of the gate at Meadows Group Campground. See BUFFALO CREEK BIKE AREA.

If you make it across 126 without getting squashed, pass Little Scraggy Trailhead, then swing west, staying out of sight of 550 for half a mile before crossing it. On the other side, the CT heads west again, then southwest, all pretty easy until you come to stream crossings. Our rating changes to moderate from now on. Your trail is designed to skirt the Meadows Group Campground (reservation only), but does cross the entrance of the campground. (Note the large new parking lot just to the right of the gate) Shortly after, at mile 9.5 you cross the stream called Buffalo Creek at FS-543. Now climb steeply out of the Buffalo Creek watershed to a yucca ridge with views of the granite outcrop called The Castle to the south.

Streamside view near the Colorado Trail

At mile 13.4, the CT drops down to cross FS-560 at the **Rolling Creek** Trailhead access and follows that access road 0.3 miles to parking for both trails.

SEGMENT FOUR, 15.3 miles one way, elevation gain 2,800 ft., loss 920; rated more difficult.

ROAD DIRECTIONS: From Denver, take Hwy. 285 south 39 miles to Bailey. Go left on County 68, which becomes marked FS-543 (called 560 on FS visitor's map, but marked 543 here). At mile 5.2 take the right fork marked for Wellington Lake). The CT crosses this road about 8.5 miles south of Bailey. From Deckers, take 126 11.3 miles to FS-550. Turn left and follow 550 (5.1 miles) then FS-543 (3.5 miles). When you reach Wellington Lake, turn right toward Bailey. Only 0.9 miles past Jeffco's Windy Peak Outdoor Education Lab, look for a little dirt road that leads west about 0.3 miles. There you'll find the shared trailhead for both ROLLING CREEK and the CT.

Bikes are not allowed in the Lost Creek Wilderness, so an alternate route for bikes will be described at the end of this segment. All others get ready for a climb because this segment gains a lot of altitude.

From 560 or 543, the CT goes 0.3 miles up an old road to a gate that closes the road to vehicles. **Rolling Creek Trail** goes to the left, the CT to the right. Almost a mile later, 1776 joins the old Hooper Trail, a logging road built by W.H. Hooper between 1885 and 1887. His sawmill in Lost Park was eventually shut down by the Department of the Interior for persistent violations, and now the Lost Creek Wilderness is so highly protected that not even the Forest Service can use a chain saw there. In fact, they're not even allowed to measure trails with a wheel!

After a climb of 1.8 miles, pass through a gate to enter the Lost Creek Wilderness, the last stronghold of wild buffalo in Colorado until the last four buffalo were killed by poachers in 1901. Turn left where the trail forks at mile 2.3. The **Payne Creek Trail** (once called Craig Meadow) comes down from your right to join the CT at mile 3.1. Continue straight ahead, climbing southwest through aspen and lodgepole forest. At mile 4.5, you cross a small stream, then leave Hooper's road to avoid Bluestem Draw, a giant bog where the log corduroy used to run for almost a quarter of a mile. Half a mile later, 1776 returns to Hooper's trail and climbs over a wooded ridge to find the long meadow of the North Fork of Lost Creek. At mile 7.8 a side trail From Lost Park Campground joins 1776 from the south (left). Notice the remains of a sawmill to the south across the creek. Lots of brook trout here. For road directions to Lost Park Campground, see our Kenosha Pass chapter.

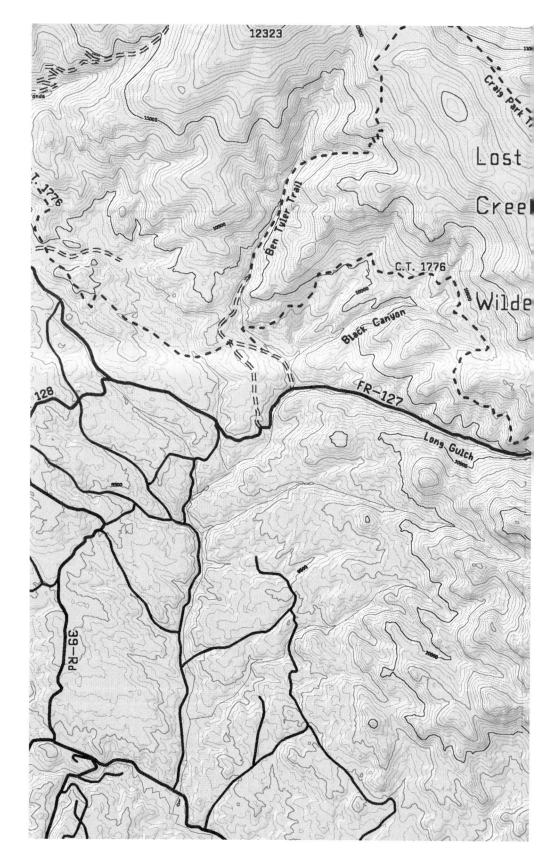

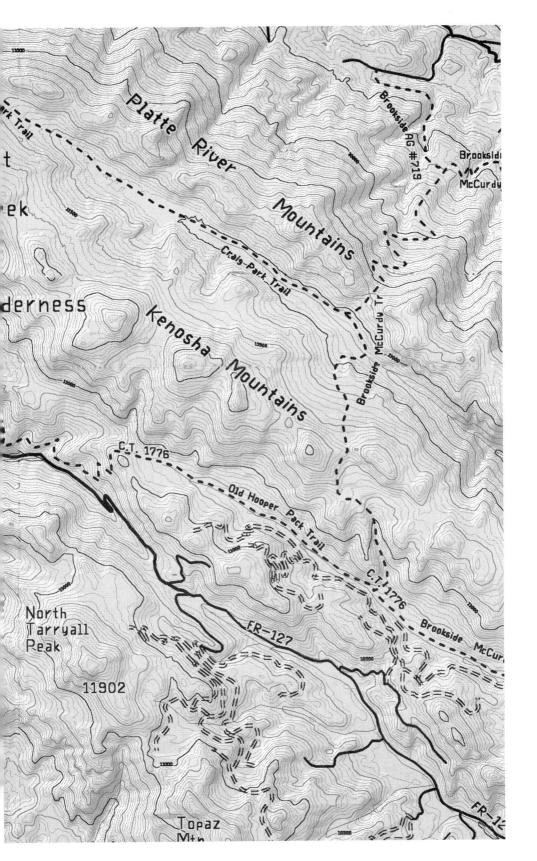

Brookside-McCurdy Trail will branch off to your right at mile 8.0, but 1776 continues straight up the open valley, a steady gentle climb with views of the Kenosha Mountains. At 10,880 ft., you mount the saddle at the head of the valley (mile 13.2), leaving the Hooper Trail and contouring through spruce forest. Glimpse the Continental Divide and then switchback down to cross a tiny stream at mile 15.2. Just past some washed out beaver ponds, you pass an eroded side trail coming up from FS- 817 on the Lost Park Road. This is a popular access. For directions see Segment Five.

SEGMENT FIVE, 14 miles one way, elevation gain 960 ft., loss 1,160; rated moderate.

ROAD DIRECTIONS, Kenosha Pass is located about 58 miles west of Denver on Hwy. 285, or about 21 miles north of Fairplay. Just 1.2 miles north of Jefferson or 3.2 miles south of the pass, turn east onto Lost Park Road (FS-56). Your first CT access is not the beginning of Segment Five. Go 7.3 miles and turn left onto F3-133, marked for the BEN TYLER TRAIL. The CT crosses this route 1.3 miles farther up; this is where mountain bikes pick up the CT once more, after detouring

Streamwater always has to be boiled or treated.

around the Lost Creek Wilderness Area. Segment Five begins at the next access along Lost Park Road, 11 miles from the highway. Turn left onto tiny FS-817, which is only about 0.2 miles long. Park and climb up this rutted road to where the CT crosses it at right angles.

Continuing through aspens above FS-817. the CT turns north and crosses the head of Black Canyon, then makes a slow descent to Rock Creek at mile 7.1. This is the point that can be accessed via the **Ben Tyler** trailhead as mentioned ear-

Pikes Peak seen in the distance from near Lost Creek

lier. Find your way through brush to cross the creek's footbridge. Follow an old road downstream for only a tenth of a mile and watch for the CT suddenly ducking into the spruce forest to your right. After passing through a gate, turn right onto another old road and look for the CT on your left a third of a mile higher. At mile 7.7 you'll cross **Ben Tyler Trail**, here a road, then descend through a meadow to Johnson Gulch (seasonal flow) and cross at mile 8.2. Posts mark your way through the grass for more than a mile until you reach timber at the head of the valley. A clearing up ahead offers views of the Black Canyon behind and the CT as it crosses the Continental Divide far ahead. Many faint roads complicate the route, so watch your markers. The last leg is through aspen forest, leading down to the saddle of Kenosha Pass, which is popular with cross-country skiers. Note: Do not park in the Kenosha Pass Campground.

SEGMENT SIX, 11.6 miles one way to Pike National Forest boundary, elevation gain 2,600 ft., toss 620; rated moderate to difficult.

ROAD DIRECTIONS: For directions to Kenosha Pass, see Segment Five. The CT crosses at the Kenosha Pass Campground, but park on the east side of 285 or at the new trailhead on the east side. To find the Jefferson Lake Road Access, go 4.4 miles south to Jefferson and turn west on Jefferson Lake Road. Drive 2.1 miles and turn right toward the lake. Find the CT crossing the road 3.1 miles farther. Parking is available a tenth of a mile farther at Beaver Ponds Picnic Ground, and overnight parking Is available 0,6 miles farther, near the entrance to Jefferson Creek Campground.

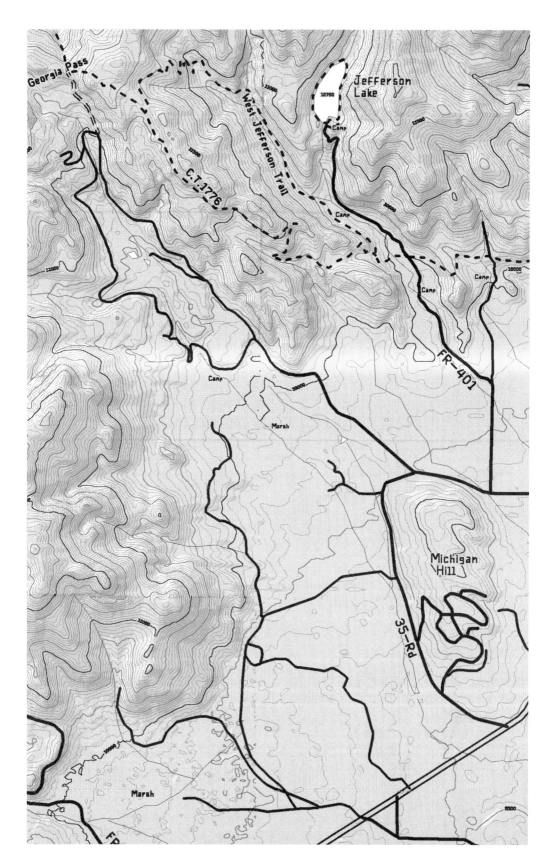

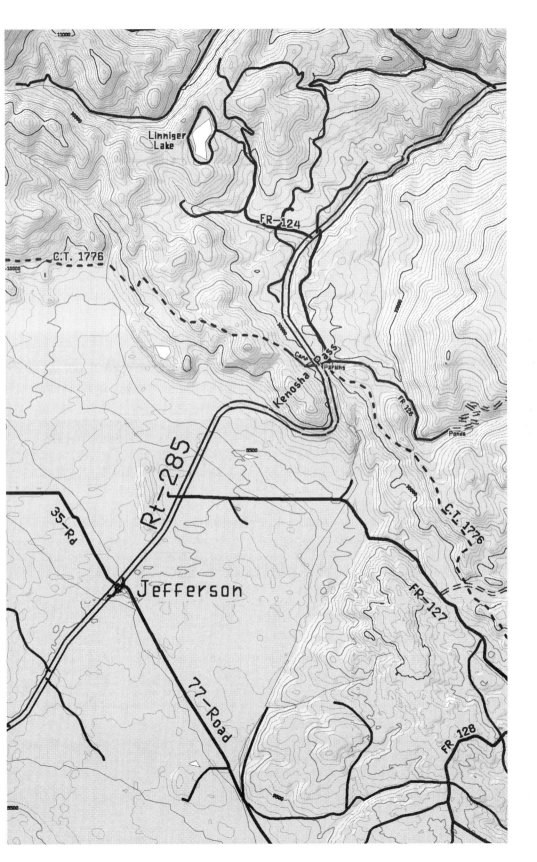

Near Kenosha Campground, the CT continues through aspens and lodge-pole. This early section is popular for cross-country skiing. The trail washboards through meadow and forest, then across Guernsey Gulch, Deadman Gulch, and past Jefferson Hill before dropping down to the Jefferson Lake Road. There are great views of South Park and distant mountains. From there 1776 switchbacks uphill again, sometimes adopting old roads, climbing through forest that changes from bristlecone to spruce closer to timberline. At 11,400 feel (mile 10.5), you find the krummholz transitional zone, where forest gives way to tundra. Here runted trees barely grow at all, their branches shaped by prevailing winds. Please stay on trail going across tundra because this delicate vegetation takes many years to regrow. At mile 11.6 (11,880) you reach the Continental Divide just east and above Georgia Pass. This is the boundary of the Pike National Forest, the end of our area, but the Segment Six continues down to Hwy. 9 north of Breckenridge.

LOST CREEK WILDERNESS BIKE DETOUR, 72 miles one way, elevation gain 3,560 ft., loss 1,240; rated moderate.

There is only one mile of pavement along this 72-mile detour around the Lost Creek Wilderness. It goes through the old mining town of Tarryall, which was known as Puma City when it was founded in 1896. If you don't mind pavement and the danger of traffic, there is a more direct route not described in detail here. Go northwest on FS-550 and FS-560 from the Rolling Creek Trailhead to Bailey, then take busy Hwy. 285 to Kenosha Pass.
Our detour begins about halfway through Segment Three, where 1776 first crosses FS-543 at mile 8.9. **Mileage figures now start over.** Follow 543 southwest 2.7 miles to Wellington Lake, then turn left onto FS-560 and climb Stony Pass (8560). About seven miles past the summit, go right onto FS-211 at mile 13.6, then right again 5.4 miles later, following signs to Goose Creek Campground. Turn right onto Park County Road 77 at mile 35.8, which is paved for about a mile. Continue through the town of Tarryall and pass the Spruce Grove Campground. Go past the Tarryall Reservoir to mile 63.0 and turn right onto Park County Road 39, also called FS-128 and Rock Creek Hills Road. Go north to Lost Park Road (FS-127) and turn right (east) at mile 68.6. About two miles farther, turn left onto FS-133 where the sign points toward **Ben Tyler**. Bike another 1.3 miles and find the CT crossing your road. This point is called mile 7.7 in the description of Segment 5 (9720). Now you're back on 1776, heading west toward Kenosha Pass.
Another popular biking route starts at the end of Segment Five at Kenosha Pass. Since bikes are allowed on the last 6.5 miles of Segment Five, some like to make a loop by starting at Kenosha Pass, pedaling east on the CT to Rock Creek, then down to Lost Park Road, returning to Hwy. 285 and then up to Kenosha Pass once more. Only the last 3.2 miles is on pavement.

BUFFALO CREEK MOUNTAIN BIKE AREA

The Colorado Trail 1776 below Green Mountain

Buck Gulch Trail
Skipper Trail
Strawberry Jack Trail
Miller Gulch Trail
Sandy Wash Trail
Gashouse Gulch
Baldy Trail
Homestead Trail
Charlie's Cutoff
AND LINKS TO COLORADO TRAIL #1776
Tramway Trail
Green Mountain Trail

Despite the fire of l996, the Buffalo Creek Mountain Bike Area continues to be the premier fat-tire adventure land for Denver and the Front Range. The fire did force changes, including trail, campground and road closures, but before the fire, authorities opened three new trails in areas that went untouched. Moreover, the addition of Jeffco's Pine Valley Ranch Park to the north created a new way to access the entire system. See our very next chapter about Pine Valley Ranch Park.

Frankly, for a long time after the fire, we avoided this area, afraid of what we would find, but now we kick ourselves for missing out because the fire left much of it undamaged. Although the blaze burned a wedge through the very heart of the area, you don't actually see its damage from your car, except from Hwy. 126. The access roads used today show you none at all! We were amazed.

Of course, we don't want to downplay the real damage. This was not one of those ground-level grass-burners that put back nutrients and made the wildflowers bloom. This was one of those tragic crown fires that burns away the organic topsoil, leaving behind sandy minerals poisoned with turpines, the kind of fire that won't let Nature rebound in our lifetimes. And as always, such unprotected sand soon washes away in any downpour, adding flood to fire damage.

Still, our reaction was one of relief as much as regret, and we truly admire the creative ways that the Forest Service has handled the problem. We also thank the Volunteers for Outdoor Colorado for doing the hard labor.

Originally intended to take pressure off the most popular segment of the Colorado Trail, this system is a maze of old logging roads with single-track connections, allowing you to design loop adventures of any length that suits you. The area is only about an hour's drive from Denver and one and a half from Colorado Springs. Mild winters at this altitude (7,000-8,000) mean that trails remain clear eight to 10 months a year. No kidding, people ride here pretty much year round!

Often, routes are marked only with a bike symbol, not trail names at this time, so it's important to keep your bearings. (There is no exclusive use for bikes here; hikers and horses are welcome.) Too, the terrain is gentle enough not to provide many looming landmarks, so--yes--we have gotten confused here more than once. To our knowledge, our guide is the only one that details this area and always has.

When describing any maze, it's always hard to know just where to begin. Our road directions may look complicated, but if you follow them carefully, you should get the grand tour. One other thing: Road maps are created in offices: Ours is done in the woods. Our road numbers will be different from those you find on official maps because our numbers are taken right off the signs you actually find in the forest. What else would help you?

The Buffalo Creek Mountain Bike Area is situated around the Buffalo Creek Recreation Area, which includes established campgrounds. Fires in the Recreation Area are always absolutely restricted to metal fire grates provided, regardless of fire danger conditions. Roadside parking is restricted by law, so watch the signs. To reserve the Meadows Group Campground, call 800-416-6992. To reserve others call 877-444-6777. You may also visit the web site at www.reserveusa.com.

For more about the fire, see Colorado Trail Segment Two.

ROAD DIRECTIONS: The community of Buffalo Creek is located on Jefferson County 126 between Deckers and Pine Junction. From Denver take Hwy. 285 south 32 miles to Pine Junction and turn south on 126. From Colorado Springs, take Hwy. 24 west to Woodland Park, take 67 north to Deckers, then turn left and cross the bridge to take 126 north to Buffalo Creek.

The most popular access to the area was always the creekside road FS-543, which started at the community of Buffalo Creek itself. That road has been closed to motorized vehicles and is now a trail, known simply by its number 543, but there is NO PARKING FOR IT ALONG THE HIGHWAY. Our road directions take you to the other end, where parking is provided. It's still a very pretty route because many of the trees along its corridor survived. (In a canyon, hot fires tend to burn upward, taking out the hillsides above but leaving creekside trees.) Go see it. It's a very easy trail through interesting rocks and beside a tumbling stream: distance 6.3 miles one way.

There is no sign of fire damage from FS#550

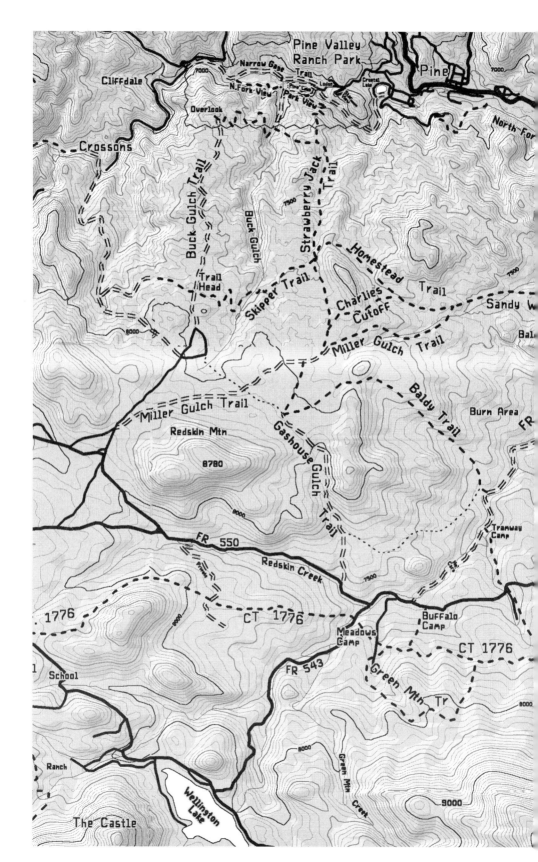

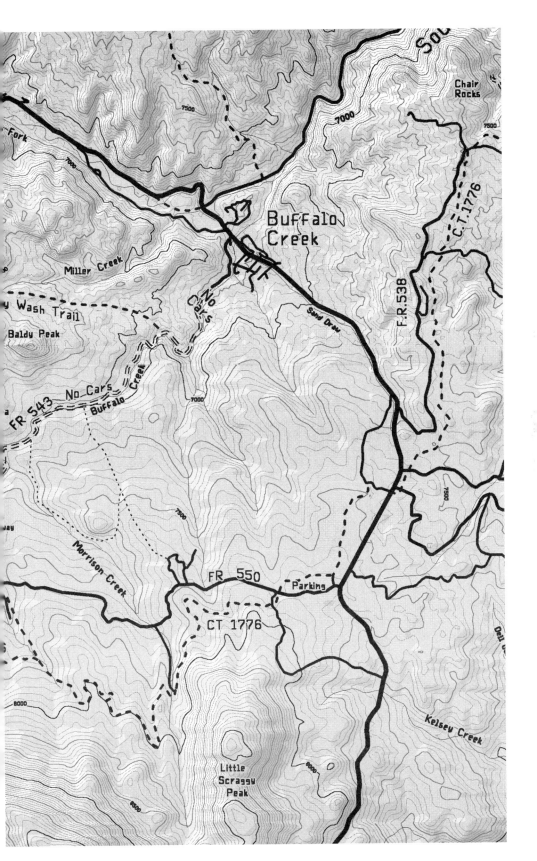

Closed to motorized use by the fire, FS 543 is an easy—and still pretty—trail along the creek.

When we heard that many people access this area from Bailey, that seemed too round-about for us, but having tried all routes, that one will be one of our favorites! We describe it later. First, however, we have to show you in the old way. Besides, you have to know your way around, so bear with us.

To access trails from Highway 126 south of Buffalo Creek, use FS-550, which begins on a hill 4.1 miles south of Buffalo Creek or 11.3 miles north of Deckers. When coming from Denver, this turnoff is hard to miss because of the big sign for the Buffalo Creek Recreation Area on your right, but when coming from Deckers, you must slow down as you top the hill and watch carefully for the turnoff to FS-550 on your left. (Note: the popular CT 1776 trailhead on Hwy 126 itself north of this intersection has been closed and replaced by a newly expanded trailhead which we describe next. CT 1776 now crosses I26 closer to 550.)

Turn onto FS-550. Shortly on your right is the newly expanded trailhead parking for COLORADO TRAIL 1776, but since this lot is often crowded with as many as 70 cars, we'll show you better parking farther down. The CT parallels 550 for half a mile (out of sight), then crosses 550 and parallels the road on the south to intersect with bike trails ahead. At mile 4.2, TRAMWAY TRAIL crosses 550. Ignore the apparent trailhead at mile 4.7. At mile 4.8 you pass Buffalo Campground on your left. GREEN

MOUNTAIN TRAIL joins 550 from the left at mile 4.9, but there is no good parking here. (GREEN MOUNTAIN has no trailhead parking of its own, being just a detour off the CT.) At mile five, the closed-to-motorized vehicles FS-543 is on your right. DO NOT PARK IN FRONT OF THIS GATE, WHICH IS STILL USED BY AUTHORITIES, EVEN IF YOU SEE OTHERS PARKING THERE. Instead, use the new parking lot near Meadows Group Campground, described next.

Our road 550 jogs left for half a mile (becoming 543 for that short distance) then takes off northwest again from 543. Along that jog you'll find the entrance to Meadows Group Campground. TO FIND NEW TRAILHEAD PARKING FOR THE CT 1776, turn left onto the sideroad marked Meadows Campground. A large parking lot, complete with restroom, has been provided just to the right of the gate, outside of the campground. Do not enter the gate or park in the campground itself. Back on the main road, there is another small parking lot just beyond the Meadows that may also be used for trails in this area, but none actually leaves from that lot.

To access more bike trails, proceed past Meadows Campground. We're actually on the 543 jog here, but 550 takes off again to your right very shortly. (If you stayed on 543 straight ahead, the CT crosses it just a short distance farther where the stream crosses. Head to your left or southeast on the CT to access GREEN

We call this Lincoln Rock along trail 543.

MOUNTAIN TRAIL.) But we're going to take the 550 turn to the right, very sloppy for a short distance in spring.

To find the trailhead for GASHOUSE GULCH, go only 0.4 miles further and turn right onto a dead-end road that leads up half a mile to the trailhead, which is guarded by a log rail fence. Back on 550, continue northwest another 1.8 miles to a fork. There 550 goes left, but you want to TURN RIGHT at the fork marked 549 and "EOS Mill." (This 549 is confusing, being a left turn later on, so just watch your odometer and keep following our directions.) Climb one mile farther and find a triangular intersection, marked Bailey and Highway 285 to the left. Go right here. You are now on FS-553.

To find MILLER GULCH TRAILHEAD, go only 0.4 miles and turn right onto FS-554. Ignore the false trail 0.1 mile up 554 and proceed on 554

one half mile to a fence with a cattle-guard gap to the left of the gate. You may find this gate open for firewood cutters, but this is the MILLER GULCH TRAILHEAD and you may not drive farther. (Actually, you've been driving Miller Gulch since the turnoff, but this is where you park, so we call this the trailhead.) This trailhead also serves to lead you to HOMESTEAD, CHARLIE'S CUTOFF and SANDY WASH and the northern end of GASHOUSE GULCH, linking with BALDY TRAIL.

To find the trailhead for BUCK GULCH and SKIPPER, linking to STRAWBERRY JACK, DON'T take the 554 turnoff for Miller Gulch, but proceed up the road you were following, now known as 553, for 0.9 miles. There you find an intersection where the well-traveled road ahead is marked Dead End. That's private property. Instead, you turn left here on a much smaller road marked 552. Go 0.7 miles farther and you'll find the trailheads for BUCK GULCH and SKIPPER on your right as the road swings left to-ward private property. Look for a large bulletin-board kiosk built by Volunteers for Outdoor Colorado using materials donated by Recreational Equipment, Inc (REI) of Denver.

See why lots of people use Pine Valley Ranch Park as an access? No matter how you get here, you have to know your way around or you'll spend as much time confused as we did finding all this out for you.

Another popular way to the same spot is from Bailey on Hwy 285, and although that may not seem direct, this a very pretty route through ranch valleys on much better road. To do it that way, turn off at Bailey onto Park County 68, which becomes FS 543. The pavement runs out at mile 2.3 from Bailey. (543 is called 560 on the FS Visitor's Map, but stick with us.) At mile 5.2 bear left at a fork marked for a lot of things, including the EOS mill. You're now leaving 543 to take 549. At mile 6.8 you cross a cattleguard, leaving Park County, and 0.4 miles later (mile 7.2 from Bailey) you find the triangular intersection. Go left, again marked for the EOS mill. Only 0.4 miles later you pass the Miller Gulch turnoff (554). You're on your way to BUCK GULCH-SKIPPER TRAILHEAD as described above.

BUCK GULCH TRAIL, Forest Service #772, 3.2 miles one way, including one mile segment within Jefferson County's Pine Valley Ranch Park, rated mostly moderate with difficult switchbacks; features stream-side and then ridge trail linking with Strawberry Jack and Skipper.

Buck Gulch is the name of a tiny stream feeding into the North Fork of the South Platte River at Pine Valley Ranch Park. At least 70% of Denverites access Buck Gulch Trail and the vast system beyond in the Buffalo Creek Mountain Bike Area via that park. For that reason we describe Pine Valley Ranch Park in our very next chapter instead of including it in the Jefferson County Open Space chapter.

The park access is so popular because you drive every inch on pavement, enjoy adequate parking, clean restrooms and have this magnificent park as a gateway. Horseriders also prefer this access because it prevents hard jostling trailering over rougher roads and because the park has a special parking lot just for horse trailers. So we're going to describe Buck Gulch Trail from the park.

Circle the lake to find Buck Gulch Trail on the far side. The park segment follows the stream itself closely, straight up a draw with mixed aspens and past a log cabin. Just beyond the park boundary, you reach an open area where Strawberry Jack comes down from your left to join Buck Gulch Trail at a culvert.

From here Buck Gulch Trail leaves the water and switchbacks up (very steeply and very washed) to a high ridge, past a rock overlook from which you can see up river, and then into an open forest composed mainly of ponderosa. From here on you have a ridge trail tracing the rim of the Buck Gulch drainage, following an ancient double-track. This is a high and sunny route. If the weather is damp, this trail stays much drier than Strawberry Jack. It ends at the kiosk trailhead where Skipper takes off to the east. If you include the distance around the lake to the trailhead, you are now about 3.5 miles from your car at Pine Valley Ranch Park.

SKIPPER TRAIL, Forest Service #790, 1.1 mile one way, rated moderate, links Buck Gulch with Homestead and Strawberry Jack.

Leaving the VOC-REI kiosk, Skipper Trail starts down past low-profile rock formations toward Buck Gulch Creek. Its switchbacks are nowhere near as steep as those on Buck Gulch Trail. This part of the drainage is far more moist and mossy and has many more blue spruce than you'll see elsewhere in the area. At the plank bridge the brook has a fairy glen look. Then you switchback up through the kind of high, sparse ponderosa that dominates the area.

From here Skipper meanders through the tall ponderosa to a strangely-shaped junction with Homestead in a fairly open area. Here Homestead appears as a double-track coming down from your right to T-junction against singletrack. This is the end of **Skipper**, but to find **Strawberry Jack,** continue straight ahead on the singletrack, which is now technically part of **Homestead's** loop. Only 125 paces farther, **Strawberry Jack** takes off at a right angle to your left. We do wish this had been designed as a simple four-way intersection.

Skipper Trail is named after a threatened butterfly.

STRAWBERRY JACK, Forest Service #790, 2 miles one way, including the 0.7 mile section marked "service road" on the Jeffco Pine Valley Ranch Park map, forms link between Skipper, Jeffco's Parkview Trail and Buck Gulch Trail.

The way we heard it, Strawberry Jack was the name of a dog at the private Crystal Lake Resort, where the Volunteers for Outdoor Colorado camped. Not every dog gets a trail named after him.

Starting from our link with **Buck Gulch** and **Homestead, Strawberry Jack** zig-zags more than we can show on our maps, always staying to the left side of a draw leading down toward the Platte. Unlike sunnier **Buck Gulch**, this can be a pretty soggy route.

Only a few years ago this whole area was cleaned of underbrush by prescribed burn. This type of intentional fire works only at ground-level, revitalizing the forest by returning nutrients to soil. thus encouraging wildflowers and grasses that benefit wildlife. It also reduced fuel load, which may prevent a more serious fire. Everywhere you look you see evidence of past burns in the upper bike area, but this is the most recent.

Along the way you'll see some aspens to your right and a few rock formations on your left. **Farther along, you start uphill, climbing to a saddle where Jeffco's Park View Trail heads up into the rocks to your right. No horses or bikes are allowed on that one, but we strongly recommend the sidetrip to the top of Park View for, well, a view of the park. It's quite a vista from atop high bluffs above the river and lake.**

For the next 0.7 miles you'll be going downhill on something called a "service road" on the park map, but which is just a wide singletrack these days. Actually, this section was used as a service road by the ranch to service antennas you'll see on Park View.

When you break out into a clearing, you'll cross the stream called Buck Gulch on a culvert. That's where **Strawberry Jack** ends. Total distance of the Skipper-Strawberry Jack-Buck Gulch loop is about 5.3 miles.

MILLER GULCH TRAIL, Forest Service #730, 3.5 miles one way, elevation 240 ft., loss 560 ft.; rated easy. Features gentle route linking directly to three other trails, which lead to many more. Open to foot, bike and horse.

7,760	3.5 miles	7,600

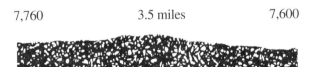

Perhaps the easiest trail in the system, Miller Gulch rolls gently through a hilltop forest. Years ago woodcutters thinned this forest, opening it up, which enhanced the wildflower and wildlife habitat. It is home to a small herd of elk and a flock of wild turkeys. Soon, Gashouse Gulch branches off to your right, and Homestead takes off to your left shortly after.

There is one switchback along the route, then a meadow. Shortly beyond, Miller Gulch reaches a stream where Sandy Wash Trail begins.

SANDY WASH TRAIL, Forest Service #730,1.6 miles one way, elevation loss 640 ft., rated moderate downhill, very difficult uphill. Features great downhill ride. Open to foot, bike and horse.

Think of Sandy Wash as an extension of Miller Gulch, for it even shares the same FS trail number. Sandy Wash is rated moderate only if you take its designer's advice and use it as a one-way downhill from Miller Gulch to the fire-closed FS-543. If you try it from the bottom, you'll find it very tough going because it is exactly what its name implies, a sandy wash. The fire missed almost all of this trail. It dives down to the Buffalo Creek drainage, joining FS-543 at the edge of the burn. From there, we recommend you take 543 southwest or upstream 2.2 miles to do a loop with Baldy Trail because **the lower portion of Gashouse is closed.**

BALDY TRAIL, Forest Service #727, 2.3 miles one way, elevation gain 880ft., loss 40, rated difficult. Features challenging climb to Gashouse Gulch. Open to foot, bike and horse.

7,120   2.3 miles   7,960

Baldy Campground is gone with the fire, but Baldy Trail nearby is still open, though its lower portion did burn. This is a tough climb up from the Buffalo Creek drainage on FS-543, now a trail, but has good views. At the top you T-junction against **Gashouse Gulch**. If you turn left or downhill on Gashouse, you'll have to use forest service road to complete any loops because the lower half of Gashouse is gone.

GASHOUSE GULCH TRAIL, Forest Service #726, now only 1.7 miles one way due to closure of lower leg, elevation gain 930 ft., rated difficult. Features challenging climb to Miller Gulch.

The fire which started near Gashouse Gulch cost us the lower leg, shortening the distance to only 1.7 miles one way. From the lower trailhead off FS-550, it goes up through aspen meadows with only a couple of steep spots, intersecting with Baldy and ending at Miller Gulch. That sounds easy, but the upper half is sandy, which is tougher on a bike. The name Gashouse Gulch was reportedly coined by local children.

HOMESTEAD TRAIL, Forest Service #728, 2.6 miles one way, elevation gain 320 ft., rated moderate. Features interesting ride past overlook rock. Open to foot, bike and horse.

Homestead forms a kind of long detour, leaving Miller Gulch, looping around a wooded hill and returning again. Put together with Charlie's Cut-off, there are several loop possibilities. We're describing it clockwise.

Homestead is mostly old logging road, but changes to single track as it arches over a ridge near its northern end. It is at that T-shaped junction, where the double-track ahead is closed off with logs, that **Skipper** comes in from your left as a singletrack. Go right from that junction on singletrack and 125 paces later, **Strawberry Jack** goes left. From here on Homestead is a singletrack. Watch for a high set of rocks on that ridge to your right. Leave the trail and climb to the top for an impressive view of Kenosha Pass, Mount Rosalie, Mount Logan, the Valley of the North Fork and much more. Descending the ridge, your trail becomes an old road again, then single track after its intersection with **Charlie's Cut-off**. From here your trail is an old cow path, following a tiny stream toward its eastern intersection with **Miller Gulch**.

CHARLIE'S CUT-OFF, Forest Service #729, 0.7 miles one way, elevation gain 80 ft., loss 240 ft., rated moderate. Features shortcut between sections of Homestead. Open to foot, bike and horse.

For some reason, Charlie's Cut-off was named after a remote weather station that is not on this trail. This shortcut is mostly single track through rocky forest. It makes the whole system more versatile, making it possible to do loops with Homestead and Miller Gulch.

TRAMWAY CREEK TRAIL, Forest Service #??? 1.1 mile one way, elevation gain 480 ft.; rated moderate. Features creekside climb to Colorado Trail. Open to foot, bike and horse.

Tramway is an old name for a yarder, a kind of ski lift contraption used to haul logs out of the woods. The tramway is gone now, and the forest has grown tall again, but the contraption is still remembered in the name of the creek and its trail. Tramway campground is gone. The trail follows the creek upstream, crosses FS-550, and eventually links with the Colorado Trail. The section above 550 is rocky, has several stream crossings and leads into the burn area.

GREEN MOUNTAIN TRAIL, Forest Service #722, 1.8 miles one way, elevation gain 400 ft., loss, 560 ft. if ridden east to west; rated difficult. Features scenic alternative along Colorado Trail. Open to foot, bike and horse.

This is a kind of looping detour off the Colorado Trail 1776 and has no trailhead parking at the one place where it meets a road. Still, its scenery makes it worth the effort. Green Mountain Trail is named after the mountain and does not actually begin at Green Mountain Campground itself.

Considered most enjoyable ridden east to west, it takes off south of the **Colorado Trail,** climbing an old logging road west of Tramway Creek. After grunting up this road, look for a big granite outcrop on the ridge. Great views from the top. Your road changes to single track for a downhill leading to a double track above the Meadows Group Campground. Follow bike trail markers around to the **Colorado Trail 1776.** A spur of Green Mountain leaves the CT shortly and goes down to join FS-550, but there is no parking there.

One of the most popular approaches to the Buffalo Creek Mountain Bike Area is across this bridge at Pine Valley Ranch Park, our next chapter.

JEFFERSON COUNTY'S PINE VALLEY RANCH PARK

Park View Trail leads to the top of these bluffs across the Platte River.

Buck Gulch-Park View Loop
Pine Lake Loop
North Fork View
Narrow Gage Trail
Star View

This is our favorite Jefferson County Open Space Park, and when you see its 100-car parking lots, you'll know we aren't alone in that opinion. Many other Jeffco Parks are described in a later chapter, but this one gets a special place next to our Buffalo Creek Mountain Bike Chapter because Pine Valley has become the favorite access for fat-tire fans heading into that area.

Road Directions: From Denver take Hwy 285 to Pine Junction and turn south on Hwy 126. Go six miles and look for the park on your right. From Colorado Springs, take Hwy 24 west to Woodland Park, then right on 67 to Deckers. Cross the bridge and take 126 north past Buffalo Creek. Just past Pine, you'll see the turnoff on your left.

At 820 acres, Pine Valley Ranch Park isn't huge, but it takes the prizes for beauty, interest and variety. Not only does it have a fishing lake, with wheelchair access docks, but the North Fork of the South Platte River meanders the length of this gentle valley rimmed with high bluffs and forest. Park View Trail, a hiking-only trail, leads to the heights across the river from which you can see the whole park: the lodge, the observatory, the gazebo and kiosk shelters, the lake and the sinuous river and the rapids downstream.

As you might expect, such delicious real estate was in private hands for a century. The latest in a long line of homesteading and ranching families was the William Baehr family. Baehr was a wealthy Chicago businessman and in 1925 he gave his architect only 90 days to build the big lodge which sits above the parking lot. Styled like a manor home from Germany's Black Forest, the lodge was completed on time, but it took 60 men working 24-hours a day to complete it.

In later years, Conrad Johnson, Baehr's foreman, added an observatory, pagoda, ice shed, barn, water wheel and tea house to the property, which had come to be known as "Baehr-den of the Rockies."

As you enter the park, watch for a workshop on your left from which the **Star View** trail takes you to the observatory. This once private observatory was erected for the Baehr family in the '30s. Public observatory programs are offered periodically through the Open Space education programs coordinated by Lookout Mountain Nature Center staff. Call 303-526-0594 for information.

At first you may not even notice the lodge to your right as you arrive. Indeed, the best view of the lodge is from the bluffs we mentioned to your left across river.

As soon as we saw the wooden staircases set high in the rocks above the river, we decided to head up there for the grand view. But since stairs are the steepest trail of all, so by far the easiest way up to those rocks is to take the long gentle trail that leads up and around from the back. To do that, go right from the parking lot and around the lake (Pine Lake Loop, only 0.3 miles if hiked as a loop), then take Buck Gulch Trail up through the forest.

This segment of Buck Gulch measures one mile, but if you're not doing the loop we describe, it continues another 1.7 miles into the Buffalo Creek Bicycle Area in the Pike National Forest to link up with a new trail called Skipper. See **Buffalo Creek Mountain Bike Area** for more on that.

Buck Gulch climbs gently along a trickling brook through conifer forest mixed with some aspen. Watch for the well-preserved log cabin on your left. One mile up, you enter the National Forest and take the obvious path to your left at a stream crossing. This wide path is marked as a "service road" on the park map, but it isn't a double-track. They just call it that because it serviced the antenna up ahead (It is now part of Strawberry Jack Trail). The forest here features large red-barked ponderosa. About a mile later, you'll top a low saddle, where a sign directs you left and uphill to Park View Trail. The unmarked trail going downhill to your right is Strawberry Jack (see Buffalo Creek Mountain Bike Chapter).

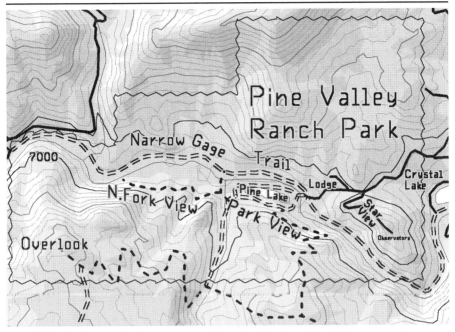

Going left, you climb to the top of the bluffs where Park View earns its name. Heading down the other side, you travel stairways, some curving, with peeled post railings. Near the bottom your singletrack switchbacks to the river again.

NARROW GAGE TRAIL, 2 miles one way, rated "rail easy," features riverside walk along historic railroad route.

This one is special to me because 20 years ago, when I began this guide, locals were amused that the government had sent me to explore Crosson's Trail, a National Forest Trail located just upstream. Crosson's Trail follows this same narrow gauge railroad route, so I knew it had to be sturdily built, winding through a deep three-mile canyon of the North Fork. I had my fishing gear and camera and expected a fantastic canyon trail, but found it cut off by private property on both ends! Wandering **Narrow Gage Trail** gives me a sense of what I missed all these years.

Oddly enough, the lake you pass was one of those used to produce ice in the l800s for shipment to Denver via the Colorado and Southern Railroad. This branch was abandoned in 1937. And by the way, the name of this trail is no typo. Gage is just another way of spelling gauge.

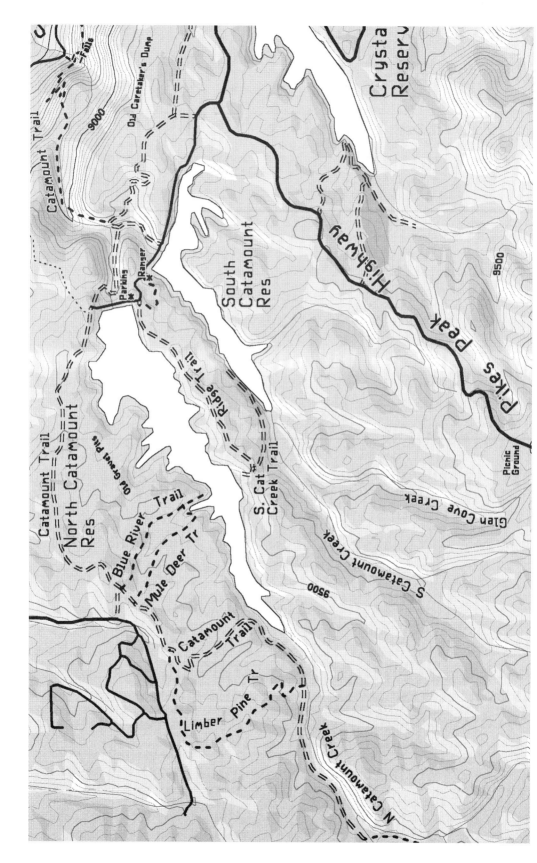

PIKES PEAK
AMERICA'S MOUNTAIN

BARR TRAIL SYSTEM:
Bottomless Pit Trail
Mountain View Trail
Manitou Reservoir Trail
Fremont Experimental Forest Trail
Manitou Incline Trail
Eagle's Nest—Mount Crest Crags
Elk Park Trail (Ghost Town Hollow)
Severy Creek Trail
Crow Gulch to Mount Esther Trail
Ute Indian Trail (endangered)
Barr-Ute Indian Loop (endangered)
NORTH SLOPE RECREATION AREA
Ridge Trail
South Catamount Creek Trail
Catamount Trail
Blue River Trail
Mule Deer Trail
Limber Pine Trail

Early pioneers emblazoned their covered wagons with the motto, "Pikes Peak or Bust!" because Pikes Peak is the one shining white beacon they could see for a vast distance out on the prairies. That made Pikes Peak so famous that it is now part of our language. Every English dictionary that I have ever seen, even the smallest, mentions Pikes Peak even though other famous mountains are left out.

Pikes Peak (now being advertised as America's Mountain) is rare among high mountains for having such convenient access. A toll highway, a cog railway and the famous Barr Trail go clear to the summit. If you don't want to climb this mountain, you can always take it as a downhill. Few peaks anywhere in the world afford you that luxury.

The Pikes Peak Cog Railway is a fascinating trip in itself. **One-way tickets** to the summit or to the Mountain View trailhead, halfway up the mountain, **are sold on a space available basis only.** Your best (and maybe only) chance of finding space available is to **avoid the peak season,** the third week of June through the third week of August, when even the 8 a.m. train is generally full. **Backpackers often have luck trying the last train of the day. No dogs or bikes are allowed on the train.. Call 719-685-5401 for details.**

You can also drive to the top via the Pikes Peak Highway from Cascade on Hwy. 24. Built by Spencer Penrose of the Broadmoor, this 19-mile marvel is very scenic and extremely expensive to maintain. Tour buses go to the summit, but they are also required to bring you back! **There is no taxi or shuttle service. The Pikes Peak Patrol does not encourage hitchhiking and does not provide taxi service.** *If you arrange for someone to meet you at the top, and they don't show*

up, be prepared to walk down. **Closing times for the toll road and Summit House vary, and bad weather may close everything early. For more information about the Pikes Peak Highway call 719-385-PEAK (7325).**

You cannot expect anything in the way of services at the top. There are no accommodations. About the only thing available on the summit are snacks and souvenirs. Civilization exists only in your pack, so bring whatever you need.

Branching away from **Barr Trail** is a complex system of trails, all closed to motorized vehicles. These branches give you many ways to get away from the crowd. Folks who go prepared generally have a world of fun, but those who don't go prepared often wind up with a new respect for Mom Nature's sour moods. Some even die, so take this mountain seriously and have a good time.

BIG NEWS about backcountry camping: Beginning in 1999, the Pikes Peak Highway began offering overnight parking passes for backpackers who want to camp in the National Forest. Ask at the gate. You must park off the Highway in specified locations and you must indicate on the pass where you are going and when you expect to return, so authorities know where to look, if you fail to return. If patrolmen find a car without such a pass, they assume that a day-hiker is lost and they call Search and Rescue. At this time there is no extra charge for the pass.

ROAD DIRECTIONS: From I-25 in Colorado Springs, take the Cimarron Exit #141 marked for Manitou and Pikes Peak. Go west on Hwy. 24.

To reach the lower trailhead for BARR TRAIL, take either Manitou Springs Exit, then drive up Ruxton Ave. from its intersection in downtown Manitou Springs. The Cog Railway Depot is located near the end of this avenue, and the lower trailhead for UTE INDIAN TRAIL is just across the street from the Cog Depot, but YOU MAY NOT PARK THERE. Instead, use the BARR TRAILHEAD parking for both BARR and UTE INDIAN, which is just beyond the depot on your right. Ute Indian Trail is open from this end, but obey any signs you find at the upper end where a landowner is trying to close this historic trail. Do not trespass.

To find the NORTH SLOPE RECREATION AREA, SEVERY CREEK TRAILHEAD, MOUNT ESTHER and ELK PARK TRAILHEADS, do not exit at Manitou Springs, but instead continue west on Hwy 24 to Cascade (9.5 miles from I-25) and take the well-marked left turn across traffic to the Pikes Peak Toll Road. THE TOLL FOR GOING TO THE NORTH SLOPE IS CHEAPER THAN GOING TO THE SUMMIT, BUT DO NOT CHEAT OR YOU WILL BE CAUGHT AT THE BRAKE CHECK STATION ON YOUR RETURN. SET YOUR ODOMETER AT THE TOLL GATE! POSTED MILE MARKERS WILL NOT MATCH YOUR ODOMETER.

Parking for SEVERY CREEK TRAIL may been moved to the Crow Gulch Picnic Ground (on your right 1.9 miles from the gate). Crow Gulch also serves as trailhead for MOUNT ESTHER TRAIL, which heads up valley.

SEVERY CREEK (TEMPORARILY CLOSED) TRAILHEAD used to be accessed by foot or bike via a closed-to-motorized roadway that is hard to see as you drive up the Pikes Peak Highway. Look for it exactly 1.5 miles from the gate (but beyond the 2-mile marker, since Toll Road measurements do not begin at the gate!) The rusted iron "No Trespassing" sign may still be in place at that turnoff, guarding the access to the City of Manitou Springs Reservoir, which is not (yet) open to the general public, but the old trailhead is located on Forest Service land, so the No Trespassing sign really belongs farther down the road. FOR FUTURE REFERENCE, USE YOUR ODOMETER TO LOCATE THIS TURNOFF AS YOU DRIVE TOWARD CROW GULCH, BUT DO NOT DRIVE DOWN IT. Instead, continue past it on the highway to Crow Gulch Picnic Ground at mile 1.9 from gate.

When SEVERY eventually reopens, it may be rerouted 0.4 miles to a new trailhead at Crow Gulch to keep hikers and bikers from traveling the pavement, which has no shoulder in some places. The old trailhead is located half a mile down the access road and is unmarked at this time but is located at the plank bridge to your right. IT HAS ALWAYS BEEN FORBIDDEN TO EXPLORE FARTHER THAN HALF A MILE ON THIS ROAD OR APPROACH UTILITY FACILITIES NEARBY. SEVERY has been temporarily closed until its rare strain of endangered greenback cutthroat trout has been successfully raised and preserved elsewhere. The stream is free of whirling disease, and even a dog that has swum in Fountain Creek, for instance, could infect it.

More than six miles up the Highway, cross the dam of Crystal Reservoir. This is the first of three NORTH SLOPE RECREATION AREA lakes. To find the others and our North Slope trails, go 0.6 miles farther and take the well-marked right turn to the Catamounts.

ELK PARK TRAILHEAD is located at Elk Park Knoll, which is a shoulder of Pikes Peak just above timberline. As you drive the Highway a mile past Glen Cove, you will see a metal gate used to close off the upper road in winter. The turnoff is located just before this gate, but it is not apparent as you approach because it dives off steeply on your left. Watch for it between iron posts on your left. There are several such posts, so be sure you have the right pair! As you enter the parking area there, a metal sign marks the trailhead on your right. Please do not damage tundra.

The summit trailhead for **BARR TRAIL** is located near the Cog Railway tracks at the Summit House. Many trails branch off of **BARR TRAIL**, and each will be described individually.

BARR TRAIL, Forest Service #620, 11.65 miles one-way according to John Cappis of the Pikes Peak Marathon who measured it five times; elevation gain 7,258 feet, rated very difficult. Features famous scenery and greatest altitude gain of any trail in Colorado. NOTE: Marathon officials found that all the old trail signs have wrong distances.

14,110 Summit   5.68 miles   Barr Camp 10,200

Whether you hike up it or down it, Barr Trail is very strenuous for the average person. For those who want a challenge, Barr Trail offers the greatest base-to-summit climb in all of Colorado, an altitude gain of over 7,000 feet! Yet unlike other trails that force you to climb, Barr can be hiked downhill, which makes it suited for those who want to experience mountain hiking in a somewhat easier manner. The catch is the word "somewhat," for the uppermost and lowest parts of this route are so steep they can be painfully difficult, even downhill.

A long steep downhill endangers your toenails, if you don't cut them short first, and shortens your calf muscle. With toes angled downhill, men learn what it must be like to walk in high heels all day!

The operators of Barr Camp, located halfway up the mountain, once estimated that fully two-thirds of the people who start up Barr Trail for the first time, expecting to reach the summit, actually turn back when they realize what they have attempted.

But there are other good reasons for taking Barr downhill. If you climb from the bottom, your strength may give out because there is less and less oxygen with every step. Going down, you have more and more oxygen with every step. And going down, you are headed toward civilization, not away from it. Our mountain weather is generally best in the morning, so if the weather turns bad in the afternoon, it is wise to be on your way down: **You don't want to be headed up above timberline when rain or hail threatens.** And going up, any delay can make you arrive late: The Summit House and Pikes Peak Highway may be closed, and your ride may be forced to leave! **Highway Patrolmen warn that anyone attempting to climb Barr Trail must be prepared to hike back down in such a case. That won't happen if you're going downhill because the lower trailhead never closes. So let's begin the safer way, at the top.**

At the summit trailhead, you have a true panorama of distant mountains and prairie. It was this very view, this "purple mountain majesty," that inspired the words to the song "America the Beautiful." As you look out over the prairies toward Kansas, with Colorado Springs spread out some 8,000 feet below, the altitude is 14,110 feet, the air is thin, and you had best move slowly, if you don't want to contract altitude sickness.

Begin by making your way down a steep series of switchbacks high above timberline. Snow may cover part of this trail until sometime in June, so inquire about conditions and the need for an ice axe in early spring.

Bighorn sheep, yellow-bellied marmots and the grouse-like ptarmigan are often seen on this slope. Both the ptarmigan and the bighorns are rock-colored in summer; but the ptarmigan is white in winter, and sometimes you spot their movement or shadow first.

This is the most dangerous part of the mountain, so you must take along the gear to weather a sudden storm. Remember that ptarmigan are found only above timberline and at the Arctic Circle. Even the plant life above timberline is the same sort of tundra found at the Arctic Circle. So what you have on Pikes Peak is a piece of the Arctic! It can be very warm in the summer sunshine and deadly cold if the weather changes.

A sign marks the edge of The Crater, which is a deep cirque where a glacier formed and scooted down, carving a pit. Return to the main trail and be sure to stay on the trail, for this high tundra is easily damaged and takes centuries to regrow. Tundra abuse also closes trails.

Three miles and some 3,000 feet below the summit, the trail finds timberline, which is marked by dwarfed trees that may be very old. Right at treeline, you pass an A-frame shelter with spring water coming from a pipe driven into the mountainside.

Now the trail dips into a world of tall spruce and fir. Watch for a turquoise-like gem called amazonite that washes out of the granite near the trail (no digging please). When you pass the sign marking the **Bottomless Pit Trail** turnoff, you are within about a mile of Barr Camp. And when you reach Barr Camp at 10,200 feet, you will have gone 5.68 miles and descended about 4,000 feet .

10,200 Barr Camp   5.97 miles   Ruxton Trailhead 6,840

Barr Camp, which is operated by permit from the Forest Service, offers overnight accommodations for a small fee. It has rustic log cabins with wooden floors, spring water (always treat or boil water before drinking) and outhouse facili-ties. The camp provides hot chocolate and bunk beds with foam pads at modest cost and a few supplies at higher cost because everything at Barr Camp must be packed in. This camp makes a convenient base from which to explore other trails in the region. Side trails provide tent camping in many other areas.

To me, the most beautiful part of this route is the gentler mid-section that extends between Barr Camp and the Incline Trail. The

The Health Dept. does not recommend paying toll to chipmunks near the "rock tunnel."

distance is over three miles, but the altitude change is only 1,200 feet.

Here the trail wanders among granite formations, with aspens and douglas fir and ponderosa pine. Sometimes you catch a glimpse of the flats to the east, or find spectacular views of the Peak itself. Along this route you will find the last of the Army's telegraph poles that carried the first communications to the summit in the 1800s.

Just over half a mile below Barr Camp is the **Mountain View Trail** turnoff, which leads to the Cog. Just over 1.2 miles lower find the turnoff for **Manitou Reservoir Trail.** Almost 1.6 miles farther down lies the intersection with the **Upper Incline** (which once led to the Incline Railway) and the **Fremont Experimental Forest Trail,** which follows a brook uphill. Go 0.17 mile farther down on **Barr Trail** and you'll find another sign for the **Lower Incline Trail** and 0.15 miles lower you pass beneath huge boulders, the "Rock Tunnel."

Below this point, **Barr Trail** is very steep. The city is visible only part of the time, and much of the trail plunges through stands of ponderosa pine, white fir and blue spruce, with views of Camerons Cone and Pikes Peak. The only branch off this lower section leads to an overlook where people used to watch the Incline Railway pass by. How we miss that wonderful machine! More steep trail takes you on down to the trailhead on Ruxton Avenue.

While you're congratulating yourself for conquering Barr Trail, you might remember Fred Barr, who shoved the rocks and moved the dirt to build the trail. You might also marvel at the Pikes Peak Marathon runners who race up and down Barr Trail. Runners actually do the full 26 miles up and down in a little over three hours, but don't even try estimating your hiking time by that. I like to take all day one way. After all, I go to see the scenery.

Imagine: When we first wrote up **Barr Trail** a generation ago, America's most famous mountain had no legal parking or trailhead at the bottom. With the FS short of funds, the El Paso County Park and Recreation Dept finally provided this marvelous facility. Please do not park elsewhere.

Bikers note: Horses and hikers have right of way, and this trail has so much traffic that bikers have to be extra cautious (and polite). Frankly, most mountain bikers wind up pushing their bikes up the switchbacks and then have difficulty controlling their bikes coming down again. Aside from not being much fun (this book has better places to ride), Barr presents a potential safety problem. For that reason, the Forest Service may be forced to ban bikes from Barr Trail.

Unfortunately, a one-way loop trail for bikes called the Barr-Ute Indian Loop has been closed (for now) by a new private property owner.

BOTTOMLESS PIT TRAIL, Forest Service #632, 2.4 miles one way, elevation gain 760 ft., beginning at 10,500 feet and continuing upward, rated difficult. Features treeline scenery with small waterfalls spouting from high cliffs

10,850   2.4 miles   11,700

Almost exactly a mile uphill from Barr Camp, you find a sign that shows the way to Bottomless Pit. This rugged climb begins with a switchback and never really levels out, for oddly enough, you must climb up into the bottom of the Bottomless Pit.

The Pit is a deep cirque, a semi-circular scoop in the cliffs gouged out by glacial ice, and when you get there, you may agree that it has very little bottom, for the land continues to fall away at an angle.

This one should be saved until mid-June or later because the trail skirts a shady ridge that keeps its snow for a long time. An ice ax and gaiters may be necessary for earlier attempts.

The trail climbs to timberline and dead-ends in a pocket where granite walls rise up to 3,000 feet around you on three sides. Many rock wall and ice climbers try their skill here, and it is a spectacular, if somewhat forbidding landscape with many waterfalls spouting from the cliffs. This flow decreases in late summer.

Bottomless Pit

MOUNTAIN VIEW TRAIL, Forest Service #671, 1.2 miles one way, elevation gain 220 ft., rated easy. Features campsites and link with Cog RR.

This short and gentle trail provides access to campsites along Cabin and Sheep Creeks. To find the trailhead, watch for a metal sign on **Barr Trail** 0.58 miles below Barr Camp, with the trail leading off to the south (left as you go up Barr Trail).

This trail has changed coarse slightly, no longer going past the roofless log cabin at Cabin Creek. Instead, it crosses Cabin Creek higher up, then crosses Sheep Creek, ending at the Cog Railway's Mountain View Station. Lucky hikers with one-way space-available tickets often disembark here

At present, you may not cross the tracks into the South Slope Watershed.

MANITOU RESERVOIR TRAIL, Forest Service #638, 3.3 miles one way, elevation gain 275 ft, loss 900 ft.; rated difficult. Features scenic vistas and camping, though not near the reservoir, which is closed to public.

9,420 Barr Trail   3.3 miles   Overlook 9,080

A sign marks the turnoff 1.75 miles below Barr Camp (4.22 miles from the bottom). This dead-end trail offers many beautiful campsites along the streams it crosses, but it is steep going as it washboards over a series of ridges.

It starts by diving toward South French Creek. There you find a meadow with large aspens and a stream. Your trail switchbacks up the opposite ridge, then drops again toward another drainage which has no name, and so it goes until you find yourself standing above the watershed for Manitou Reservoir, which is closed to the public.

This is drinking water for the City of Manitou Springs. Do not approach the lake. As soon as you see the lake ahead, you must turn around and backtrack to Barr Trail because the area surrounding the lake is closed to all (public) recreation, and there is no public access to that end of the trail. A caretaker lives at the reservoir, and the area is vigorously patrolled with security dogs.

FREMONT EXPERIMENTAL FOREST TRAIL, Forest Service #702, 0.5 miles one way to end of Experimental Forest or 1.5 miles as part of loop; elevation gain 380 feet, rated moderate. Features campsites and ruins of experimental station.

A brook crosses Barr Trail at a complex intersection where Fremont Experimental Forest Trail begins. Here the upper Incline Trail, a single track, comes down to join Barr at the stream crossing. If you follow the brook upstream, you will be traveling an old road into the Fremont Experimental Forest, where the Forest Service once planted exotic evergreens to see if any would do well in this area. (Apparently, they didn't.) Only the foundations of the station buildings remain now.

When hiking **Barr Trail** from the bottom, this area offers the first good camp-sites, so it receives a lot of use. This route has been used as a road to haul fencing for Barr Trail, so it is wide and leads to Long Ranch Road. Keep to the right as the brook curves away to the left. You climb a short, steep section and arrive at a ridgetop where **Fremont** T-junctions against Long Ranch Road. This is the end of **Fremont Trail** itself, but if you turn left onto Long Ranch Road (#329), you can make a 1.5-mile loop going up to **Barr.**

Note: The rest of Long Ranch Road is technically open for a long way, but leads downhill to a trespass situation near Ute Pass, where a new property owner has closed off access to the Pass and to the historic Ute Indian Trail. That may change. Obey all signs.

MANITOU INCLINE TRAIL, Forest Service #627, 0.5 miles one way, elevation gain 120 feet, rated easy. Features gentle trails to site of the old Incline station, now gone.

You won't find this spot on any main trail. It is on Pikes Peak.

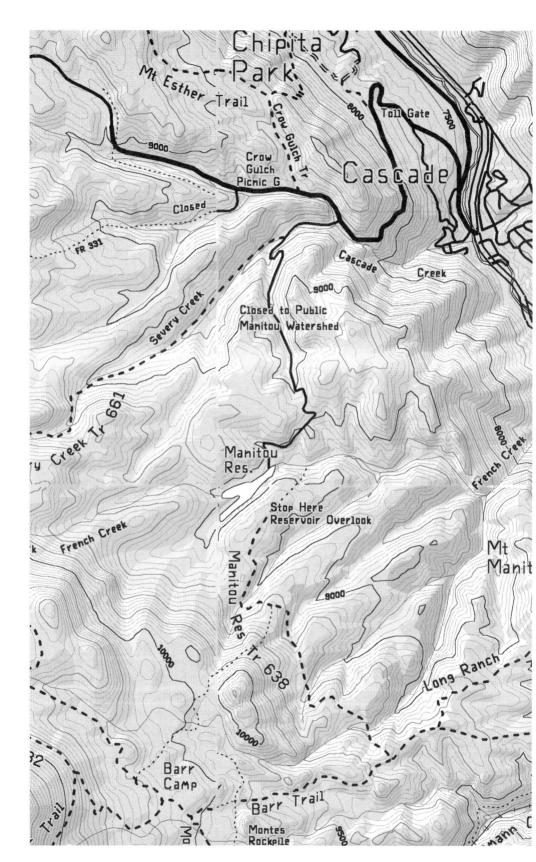

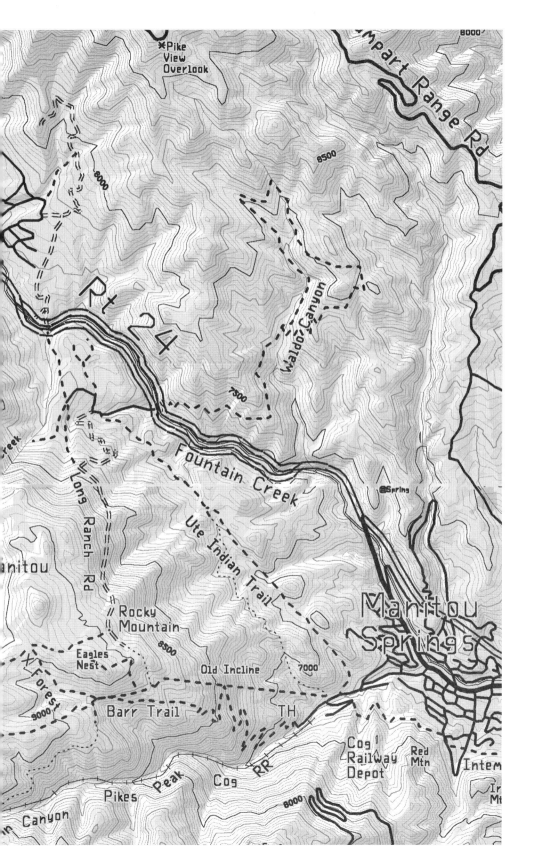

There are actually two Incline Trails, but since they parallel each other closely, they share a common trail number. The upper trail is a single track that passes beneath a huge boulder that spans the trail, an excellent shelter on rainy days. The lower trail is a continuation of the Fremont Experimental Forest Trail-road, and it leaves Barr Trail just below the stream crossing. Both meet up higher up and continue to the site of the closed Incline Railway station, which is now being reclaimed.

The Incline Railway was built in 1906 to haul men and equipment to build the Manitou pipeline and it operated as a tourist attraction for many years with a perfect safety record, but was closed to make more parking available for the Cog. The loss of this mountain access—and safety line—will be mourned for a lifetime.

EAGLES NEST AND MT. CREST CRAGS, Forest Service # 623, 0.1 mile to Eagles Nest and about 0.5 mile to Mt. Crest Crags; elevation gain 650 ft., rated easy to moderate. Features climb to overlook.

This trail climbs Rocky Mountain. Starting from where the Manitou Incline's station used to be, it turns right toward Eagle's Nest and Mt. Crest Crags. The path heads north, but a side trail soon branches off and heads uphill toward a clump of rocks. This is called the Eagle's Nest. The main trail wraps around the mountain and begins a series of switchbacks to a higher set of rocks known as Mt. Crest Crags. From there you can see the white bluffs of Williams Canyon, the Rampart Range beyond, and even portions of the Ute Indian Trail that runs between Manitou and the Long Ranch Road near Cascade.

ELK PARK TRAIL, Forest Service #652, 5.2 miles one way, elevation gain 200 ft., loss 1,680 ft. from Elk Park Knoll, rated easy from Elk Park Knoll, more difficult from Barr. Features tiny ghost town and large spring flowing from mine tunnel, access to Barr Camp. No camping in Manitou's North French Creek Watershed, including Ghost Town Hollow.

| 11,820 | 5.2 miles | 10,200 |

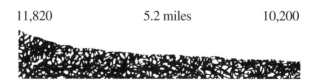

This is the back way to Barr Camp, leading downhill from Elk Park Knoll off the Pikes Peak Toll Road to Barr Camp, and it goes to an area romantically called Ghost Town Hollow. The so-called ghost town was a tiny mining and lumber camp, something like a half dozen cabins. Just above is the Cincinnati mine, which struck water instead of gold. The headwaters of North French Creek

Ghost Town Hollow's tunnel and steam engine.

pour out of this tunnel in the granite, providing part of the drinking water for the City of Manitou Springs.

The City of Manitou bans horses and overnight camping from the North French Creek-Ghost Town Hollow area. However, camping is available in other drainages nearby. Do not follow North French Creek downstream toward Manitou Reservoir, which is closed to the general public and is vigorously patrolled with security dogs. Stay on trail through this sensitive area.

Starting at Elk Park (see road directions), you follow a badly washed roadway that curves down from timberline through forest to North French Creek. At the bottom, you find a fork with a sign pointing left, or down creek, toward Barr Camp (4 miles), and straight ahead toward the Oil Creek Tunnel (1/4 mile).

To see the mine, walk up a gentle valley that is heavily forested. Soon you pass a few crumbling log cabins. The roofs are gone, the walls collapsing, and wildflowers bloom from the floor spaces. Visitors have carried away everything but the most uninteresting rusted garbage. The mine is just above, still producing a valuable flow of water. In the winter, this produces weird ice sculptures. **All of the mine timbers have rotted away, so exploration would be very dangerous. A huge iron boiler stands outside, shown here.**

Backtrack to the trail fork. From here, **Elk Park** heads downstream for a short distance, but actually climbs slightly, following a sunny ridge above the stream. Then your trail forks again. **Elk Park Trail** turns right to cross the creek, while the trail ahead (**Severy Creek Trail**) leads over the ridge.

After crossing North French Creek, **Elk Park** switchbacks up the opposite ridge. This climb is fairly gentle and soon the trail almost levels out, skirting the end of the ridge with Manitou Reservoir visible below. Next you cross a high park meadow, then drop down into the South French Creek watershed.

Your trail follows the creek downhill a short way through dark and mossy timber, with the creek just out of sight to your right, and then you find a shallow crossing. On the other side, climb to the left and find yourself walking a ledge on a cliff's side with the creek roaring below. Your trail goes past a prospect hole, over a rise, then descends to the cabins of Barr Camp. You arrive just a few yards above the cabins themselves.

SEVERY CREEK TRAIL, (TEMPORARILY CLOSED) Forest Service #661, about 4.9 miles one way, if its new trailhead is relocated to Crow Gulch Picnic Ground, elevation gain 2,550 ft., rated moderate. Features beautiful trail along high mountain stream, linking with Elk Park Trail. All visitation is temporarily banned because of a special DOW study.

9,320   4.0 miles   10,960

Severy is one of my favorites, and it is rare for me to approve of a trail closure, but this one is necessary and only temporary. Our 1999 version of the Sixth Edition kept the DOW's secret that a unique strain of the endangered greenback cutthroat trout (Colorado's only native trout) had suddenly been discovered in Severy Creek. At first, authorities just banned fishing and made it more inconvenient to explore Severy, so that's what we printed. Then, just after press time, authorities reluctantly closed Severy when they realized that even a dog that had first swum in Fountain Creek, for instance, could spread whirling disease to Severy and, thus, infect the strain before it could be successfully raised elsewhere. The closure may last several years.

Severy Creek has long been considered one of the region's most beautiful trails, but it remained closed to the public from 1913 to 1990, supposedly to protect the water supply for the community of Cascade, which lacked a modern filtration facility. Yet in the fall of 1990, Cascade switched to municipal water from Colorado Springs. The Forest Service championed this trail for generations, even spending precious funds to maintain it while closed, and the FS now considers Severy a "system trail."

Severy is best approached via the Pikes Peak Highway, which means you must pay the toll. The only other route is via **Elk Park Trail** to Ghost Town Hollow, then down **Severy Creek** and back again.

The creek itself originates below Elk Park Knoll off the Pikes Peak Highway, but please do not spoil the tundra by bushwhacking down from there. If you want to take **Severy** as a downhill, it is actually easier (good trail with no altitude gain!) to start at Elk Park Knoll and go down the Elk Park Trail to North French Creek, where you will find the upper trailhead for **Severy**.

The best way to see Severy is from the bottom. (see ROAD DIREC-TIONS). That way you can explore up as far as you like and have an easy downhill to your car at Crow Gulch.

Once you start down the access road from the Highway, ignore the left turnoff that leads to a utility facility and instead go straight down the access road. Half a mile from the Highway, you'll find a plank bridge on your right that takes you across a tributary and through the willows to cross Severy. This bridge was built by the Volunteers for Outdoor Colorado.

Beyond the willows, you enter the world of mossy evergreens. Rated as moderate, the trail has many easy stretches mixed with short steep sections. The creek is often in sight, tumbling between boulders, forming a number of charming cascades. You pass through aspen glades, crossing and recrossing the creek. As you mount one group of giant boulders, Pikes Peak suddenly shows itself towering above.

In a broad meadow just below 10,000 feet, the trail leaves the creek and switchbacks up the ridge separating Severy from the North Fork of French Creek. Rounding that ridge, you continue above French Creek to link up with **Elk Park Trail** below Ghost Town Hollow.

Overnight camping may be allowed along part of Severy Creek itself, but IS NOT allowed in Manitou's North French Creek (Ghost Town Hollow) watershed at the upper end of Severy Trail. Remember that you must have the new pass to leave a car overnight anywhere off the Pikes Peak Highway. Horses have no access to Severy.

NOTE: The DOW has discovered endangered greenback trout in Severy and has banned fishing, at least temporarily, while the fish are studied.

CROW GULCH TO MOUNT ESTHER TRAIL, FS #754A, about one mile to the intersection with Mount Esther #754 from Chipita Park, then about 1.5 miles farther to "end" at Utility service road, rated very easy from Crow Gulch, with elevation gain of only 600 feet to Utility service road. Features easy aspen meadow walk.

Mount Esther #754 is described in detail in our next chapter, Ute Pass Area, but this one-mile spur off the Pikes Peak Highway trailhead at Crow Gulch offers by far the easiest way to enjoy the upper portion of the trail. Notice its number, 754A, indicating that this is an extension of 754. This beautiful and easy aspen walk does not take you to the summit, however. It stops short. See Ute Pass Area.

UTE INDIAN TRAIL, Ute Pass Historical Society Trail, 3.2 miles one way; elevation gain 1,040 feet, loss 340 feet; rated moderate. Features historic foothill and mountain route, west trailhead now endangered.

The west end of this historic trail has been closed by a private property owner, but former Judge George Gibson believes that the trail is not even on private property, as alleged. Obey all signs until this can be worked out.

The Ute Indians believed that the gods lived below the springs at Manitou, that their breathing caused the bubbles in those mineral waters. So the Utes made pilgrimages to these springs over an ancient trail that extended from Utah. This trail was used by trappers, by mountain men, and later it carried wagons toward the mining areas in the mountains.

Our description begins at the southern trailhead across from the Cog Railway at the site of the old Incline station on Ruxton. Travel around the base of the mountain, following a road-like path up Rattlesnake Gulch. Your trail washboards over a series of ridges where the land is somewhat arid at first, dominated by Gambel's oak and yucca, and then the evergreens close in.

An iron sign marks the point where the Ute Wagon Trail joined the Ute Indian Trail, and further on you pass under a pipeline that crosses the trail on a steel trestle. Several utility lines follow this trail toward Cascade, and much of the right-of-way belongs to the City of Colorado Springs Utilities Department. As you walk by steel pipes that jut from ridges, listen for gurgling caused by pressure changes in the water pipelines.

Cross-country skiers often turn back just before the last downhill section that takes you into the French Creek watershed. The trail should end near Highway 24, one-half mile east of Cascade, but obey the signs you find.

This trail was built through the efforts and cooperation of the Chipita Park-Cascade Bicentennial Association, the Ute Pass Historical Society, the National Hiking and Ski Touring Association, Boy Scout Troop 18 and Explorer Post 24, the Lions and Kiwanis Clubs, the Colorado Springs Utilities Department, the Fourth Infantry Division of Fort Carson, and of course, more thoughtful and public-spirited private land owners. **We wonder how all these people feel about the closure!**

Horses are not allowed on Ute Indian Trail.

BARR—UTE INDIAN LOOP, Forest Service and Ute Pass Historical Society Trail, 11.2-mile loop, elevation gain-loss 2,650 ft., rated difficult and then easy Features one-way uphill-only bicycle access to Barr Trail, forming a loop by coming down Long Ranch Road and then down Ute Indian Trail to Ruxton Avenue near Barr trailhead.

As mentioned above, the west end of Ute Indian Trail has been closed by a private property owner. This effectively cuts the center of the loop we describe, but both ends are still open to back-and-forth exploration. Obey signs until this can be worked out.

Not just for mountain bicycles, this trail was designed with bikes in mind for increased safety and fun. If approved, the Barr-Ute Indian Loop should eliminate the danger of bikes coming down steep switchbacks on lower Barr Trail and legally open a scenic back route. If you have not seen media reports of this trail opening, check with authorities before starting out.

Park at the Barr trailhead on Ruxton Ave. and climb **Barr Trail.** About a mile past the **Experimental Forest** turnoff, where the trail is fairly flat, Pikes Peak comes into view and a single track takes off to your right, turning into a double track within about a third of a mile. This is Long Ranch Road, built by Fred Barr and R.A. Long to haul timber from this area. The top of **Experimental Forest Trail** (also a road) comes up from your right and T-junctions against Long Ranch Road, but stay on Long (straight ahead). You pass between Rocky Mountain and Mount Manitou and then begin a long descent toward Ute Pass. Near the bottom you will come to a gated fence and perhaps some No Trespassing signs.

Do not go all the way to Hwy. 24. You will come to an intersection where a gated road is on your left and Ute Indian Trail is on your right (see Ute Indian Trail). Take the Ute Indian Trail back to Manitou. The most difficult part of the trail is at the bottom, but future trail work may improve this very steep section, if the trail can be approved. Then go up Ruxton Avenue to the **Barr** trailhead.

Pikes Peak North Slope Recreation Area

Ridge Trail
South Catamount Cr
Catamount Trail
Blue River Trail
Mule Deer Trail
Limber Pine Trail

Just before the North Slope Recreation Area opened in 1992, a City of Boulder water official predicted disaster for this Colorado Springs watershed, saying it would be "trashed in no time." Well, years of public use and park management has left Pikes Peak's North Slope even cleaner than I found it before opening! All the agencies involved are extremely pleased and proud.

Wheelchair accessible fishing dock at Crystal Reservoir, six miles up the Pikes Peak Highway. The summit of Pikes Peak seen here in the background is another 13 miles up the highway.

Graced by the three largest lakes on Pikes Peak, the North Slope Recreation Area consists of 2,267 acres, a place where families enjoy fishing, boating, picnicking, hiking and mountain biking amid world famous scenery. Even more important, the park is a model of what the rest of mountain will offer someday when its four other watersheds are opened to the public. (So don't mess it up!)

Kids are free and adults pay a reduced toll at the Pikes Peak Toll Gate, but don't try to cheat and drive to the summit on the cheaper ticket or you'll be nabbed on the way down when officers check your brakes at Glen Cove.

Amenities include modern restrooms at North and South Cat, floating docks for wheelchair access and a mini Visitor Center at Crystal where folks can buy fishing licenses and snacks and can even rent fishing gear and small boats.

Most service roads are closed to public vehicles, but are open to hiking and biking and have been given trail names. So you drive to the lake of your choice, park in the lot near its dam (rangers will ticket cars parked elsewhere), then hike or bike from there. The father you go, the fewer people you'll find!

Mountain biking is restricted to designated trails and roadways. You're not allowed to bike along the water's edge because of erosion, but bikes do provide a quick way to reach the far end of North Catamount Reservoir, for example. Some trails are old logging roads: Our maps show them all.

How's the fishing? Boom and bust like all high lakes: Either they're biting or they're not. But the lake trout grow to 30 inches, the brookies to 22 inches, and the DOW stocks the lakes with many thousands of cutthroat and rainbows. The best fishing is spring and fall.

Bait fishing is allowed at both Crystal and South Catamount, but North Catamount is fly and lure only. No fishing is allowed from the dams of Crystal or South Cat because of the steep and dangerous faces. North Cat's rip-rap dam is open to fishing and provides shore fishermen with access to some pretty deep water. Ice fishing is banned at all three lakes because winter draw-down can make the ice dangerous.

Special fishing limits have been established and will be adjusted to protect fishing quality, so heed the signs.

Since trailers are not allowed on the PPH, boats must be hauled on your vehicle. Only electric or muscle-powered craft are allowed, including belly boats, of course. Gasoline motors are banned to prevent both water and noise pollution. Small boats can also be rented at the Visitor Center for use on Crystal. Watch the weather closely because these high mountain lakes can get dangerously windy. A spill can be deadly, even for the best of swimmers, because the water is so cold.

Old poacher's paths extend from the Crags, but these have yet to be improved or designated, so they cannot be recommended yet. The **Lower Catamount Trail** from Green Mountain Falls, however, is well underway and is described in our Ute Pass chapter. **There is no fee for those who access the area on foot.**

Do not use Ed Lowe Road for access. This dangerous route is the only access for a residential area and any increase in traffic may wind up hurting a load of kids, so residents are very alert—and serious—about any strange vehicles parked in the area.

You can help expand your freedoms by respecting park rules and by treating the place as a living museum where the wildlife, wildflowers and other natural features remain undisturbed. Finding a baby elk curled up on the ground made us realize how important it is to keep your dog on a leash. Baby critters can't run, so they can only crouch and hope no predator finds them. Your dog's hunting instinct kicks in when wandering the wilds. Don't kid yourself about that.

No swimming or wading or other water-body contact is allowed. Cook only with charcoal, never wood, and only in established fire grates. No firearms, no fireworks, no littering. You may blanket picnic in remote areas, but in popular areas, please use the tables provided. Please pick up any litter that you see.

Since camping is not yet allowed even on the federal portions of the watershed, this day-use park closes when the Highway closes and that is a major source of complaint. Just when fish start jumping toward evening, patrol officers have to start telling folks to head back! Opening and closing times vary, so call 710-385-PEAK (7325) for current times. After dark, according to regulations, you are a trespasser, even if you hiked in.

The North Slope Recreation Area has blossomed into a model of what other closed watersheds can become when opened to public recreation. Its iron curtain of barbed wire borders and "no trespassing" signs has been transformed into a "welcome" for the families of America. Through careful management, the Colorado Springs Parks and Recreation Dept. and the Watershed Advisory Committee is determined to protect this fabulous environment, while providing quality recreation for all.

But here's what's at stake: If we simply leave all the government lands on Pikes Peak under the same authorities, but cooperate a little, we can create a regional park of well over 100 square miles! That means leaving the boundaries the same on all maps, but tearing down the barbed wire borders in the forest, converting guards into park rangers. With a little neighborly good will, we could truly Americanize America's mountain, build a trail out of old routes circling the mountain below timberline, a 50-mile trail linking that sapphire necklace of 13 lakes to produce a world-class regional park.

Local cities would have much to gain. At present, you cannot buy mountain bikes, hiking gear or fishing gear in Manitou, Victor or Cripple Creek. That's our dream for Pikes Peak. Is it yours? Tell your mayor.

But since this is a somewhat official guide, I must disclose that this vision is my own and that of the Pikes Peak Trails Coalition and does not reflect the official position of any city or its utility department.

HERE'S A BRIEF RUN-DOWN ON THE LAKES:

CRYSTAL RESERVOIR Crystal flirted with visitors for generations. While the rest of the peak's sapphire necklace of 13 forbidden lakes were generally hidden or only glimpsed from a distance, Crystal always flaunted herself for every local and tourist that drove her long dam. Crystal sprawls in full view, with no hidden arms, always sparkling, alluring, as inviting as a postcard (and the subject of many) with a close-up of Pikes Peak as her backdrop. She has 136 surface acres, after a few drinks, with a maximum depth of 55 feet, and was built in 1935. Her northern banks (the Visitor Center side) slope gentle, soft and grassy, so it's a great place for kids. The opposite side of the lake, however, is steep and unwalkable in places. Please help prevent erosion there. The shoreline measures 3.3 miles.

SOUTH CATAMOUNT The baby sister of the family, she's known by the nickname South Cat, but as mountain lakes go, she's no baby: 120 surface acres, 65 feet deep at the dam, built in 1937 at an altitude of 9,225 feet. She is reached via the turnoff 0.6 miles beyond Crystal on the Pikes Peak Highway. Within a tenth of a mile you come to a fork which is part of a one-way loop system enjoyed by mountain bikers. The road ahead (leftish fork) takes you along its shoreline and across its dam, very scenic. It's shoreline measures about four miles. The worst spot is a scree slope right across from the southern end of the dam, so if you wander that side you'll have to hike up and around that cove.

NORTH CATAMOUNT RESERVOIR Big sister North Cat is the largest lake on the mountain: 210 surface acres, 135 feet deep, a fine figure of a lake measuring 6.6 miles around and every inch of that walkable. She's our fly-and-lure lake where trophy fish lurk, including lake trout up to 30 inches. North Cat is NOT actually a catch and release lake, but DOW surveys report that most of its fish are returned to the water by sportsmen grateful for the experience. A friend tells us that a day spent belly-boating here during the fall laker spawning was the best day's fishing he's ever had. Remember, flies and lures only at North Cat.

AND NOW THE NORTH SLOPE TRAILS:

RIDGE TRAIL, 1.1 miles one way, rated easy breezy. Features access to both North and South Cat.

This closed service road traces a ridge between the two Catamounts. Starting next to the North Cat dam, this road leads back 1.1 miles to a four-way intersection. Ahead leads only a short distance to an overlook of North Cat, but will someday be part of a trail circling that lake. With a bit of bushwhacking, you can pick up an old poacher's path that only needs to be developed. Or you can simply take advantage of the fact that every inch of North Cat's shoreline is walkable.

Going right from the four-way leads down to a cove on North Cat, but going left takes you to the South Catamount Creek inlet and that's what we're describing next.

SOUTH CATAMOUNT CREEK TRAIL, 0.5 miles one way, rated moderate at worst, features access to inlet fishing on South Cat.

Turning left from the four-way on Ridge Trail, **South Catamount Creek Trail** switchbacks downhill to the inlet, then doubles back along South Cat's upper shore, one of our favorite blanket picnic areas. If you wish to hike the opposite shoreline, you'll be surprised to find that the creekbed is very firm gravel, not muddy at all.

CATAMOUNT TRAIL, 3.5 miles one way from North Cat's dam to its inlet, but continues upstream an indeterminate distance (because an unofficial poacher's path sort of links to the Crags. See Cripple Creek). Features a spine trail access for other trails in the northern area, plus access to the inlet. For its link to Green Mountain Falls (foot only) see Ute Pass Area.

Long before South Cat was built in 1937, hikers from Green Mountain Falls used to claw their way up from the falls of Catamount Creek to—well, sneak into this area that had been closed since 1913. Then in 1997 locals and the Volunteers for Outdoor Colorado began building a real trail. Best of all, we're happy to see that the long access road around the northern shore of North Cat has been named Catamount Trail to make it all one long route! We think those early "visitors" would be honored.

Unfortunately, this wide access road begins by looping way out from the shoreline, so you go quite a ways without seeing any water. If you're not cycling too fast, watch for one spot on a rise where you do get a view of the lake with Pikes Peak behind it. Starting at the dam, this high ridge rollercoaster rolls two miles before finding a major four-way intersection with concrete utility works in the middle.

Going to the right from that four-way would lead to Ed Lowe Road, a serious no-no! Going left is the Blue River Trail, which we describe next. So we continue on Catamount by going straight. Within a few yards, you pass the trailhead for Mule Deer Trail, then roll on for 1.5 miles to the inlet, 3.5 miles from the dam.

Again, you don't see the lake until the road starts switchbacking down. But when you get there, the shore is gentle and grassy where the road skirts the lake, a nice spot for a blanket picnic. The single-track that you can see across the lake at that point is, quite frankly, the result of game and sneak-in fishermen, but not necessarily in that order. You'll have to go farther up the road to cross the inlet creek to access that trail. We hope to extend it all the way around the lake by linking with Ridge Trail that leads between the Cats.

If you continue up the valley for another half mile, you'll come to a stream gate area where satellite transmission gear keeps tabs on North Catamount Creek's flow. South Cat has the same gear, relaying information downtown. When streams start rising, experts know within minutes.

BLUE RIVER TRAIL, 0.6 miles, rated moderate. Features visit to lake's cove. Part of Blue River/Mule Deer Loop.

You don't find many four-way intersections in the woods that have a square concrete utility box in the middle, but that serves the pipeline buried beneath Blue River Trail. This trail takes its name from the source of the water fed into the lake from the pipeline that goes almost to Breckenridge.

You see, the North Slope lakes are part of an elaborate plumbing system. The little creeks feeding them could never sustain lakes so large. Most of their water actually comes from very far away, via Montgomery Reservoir (open to fishing) on Hoosier Pass. Gravity takes it all the way across South Park to North Cat, and then on to South Cat and Crystal via underground piping. Thanks to such wonders, Colorado Springs will continue to grow while other communities cannot.

The trail is itself is an unremarkable tour down through the woods, except its destination is a beautiful cove. This makes a great loop with Mule Deer.

MULE DEER TRAIL 0.7 miles one way, rated moderate with a difficult spot, part of loop with Blue River Trail.

Starting at the cove, this old logging road loops up through the woods, forming a designated bike trail. It starts up the draw to the right (west) at the cove, then does a hard left, grunting up a steep and eroded section before topping out in the trees, where the rest is pretty gentle. It takes you back to the main road within a few yards of the big intersection.

LIMBER PINE TRAIL, 1.5 miles one way, rated moderate. Mixed aspen tour created to form longer loop with Catamount Trail.

Going straight ahead from the big intersection, Catamount stays high until it's intersection with Limber Pine Trail. Watch for it on the right just before Catamount starts downhill. Limber Pine was only partly created from logging roads. It's a pleasant adventure through aspen and evergreens with a visit to the chimney remains of an old Boy Scout lodge. It follows a finger ridge back down to Catamount.

This trail is named after a valued pine that is often mistaken for bristlecone, but limber pine is much less sticky, which also means they produce far less resin. Their name comes from the fact that their branches are so flexible, and their special value comes from the fact that they're not as prone to burning. A mix of aspen and limber pine is often used as a kind of natural firebreak. They will burn, of course, but are far less prone, and when it comes to fires, anything helps.

UTE PASS AREA

The Garden of Eden, Catamount Trail

Waldo Canyon Trail (For maps of these trails see Pikes Peak)
Mount Esther Trail
Thomas Trail
Catamount Trail

A cliff-edged notch in the great wall of the Front Range, Ute Pass itself is one of Colorado's most ancient trails, first serving the Ute Indians traveling from Utah on their pilgrimages to the springs at Manitou: Then came trappers, mountain men, soldiers, miners, lumberjacks and ranchers. Today it is still one of the most important routes into the mountains.

ROAD DIRECTIONS: From I-25 in Colorado Springs, take the Cimarron Exit #141 marked for Manitou and Pikes Peak. Go west on Hwy. 24. To find the trailhead for WALDO CANYON, drive 2.2 miles west of the Cave of the Winds exit at Manitou Springs on Hwy. 24 and watch for the large parking lot on your right.

To find MOUNT ESTHER TRAIL, CATAMOUNT and THOMAS TRAIL, continue on Hwy. 24 west and just beyond Cascade (where you see the turnoff for Pikes Peak) take either exit for Green Mountain Falls.

To find MOUNT ESTHER TRAILHEAD, double back east (left) along the main street, which is Chipita Park Road, and turn right onto Picabo. Follow Picabo uphill (very steep and not recommended in winter). When the pavement runs out, make a hard left onto gravel Mountain Rd and about 50 feet farther you'll see MOUNT ESTHER TRAILHEAD marked on your right. Park to the left, without blocking the road There are more pulloffs up ahead. Please respect private property and stay on trail. NOTE: MOUNT ESTHER can also be accessed via the Crow Gulch Trail from Crow Gulch Picnic Ground on the Pikes Peak Toll Road. See PIKES PEAK ITSELF.

To find the THOMAS and CATAMOUNT trails, go straight at the main road off the first Green Mountain Falls Exit. Go past the school 1.6 miles to the town of Green Mountain Falls. Park at Lake St. near the gazebo. DO NOT PARK IN RESIDENTIAL AREAS. We strongly recommend that you hike THOMAS from east to west, ending at the CATAMOUNT trailhead because that provides a more gradual grade and a more spectacular approach to Catamount Falls. Leaving Lake St., hike south along Ute Pass Ave. and turn right onto Hotel St., then left on Park Ave., right on Boulder to find the THOMAS trailhead at the end of Boulder.
To find CATAMOUNT trailhead, hike one block west of the lake along Ute Pass Ave. and turn left onto Hondo Ave. Hike up Hondo past a gate that blocks off vehicular traffic, and cross Catamount Creek at the bridge next to the water tank (0.68 miles from your car). The trailhead for both CATAMOUNT and the end of THOMAS is marked on your left. Both trails share route for a short distance, then branch. Follow yellow markers for THOMAS and blue markers for CATAMOUNT.

WALDO CANYON TRAIL, Forest Service #640, 7-mile balloon loop, including about 2 miles to beginning of 3-mile loop, then 2 miles return; elevation gain 1,280 ft., rated steep at first, then easier. Features scenic route through wooded canyon.

7,040   7-mile loop   7,040

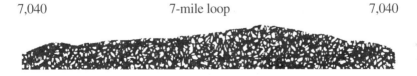

According to trails researcher Gwen Pratt, Waldo Canyon used to be the site of Waldo Hog Ranch, and Waldo used to haul garbage from Manitou to feed his stock. The mortgage was owned by a man named Jones, and one day the two men had a falling out. Waldo demanded to see the mortgage document, but when Jones handed it to him, Waldo ate it!

Such is the history of this scenic canyon that now features one of the region's most popular trails. Indeed, it's popularity is its major protection and its major problem. Its popularity helped prevent the threatened expansion of a nearby gravel strip mine, but the notoriety and its prominent situation on a busy tourist highway has resulted in large numbers of people visiting Waldo.

This trail is generally crowded! Weekdays, early mornings, especially off season, offer the best chance of beating the rush. It is also fair to say that many people visit Waldo Canyon over and over again simply because they simply don't know anywhere else to go, and it is our hope that this guide will help solve that problem by offering more choices. Share your copy.

Waldo begins with a set of switchbacks, but then becomes more gentle. The first couple of miles are arid, but this "string" leads to a "balloon loop" within a moist canyon. The canyon loop is three miles in itself, a beautiful route through ponderosa pine with a brook along the west side. **The loop is more gradual if hiked clockwise because the opposite way begins with a set of switchbacks.**

MOUNT ESTHER TRAIL, Forest Service #754, lower leg is close to one mile long, the upper leg is about 1.5 miles long one way, elevation gain 1,320 feet from lower trailhead, rated fairly difficult from Chipita Park, but is rated very easy from Crow Gulch (FS#754A), with elevation gain of only 600 feet to Utility service road. Features aspen meadow walk.

We go to some trouble to keep you out of trouble, so we could never publicize this old trail until it had been legalized. It's former trailhead trespassed on private property, but thanks to the cooperation of a new landowner and to neighborly negotiations by Dan Cleveland of the Pikes Peak Trails Coalition and Rick Ellsworth of the Forest Service, a new trailhead has been established, with signage and a wooden staircase. Thus, Mount Esther has finally earned Forest Service designation. We owe a debt to everyone involved.

This is a beautiful and varied trail that won't disappoint you unless you're expecting a great view from its summit. In fact, the trail does not even go to the summit, and if you bushwhack the rest of the way, you'll find that thick timber atop the mountain obscures the views you might expect to see. Tiz the journey and not the destination that makes this one so much fun.

Because of its Y-shape with 754A, there are two trailheads. We'll start with the new one, the low one, the one that's free of charge. Any trail that begins with a long series of switchbacks up a steep slope is usually a grunt, but the newest switchbacks are incredibly gentle. Only farther up, where more work awaits on washed sections, do you find it tiring. This section is in thick timber and gives you loftier and loftier views of Ute Pass. At the top of the ridge, you find an intersection at the edge of a grassy meadow.

Going left would take you down a long grass-walk, past aspen glens and interesting rocks, to the Crow Gulch Picnic Ground on the Pikes Peak Toll Road. Good parking there. That approach has always been legal, but authorities feared that if we announced that Mount Esther was "open," folks would use the illegal trailhead also and make matters worse in Chipita Park. If you're looking for an easy hike, however, we do recommend paying the short toll as if you're going fishing at the lakes and then you can use the Crow Gulch Trailhead. That will boost you 720 feet in elevation and provide a long meadow walk.

Just to ease confusion, we're calling the upper (southern) leg Crow Gulch Trail, but its FS trail number 754A shows its relationship with Mount Esther Trail #754. (By the way, the gulch is named after the Crowe Ranch, but the "e" was long ago dropped and the new spelling is now considered the official usage.)

When you come up from Crow Gulch, don't be surprised that the valley forks. Old topos show the stream coming down from the right fork, but actually it comes from the left fork. At that point your trail leaves the tiny stream and follows the drier fork to the right. The wetter valley has no trail.

Now imagine that we're back at the Y. Going uphill on the Y takes you up oh-so-gently. Shortly afterward you'll see a side trail to your right that takes you out to a point of rocks where you can see for miles up Ute Pass. Well worth seeing! Return to the main trail and wander up through aspen, all well-chewed by elk.

High amid the aspen, you cross a trickling tributary near an old lean-to made of logs. Still higher up you angle right to approach the lip separating you from Ute Pass and suddenly encounter a Utility service road beneath power lines.

For my money, this trail ends right there. But if you're curious, here's what to expect by turning left and going uphill on the road. First of all, make sure you memorize that intersection because we missed it coming down again. Don't worry, it doesn't go far, even if you do miss the turn. But as you go up, watch for a tall stump downhill to your right that has been chain-sawed to look like a smiling cat. Where the road starts to pitch downhill, Mount Esther is that jumble of timbered rocks to your left. We did find a balanced rock up there, but it's hard to tell you how to find it. Dick Bratton, trail activist and Mayor of Green Mountain Falls, tells us that no one ever pushed a trail to the very top, perhaps because there never was a great view from up there. Tiz the journey, not the destination.

THOMAS TRAIL, 3 miles one, way including street access; elevation gain 737 ft., rated moderate. Features forest hike from Crystal Falls to Catamount Falls.

Back in the 1890s, when hiking was the major recreation for tourists in Pikes Peak Country, men used to sprinkle pine needles on trails so ladies

wouldn't soil the hems of their long dresses. **Green Mountain Falls is now working to rebuild its historic trail system.**

Using the Pikes Peak Atlas, local architect and Mayor Dick Bratton discovered traces of Felton's old trail above his home and spearheaded a community effort to rebuild the route. Renamed the Thomas Trail in honor of the present owners of the land it crosses, this historic path (along with two short urban trails) was dedicated in 1990 at the town's centennial celebration.

The two shorter loops, Crystal Falls and Catamount Falls, are mostly gravel street routes, leading directly to the Thomas Trail and the falls at each end of town. These are popular walks for those unable to do strenuous hiking. Crystal Falls Loop is one mile long; Catamount Falls Loop is two miles long.

The Thomas Trail, on the other hand, is no urban trail, as you'll see. Bikes and horses are not allowed because of erosion concerns and because the trail is too rough and narrow to be appropriate.

Please do not try to shortcut by parking in residential areas. Besides, the shady gravel roadways which form the two loops that lead to Thomas Trail are pleasant walks with a dozen points of interest. For example, the House of Fortune is a quaint Victorian home where miners came to weigh their gold. And the owner of Tanglewood, an historic log home, is restoring the Iron Spring Gazebo just for the comfort of passing hikers. Ask any merchant for a free map listing points of interest.

If you've ever wondered, "Where are the falls in Green Mountain Falls?" you're about to find out. Right away your singletrack is climbing up along the waters of Crystal Falls (pretty steep here). Farther along, the middle portion of the trail levels out, contouring along a steep wooded hillside. A small cave niche along the way has been a traditional shelter during rains.

Your path rolls along, studded with rocks and roots, fairly gentle until it finds Catamount Falls cascading down a high-walled gorge. Here the path is at its steepest, crossing the creek and climbing down along it to a plank bridge and joining Catamount Trail, heading down to Hondo at the water tower. Here you can recross the creek and head east along Hondo Avenue to the lake or you can take Hondo north 0.2 to Belvidere Ave. and then to Ute Pass Ave., the main street leading to the lake. Trailhead to the lake in this direction is l.2 miles.

CATAMOUNT TRAIL, this chapter describes only the 2-mile segment leading to the lakes, rated difficult at present because of fallen timbers; features mossy forest climb to pretty valley, followed by scramble through logs to lake access. This segment open to foot only. Leads to much longer portion of Catamount at the North Slope Recreation Area, open to bikes and foot.

Catamount Trail was little more than a dream when Green Mountain Falls Mayor Dick Bratton first pointed it out to us years ago, but in l997 the

Garden of Eden, Photo by Dick Bratton

Volunteers for Outdoor Colorado, including Deb Acord of the CS Gazette, did a masterful job of restoring and building the lower switchbacks, making them look absolutely ancient! With loving care they took lichen-clad shelf-rock and built little stairs at the switchbacks, some of them curving and having as many as ten steps, incorporating roots and moss and planting vines so as to make this journey look like something out of a fairy tale.

The first few feet of trail give you a taste of what a gnarly singletrack this really is. Beginning among the roots of a large tree, it climbs like a natural staircase, sharing trail with **Thomas** until higher up, where the yellow markers take you left on **Thomas Trail** and the blue ones to the right take you to **Catamount's** many switchbacks. At nearly mile 0.8 there is a sidetrail to the left that takes you 300 feet to the spectacular town overlook.

Back on the main trail, we climb only a little higher and cross a saddle into the Garden of Eden, a grassy valley guarded by high granite formations, lush with flowers, where the creek gurgles along through coyote willows. There Dolores produced some apples and we sat admiring The Tree, the largest ponderosa we can remember seeing south of Evergreen. Dolores and I could not hold hands around it! And nary a snake in sight.

The trail earns its temporary, difficult rating higher up where it scrambles through rocks and roots, barricaded by fallen snags. Future work will improve that, but it's a very strenuous struggle at this time, actually dangerous when iced.

Farther on you pass through an aspen glen a third of a mile before reaching barbed wire left over from the bad old days when the North Slope Watershed was forbidden fruit. Immediately beyond there is one of the newer 6x6 gates marking the access roads at the confluence of North and South Catamount Creeks.

From here you can access South and North Catamount Reservoirs, and there is no fee for you because you earned this visit with your feet! To reach the lakes, keep heading more or less straight ahead, avoiding left and right choices. That middle road follows South Catamount Creek to the base of South Cat's dam, then switchbacks up to the top of South Cat's dam at the spillway: Distance from the singletrack gate is only one-half mile. To reach North Catamount Reservoir, turn right at the top of the spillway and go only another 0.3 miles.

In case you're curious, here's where the other access roads go. If you went left from the gate, you'd be taking the one-way loop back toward the T-junction with the main entrance road from the Pikes Peak Highway. If you took the upcoming right turn, you'd only dead-end below the spillway of North Cat, a massive wall of difficult rip-rap that nobody wants you climbing. Again, topos are wrong.

By the way, the access road that leads all the way around the north side of North Catamount Reservoir and clear up to its headwaters is now called **Catamount Trail** also. You can think of it as one long trail, closed to public motorized use. Frankly, most people who make the climb from Green Mountain Falls find themselves wanting a bike when they confront that extra 3.5 miles from North Cat's Dam to the end of the trail. If you did every inch, the up and back to Green Mountain Falls would be almost 13 miles, a hearty distance on foot, considering the climb and the fact that the North Slope is day-use only. **See Pikes Peak, North Slope Recreation Area.**

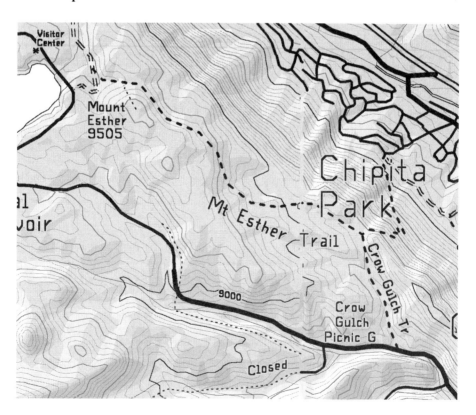

COLORADO SPRINGS AREA

*Legend holds that the Indians of the plains and the Indians of the mountains agreed **not** to fight each other here, so they might both be able to enjoy the* ***Garden of the Gods.***

Palmer Park
Garden of the Gods
Rock Ledge Ranch Historic Site
Bear Creek Regional Park

Colorado Springs has the rare honor of having been founded as a resort community. In 1869 General William Jackson Palmer camped here while exploring railroad routes. He became fascinated by the region's beauty and climate and realized that he had discovered a well-watered crossroads, a place destined to become a big city someday. He laid out streets wide enough for his wagon to turn around in a circle. He set aside what is now Palmer Park and he planted 10,000 trees, as well as the seeds of many people's dreams, including ours.

In the last days of his life, General Palmer said his greatest regret was not setting aside even more open space, but visitors from other cities are generally astonished at the wild mountain nature of three parks located within the city limits.

Trouble is, Palmer Park and Garden of the Gods have so many, many trails packed together that the kind of detailed descriptions done for other park systems is not practical here. Signage is good and these parks are fairly surrounded by development, so you are unlikely to get lost.

ROAD DIRECTIONS: Palmer Park is located in northeastern Colorado Springs and may be approached by Paseo Road off Chelton or by Maizeland Road. From I-25 take Garden of the Gods Exit, but then go EAST. That changes to Austin Bluffs, but just keep going until you find Academy. Turn right on Academy, then right again on Maizeland. A major entrance is your next right turn.

To find the main Gateway entrance to the Garden of the Gods, take the Garden of the Gods Exit west off I-25 and follow signs. You will turn left on 30th St. The Visitor Center is on your left and the entrance is on your right.

The Rock Ledge Ranch Historic Site is located near the Gateway entrance.

To find Bear Creek Regional Park take the Cimarron Exit marked for Manitou and Pikes Peak. Take Hwy 24 west and turn left on 26th St. Go two miles to Bear Creek Road. Follow signs.

PALMER PARK TRAILS, City of Colorado Springs Parks and Recreation Dept. Four different trails up to 2 miles long, rated moderate for hiking, very technical for mountain bikers. Features interesting nature trails and geologic formations. Horses are permitted in the park.

Despite its location, this is no urban park! Palmer Park is a sprawling mesa area with evergreens and sandstone formations. A maze of gravel and paved roads lead to picnic areas scattered through the rocks, some on overlooks with views of the city and mountains and plains. Nature trails lace the area. Mountain bikers will find some very technical riding, but please stay on designated trails and roads to minimize environmental impact. The City has developed wonderful maps displayed on the trailhead signs that divide easy from moderate from difficult trails. We found those maps hard to duplicate in this book, but we doubt you'll have much trouble within such a limited area.

Geologic oddities include sandstone boulders weathered into odd shapes, some resembling mushrooms, and ball-shaped rocks called mud rollers that were created by material rolling downhill through mud and sand during prehistoric storms.

The top of the mesa is a botanical reserve called the Yucca Area, where thousands of yuccas blossom each June.

Balanced Rock in the Garden of the Gods

Palmer Park opens at 5 a.m.and closes at 11 p.m. (May 1 to Nov. 1) and at 9 p.m. otherwise. Dogs must be on leash. No open fires (grates only and charcoal only, no wood), no firearms or fireworks, no alcoholic beverages, no overnight camping. The Lazy Land, Council Grounds Youth Camp and Meadows Picnic Areas are open by reservation. Call 719-634-6666.

GARDEN OF THE GODS PARK, City of Colorado Springs Park and Recreation Department, short nature trails, some of which are now open to mountain bikes and horseback riding, features colorful and majestic geologic formations.

Millions of years ago, ancient seas and rivers laid down sediment layers that turned to sandstone. Then Pikes Peak and other rocky mountains rose from below, not as volcanoes, but as granite masses formed deep in the earth and thrust upward by the buckling of the earth's crust. Granite from deep in the earth now towered above rock which had formed on the ocean floor! And at the edge of this upheaval, giant sandstone slabs were broken and tilted up on end to form the Garden of the Gods.

Even today, after centuries of erosion by wind and water, these slabs stand on edge, the largest some 300 feet high.

This exotic garden was fully appreciated by Indians of both the mountains and plains. The Utes visited here as part of their pilgrimage to the sacred springs at Manitou: Ute Pass was their path. And the plains Indians made a trail that led to the Garden from the east; a stone marker erected by the Daughters of the American Revolution stands at the eastern edge of the park, marking that path. Today the City of Colorado Springs owns and takes care of the Garden.

Mountain biking is legal in the Garden! Not just on 5.3 miles of paved roads now marked with bike and foot lanes, but also on 4.6 miles of designated

off-road honest-to-grunt-goodness trails! Mountain biking trail maps are available at the Visitor Center.

We hasten to add that this new freedom is experimental and we need to remind each other not to mess it up. Please stay on trail, for the area is very delicate, and be courteous to the hikers, horsebackers and joggers who share the paths. Never shortcut between trails. Heavy use means everyone has to be neighborly or this experimental freedom won't last.

By the way, horses are available from nearby stables, but don't be confused by the name: The Academy Riding Stables are very near the Garden of the Gods, not the Air Force Academy, which also has stables. Horses are not permitted in the heart of the park where rock formations are largest, but the trails they use offer great views. Seeing the Garden on horseback is an unforgettable experience.

The Visitor Center just outside the park is an educational showcase with fascinating exhibits about the geology, history, flora and fauna of this world class park. The Visitor Center also serves to move commercial interests outside the park, leaving the park itself to Nature. Hours are 7 to 9 daily, May through September, and 8:30 to 5:30, October through April. Closed Thanksgiving and Christmas day. The Center also offers food service and sales.

Garden of the Gods Park opens at 5 a.m. daily, but closes at 11 p.m. in summer and at 9 p.m. Nov. 1—April 30. No camping, no hunting, no collecting, no open fires (grates only and charcoal only, no wood), no firearms or fireworks. Dogs must be on leash, and no alcoholic beverages are allowed.

Daily nature hikes are led by naturalists throughout the summer (no reservations required). Group nature tours can also be arranged. Call 719-634-6666.

Photographers will find the colors most vivid near sunrise or sunset. In late winter or early spring, watch for bighorn sheep that graze on the hogback ridge immediately north of the Garden.

ROCK LEDGE RANCH HISTORIC SITE, Colorado Springs Parks and Recreation Dept., features short Living History Trail and wheelchair accessible nature trail with raised lettering on signs.

You can step back in time at the Rock Ledge Ranch, where life still goes on much as it did in the late 1800s. The interpreters dress in period clothing and illustrate the historical development of the Pikes Peak region by interpreting an 1868 homestead, an 1895 working ranch and a 1901 country estate.

Walter C. Galloway first homesteaded the Ranch in the 1860s, and his cabin has now been rebuilt in the old ways, using square nails and fittings made by the resident blacksmith. Robert Chambers operated his Rock Ledge Ranch here in the 1890s, growing vegetables for the plush Antlers Hotel. His asparagus now grows wild along the Living History Trail, and the Chambers garden is still being tilled by hand, though now the vegetables are sold to the public in the Ranch's general store.

While there, you'll deal with people in period costume who really play the part. There's no use asking them about the Denver Broncos: They'll just pretend you're asking about bucking horses from Denver.

This used to be called the White House Ranch, named after the elegant "white house" (actually called the Orchard House) built in 1907 by General Palmer for Mrs. Palmers half-sister. The house is only part of this historic site, of course, and remains open for public tours during the summer and at Christmas. The historic site itself was renamed Rock Ledge Ranch in 1995 in keeping with the "step back in time" theme of the ranch, which tries to recapture what it was like during the Chambers era of the 1890s.

In the working ranch you can see ranch animals and a working blacksmith. A 1/4-mile Nature Trail is paved and has signs with raised lettering for use by the visually handicapped, describing the plant life surrounding a picturesque pond.

Rock Ledge Ranch Historic Site is operated with assistance from the Rock Ledge Ranch Living History Association. The Ranch is open Tuesday through Sunday, 10 a.m. to 4 p.m. from early June through Labor Day and weekends from September through December. There is an admission fee to the historic area.

BEAR CREEK REGIONAL PARK and NATURE CENTER, El Paso County Parks Dept. Features Nature Center with interpretive programs and trails, an active use area, plus a lengthy regional trail linking the Penrose Equestrian Center and National Forest.

Located in southwest Colorado Springs off 26th Street and Lower Gold Camp Road, this 1,235-acre park, set in the foothills of the Pikes Peak region, offers a pleasant escape from the crowded city and supports a variety of plants and wildlife including red-tailed hawks, black bears, Peregrine falcons, deer, and coyotes. Scrub oak thickets, ponderosa pines, native grasslands, a mountain creek, cottonwood riparian areas, and sparse wetlands give this park its varied natural character.

As a window to the foothills life zone, Bear Creek Nature Center offers a wildlife viewing area, a large-scale topographic map of the Pikes Peak region, and a foothills wildlife diorama including a full-sized black bear. Interpretive exhibits feature local foothills history, geology, weather, plants and animals. Throughout the year, the Nature Center features interpretive programs, special events, media presentations, outdoor recreation activities, group tours and environmental education programs for area schools. Call 719-520-6387 for more information.

There is plenty to see along the 2.6 miles of trails through this lovely foothill environment. All trails are well marked and have station signs describing flora and fauna. Here's a rundown.

SONGBIRD TRAIL, 0.1 mile. This wheelchair accessible trail passes under vine-covered cottonwoods and features a large bird feeder that attracts a variety of Front Range birds. Look for the squirrel nests.

MOUNTAIN SCRUB TRAIL, 0.5 miles. This loop climbs through a meadow interspersed with scrub oak thickets. Acorns from these minia-ture oaks are a rich food source for wildlife.

CREEKBOTTOM LOOP, 0.8 miles. Tall cottonwoods, thorny locust trees and a sparkling stream make this a shady retreat. The climb up a steep, narrow ravine is rewarded by a big view of Colorado Springs.

COYOTE GULCH LOOP, 1.2 miles. Following the meadows to the crest of the hill, you'll find abundant wildflowers as well as prickly pear, hen and chickens and ball cacti.

Bicycles, horses and dogs are prohibited from the nature trails, but are allowed on the Regional Trail which extends from the Penrose Equestrian Center through the park to access Bear Creek Canyon Trail, El Paso County's Section 16, the Palmer-Redrock Loop and the Intemann Trail. Trails are open from dawn to dusk every day.

The park is open from 5 am. to 11 p.m. No hunting, no firearms or fireworks, no open fires (grates only), no picking of lowers or collecting of artifacts or other souvenirs. Dogs must be leashed in areas where they are allowed. Playfields and group picnic facilities can be reserved by calling 719-520-6375.

ROXBOROUGH STATE PARK

Denver's Roxborough State Park, looking south.

Fountain Valley Trail
Lyons Overlook
Willow Creek Trail
South Rim Trail
Carpenter Peak Trail
Roxborough Loop Trail

Located south of Denver's Chatfield Reservoir and snuggled up against the Pike National Forest, Roxborough—"a city of rocks"—is a unique state park dedicated to nature walks and cross-country skiing. Its unusual geology and its position as a transition zone have created microclimates for seven different plant communities, plus an unusual richness and variety of wildlife. *So at Roxborough, even more than at other parks, the watchword is preservation.*

This is the kind of special place where naturalists tread very softly. At Roxborough, it is especially important for you to stay on trails as much as possible, to pick up litter, and try not to change anything. That's why no pets are allowed, no horses, no mountain bikes, no rock climbing, no fires, no camping, no firearms, no hunting. Even picnic tables are not provided, though visitors are welcome to bring a meal and eat at one of the benches at the Visitors Center or along the park trails. Please don't spread blankets on the wildflowers, however.

This is an especially good place to view wildlife. The ban on dogs has made wildlife feel more secure and has prevented the park from being scent-marked as dog territory. Even bear and mountain lion are seen here.

Perhaps the best way to appreciate Roxborough is to arrange for a tour with volunteer naturalists. You'll learn from experts about the plants and animals, birds and mushrooms, history and geology, even a little "belly botany," the close-up study of tiny plants. Call 303-973-3959 to arrange tours or group activities. A day pass is required. Hours are posted and change with the season. If you return to your car after closing, you may be ticketed, so watch the time. Drinking water is available only at the Visitors Center. There are no restrooms along the trails. Restrooms are located at the first parking lot and at the Visitor Center. The Visitors Center also offers exhibits, interpretive signs and educational materials.

Be aware that Roxborough is home to poison ivy and a few prairie rattlesnakes, another good reason to stay on trails.

Because of its low altitude, Roxborough can be enjoyed year round. Each season brings a different beauty. When fall colors fade, for example, elk start moving down into the area, and winter storms only open up the area for cross-country skiing. Ski trails are not groomed, but the park road is plowed.

ROAD DIRECTIONS: From Denver, take Hwy. 85 (Santa Fe Drive) south to Titan Road. From Colorado Springs, take 1-25 north to the Sedalia-Hwy. 85 Exit just north of Castle Rock. Titan Road is located 5.8 miles north of Sedalia on 85. Titan heads west from 85. After three miles, Titan turns south. Follow it. Near the entrance to Roxborough housing estates, you'll see park signs directing you to the left. Follow signs.

FOUNTAIN VALLEY TRAIL: 2.25 mile loop, elevation gain 240 ft., loss 240 ft., rated gentle to moderate. Features unusual geology with fairly easy hiking and cross-country skiing.

This loop begins at the Visitors Center and winds northward through spectacular rock formations. The red rocks studded with gravel are called the Fountain formation (also found in Red Rocks Park and Garden of the Gods). Their color comes from iron compounds, and they were formed from stream sands and gravel eroded from the ancestral Rockies 300 million years ago. The yellow-orange sandstone is the Lyons formation, once a series of sand dunes and stream deposits along the shores of ancient seas. At the far end of the trail is a group of buildings dating to the turn of the century when Henry S. Persse had a summer home here. He planned to develop a resort, but eventually sold the land to a cattle ranching family, the Helmers.

LYONS OVERLOOK TRAIL: 0.5 miles, elevation gain less than 100 ft., rated moderate. Features spectacular views.

This is just a short spur off the Fountain Valley Trail, climbing up to an overlook. From there you have a view of the Fountain and Lyons formations, plus the Dakota Hogback to the east. The hogback is sandstone formed 135 million years ago from beaches and floodplain sands. All of these formations were laid down horizontally, then were tilted up on edge when the Rockies rose from below.

WILLOW CREEK TRAIL: 1.8-mile loop, elevation gain nil, rated easy; features easy hiking or cross-country skiing.

Starting at the Visitors Center, this is naturally one of the easiest and most popular routes for hikers and cross-country skiers. It takes you through the streamside environment of Little Willow Creek, with its cottonwoods and box elders and meadows with tall grasses. It also serves as a link to longer trails beyond.

SOUTH RIM TRAIL: 3 mile loop, elevation gain-loss 360 ft., rated moderate. Features scenic overlook.

6.160   *3.0 miles*   *6.160*

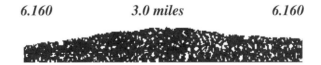

South Rim takes off from the Willow Creek trail not far from the Visitor Center. The first part is gentle enough for cross-country skiing. Soon it enters an old hay meadow where a huge cottonwood stands. Nearby Carpenter Peak Trail branches away to your right (west). South Rim then crosses Willow Creek, which is often dry in August. In spring, this is a lush cool spot. The trail rises to open meadow again, then climbs to the top of a ridge (Lyons formation) where you have a good view of the park and its formations to the north. Make sure children stay on trail; there are some drop offs here. Your path then winds down to drier prairie terrain and and joins Willow Creek Trail at the road.

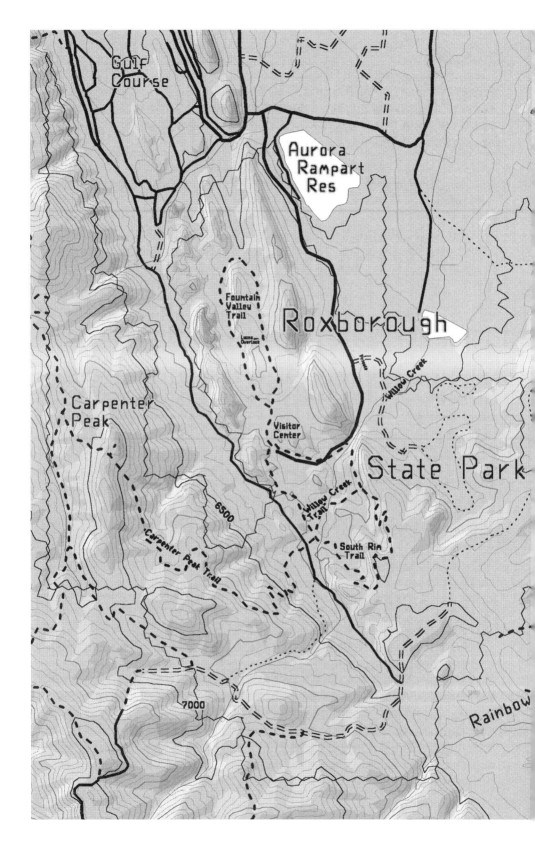

CARPENTER PEAK TRAIL: 5.5 miles round trip to summit from visitor center, 7.7 miles round trip to fork of Roxborough Loop, elevation gain 960 ft. to summit, rated moderate to difficult. Features hike to mountain summit and on to the Roxborough Loop.

6,220 S. Rim   *2.8 miles*   *7,710*

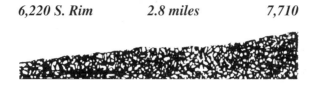

This one is so long that rangers want to remind you about getting back before closing time. Carpenter Peak Trail branches off the South Rim Trail and soon crosses a dirt road that leads to private property. From here you can see an old brick farmhouse called Sundance Ranch. Skirting the Fountain formation, your trail climbs switchbacks and ducks in and out of ravines. There are many clumps of Douglas fir and Pondcrosa along here. Past a meadow with views of the summit, the trail avoids a big ravine to keep elevation and goes through a jungle of large scrub oak. Here the rocks are gneiss (pronounced like the word "nice"), a beautiful metamorphic stone that glistens in the sun and has banded colors. Carpenter Peak has some very nice gneiss!

From the top you have a grand view of downtown Denver, the plains to the east and the mountains to the west. A tenth of a mile below the rocky summit, you find what we used to call the Roxborough Link trailhead. That leg is now called Carpenter Peak also, all the way to the fork that begins what is now called the Roxborough Loop Trail.

ROXBOROUGH LOOP: Pike National Forest, Colorado Division of Parks and Outdoor Recreation and the Denver Water Board, a triangle measuring 4.5 miles with the CT as its third leg or 12.2 miles round trip from the Roxborough Visitor Center; rated moderate to difficult. Features backcountry link with CT 1776. SEE COLO TRAIL 1776 FOR MAP.

Perhaps this loop should be named something else, because none of it is located within the State Park and, since *Roxborough State Park is no bike and no horse***, only hikers can reach it via the park's Carpenter Peak Trail. In fact, it probably gets more use via Colorado Trail 1776 (a much longer journey, but open to both bikes and horses), so perhaps we'll move it to that chapter in our next edition. Be sure to camp only within the National Forest (not within Denver Water Board property and not within the park itself).**

This loop is a long way from anywhere because you can only reach it by starting on other trails. See COLORADO TRAIL 1776, Segment One, for directions via Waterton Canyon.

This brings up some practical problems. If you want to hike from the park and do the entire Roxborough Loop, your total distance round trip will be about 12.5 miles-and if you're not planning an overnighter, that is a very tough day hike, especially considering that you must return to your car before closing.

However, if you start from the National Forest, you have a six-mile trip along Waterton Canyon before you reach Roxborough Loop, so doing the entire trail from that end would be a round trip even longer, 16.5 miles. Either way it's a long way, but at least the Waterton Canyon parking area does not close.

Still, the shorter way is from the park, so we'll begin there. Starting down from the summit of Carpenter Peak, you soon find an old four-wheel track that leads down along a ridge. This takes you over the Aurora Rampart Tunnel and down to a meadow area owned by the Denver Water Board. After leaving the meadow, the trail splits. This is the beginning of the Roxborough Loop.

The right branch heads west down a ravine 0.8 miles to the Waterton Canyon access road, arriving near a DWB caretaker's home. If you want to make a balloon loop, turn left on that access road and go 0.4 miles uphill to the trailhead for CT 1776 and climb the switchbacks another 1.1 miles to a saddle ridge where you'll find the other leg of Roxborough Loop. This next branch (2.2 miles) starts out in scrub oaks and pines and wraps around a hillside before starting down into Stevens Gulch (water undependable). Then it heads due north along an old horse trail through the gulch, hugging a hillside on its way back to the loop intersection. From there you return the way you came.

Watch your trail markers because there are a quite a few social trails in this area that locals have used for years, especially near the park boundary. These spurs soon take you into private property trespass situations. Never trespass. There are plenty of legal places.

The Roxborough Loop was built with volunteer labor from the Colorado Trail Foundation, Martin Marietta Corp. and the Boy Scouts. Volunteers for Outdoor Colorado helped on other trails as well.

Millennium Update: Roxborough State Park has expanded by adding lands from the South. It's current trail system is unaffected, but users can expect even more in the future.

CASTLEWOOD CANYON STATE PARK

Canyon View Nature Trail
Inner Canyon Trail
Rim Rock Trail
Homestead Trail
Creek Bottom Trail
Lake Gulch Trail
Climbers Trail
Cave Trail

Working in a downpour, the caretaker was trying to relieve the mounting pressure on Castlewood Canyon Dam when he heard a rumbling noise. He drove immediately to the switchboard operator and gave the alarm as the dam burst. The 400-acre lake emptied in a deluge that swept away bridges for miles, doing a million dollars in damage and taking two lives. Without the caretaker's alarm, more lives might have been lost that August of 1933.

The dam was never rebuilt, and today you can still see the dam ruins and evidence of the flood's scouring downstream. Yet the area is now a beautiful and charming park where visitors picnic, hike, climb rocks, observe wildlife, and snowshoe amid 873 acres of unique geology—now increased to 1,631 acres with the acquisition of the East Canyon Preserve Area. The undeveloped East Canyon Preserve Area across Hwy. 83 is currently open only for guided nature tours.

All trails are for foot travel only (cross-country skiing is permitted, but not encouraged because the rocky terrain makes it difficult to maneuver and because canyon edges are not always visible when covered with snow.) Eventually the Cherry Creek Bike Path will link Cherry Creek State Park with Castlewood. Horses and bicycles will be allowed on that trail.

We often think of forests standing above prairie, but Castlewood Canyon turns that notion on its head. This is the northernmost portion of the Black Forest ecosystem, but here the canyon is largely surrounded by grassland. Castlewood is a crack in that grassland, a moist corridor where Douglas fir and Ponderosa pine thrive. Through it flows Cherry Creek on its way to Denver. From the bridge on Hwy. 83 you get just a peek of the canyon.

Its steep cliffs are composed of Castle Rock conglomerate, a kind of sedimentary cement studded with hard gravel and cobblestones. Where cobblestones fall

The stream at Castlewood Canyon

out, the pockets left behind form hand-holds that climbers call huecos (Spanish for hollow). The cliffs are not gigantic, but are very popular training climbs because of their many interesting situations. Bolting is not allowed. Free climbing is allowed, but beware of letting your children imitate the experts.

No hunting or firearms are permitted. **Dogs must be on a leash no more than six feet long.** Visitors are encouraged to stay on trails to help protect delicate plant life. (Too, there are a few rattlesnakes to watch out for.)

A day pass is required. Vehicles must stay on roads. No camping or ground fires (self-contained grills or camp stoves are permitted). Only 3.2 alcohol is permitted in the park. Picnic tables are available. Hours are sunrise to sunset. **Don't forget this is a low-altitude park enjoyable at all times of the year.** Guided nature tours and group presentations can be arranged.

The Visitor Center features wonderful interpretive displays about the park's ecology and the Castlewood Dam. There is also a 15-minute slide show that introduces visitors to the natural wonders they will discover in the park and which vividly describes the dam's failure.

Three new group picnic shelters have also been completed; these can be reserved for family reunions, company picnics, etc. **Call 303-688-5242 to reserve shelters or nature tours. You may also visit the web site for all State Parks at**

www.coloradopark.org. And by the way, much of the initial trailwork throughout the park was completed with help from Volunteers for Outdoor Colorado.

ROAD DIRECTIONS: From Denver or Colorado Springs, take I-25 to Castle Rock and drive six miles east on Hwy 86. The original (now the backdoor) park entrance is located on Hwy. 86 just west of Franktown at the Cherry Creek bridge. To find the main entrance and Visitor Center, proceed to the intersection of 86 and Hwy 83 and turn right (south) The main entrance is five miles south of Franktown, immediately south of the other Cherry Creek bridge. From Colorado Springs, the most scenic route is Hwy. 83, a drive of 30 miles north from its intersection with North Academy. Blvd.

CANYON VIEW NATURE TRAIL, about one mile in all, elevation gain nil, hard-surface trail system features handicapped access.

Used by visitors of all abilities, the Canyon View Nature Trail is a handicapped accessible sidewalk trail stretching along the southwest rim of the canyon. Starting at the Visitor Center, this is actually a trail system connecting parking lots, restrooms and picnic areas, and includes short spurs taking visitors to overlooks. There are four canyon overlooks in all. This trail is especially popular with families with young children in strollers. It also connects to the Inner Canyon Trail and Lake Gulch Trail.

INNER CANYON TRAIL, one mile one way, elevation loss 200 ft., rated easy to moderate. Features scenic walk down into canyon.

This trail switchbacks down through Douglas fir and Ponderosa to the floor of the canyon, where it crosses the creek and continues downstream on the other side. Rhyolite is found as pieces within the conglomerate and loose on the ground. It occurs in several colors, one almost purple. Denver's brownstones are made of rhyolite. Watch for watermarks on the rocks showing the level of the old lake. Near the end of this section, you'll see **Lake Gulch Trail** branching off to your left, crossing the bridge to loop back to your starting point, but we'll describe that one later. Right now continue on Inner Canyon to the next intersection.

RIM ROCK TRAIL, 1.9 miles one way, elevation gain 160 ft., loss 340 ft.; rated easy to moderate. Features great views of the dam and the Front Range from Pikes Peak to Longs Peak.

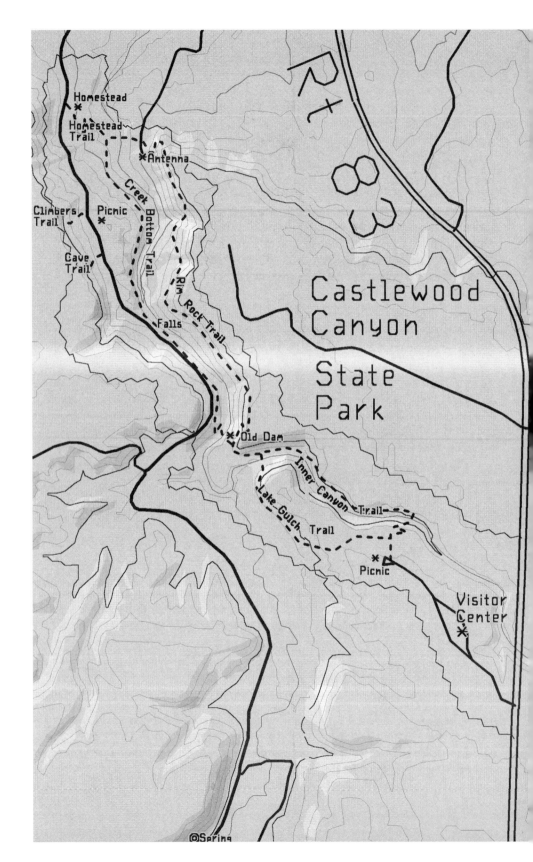

Close to the dam at the bottom of the basin once filled by the lake, we find a fork. To the left is **Creek Bottom Trail** and to the right is **Rim Rock Trail**, which together form a loop. We'll take **Rim Rock**, a steep climb at first. Because of its sunny rocky terrain, **Rim Rock** is a good place to watch out for rattlers. As you climb the switchbacks, a full view of the dam construction unfolds. This is a cliff-edge walk, close enough to give great views but not close enough to be scary. Ponderosa and juniper line the rim, as well as many hardy plants that survive in shallow soil.   Near the end you'll see a gauging station, which looks like a metal chimney near the creek. Beyond lie the ruins of the Lucas homestead. Descend through trees to the creek, where you'll find a fork in the trail. Downstream is **Creek Bottom Trail**, continuing our loop, but first let's explore the other fork, **Homestead.**

HOMESTEAD TRAIL, 0.4 miles, elevation gain 60 ft.,rated easy to moderate. Features link to old county road entrance through Lucas homestead.

Before the new entrance was established, this was the major gateway to park trails, but is now only a short spur connecting the back loop with a county road parking lot. It climbs up from the creek bottom through the stone ruins of the Lucas ranch homestead.

CREEK BOTTOM TRAIL, l.5 miles one way, elevation gain 280 ft., rated easy to moderate. Features stream and forest walk past waterfall.

As you follow the stream, notice the mudstone layer cut by the 1933 flood. Soon you'll find a 20-foot waterfall. Springs oozing beside the falls sometimes form an ice sheet that is enjoyed by ice climbers. Most years, however, there is not enough ice to climb. Hiking is easy until you get to the base of the dam, where a moderate climb takes you to the top. An overlook position is marked atop the dam, but please do not go out farther on the dam. This has been the scene of sad accidents. You complete this loop by hiking down to the intersection with **Inner Canyon Trail**, and you complete the next loop (the one we began at the parking lot) by crossing the creek onto **Lake Gulch Trail.**

LAKE GULCH TRAIL, 0.65 miles one way, elevation gain 200 ft., rated easy to moderate. Features rim trail to main entrance parking.

Beginning at the footbridge, **Lake Gulch** soon leaves the gulch, but offers a fine view of the basin once filled by the lake. Notice the cottonwoods that once lined the lake. Now growing in drier soil, they look as if they're becoming shrub-bery. The trail takes you back along the south rim to the main entrance parking.

CLIMBERS TRAIL, 0.9 miles one way, elevation gain 110 ft., rated short but steep. Features access to popular climb.

This shorty starts at a picnic ground on the old entrance road and climbs up to a cliff called the Grocery Store Wall, popular as a top-roping area. Rock climbers are welcome, but visitors without training should think twice. There is a distinct path linking this area with the **Cave Trail**.

CAVE TRAIL, less than a mile, elevation gain 120 ft., rated short but steep. Features access to shelter cave.

This one is very much like the **Climbers Trail**, leaving another picnic area on the old entrance road and climbing steeply to the cliffs, but its destination is the large-looking cave that can be seen from below. Actually the cave is quite shallow, only going back about a dozen feet. The climb to the cave is moderately technical, however, and most climbers require equipment to reach it. The newest trail in the park is an L-shaped shorty called Cliff Base that simply links Cave Trail to another picnic ground on the west road.

MONUMENT/PALMER LAKE and BLACK FOREST AREA

Monument Rock as seen across a small pond. Photo by Andy de Naray.

Monument Trail
Mount Herman Trail and Bottomless Pit
Palmer Lake's Upper Reservoir Trail
Fox Run Regional Park
Black Forest Regional Park

Located south of Castle Rock and north of the Air Force Academy, the Monument/Palmer Lake and Black Forest Area continues to see a rapid increase in trail use, both official and unofficial. We are especially pleased to see Palmer Lake's officially permitting bicycles on its Upper Reservoir Trail and allowing the Division of Wildlife to stock that beautiful mountain lake for public fishing: More on that later.

The big news in Monument is too much trail!

Unplanned social trails are actually becoming a problem in one of the area's most popular spots, the **Monument Preserve, a 1000-acre open space one and a half miles west of the community of Monument.** Indeed, we almost left this out of our current edition, but you do need to know what's going on. You might even be able to help.

The Monument Preserve contains the trailhead for the old **Monument Trail, which is the only trail we will describe here.** Rich in history, the Preserve was used as a tree nursery from 1907 to 1965. Old irrigation ditches, building foundations and planted rows of various conifers can still be seen, and its historic stone buildings serve today as the Monument Fire Center, home of the elite Helitack and Hotshots Firefighting crews.

When the nursery shut down, locals began to recreate in the area without any real management. Social trails multiplied into a nonsensical lacework of parallel paths and shortcuts that actually trample the environment. (**You see, a trail is actually a deliberate path of ruin designed to protect everything on either side of it. Too many trails spell too much ruin.**) Organizing this system requires shutting down some paths, which is supported by the majority of locals, but some die-hards continue to reopen closed routes, ruining the effort. If you should see such vandalism, please report it.

While open to all, we CANNOT RECOMMEND RUSHING TO SEE THE MONUMENT PRESERVE because it is simply not ready for more use. Trailhead parking and signage are practically nonexistent. Put this on your "someday list" and consider donating to the Friends of Monument Preserve (PO box 364, Monument, 80132) because funding is also a problem. Meanwhile, the Forest Service has published an implementation plan and public meetings have been held.

We will guide you only to the **Monument Trailhead** that we have always described, but again, we do not recommend this trailhead at this time. Instead, we'll show you two other ways to access the upper portion of **Monument Trail**, including the newly bikable **Palmer Lake Upper Reservoir Trail**.

Fortunately, none of these problems afflict the fully developed Fox Run Regional Park in the Black Forest nearby, nor the Black Forest Regional Park, both operated by El Paso County Parks. These parks have miles of well-planned trails for hiking, biking, horseback riding and cross-country skiing, complemented by plenty of parking and good facilities.

ROAD DIRECTIONS: Take I-25 to the Monument-Palmer Lake Exit #161 west. To find MONUMENT and MOUNT HERMAN TRAILS go the Seven Eleven and turn west on Third St. Drive through the town of Monument. Go left onto Front Street, go right on Second, cross the railroad tracks and turn left on Mitchell Ave. Go past the turnoff for Monument Lake (private) and turn right on Mount Herman Road.

To find MONUMENT TRAILHEAD at Monument Preserve go 0.6 miles and turn left onto Nursery (where the pavement ends). (This becomes Schilling.) Driving 0.6 miles on gravel, stop at the intersection with Linbergh (which goes left) and park as best you can near the gated fence with a stile in it. Horseriders will find an entrance by going through the trees to the right of the gate. No signs, no real parking.

To find MOUNT HERMAN TRAILHEAD and another access to MONU-MENT TRAIL, do NOT turn left on Nursery but stay on Mount Herman Road and note your odometer when you cross the National Forest boundary. Drive 1.6 miles and turn left at the fork. Go another 2.7 miles and watch for the trailhead on your right as you make a tight curve at a drainage area leading down toward Beaver Creek. Overall distance from the National Forest boundary is 4.3 miles. To find the MIDPOINT OF MONUMENT TRAIL, go just a little higher to the next hairpin as shown on the map. Your trail shares a four-wheel road for about a third of a mile. The road continues, so watch for the spot where the trail cuts northwest and into Limbaugh Canyon.

To access the far end of MONUMENT TRAIL, please do ignore the Palmer Lake trailhead shown on all maps we've seen because it is illegal, trespassing on private property. Yes, locals use it, but they have permission and if the public at large bugs those folks seeking permission, maybe nobody can use it, so stay out of trouble and let us show you a much prettier and legal Palmer Lake alternative, which follows:

To find the newly bikable PALMER LAKE UPPER RESERVOIR TRAIL, which leads to MONUMENT TRAIL, from I-25 take the same Monument-Palmer Lake exit #161 WEST and turn right and head for the mountains. You'll soon pass the Palmer Lake city limits sign, but town is about 3 miles farther. Just as you reach the outskirts, watch for South Valley Road going sharply uphill on your left (next street past Vail). Turn left on South Valley and then left on Old Carriage Road, a one way going downhill. On the hairpin you'll see the trailhead on your right. There is much more parking just downhill, again on your right.

MONUMENT TRAIL, Forest Service #715, 8.2 miles one way, elevation gain 1,360 ft., loss 600 ft.; rated moderate going, more difficult coming back. Features varied scenery.

7,040   8.2 miles   7,860

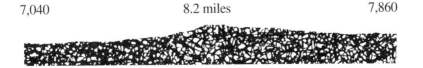

A mountain biker climbing Mount Herman Road above Monument Preserve

Park as best you can at Memorial Grove, where a plaque and planted trees memorialize dead Forest Service personnel. Go through the stile in the fence and up the road for a very short distance before turning left (south) onto the trail itself. Please sign the trail register there. This first section is flat enough to make good cross-country skiing and is also popular among local joggers. It leads through Scrub oak, eventually climbing steeply beside the creek that flows below Mount Herman Road.

Crossing Mount Herman Road, (see road directions) your trail shares a four-wheeler route for about a third of a mile and cuts northwest off the road just before the road hooks back southwest. Now your trail narrows and wanders down through aspen until it connects with Monument Creek in Limbaugh Canyon, lovely place! It follows the creek through willow-brush and aspen meadows for about a mile and a half, then forks. We'll describe the left fork in a moment. The right fork continues downstream for 1.1 miles to the Forest Service boundary, well worth seeing if you have time. Beyond this point is private and utility property, so the trail dead-ends at the Forest Service boundary.

The left fork leaves the creek and climbs up to a saddle where it four-way-junctions with the **Balanced Rock** four-wheel drive road. The altitude gain on this short section is only 250 feet, but is a very steep climb up through dense ponderosa. This is one of those ancient roads with a deep wash down the middle, but it leads to another lovely place. At the four-way, go straight over the saddle. The right turn is a short uphill and the left turn takes you to **Mount Herman Road** via the long and very rugged **Balanced Rock** stage coach road, which is described in the MORE RAMPART AREA chapter.

As you head down over the other side of the saddle, you are really traveling the end of **Balanced Rock**, heading down toward the gate guarding Palmer Lake's Upper Reservoir, which we describe in this chapter. This connection takes you down through aspen with distant glimpses of huge rocks and the lake itself. There are some side routes to the left, but just keep bearing to the right until you reach the lake, where you want to turn left to cross the creek and find the main route out to Palmer Lake.

Horses stop here. Bikes are okay on the watershed, but horses are not. And if you have a dog with you, it must be on a leash: Verbal control is not recognized. Use the leash or pay the fine. See Palmer Lake in this chapter.

MOUNT HERMAN TRAIL, Forest Service #716, about 2 miles one way, elevation gain 1,000 ft., rated moderate. Features hike to summit of Mt. Herman. See special warning about dangerous Bottomless Pit.

Starting up from the Mount Herman Road, your trail follows a tiny tributary for a short way, then turns right, switchbacking up the mountain. Your path is washed and rocky. It grows gentler on top, leading to a popular outlook where the Great Plains are laid out below you. You can also see the Kenosha and Tarryall mountains to the west, Long's Peak to the north and, of course, Pikes Peak to the south. One of the very best views in the entire area.

The trail does not visit the mountain's lower peak just to the south, but since people do scramble over there to visit its more interesting rock formations, **there is one formation so dangerous that we have to warn you. It's called Bottomless Pit, and unlike the one on Pikes Peak, this one really is a pit, a natural shaft in smooth granite, very deep and dark, every bit as dangerous as a mine shaft.**

PALMER LAKE'S UPPER RESERVOIR

Named for its popular downtown fishing lake, the community of Palmer Lake also has two reservoirs hidden in the woods above town. We delayed describing this gorgeous route in our *Trails Guide* because there was always a huge parking problem, the rules were in flux and the lakes were being drained and repaired. Now, with repairs finally done, with new parking lots ready, and with the new Emory Hightower trailhead provided by lottery funds, everything is ready to welcome America.

Bikes are now welcome on the trail! Furthermore, the Division of Wildlife will stock the Upper Reservoir with fingerlings for the first time in the summer of 1999 (fingerlings mature in 2000). At the time of this writing, there are still some "no bike' signs high in trees, but this report has been cleared with city authorities. Bikes are definitely okay, which opens this as a biker's route to Monument Trail to Limbaugh Canyon and to Balanced Rock!

Yet since this is a drinking water watershed, there are the usual no-nos, plus one that is different than you may expect. At this time there is no single sign listing all the rules, so this is your guide: No motor vehicles, no horses, no firearms or fireworks, no camping, no campfires, no glass bottles, no persons or pets in the water. **Plus, dogs must absolutely be on a leash at all times no matter what. This is strictly enforced. If you claim your dog is under verbal command, you will still get a ticket for not having it on a leash. No exceptions. No fishing in the lower reservoir (which is small anyway), but fishing is allowed in the Upper Reservoir with valid Colorado license.**

PALMER LAKE'S RESERVOIR TRAIL, 1.2 to Upper Reservoir dam, plus half a mile farther to the lake's inlet. Single track around far side of lake is about one half mile one way. Rated moderate to easy. Features scenic canyon tour with picturesque fishing at lake.

This trail begins as a singletrack through large ponderosa, then joins the service road after crossing the creek. Calling this narrow track a "service road" gives you no idea of how beautiful this route really is. Every bit of this canyon is scenic.

Not quite so scenic is the new chain link fence around the small Lower Reservoir. This little lake, also fed by Ice Cave Creek, was recently drained and dredged. The huge boulders that cross it are designed to help keep sediment from building up in the deep end near the dam. It had gotten quite shallow before this work was done. No fishing here, but you won't mind when you see what awaits you upstream.

When you first glimpse the small curving dam of the Upper Reservoir, imagine several feet of flood water pouring over the top. That would have destroyed most dams, but this mightily little wonder, built by the Army Corps of Engineers, survived the flash flood of 1965. That flood also rearranged some boulders in Ice Cave Creek nearby and actually blew away both of Victor's reservoirs. You'll see evidence of the flood up and down this trail and along other trails in our region.

After a test like that, you'd think this dam would be trouble free, but excavations to provide a proper footing for a new membrane somehow broke into a natural fissure in the granite formation on the far side of the dam. So when the lake refilled, it started to leak, gushing from rocks well below the dam. Fixing that proved difficult. The lake had to be drained three years in a row. It finally took six loads concrete pumped underground before concrete started gushing from the same opening below the dam.

As mentioned before, the DOW will stock fingerlings here for the first time in 1999 and those fish will mature by 2000. But when I fish a lake this beautiful, I don't care whether I catch anything or not. Biologists say it has great potential. Retired Road and Water Supervisor Bob Schroeder knows it does: "When we first drained Upper Reservoir, we found trout 15 and 18 inches long."

Notice the fisherman's singletrack on the far side. That's a great little hike in itself. It goes past a rock formation on the far side that has a little caveman shelter built inside. But do return the way you came. DO NOT ATTEMPT TO CROSS THE DAM.

Upstream you'll find old four-wheel tracks. The one farthest south switchbacks up to a saddle where you'll find the four-way intersection described in the **Monument Trail** section of this chapter, a great access to Limbaugh Canyon. At the four-way you are 2.6 miles from the car (0.9 from the inlet).

FOX RUN REGIONAL PARK

ROAD DIRECTIONS: To find Fox Run Regional Park, take the exit south of Monument-Palmer Lake, marked Baptist Road Exit #158 EAST from I-25. Pass Gleneagle, pass Desiree and just as this straight road begins to curve left, turn right onto Tari Dr and immediately turn left on Becky Lane. Go one half mile to its intersection with Stella Drive and

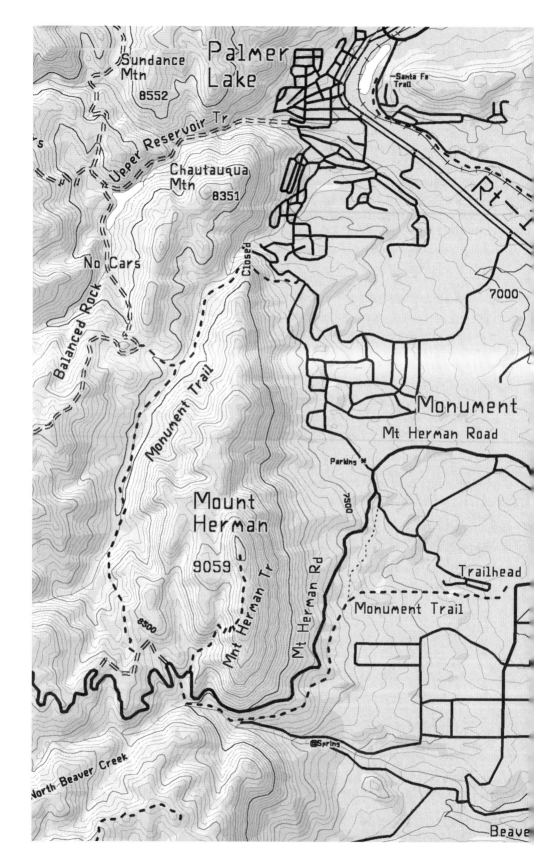

turn left. Follow Stella for another 0.6 miles to find the main entrance to Fox Run Park. To find the north trailhead, proceed on Stella and turn left on Rollercoaster Road. Parking is on the left.

Once a part of a fox ranch, Fox Run Regional Park offers gentle trails for cross-country skiing, hiking, horseback riding and mountain biking. The entrance looks like an urban park, with flower beds and mowed lawns, pavilions for picnics and areas for games, but 90% of its 410 acres have been left in a natural state called the Fallen Timbers area.

Fox Run three excellent self-guided interpretive trails. If you don't learn something from these interpretive signs located along these trails, you deserve some kind of honorary degree.

Wide and well-marked with frequent "You are here" maps, the trails tunnel through dense ponderosa so typical of the area. Two trailheads, one in the center of the wilderness and the other on Rollercoaster at the north end of the park, each provide restrooms, parking, potable water, picnic sites and interpretive displays.

The usual park rules apply: No hunting, no firearms or fireworks, no open fires (grates only), no camping. Dogs must be on a leash. Bikes, horses and dogs are permitted on the loop trails, but are prohibited from What's In A Name Trail.

Here's a run-down on its trails:

NORTH LOOP, 1.5-mile loop, elevation gain nil, rated easy. This is really two loops because of an extra north-south route that cuts across it. If you use that extra section to make two loops, the eastern loop measures about a mile by itself and the other half measures about 1.25 miles by itself. All of the park's trails are easy, but this one is almost flat. This kind of evergreen forest extends into the plains because of a layer of sandstone beneath the surface that traps enough water to make trees grow.

WEST LOOP, almost 2 miles, elevation gain negligible, rated easy to moderate. A little more challenging for skiing and biking, West Loop is more hilly than North Loop, and bikers will find it sandy in spots. Still, these hills only make gentle rolling trail; there are no switchbacks. Don't miss the interpretive signs along the way.

WHAT'S IN A NAME TRAIL, 0.25 miles one way, elevation gain negligible, rated easy. Bikes, horses and dogs are prohibited from this short trail because of heavy use. Interpretive signs highlight aspects of history, geology and wildlife as revealed in their names. The trail circles Aspen and Spruce lakes (which are small enough to be called ponds), offering a picturesque view of Pikes Peak.

BLACK FOREST REGIONAL PARK

Road Directions: From Highway 83 (a scenic route running parallel east of I-25 accessed from several exits) take Shoup Road east. Shoup is located south of North Gate Road and north of Briargate Parkway.) Go east on Shoup to Milam Rd and turn left (north). The park entrance is on your right off Milam.

Smaller than Fox Run, we like to think of this one as Son of Fox Run, for they are both remarkably similar. Like Fox Run, all of the development is concentrated in one small area with the vast majority of its 240 acres reserved for non-motorized use. The ponderosa forests in both parks get more snow than most other areas of similar elevation because Monument Hill is a kind of mini-continental divide running east at a right angle from the Front Range. This geological feature tends to manufacture weather. Indeed, if I-25 is closed anywhere in Colorado, it is generally at Monument Hill.

One difference: Although El Paso County Parks operates Black Forest Regional Park, the land is actually owned by the Forest Service.

AIR FORCE ACADEMY AREA

Five different trails lead to Stanley Reservoir above the Air Force Academy.

Stanley Canyon Trail
West Monument Creek Trail
Falcon Trail

As the Air Force equivalent of West Point and Annapolis, the US Air Force Academy is quite a tourist attraction. Set in a beautiful foothills area between Monument and Colorado Springs, it has three public trails, two of which (Stanley Canyon and West Monument Creek) extend into the Pike National Forest.

ROAD DIRECTIONS: From I-25 south of Monument, enter the south gate of the U.S. Air Force Academy. Proceed 2.2 miles and turn left onto Pine Drive. To find the trailhead for FALCON, follow Pine Drive for 3.6 miles and turn right onto Community Drive. At the top of the hill, a distance of almost a mile, turn right and find your way back to the Youth Center, Building #5132, which is the small building on the southwestern corner of the complex. The trailhead is located behind the building and a large blue sign marks the spot.

To find the lower trailhead for WEST MONUMENT CREEK TRAIL, follow

Pine Drive only 4.8 miles from south gate. Turn left onto gravel road immediately beyond the Fire Station' where the sign points toward the water treatment plant. Horse trailer parking is near a westward curve past the creek. All others continue . At mile 5.9 from the south gate, look for a sign on your right for Trail 713 trailhead parking. Enough room for about six cars.

To find the STANLEY CANYON trailhead, follow Pine Drive another 1.4 miles past the Community Drive turnoff. The paved road will rise on a hill until it overlooks the Academy Hospital on the right. There, on the left, is a gravel turnoff that leads back 0.9 mile to the parking area for STANLEY CANYON. Follow the markers. There is limited parking, but more is available at the Academy Hospital. The Hospital lot is constantly patrolled and is considered safer for overnight parking.

Remember that the public may enter Academy gates only during day hours that vary seasonally, though you may park overnight for pack trips into the National Forest. No camping is permitted on the Academy itself. You may leave the Academy at any time.

STANLEY CANYON TRAIL, Forest Service #707, 3 miles one way to lake, another 1.7 miles to Upper Stanley TH; elevation gain 1,330 ft., rated moderate to difficult. Features climb through spectacular canyon. Not recommended for bikes, horses or children.

7,480   3.0 miles   8,840

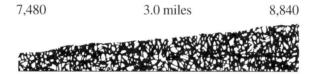

If you want to fish Stanley Reservoir (which won't be up to maximum potential until 200l), most people think of climbing Stanley Canyon Trail, but #707 is only one of five trails that go there. We rate #707 as the second toughest of them all. Fishermen should try one of the others.

Billy Jack Barrett, who runs the AF Academy's stables, told us that he would only take a horse up Stanley Canyon if he had a hundred screaming Indians after him. It's not a good trail for horses or bikes or small children, but it is very very pretty.

Beginning on Academy property, #707 quickly climbs into National Forest, following the stream that pours down Stanley Canyon. Within 1/4 mile you reach a bend in the trail where the trees open up, revealing an overlook of the surrounding country. Higher up, where the canyon grows most narrow, you have another view of the distant prairies framed in granite.

Be careful making your way up through the streambed narrows, for is still a somewhat treacherous spot, especially when icy or rainy. Then the canyon turns sharply, shutting off the view. Your trail grows more gentle after that, leading through forest and narrow meadow toward Stanley Lake. When you cross a little tributary trickling from a grassy draw to your right, notice the little singletrack there. **That's Upper Stanley Trail, by far the easiest route to Stanley** (but with a rough road leading to the trailhead. See WOODLAND PARK AREA, Deadman's Trail #313.) **For bikes, kids and horses, that's the way to get here.**

The best camping spots are downstream or upstream from the lake; camping very close beside the lake is prohibited and would be unecological anyway. Heed the new signs, if there are any.

This beautiful lake is owned by Colorado Springs. It is now open to both the public and Academy personnel, but a special problem means that it's fishing potential won't peak until the year 2001. See WOODLAND PARK AREA.

WEST MONUMENT CREEK TRAIL, Forest Service #713, estimated at 5.5 miles one way, rated difficult. Features canyon climb toward Stanley Reservoir. Okay for horses, but no good for bikes, kids or acrophobics.

| 7,800 | 5.5 miles | 9,120 |

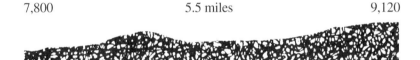

We waited a long long time for this one! We always included West Moment Creek Trail #713 in previous editions, just to keep it from being forgotten, but it was effectively closed for many years. Utility construction in the mouth of the canyon had sealed off its main access, and the opposite end was always nearly impossible to find. But thanks to work done by Colorado Springs Utilities, a new access has been designated and this rugged adventure is attracting explorers again.

But #713 is a toughy! Very primitive in high places, very steep in places, very narrow in places, sometimes across crumbling scree—no place for bicycles or children or people who can't tolerate heights.

We like to do it on trail horses rented from the Air Force Academy because they actually know the way better than anyone. (Don't confuse this with Academy Riding Stables at the Garden of the Gods.) These sturdy steeds know the hard spots and actually seem to relish the struggle. Not only that, but one of your mounts will have a real live cadet guide on its back. It's a hoot! Any member of the armed services, active or retired, can rent horses and bring guests with no such affiliations. That means almost anyone can arrange to go. Call 719-333-4607.

Once you park at the trailhead, ignore the track that parallels the road and take

West Monument Creek Trail, a horseman's favorite.

the one that leads down across the stream. You are now traveling part of the Falcon Trail, but not for long, because less than a hundred yards past the stream, #713 strikes off on its own. Last time we looked, there was no sign at this junction, but you're looking for a double track on your left that heads up to a group of power line poles.

This part of the journey is across as grassy hillside. One of the power lines is almost reachable by people on horseback, but surely I don't have to tell you not to touch it. Then the trail snakes into Gambels oak, now more of a single track, skirting the high edge of a ridge. There are plenty of #713 signs to guide you here.

They lead you to pavement in front of the new tunnel, which looks like a concrete box set into a rock hillside that has been coated black. That tunnel replaces the large pipeline that lay buried in the floor of the canyon, bringing water from Rampart and Nichols and Northfield down to the new McCullough treatment plant at the Academy. It repairs the damage done in 1965 when a freak flash flood blew away the old pipeline, plus the Victor reservoirs, plus the Palmer Lake pipeline and much more. That was a wild year.

Head downhill on pavement almost a tenth of a mile and watch for a #713 marker to the right. That takes you to gravel once more.

Soon you reach the mouth of the canyon which is sealed off with cyclone fencing and a locked gate. The canyon road beyond the gate looks so inviting that lots of folks are annoyed that you can't simply take it instead of the next high adventure, but there's a reason: Just out of your sight that road is ripped up and ruined, a jumbled mass of boulders left over from the flash flood of 1965. It was not considered worth fixing, so the trail to your right was built to skirt this problem.

To your right is another gate meant to keep away vehicles. The foot-and-hoof-path at the edge of the fence leads up around it. You are headed up a very steep gravel route that serves a utility facility higher up. You'll see it on your left. Just above that, the double track suddenly reaches a strange T-junction.

At that junction, the route to your left looks plain, but is somewhat blocked by a series of rocks meant to warn you that the left turn is the wrong one. We need another sign here, but visitors have arranged rocks in the trail to point to the right, which looks like a dead end but isn't. Hidden in the brush to your right is a single track. Just push your way in. Right away it gets plainer and much steeper as it switchbacks right up the canyon wall.

You'll see now why we warned people afraid of heights: Your singletrack is narrow, steep, with lots of sheer drop below, but the views are great. Your path struggles along the high canyon wall, through forest, across short scree slopes, but just when you think you're about to near the top of the canyon, it starts down again with more dizzy switchbacks, finally leading to the canyon floor. The last few feet are on scree, very treacherous, so beware.

If you're coming back this way, take a good look at this junction because it doesn't look like much and is easy to miss. Another sign here would be helpful. Just remember that it is located just below a mass of industrial stuff, including a large water tank and venting station that you'll soon pass on your way up canyon.

Armchair environmentalists often imagine that utility property is pristine wilderness, untouched by human impact, but utility projects are just as utilitarian as the name suggests and require lots of industrial-strength development. They are, in fact, industrial parks with some wilderness left over. Any attempt to photograph the marvelous rock formations in this beautiful canyon will often have to include a lot of power lines and such because power goes up this route to the old plant at Northfield Reservoir below Nichols and Rampart Reservoir.

The canyon road crosses and recrosses the stream. In fact the stream is on your right when you find the place where #713 leaves the road and crosses it on a kind of log and plank footbridge. You could miss it, so look for an iron sign that says "No Trespassing Violators Will Be Prosecuted" located on your right just ahead of the plank bridge. That sign means that you are not supposed to explore the road any farther, but the trail is okay.

This Boy Scouts bridge is no good for horses, so horses cross just upstream. Now you're on singletrack again, very rock at first and sometimes wet where a tributary oozes down. Then you break out of thick timber into sparse timber, including small aspen, and every step gives you a loftier view of the canyon. Higher up,

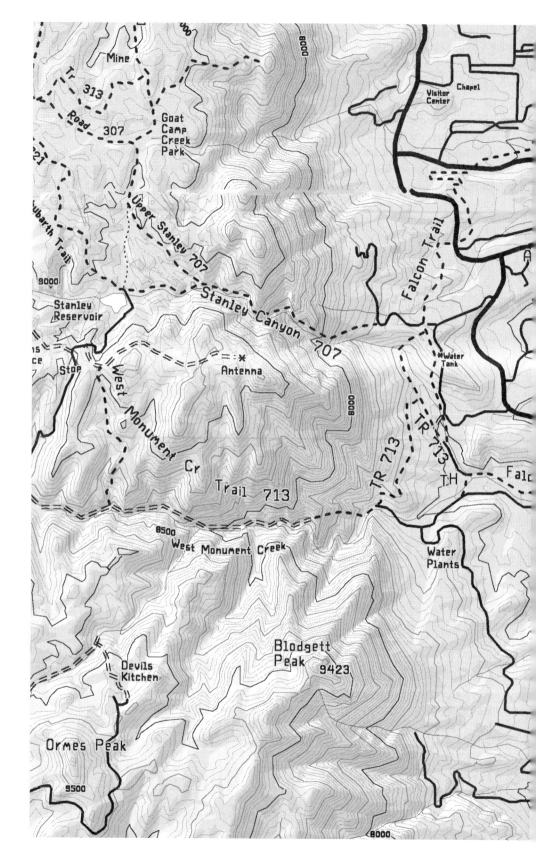

you'll travel beneath small transmission wires that go to a microwave tower. Notice the grove of very tall and straight aspen to your right, a charming rest area.

Still higher up, you angle left and go down into a grassy meadow. Your path goes right up the middle of the meadow, then takes off into sparse timber to your left. Soon you T-junction against a utility road that goes to a microwave station.

This is the end of West Monument Creek Trail, but of course, anyone going here is probably going somewhere else, such as Stanley or Rampart Reservoir. So our description will continue, but first take a moment to memorize this spot because there are confusing forks nearby. If you turned right here, you'd be on your way to a dead end at the microwave facility. Notice the sign nearby marking a buried fiber optic cable. That's your only landmark.

Now look left. The road to your left forks. Don't take the left fork going down toward the locked gate north of Northfield Reservoir, still closed to the public. The fork you want is the right one that climbs. Follow that just a short way and you'll find yourself in a wide place that looks like a small gravel pit with a low rock in the middle. From here you can proceed two ways legally.

Face north. If you head down the road to your right, you'll soon find Stanley Reservoir. You are allowed to used this portion of the utility road. There is another route less obvious to your left, an old road marked with a series of large boulders along its right side. **That is the trail we named Stanley Rim, now officially designated as Stanley Rim Trail FS#722, that leads to Zoltan's Terrace, then on to the trail we named Backdoor, now officially designated Backdoor Trail FS#723, thence to a trail we named Boatman's Trail, both of which lead down to Rampart Reservoir.** These are excellent bike routes (also open to horse and foot) that provide more ways to reach Stanley. For complete instructions see WOODLAND PARK AREA.

FALCON TRAIL, Air Force Academy Trail, 12-mile loop; elevation gain 880 ft., rated easy. Features well marked nature trail with varied terrain and wildlife, plus a restored settler's cabin.

This long and varied trail is maintained by the Boy Scouts, but is open to all hikers for day use. No firearms or fires are permitted. Hikers no longer need to register, but the Academy warns hikers to stay on the trail to avoid military training and construction that may be in progress nearby. The trail is marked with signs showing a white falcon against a blue background.

Falcon Trail begins on a hill at the Community Center's Youth Center Building. It first descends the wooded hillside, crosses Pine Drive and enters grassland. Then it climbs behind an arid hill with Blodgett Peak towering to the west and crosses the gravel road that leads to the filtration plant. Here you enter the trees once more, cross a stream on a wooden bridge, and join another stream, the one that flows from Stanley Canyon.

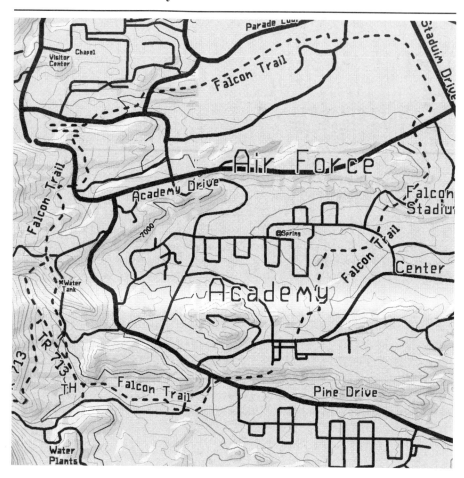

In this area Scouts have built small dams to help prevent soil erosion and to provide shelters for aquatic life. Fourteen signs point out natural and man-made features along the way, and the Academy Visitor Center provides brochures to explain the points of interest.

Your path wanders through ponderosa pine and Gambel's oak. It crosses Academy and Interior Drives and then skirts a small marsh where cattails grow. After crossing another road, the path climbs again to follow a pine-covered ridge that overlooks a reservoir, eventually leading past a pioneer cabin.

This log cabin has been so well preserved and restored that it looks almost as if the pioneer family has locked it up to go visit friends. Wooden tombstones in the yard mark the graves of family members.

The trail ends where it began at the Youth Center. Remember that rattlesnakes are among the many kinds of wildlife seen along Falcon Trail. If you visit in the fall, be aware of a limited deer hunting season and wear orange reflective clothing.

CHEYENNE CANYON/HIGH DRIVE AREA

Helen Hunt Falls in North Cheyenne Canyon

Columbine Trail
Mount Cutler Trail
Seven Bridges (North Cheyenne Cañon Trail)
Pipeline Trail
Seven Bridges Spur (N. Chey. Cutoff to Bear Creek)
Bear Creek Trail
Jones Park Trail from Capt. Jack's Trailhead
Buckhorn Cutoff Loop
Penrose Multi-Use at Capt. Jack's Trailhead
St. Mary's Falls Trail
Palmer-Redrock Loop to Section 16
Paul Intemann Memorial Nature Trail

**My, how things change! Back in 1994, the Forest Service began reorga-
nizing this system to reflect how people actually use its trails. The old system**

Deadly to approach, Spoon Falls should be called Fool-Killer Falls

had routes switching rules halfway along. You may continue to find some old names on signs, and locals still use some old names, but what we describe is now official.

The new system really works. In this area there are motorized trails woven though the system that have become very popular with other users. We generally see **more mountain bicycles** than motorcycles here, so we'll show you the whole system. **Trail courtesy has created trail tolerance, and that has opened up incredible new areas for people who used to refuse to go there!**

One caution: Always yield to motorcycles, not as a courtesy (because right-of way could be debatable) but as a safety issue. As a matter of fact, bikers, hikers and horseriders can hear a motorcycle coming, but motorcyclists can't hear much at all. Motorcycles have the "right of weight" because they can't stop as fast or get off trail as fast, so just watch out for them. These are not opposing groups of users any more: We know folks who enjoy both. Lighten up and enjoy this playground.

Located on the southwestern edge of Colorado Springs, this area offers a fascinating variety of beautiful mountain trails under the jurisdiction of city, county and federal governments. Closure of the St. Mary's Tunnel also closed eight miles of the Upper Gold Camp Road, so that section of the gentle old railroad grade is now popular with mountain bikers, horse riders and cross-country skiers, though you have to climb over the damaged tunnel to use the whole route. Reopening this historic tunnel is now the subject of debate.

Cheyenne Cañon is a famous practice area for technical rock climbers and has signs showing the best routes up the cliffs, but **climbing is prohibited without full**

equipment. Unfortunately, visitors sometimes disobey this rule with bloody or fatal results, risking their lives, a $500 fine and up to 90 days in jail. The same is true of the extremely slippery rocks beside Silver Cascade (Spoon) Falls above Helen Hunt Falls. The short path leading you there needs no description, but **violating its warning sign carries the death penalty. If they're going to rename things, we suggest they rename that beautiful slide Fool-killer Falls.**

ROAD DIRECTIONS: From I-25 going south take the Tejon Exit. Turn left at the T-junction, then right onto South Tejon. This jogs right to become Cheyenne Blvd. Go west until you find the Discovery Visitor Center at a fork where right would take you into North Cheyenne Cañon and left would take you to the magnificent and spectacular Seven Falls, which is absolutely worth the price of admission.

COLUMBINE TRAIL begins at the Discovery Center here at the canyon mouth. (Note the mountain tracks in the concrete steps leading into the Discovery Center. You'll see why the instant you step inside!) To find COLUMBINE's mid-point trailhead, drive the right fork leading into North Cheyenne Cañon and travel along the city picnic grounds that line the creek for 0.9 miles. The mid-point trailhead is on your right. MOUNT CUTLER TRAILHEAD is 0.5 miles farther and is on your left. Helen Hunt Falls (No admission fee) is another 1.2 miles distant, and there you find the short path leading up above Helen Hunt Falls to Fool-killer Falls—I mean, Silver Cascade or Spoon Falls The western end of COLUMBINE meets the road on a switchback just above Helen Hunt Falls.

Continue up the road and you come to a large intersection where you join the High Drive and the closed portion of the Gold Camp. Good parking. To find trailheads for SEVEN BRIDGES (NORTH CHEYENNE CAÑON) and ST. MARY'S FALLS, park here and start up the closed Gold Camp on bike or foot or horseback. SEVEN BRIDGES trailhead is on your right 0.6 miles from this intersection, where the first creek crosses. ST. MARY'S trailhead is 1.2 miles from the intersection.

To find the trailheads for JONES PARK (formerly Buckhorn), PENROSE MULTI-USE (upper trailhead), BEAR CREEK and PALMER-REDROCK LOOP, start at that intersection above Helen Hunt Falls and take the one-way High Drive (closed in winter). One mile up you top the rise and find a parking lot on your right across from a rock wall marked "High Drive Altitude 7867 C.W.A. 34." That's Captain Jack's trailhead for JONES PARK (left) and the upper trailhead for PENROSE 'MULTI-USE' MOTORIZED TRAIL (right). Road directions to the lower trailhead are later in this chapter.

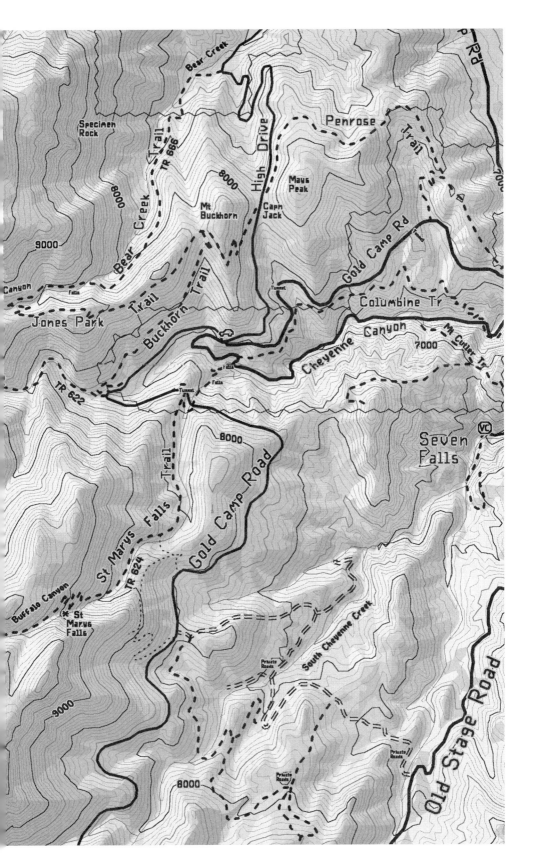

Continue down the High Drive another 1.4 miles (2.4 miles from the start of the High Drive) to find **BEAR CREEK'S** trailhead on the left at a metal gate where the next stream appears. Only roadside parking is available, but the old caretakers parking lot at the base of the High Drive has space for another 10 cars and is often used when the High Drive is closed.

The upper trailhead for **PALMER-REDROCK** is 2.7 miles from the High Drive start, roadside parking only. To find the lower trailhead, continue downhill on the paved portion known as Bear Creek Road and turn left at its intersection with the Lower Gold Camp Road. Proceed 0.2 miles and watch for it on your left. It's marked Section 16 Trailhead.

INTEMANN TRAILHEAD is located on the lower **PALMER-REDROCK TRAIL** itself, 0.5 miles up from the Section I6 trailhead. INTEMANN has another trailhead on Crystal Park Road in Manitou. Find the entrance to Crystal Park Road next to the Super 8 Motel and across from the Manitou Springs Swimming Pool. Drive up I.5 miles and park beyond the Kangaroo Campground. The trail can also be accessed from several points in Manitou Springs.

COLUMBINE TRAIL, City of Colorado Springs trail, 3 miles one way, elevation gain 1,080 ft.; rated tough on switchbacks, then easy. Features an overlook of canyon and falls.

6,200 ft   3.0 miles   7,280

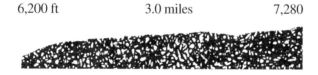

The upper part of this trail is downright beautiful, but even neighbors sometimes ignore it, thinking that it only follows a hillside above a roadway. Wrong. You rarely see the roadway once you start climbing.

From the Discovery Center, Columbine follows the creek upstream, crosses the road, then switchbacks up a scree slope for three quarters of a mile. This is a good winter adventure because sunny southern exposure helps keep it clear of snow. Higher up find Columbine Spring flowing except in the driest times.

The final mile is the most beautiful, with views of Silver Cascade and Helen Hunt Falls and majestic rocks. The trail ends on the road just above Helen Hunt Falls. Mountain bikes are allowed on this trail, but it is so narrow, steep and its switchbacks are so sharp that it should only be attempted by expert bikers. Hikers need to be especially careful along the scree section, where it is difficult to get off trail when bikes come along. Use good trail etiquette.

Like some other well-built trails in the area, this was constructed as part of a Civil Works Administration project in 1934, and the work was so difficult that a blacksmith labored under the evergreens, resharpening 100 picks a day.

The columbine is the Colorado State Flower and grows in the moist shade of evergreens near Columbine Spring. Look for them blooming in late June and early July. It is illegal to disturb them. And Helen Hunt Falls was named after Helen Hunt Jackson, a local poet, novelist (Ramona) and defender of American Indians (A Century of Dishonor). She is buried in Evergreen Cemetery downtown, not in the gravesite meant for her above Seven Falls.

MOUNT CUTLER TRAIL, City of Colorado Springs trail, 0.8 mile one way, plus 0.2 mile for Muscoco spur; elevation gain 600 ft., rated moderate. Features overlooks of Colorado Springs and Seven Falls.

This is one of the few trails that we recommend for a night hike because it is short and wide and has no really confusing points—and because it offers a view of Colorado Springs that looks like a carpet of jewels. In the summer, Seven Falls is illuminated with colored lights as well, so this can be a fine adventure, if you're careful and take good flashlights. This is not recommended for children because the overlooks have steep drop-offs.

Near the top, the trail forks. The right fork climbs Mount Muscoco for a view of the seven distinct cascades in South Cheyenne Cañon. **A private tourist attraction, Seven Falls is more grand than any other waterfall in Colorado.**

The left fork wraps around Mount Cutler itself, passes a white quartz outcrop-

First bridge on the Seven Bridges Trail. The others aren't much better.

ping and dead-ends at no particular spot on top on top. People just wander around and gawk. The Broadmoor lies 900 feet below.

SEVEN BRIDGES (former NORTH CHEYENNE CAÑON TRAIL), Forest Service #622, now 1.5 miles one way; elevation gain 1,520 ft., rated moderate to difficult. Features streamside walk over numerous bridges, 25-foot cascade.

7,600   2.0 miles   8,800

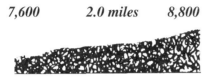

This is the trail that keeps changing names more than any other we know. It used to be called Lovely Corners after John Lovely, a Frenchman who lived in a tent in this canyon and who homesteaded there in 1902. Later it was called Six Bridges, then Seven Bridges, then North Cheyenne, but current plans are to remove that sign and go back to Seven Bridges because the upper motorized section has been designated as Pipeline Trail #668.

By any name it's still the same Lovely trail with seven log crossings up North Cheyenne Cañon. We cringe to mention that there are no actual bridges because we don't want it renamed again. These crossings give you close views of the creek as it pours and splashes over polished stones. Near what we call the end of this trail, the stream slides down a steep granite face for 25 feet or more, forming Undine Falls. As you climb the trail overlooking the cascade, however, beware of a dangerous spot where a slab lubricated with gravel slants toward a drop-off.

There are campsites farther up near a tributary that joins from the north. Your trail leaves the creek here and skirts the base of Kineo Mountain, heading up that tributary toward a trail now called Seven Bridges Spur (old North Cheyenne Cutoff) that goes to Jones Park. Seven Bridges Spur is non-motorized.

Seven Bridges, however, crosses that tributary and continues up the headwaters of North Cheyenne Creek a short and rugged distance to where the Pipeline motorized trail joins from the right.

The area ahead has always been motorized, so this is now the official end of Seven Bridges. The motorized section up North Cheyenne has been added to Pipeline Trail, leading up to Frosty Park. (See Gold Camp Road Area)

Hikers and horseriders can make a long circuit by going up Seven Bridges to the Seven Bridges Spur and take that to Bear Creek and down again: Bikers do it the other way around, counter clockwise, because the High Drive is one-way. See Seven Bridges Spur.

PIPELINE TRAIL, Forest Service Motorized #668, now 3 miles one way, elevation gain 1,220 feet, rated moderate for motorcycles, features link from Jones Park Trail to Frosty Park on Almagre Road.

9,020 Jones Park   About 3.0 miles   Frosty Park 10,240

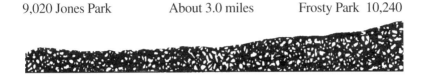

Cartographer Robert Houdek tells us that he never intended to name this trail Pipeline. His Ormes Pikes Peak Atlas only meant to point out that a straight section of one old trail is where a pipeline is buried, but that's now the name of a longer old route that zig-zags from Jones Park Trail clear up to Frosty Park on the Almagre Road.   See Gold Camp Road Area for road directions there.

As it climbs what used to be the upper section of North Cheyenne, this trail visits Nelsons Camp. Nelson was a prospector and his old cabin, built in the late 1800s, remained intact with bunk beds and metal stove until vandals destroyed it in the early 1970s. This section is very rocky and rugged, no good for bikes.

SEVEN BRIDGES SPUR (former NORTH CHEYENNE CUTOFF), Forest Service #622A, 0.5 mile, elevation gain 200 ft.; rated easy. Features saddle link between North Cheyenne and Bear Creek Trails.

We're describing this clockwise because it's a little easier to find that way. It follows a tributary that joins North Cheyenne Creek from the north, climbing past the north slope of Kineo Mountain. Keep to the Kineo side of the brook.

Soon you find a grassy area with scattered evergreens. Look for a distinct path that cuts away to the right, leading away from the tributary and up into the trees. Now you are crossing the saddle between Kineo and the high ground to the west, dropping down to Bear Creek. This is Jones Park, a high grassy area graced by evergreens, aspen and wildflowers. Your trail ends at Bear Creek, where the trail has been renamed Jones Park Trail. Bikers do this circuit counter-clockwise from Bear Creek Trail because High Drive is one-way.

BEAR CREEK TRAIL, Forest Service #666, 2 miles one way from High Drive, but add one mile for winter trailhead below High Drive; elevation gain 1,420 ft., rated moderate to difficult. Features historic climb through a scenic canyon.

Bear Creek's Josephine Falls

In 1873 the U.S. Army Signal Corps built the highest signal station in the world atop Pikes Peak, and its trail led through Bear Creek Canyon, winding 17 miles up through Jones Park and the Seven Lakes Area on the forbidden South Slope. The popular Lake House Hotel at Lake Moraine burned down long ago. Bear Creek Trail is all that remains of this historic route.

As you leave the summer trailhead on the High Drive (winter users must hike up to this point from where the road is closed below). Follow the creek bottom for a short way, then begin climbing a steady path up the side of a ridge. Soon the creek is nothing but a sound below. Raspberries, dog roses and juniper grow in the loose rock beside the trail.

7,100   2.0 miles   8,520

Bear Creek Trail's Contour

Another trail on the opposite slope provides a side trip to the area just below Josephine Falls, where it is necessary to cross over to the main trail to continue on.

Above you and to the right stands Specimen Rock, a natural breeding area for peregrine falcons. This high area is closed until July 15 each year to protect nesting, so please stay on trail.

All this climbing leads you to a high overlook where bluffs tower overhead and the falls roar below you—not really within sight, unfortunately. But from this high ledge you can see a great deal more, all the way to the Black Forest.

Now the canyon narrows and you return to streamside. You pass the remains of an old toll road bridge built in 1891 to carry wagons and workers on their way to build reservoirs in the Seven Lakes area. Higher up the old Buckhorn Motorized Trail, now called **Jones Park Trail,** crosses the creek. This junction is now the end of **Bear Creek Trail.**

JONES PARK, Forest Service Motorized #667, 6 miles one way rated moderate for motorcycles, elevation gain 1,293 ft., features both ridgetop and streamside adventure, visiting aspen valley, excellent for mountain bicyclists, hikers and horse riders.

7,867	About 6.0 miles	9,160

Pieced together with the addition of the old Buckhorn and upper Bear Creek Trails, this route is a marvelous adventure for anyone, motorized or not. It starts from Captain Jack's Trailhead, but since many locals have always called *both* trails that start from here "Captain Jack's Trail," that has led to confusion. Where would Search and Rescue look for you, if you left word that you were going to be traveling "Captain Jack's?" They wouldn't know which way to go. Remember, this book is their field reference, so it is always best to use the official names.

But here's the real story about Captain Jack:

Mrs. Ellen Jack was a prospector who found and sold a valuable mine, then moved to early-day Colorado Springs and built some tourist cabins on this spot. She always wore a six-gun and a pick-ax in her belt and claimed to bear a scar from a poisoned tomahawk dating from the last Gunnison Indian uprising. The real Captain Jack was her husband, who was just a memory when Ellen

Louds Cabin just off the Jones Park Trail

Blasting down Buckhorn Cutoff

arrived, *yet people called her Captain Jack!*

Ellen Jack wrote a book about her experiences on the frontier, but apparently she was quite a spinner of tall tales, for according to Debbi Mikash of the Penrose Public Library's Local History Dept., her book is listed as fiction! Nothing remains of her place but the parking lot itself, so we call this Captain Jack's Trailhead.

Starting there, you switchback up and around the summit of Mount Buckhorn. At the saddle on the other side, the **Buckhorn Cutoff** joins from your left: That leads down to the **Seven Bridges** trailhead on the Gold Camp, but since that whole area is non-motorized, motorcycles should avoid the cutoff. We describe that route in this chapter as the **Buckhorn Cutoff Loop.**

Jones Park Trail continues along a ridge with great views. At mile 2.1 it dives down to cross Bear Creek (the end of **Bear Creek Trail**), then continues up the creek, sometimes right in the water, to Jones Park. Your trail dead-ends at the Utility Dept. gate that guards Moraine Lake and six more. At the time of this writing, the South Slope watershed is forbidden to ordinary citizens, but you can turn south and take **Forester Trail #701** clear to Frosty Park. See GOLD CAMP AREA because we suggest using **Forester** as a reverse adventure downhill clear to the lower Gold Camp via the Penrose "Multi-Use" Motorized Trail #665. For mountain bikers, this is a long and thrilling downhill that will leave you grinning!

But while we're in this area, check out this next loop!

BUCKHORN CUTOFF LOOP, segment measures 0.4 miles, but loop measures 3.9 miles. Rated moderate, with some parts easy. Part singletrack, part road, but scenic all the way.

7,867   3.9 miles   7,867

Another guide has an illegal version of this loop because it involves going the wrong way on the one-way High Drive. Since Mount Buckhorn's cutoff has no official name, we're calling it the **Buckhorn Cutoff.** The entire loop is open to motorcycles and ATVs, but it's far more popular with mountain bikers.

Park at Captain Jack's Trailhead and start up Mount Buckhorn on **Jones Park Trail.** From the rocks atop the mountain, you can easily see the **Buckhorn Cutoff** trail across the ravine to the west. To reach it, just continue down the backside of the mountain and you'll find it at the first saddle at mile 0.9.

This trail is much smoother than **Jones Park** itself, but beware of going too fast because there are some tight spots and sharp turns where you could take a digger. At O.4 you'll cross an eroded scree slope and shortly beyond lies a nice view of the Gold Camp and Cheyenne Creek area. Sharp switchbacks follow, taking you down through evergreen forest. At mile 1.3, you T-junction against North Cheyenne Trail, which is closed to motorized vehicles going uphill at this junction. Turn left and within a tenth of a mile you'll turn left again onto the Gold Camp Road. From there it's an easy 0.6 miles to the High Drive intersection. Hang a left and go one mile up the High Drive to Captain Jack's parking lot.

PENROSE MULTI-USE TRAIL AT CAPTAIN JACK'S, segment measures 1.7 miles, but 5.4 miles as a loop with Lower Gold Camp and High Drive, rated very difficult. Gonzo downhill for skilled riders.

7,867   1.7 miles   7,200

You have to be quad monster to pedal up this trail, but people do it, sharing trail with motorcycles and a very very few hikers. Yet by far the most popular way to do this one is to bike it downhill from Capt. Jack's Trailhead, usually as part of a 5.3-mile loop using scenic mountain roadway. Because we like to do our uphills first and because there is more parking down below, we prefer to park at the large lower trailhead on the Gold Camp Road.

Warning: This is a very technical trail, requiring a lot of skill and is dangerous for beginners. Also, the trail is so steep and slippery that some mountain biking shoes don't have enough tread to hold you. Don't buy those ballet slippers. We recommend tread!

ROAD DIRECTIONS: To find Penrose Multi-Use Trail's Lower Trailhead, start at the High Drive intersection on Gold Camp above Helen Hunt, but instead of climbing High Drive, take the other fork down. This is the Lower Gold Camp, which is two-way and very narrow, so watch for oncoming traffic. You'll pass through two tunnels and at mile 1.7, just beyond the second tunnel, you'll find the large parking area for the Multi-Use Trail to Captain Jack's. Park there to do our loop.

Okay, instead of going uphill on Penrose, we're going to leave our car here and double back on the Gold Camp, then ride up High Drive to Capt. Jack's and gonzo down Penrose Multi-Use to the car.

Leaving the Captain Jack's parking lot, your trail starts out gently enough as it contours around Mays Peak, yet even here the path is rutted into a V shape which makes it easier to hike than it is to ride. Lots of ponderosa and fir here.

After a half mile the drop begins in earnest, yet the track has some steep uphills, too. At mile one you make a sharp turn where moisture from Mays Peak starts trickling to form Sesame Creek. We couldn't find the old side trail that once led down Sesame to Bear Creek. Many such routes have faded away.

From here on the route becomes worse and worse with giant ruts and deep sand in addition to the usual roots and rocks. The biggest rut is about mile 1.2, a curving narrow channel as deep as a grave! Remember to stop and listen for up-coming traffic before entering this chute. You wouldn't want to meet anyone in there.

After surviving that, ahead lies a steep uphill fitted with rubber water bars that fold down when wheels pass over. Push to the top and go out on a tiny side trail to your left for a view of city and mountains. There are several such overlooks.

Mountain bikers are often so attention-glued to the trail itself that they miss a number of such views. Stop and enjoy. You may never notice a side route that takes off from a high point (close to mile two) and simply takes another somewhat parallel route down to the Gold Camp. That's original route of the old Penrose Trail, but is now only a minor route that plunges down a ridge to the Gold Camp where it has no parking or actual trailhead. Our main trail, the Multi-Use ahead is an improvement, leading to good parking.

Soon Mount Muscoco pops into view as the trail angles down steeply. Making a switchback, our trail crosses, then recrosses a ravine before climbing slightly to the parking lot.

ST. MARY'S FALLS TRAIL, Forest Service #624, 1.6 miles one-way to the falls, plus 1.2-mile road walk; elevation gain 1,700 ft., rated moderately difficult. Features large cascade and view of Broadmoor.

When the light is right and you know where to look, you can see St. Mary's shining from the city.

St. Mary's Falls is a water slide that churns about 40 feet down the side of Stove Mountain. The trail that leads there from the Gold Camp climbs 1,200 feet in 1.6 miles, but starts out fairly gently, so the last section to the falls is quite steep. (Our graph includes the Gold Camp walk of 1.2 miles).

This trail is changing at both ends. The closure of the tunnel adds 1.2 miles to your journey, but the top part is so confusing and in such bad shape that for now the Forest Service is considering the falls to be destination of St. Mary's Falls Trail. The route to Frosty Park is still technically open for those who wish to explore, but plans call for rerouting that section to use the higher Nelson Trail, which also leads to Frosty Park. Volunteer work is needed.

Starting at the tunnel, St. Mary's Trail follows Buffalo Creek upstream through pines and blue spruce. Higher up there are some small campsites. Eventually the trail leaves the creek and switchbacks up the hillside. A metal sign says "Base of Falls 500 feet," pointing left and "Top of Falls 0.2 mile," pointing right.

Both the base and top of the falls share an overlook of the pine and blue spruce drainage that slants toward the Broadmoor. Be especially careful of falling rock, for anything dislodged from the top would hit just about where people stand at the bottom. If you learn where to look, you can actually see the falls from downtown.

For those who wish to explore higher, the traditional route continues up Buffalo Creek, then switchbacks up to a road called FS-381 and follows the road

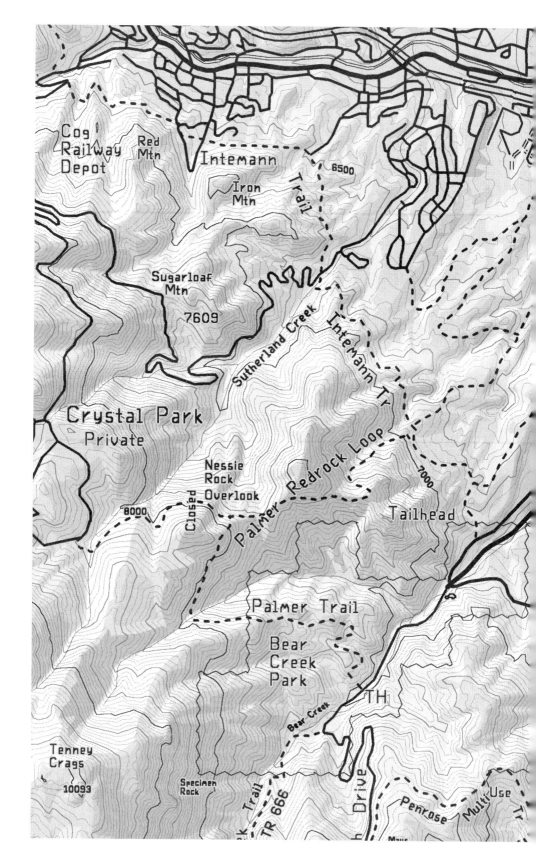

before branching away toward Frosty Park, but **this is a very confusing route.** For road directions to Frosty Park (FS-379), see GOLD CAMP ROAD AREA.

PALMER-REDROCK LOOP (SECTION 16), El Paso County Park Dept., 4.7 miles one way (from winter trailhead, add 0.7 mile); elevation gain 800 feet, loss 1,160 feet; rated moderate. Features forest route through area of geologic interest.

7,000 ft.   4.7 miles   6,640 ft.

Though the paperwork is not absolutely ironclad yet, we seem to have won our fight to keep Section 16 County Park from being traded away to developers for construction of luxury homes. I was proud to help out as spokesman.

Because the lower part of this trail is steep, many folks begin at the higher trailhead and travel the lower part downhill. The trail is much more difficult if done the other way around. Mountain bikers find it especially challenging.

Starting at the Palmer trailhead on the High Drive, you enter an aspen grove and soon find a place where the main trail doubles back to the right and begins climbing. If you continue in the meadow instead of climbing, you will find a chimney from an old Boy Scout Camp and a dead-end below Sentinel Rock.

Your path gains altitude, snaking through evergreens, then curves west through a mossy forest, keeping high on the mountainside to maintain altitude. You cross an intermittent brook called Hunters Run that drips off a large rock near the trail. Climb very gently from here and find an intersection on a small saddle ridge. The left fork is more of Palmer Trail and the right is Redrock. Going left soon takes you to private property trespassing, but we have good news.

Palmer Trail was one of the old General's favorite rides and leads to Crystal Park, now a private 2000-acre preserve and home owner's association. This gated community is very strict about trespassing. By the time you find any sign you are already in trouble, so here's a great way to know when to stop and enjoy the views.

We gained permission from a neighboring Crystal Park estate for you to stop and enjoy the views from what we call Nessie Rock. This trailside overlook features a small granite column that looks like the famous picture of the head of the Loch Ness Monster framed between larger rocks. Nessie Rock is well worth the side-trip and offers great views of Crystal Park's Sutherland Canyon. This makes a satisfying and obvious stopping point. For more information about Crystal Park, call Zoltan your realtor at Heritage Realtors.

Return to the intersection and take Redrock to complete the loop. Redrock heads east along a ridge saddle, but soon begins to angle downward and then dives along an old four-wheel track to end on the Lower Gold Camp Road at Section 16. On the way, you pass the trailhead for Intemann. Turn right on the Gold Camp, then right again and you're headed back up to Palmer trailhead. But since the High Drive is one-way, mountain bikers should walk their bikes up that short section.

INTEMANN TRAIL (mostly completed), eventually over five miles one way, elevation gain-loss nil, rated fairly easy. Features scenic link between Section l6 of the Palmer Redrock Loop and Pikes Peak Barr Trail in Manitou Springs.

Paul Intemann dreamed of linking several social paths and unused rights of way following the contours of Red Mountain and Iron Mountain, creating a wild trail near urban centers. Tragically, this Manitou Springs city planner died in l986, yet now hundreds of volunteers have worked to fulfill his dream. And thus the formal name is Paul Intemann Memorial Nature Trail.

Now mostly complete, this path will connect Section l6 of the Palmer-Redrock Loop and (virtually) the Pikes Peak Barr Trailhead in Manitou Springs, a distance of over five miles. Low altitude (about 6,700 ft.) and sunny exposures make this a pleasant outing on any but the hottest days. Intemann receives considerable winter use. Except for occasional short switchback sections, the trail rolls along mountain contours. It repeatedly ducks into forest, then returns to hillside brush, passing red sandstone formations like those in the Garden of the Gods. There are many views of the city, making it a pretty night hike.

Though the trail is not steep, there are narrow portions, so its builders recommend Intemann for more experienced mountain bikers and horse riders. The unusually flat area downhill in Red Rock Canyon is an old landfill, now reclaimed. Locals have their own paths leading up to this trail, so be sure to stay on the main trail, because those other paths quickly take you into trespass situations. Below Crystal Park, the trail switchbacks down steeply to cross Crystal Park Road, then continues to an overlook.

At the time of this publication, the Iron Spring trailhead portion has made great progress and the two ends of the trail are within sight of each other! Yet the remaining half mile in the middle is the toughest and a legal easement has yet to be worked out, so it may take several years to finally complete Paul Intemann's dream.

GOLD CAMP ROAD AREA

Bluffs above Cathedral Park (private) as seen from the Gold Camp Road

Emerald Valley Trail
Gray Back Peak Trail
St. Peter's Dome
Penrose-Rosemont Trail
Almagre #379 to Stratton Reservoir
Seven Steps
Forester Trail Downhill to Jones Park

Teddy Roosevelt called the Gold Camp Road the route that bankrupt the English language, simply too beautiful for words. This was the route of a narrow-gauge railroad hauling gold ore down from Cripple Creek to the smelter in Colorado Springs. You can still see the smelter smokestack from Highway 24 near 21st Street. Eroded Gold Hill is made of its tailings and Van Briggle Art Pottery nearby was the railroad round house. As you drive the Gold Camp, sometimes you'll see railroad timbers showing in the roadway where tall trestles were filled with rocks and dirt to make the road.

Now the subject of controversy, the St. Mary's Tunnel cave-in closing eight miles of the Gold Camp above Helen Hunt Falls. The closed section is enjoyed by mountain bikers, equestrians and cross-country skiers, but this also means that you must park farther from nearby trailheads and people must drive the more dangerous Old Stage Road to access the Gold Camp just below St. Peter's Dome. Some want to repair this historic old railroad tunnel: Others like it closed.

The Old Stage Road is much steeper than the Gold Camp because horses could climb a steeper grade than slick-wheeled locomotives. Both roads must be driven with extreme caution because they are very narrow, have many blind turns and are traveled by folks who are naturally distracted by scenery.

ROAD DIRECTIONS: From Denver or Colorado Springs take I-25 to the Circle-Lake Avenue Exit #138 in Colorado Springs and go west to the front of the Broadmoor Hotel. Turn left and follow the street that skirts the hotel and its golf coarse. At the intersection with Penrose (where you would turn left to go to the Cheyenne Mountain Zoo), simply go straight across the intersection to enter the Old Stage Road. The pavement ends at the National Forest boundary. START ODOMETER HERE. (CAUTION:The very next turn at the base of a bluff is one of the most dangerous on this steep and narrow road. Go slow.) To find Emerald Valley and Gray Back Peak Trail, go 5.4 miles from the FS boundary and turn left at the sign for Emerald Valley.

The trailhead for GRAY BACK is on your left within a quarter mile, where the road tops a rise. Ignore the old 4-wheel road that angles downhill from this tiny parking area. GRAY BACK is the faint trail that climbs. No sign.

To find EMERALD VALLEY Trail, continue down this road. The Emerald Valley Ranch gate is about l.5 miles. Do not block or enter the gate, but go straight ahead. From here on the primitive and rocky roadway itself is our trail and gets worse and worse (and worse!), so park beside the road.

To find more trails, continue up the Old Stage to the Gold Camp, which is closed to your right. Go left and a mile farther find the popular overlook ST. PETER'S DOME and its short trail. RESET YOUR ODOMETER.

Continue for another 2.6 miles and ignore FS-381 at the Wye Campground; this four-wheel drive route leads to the future (we've been waiting for years) midpoint of St. Mary's Falls Trail, but you will probably get as confused as we do up there at this time. At mile 3.5 from St. Peter's Dome, you'll find a parking lot on the right for PENROSE-ROSEMONT RESERVOIR FISHING TRAIL.

To find FS-379 ALMAGRE TO STRATTON RESERVOIR, SEVEN STEPS and FORESTER, (plus the future—we've been waiting for years—terminus of St. Mary's Falls), go another 1.3 miles (4.8 miles from the Dome) to find FS-379 on your right, at the stream that feeds Penrose-Rosemont.

Emerald Valley and Gray Back Peak

Real emeralds are green and beautiful, rare and valuable, and strangely fragile, being brittle and easy to break. All that is also true of Emerald Valley off the Old Stage Road. It's a very special place—so special that Spencer Penrose, who built the Broadmoor Hotel, also built a wonderful guest ranch in Emerald Valley. (And he could certainly have his pick of the best real estate anywhere in the region.)

The guest ranch is still in operation under a long lease from the National Forest and caters to groups up to about 44 persons, not to individuals. Please respect the privacy of the guests and the couple running the ranch. **Do not call them with trail questions and do not just drive in!** The trails we describe here are in the National Forest outside of the ranch. Don't block the roadway.

But one story first: Like the Wizard of Oz in the Emerald City, Spec Penrose had a secret microphone and hidden controls so he could surprise his guests. Hunting trophies that lined the walls of the party room were wired with sound so he could roast his guests by having the animals seem to talk to them. When the party got in high spirits, a stuffed deer would suddenly start turning its head, eyes lighting up, mouth moving, as it poked fun at friends.

CAUTION: A great deal of trespassing has been going on in this area for years. The routes we show you are entirely legal, but your friends and other publications may suggest another route that is illegal. There are two more traditional trailheads as you first drive into the valley, but both trespass on private land near Cather Springs. We have talked to the owners, who have

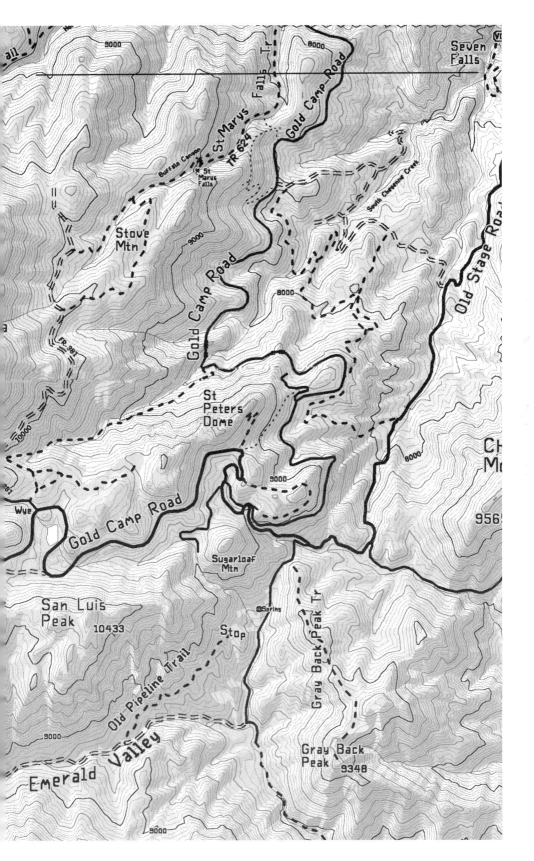

surveyed their property, and it is definitely NOT all right for you to continue to use these old entrances. Just because a trail appears on a map does not mean you may go there. It is not a map-maker's responsibility to show permissions and easements. That's what good guidebooks are for.

EMERALD VALLEY FS#371, 5.7 miles up and back, rated easy for hiking and moderate for mountain biking, this route also open to horses, motorcycles and high-ground-clearance vehicles.

8,160   2.85 miles   9,120

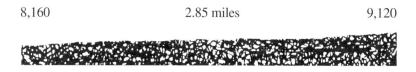

We park just beyond the ranch gate in order to enjoy the full length of this trail by mountain bike—and also to save our vehicle from the rocks ahead. In fact, a passing motorist was on his way up to retrieve the drive train that he had ripped out on his previous visit! You'll see some expensive scrape marks on rocks ahead. We're starting our odometer here.

This route is a fairly easy hike but steep enough and loose enough to make an intermediate bike trail. The forest is mixed conifer with more and more aspen as you climb. The tumbling stream beside the trail is often in sight and always within earshot, adding special charm. There are a number of pull-offs where people have camped and built large fire rings.

Which brings up a point. This trail is famous for its litter because so many people car camp up here, so do your part by taking home more than your own.

Indeed, there was talk of closing this area to vehicles because of such abuse and because of the delicate flora. This area is graced by unusual plants, including the orchid called the Yellow Lady Slipper. Never pick flowers and tread lightly when off trail.

At 0.8 some large rocks have tumbled into the roadway, and just beyond mile one there is an elaborate chimney and stone foundation of the old boy's ranch that burned down. At mile 1.3 you'll see a cairn and little sidetrail to the right with the remains of wooden flooring, more of the old boy's ranch. The overgrown track that goes past that flooring merely returns to your main track, but there at the cairn is a more faint track that angles back sharply along our main track.

Take note: That path is the pipeline trail that leads back to the illegal trailheads near Cather Springs. You can hike it legally for more than a mile from here, and it's a very pretty trail, but too rocky for bikes. It is very overgrown from this end, but only a few yards up you'll find the first of many two-foot concrete squares that support the pipeline buried beneath it. **Trouble is, at present there is no way to tell you where to turn back because the private property at**

the other end is not yet fenced, but Colorado law does not require that you cross a fence or violate a sign to be fined for trespassing, so if you explore that, be careful and don't go far.

From here on, our main track is also the route of the pipeline from Penrose-Rosemont Reservoir and many times you'll see it surface in the roadway! You'll also find water in the road. Indeed, **our path is absolutely entwined with the creek and its tributaries.** At almost 1.6, about half the creek runs down the road. We waded it barefoot and ate lunch while our feet dried. A downy woodpecker telegraphed from a huge fir all during lunch, and we saw scat from a bobcat.

At 1.79 there is another big ford just below a pair of beaver ponds, then another at mile two, then another just beyond. And that's the way it goes, ford after ford, aspen glade after aspen glade, until you reach what we call the end of our trail at mile 2.85. At that point, you'll see two blue ceramic pipes about ten inches in diameter right in the roadway, protecting pipeline valves. Ahead, the pipeline "trail" rockets uphill as a single track. Tracks on either side are only scars from where motorcycles and four-wheelers have tried to scramble up steep slopes.

From here up the pipeline is much, much steeper and rocky, no good for bikes. It is not a recommended route, being unmarked and very rough.

So we recommend that you turn back from mile 2.85 and return the way you came. Bikers can power-splash through some of the upper fords and enjoy the whoopy-bumps. It's a great downhill.

GRAY BACK PEAK TRAIL, 3.5 miles round-trip, rated moderate. Forest ridge trail leading to views of plains and foothills.

8,720   3.5 miles   9,348

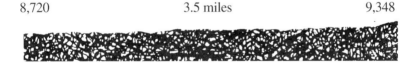

This little-used path leads to a spectacular summit with views of plains and foothills. It is open to mountain bicycles, but is blocked by so many fallen timbers that we found our bikes more trouble than they were worth!

At first the trail looks like a water crease full of pine cones. It climbs steeply below the brow of a ridge with Emerald Valley laid out below. You cross a short scree slope and continue up to a minor peak with many weathered snags and lots of knickenick.

What looks like a fairly flat route across a saddle turns out to be a series of ups and downs, some of them pretty steep. There are a number of places where you can leave the trail and find lookouts. The rocky mountain across the valley is Mount Vigil and the tree-covered mountain to its right is Sugarloaf. Notice the old mine at the base of Mount Vigil.

Before you've gone a mile the trail switches sides on the saddle ridge, giving you glimpses of the prairies. This side of the mountain is much wetter and has orchids, mushrooms and mosses. There are only a few aspens amid this old evergreen forest. Two grouse perched on a limb to watch us pass.

Higher up the path begins to switchback up through mossy forest. Practically every stone you pass here is a kind of slushy gray quartzite. When you reach the summit, the rock turns to granite and gneiss with a number of view points, the first of which offers almost a 180-degree view of the plains with Fort Carson, Hwy 115, etc. The highest views are of Blue Mountain and Emerald Valley, etc. When we visited in early August there was a lady bug convention on this summit. Low bushes and rock crevices were absolutely red with millions of lady bugs.

According to the folks at the ranch, rattlesnakes have twice been seen in the high rocks of Gray Back Peak.

ST. PETER'S DOME TRAIL, Forest Service #621, 0.7 miles one way; elevation gain 100 ft., rated easy. Features short and pleasant hike from scenic overlook of Colorado Springs and Great Plains.

Black and white can't do justice to fall glory at Penrose-Rosemont

Future improvements may restore this trail to its picture postcard glory, but the iron stairway leading to the top section was destroyed by vandals a generation ago, so visitors have no safe way to reach the lookout that made this trail famous.

The path begins at the St. Peter s Dome overlook on the Gold Camp Road and gently wraps around the wooded hillside before reaching the short cliff where the stairway once stood. Oddly enough there are no spectacular views of the city from this pretty trail because the lookout view featured in picture books is only visible from atop the rocks above.

PENROSE-ROSEMONT RESERVOIR TRAIL, Colorado Springs Dept. of Public Utilities, Colorado Division of Wildlife and Pike National Forest, less than one half mile one way, elevation loss 100 ft., rated easy. Features walk-in fishing access to mountain lake, where no other type of recreation is permitted, not even hiking or picnicking.

Almost every tourist who has ever driven the Gold Camp Road has taken snapshots of Penrose-Rosemont Reservoir. This mountain lake was once the private fishing hole for Broadmoor Hotel guests: Celebrities such as Boxing Champ Jack Dempsey were photographed fishing there.

After becoming part of the Colorado Springs water system, it was closed for many years, then experienced a dam leak after the City opened it to fishing once more. Yet now the dam is fixed, the lake has refilled and is regularly stocked for public fishing. A friend of ours caught his limit in only twenty minutes!

Opening this lake was a cooperative effort. The city provided legal work, the Pike National Forest built the parking lot and fishermans trail, and the Colorado Division of Wildlife provided concrete vault restrooms, litter barrels and stocker trout. Public cooperation is also necessary to protect this vital resource.

All drinking water reservoirs have special rules, but this one needs extra protection because it is so small, only 83 acres. Many forms of recreation are outlawed to keep human impact down. No dogs are allowed, no horses, no mountain bikes, no skiing, no camping, no open fires, no wading, swimming or water-body contact of any kind; no boating, no floatation devices of any kind, no firearms or fireworks, no alcohol, no ice fishing and no picnicking. And if you can think of anything else you'd like to do, that's probably not allowed either.

All kidding aside, by law, fishing is the only recreation allowed at this picturesque lake. That's why the trailhead sign says, "Trail for Use of Fishermen Only." And there is a very good reason for it!

True story: As chairman of a committee organized by local attractions to open these lakes, I was naturally anxious to explore here because Penrose-Rosemont was the first such forbidden lake ever opened in the system. So Dolores and I hurried to see the new fishing trail and restrooms that had just been completed. Not wanting to jump the gun on the public, of course, we took no fishing gear along.

Suddenly the caretaker roared up and announced that we were under arrest! When we protested that we had no fishing gear, he said *we were under arrest for not fishing!*

We hadn't seen the final version of the lease, wherein it was recognized that fishermen would never be able to use the tiny parking lot, if tourists were allowed to park there to walk around the lake. You see, all the improvements are paid for by fishing license fees. When we showed him our fishing licenses, he let us go, but we had to promise never to come back without a rod. **I never thought I'd get busted for *not* fishing! Moral of story: At least pretend to fish.**

For example, no picnic facilities are provided, and picnicking is specifically forbidden. The only legal way to picnic here would be go fishing. Every member of your party over the age of l6 must have a valid Colorado fishing license and must carry a fishing rod.

The trail leading down to the lake is short and easy, and the trail along the shore is almost flat. It is an exceptionally beautiful stroll, but you must fish. Do not approach the dam, the caretakers house or private property on the north side of the lake. A fence and sign about halfway along the northwest edge mark where you must stop. The trail on the southeast side goes almost all the way to the dam.

This is a day-use area only, open from 5:30 a.m. to 9 p.m. Due to icing, the lake is open only during the warmer months, May 11 to October 31. **Flies and artificial lures only.** The area is well patrolled. Report any violations. Your cooperation and care may help to open other such areas in the future.

ALMAGRE—SIGNAL MOUNTAIN. AREA

Imagine a series of high mountain valleys with streams and wildflowers, with level campsites and even a public lake with a sand beach at the top of a mountain that you can see from downtown Colorado Springs! This area has a lot to offer. It's spine trail is the old Forest Service Road #379.

Road Directions: At mile 4.7 from St. Peter's Dome, find East Beaver Creek, which feeds the reservoir, and here you turn right onto FS #379, which follows the creek uphill. Vehicles with high ground clearance may continue upward, fording the creek. This section is sometimes called Frosty Park Road, but the park itself is only a little more than a mile up, a popular place for picnics and camping, cross-country skiing and horseback riding. At mile 1.75 you'll leave the park and find a wide fork where FS #701 Forester's Trail branches downhill to your right. To go higher, bear left. Up through more forest, you next find High Park with beaver ponds on your left.

At mile 4.6 from the bottom, you find another big intersection. To find SEVEN STEPS to Deer Park and Elk Park, go straight at this fork. To climb toward STRATTON RESERVOIR, take the hard right that climbs

steeply. This is a shelf road that ends at a steel gate at mile 6.4 from the bottom. Stratton Reservoir is only about another 10th of a mile beyond the gate. No permit required.

ALMAGRE ROAD TO STRATTON RESERVOIR FS# 379, 13 miles round trip to the gate just outside of Stratton Reservoir. Scenic climb to timberline lake.

| 9,720 | 6.5 miles | 11,56 |

Bring your bucket and spade and suntan lotion, because the finest beach in the Rockies is at Stratton Reservoir high in the saddle between Mount Almagre and Signal Mountain. The water is fairly shallow and beautifully clear, but at nearly 12,000 feet, where even trees can't grown, this abandoned reservoir is a mixture of snowmelt and spring water and is very chilly!

Still, when the wind isn't blowing, the beach attracts sunbathers, sand-castle builders, toe dippers and a few brave swimmers. Watch out for rocks.

No permit is required because Stratton is no longer part of the Colorado Springs drinking water supply. The stone masonry dam looks strong enough, but state inspectors didn't like the design of the spillway, so engineers pulled out the valves to make a permanent leak. They didn't actually drain the lake, but made it shallow enough to satisfy inspectors worried about flash floods.

Because it sits in a bowl, there is no lofty view from the beach itself, but you can see the city from its dam. For a truly grand view, cross the dam (watching out for the steel rebar pungee stakes) and take the path up Mount Almagre (12,367 ft). From there you can see the forbidden Seven Lakes Area (City of Colorado Springs South Slope Watershed), the Sangre de Cristo Range, etc., but **be sure to stay on paths to protect the delicate tundra.**

Across the lake to the south is Almagre's sister peak, Signal Mountain, only 18 feet lower and crowned by microwave antennas. Please stay away from that high energy gear. Besides, you can get almost exactly the same view from Almagre.

The next bump southeast of Signal Mountain at 12, 226 feet is marked "Baldy" on USGS maps, and here lies some confusion. The whole Almagre-Signal summit is bald because it's all above timberline. Indeed, you can see this massive from Colorado Springs as the next bald mountain south of Pikes Peak and our FS #379 leading up it is also visible from town, something unusual for our trails.

Residents have long called the whole thing "Baldy," even though Baldy itself is just a blister on the sister and is not visited by the road. We discourage this usage because it is incorrect and because there are other Baldies in Colorado. There are no other Almagres. (In Spanish, Almagre means "red ochre.")

Pausing on Seven Steps.

Reaching this lofty spot is an exercise in freedom. That is, you are free to get all the exercise you want. Some bikers and hikers park at the Gold Camp entrance and do the entire 13 miles round trip. For mountain bikers, it's quite a gonzo down again. Parts are very rocky, narrow and rough, so if you try it in a four-wheel, you must have high ground clearance. Just remember that you may have to back up when meeting someone, and it's harder to watch for rocks in reverse!

This whole area is open to horses, but it's unwise to ride a horse to the summit. The top section is so narrow and shelf-like that there are many places where I would hate to sit a horse while a vehicle inched past. A perfect place for Pegasus.

SEVEN STEPS ROAD-TRAIL, about 4 miles round trip, rated moderate and easy. Big valley country.

What looks like the "main road" at the high intersection described in our road directions is really the turnoff to a huge meadow area called Deer Park and Elk Park. Actually, they look more like one massive meadow, for there is nothing separating the two parks but a bog where Gould Creek begins.

As you leave the intersection 4.6 miles uphill from the Gold Camp, you bear to the left. The road rises 0.1 mile to top a ridge where you'll see another prominent route branching to your right. This right fork leads to the very same place, but taking it means missing a great view of Pikes Peak.

Heading downhill on the main route, the track becomes extremely washed and rocky, a real four-wheeler rut that's gonzo fun on a mountain bike. Soon you'll find a very sharp turn to the right where a small high meadow appears on your left. You'll see Pikes Peak standing tall above the parks below.

Head down to the park and cross a small stream. The route to your right is the other end of that side-route we mentioned earlier. We're heading down to the left, following the stream at the high edge of Deer Park, which becomes Elk Park later on. Despite the names, we see very little deer and elk sign here, possibly because the area is heavily hunted. Wear orange in the fall, however.

These huge meadows are bigger and lovelier than any of those below. We spread out our picnic on green grass, surrounded by rocks and forest. At the far end of Elk Park the road is supposed to end. We expected a barrier, but instead found nothing but more grass. A route leading northwest into the trees soon washes out and meets a Utility Dept. fence guarding the forbidden Seven Lakes Area on the South Slope of Pikes Peak. If we can open this forbidden area to hike-in fishing, Elk Park would be a great place to camp and hike from.

Back at the grassy area, you can see the old **Seven Steps** revives itself to the south, skirting the edge of the park and then climbing as an extremely rocky and braided track. leading up and over a hill to the Middle Beaver Creek Rd FS #376. We did it, but it was so rocky and eroded that it wasn't much fun.

Forester Trail FS #701, Forester Trail segment measures 4.0 miles; entire downhill route measures 10.3 to the High Dr. parking, rated easy but long.

Many Rocky Mountain trails seem to go uphill *both* ways, but this thrilling ride is downright downhill, with only a few short ups for variety. Forester Trail #701 is a wonderful but eroded motorcycle trail that is now very popular with mountain bikers, and it's the easiest way you'll ever find to explore the beautiful Jones Park. You can't believe how easy it is until you go.

Your trail begins at a big intersection in the woods just above Frosty Park, well marked by a new sign provided by motorcyclists. Obviously it's an old doubletrack here, but that soon changes. A few yards down from the intersection you'll find a big rusted iron sign on your left that reads, "North Cheyenne Cr. 1.1, Jones Park 3.2, Deer Park 0.1," (but they mean Frosty Park) and "Rosemont 1.7."

We roll down through dense climax forest and cross water for the first time at mile 0.7. You'll cross other fingers of North Cheyenne Creek while we contour around and hop over each ridge that separates them.

Just beyond one crossing, you'll see an old trail to your right with a post near-by. That's a trail that goes down to Nelson's Camp on North Cheyenne Creek, too rocky for good biking. Stay on our main track and climb a little. Your first big view is at mile 2.2 where there is a big rock next to the trail: Scenic place for lunch. Mt. Rosa is to the left, Almagre in front of you and Runs Down Fast Mountain is on your right. At mile 3.0 the faint track coming up from your right is due to be closed.

At mile 4.0 Forester Trail #701 ends at Jones Park Trail #667 (formerly part of the old Bear Creek Trail) in an aspen valley located upstream from Jones Park itself. Gorgeous spot. So now we can keep heading to civilization on the Jones Park Trail, then to the Buckhorn Cutoff to the Gold Camp.

We cross the creek and go downstream on the smoothest, most beautiful ride, gently downhill through a glorious aspen glen with little whoop-tee-doos. Then it gradually gets a little steeper and bumpier and crosses the creek at mile 4.8. Notice that the creek has been diverted here to keep it off the trail, for the trail is actually below the level of the creek at that point.

Soon a tributary joins us and runs in the trail and the path ahead grows rocky and wet in places. At mile 5.2 there's a side trail that crosses the creek, then widens out and goes on down to join the **Pipeline Trail.** We keep to the main track, rolling through more grassy aspen. The trees open up at mile 5.7 and we find an intersection with a trail that goes left to Mount Garfield and Arthur. We cross a tributary here and roll on to a big grassy clearing at 5.9, which is the heart of Jones Park.

There is an intersection here. If you cross the creek going south, the side trail forks, the right fork being the **Pipeline Trail** (see CHEYENNE CAÑON/HIGH DRIVE) and the left being the official North Cheyenne Cutoff Trail FS #688, linking this with North Cheyenne Cañon Trail FS #622. We don't take it.

We don't cross but head downstream. At 6.5 we cross a trickle from Tenney Crags, and from here on down the trail gets even worse, extremely cobbley, sometimes with water running in the track. **Watch for a trail coming down to cross the creek from your right at mile 7.0. That's actually the continuation of our Jones Park Trail, which used to be called Buckhorn.**

You'll get down no matter which way you go, but Bear Creek goes to the High Drive and we want to head for the Gold Camp, so we're crossing the Creek and pushing up the very steep switchback to its ridge top.

Now we ride along the ridge, a high scenic route, down to a saddle beneath Buckhorn Mountain. There at mile 8.3 we take a right onto the Buckhorn Cutoff. This smooth trail takes us to the Gold Camp at mile 9.6. Turn left onto the Gold Camp and reach the big High Drive Parking lot above Helen Hunt Falls at 10.3.

CRIPPLE CREEK AREA

The Crags between Divide and Cripple Creek

The Crags Trails
The Crags-Banana Rock Trail
Horsethief Park Trail
Horsethief to Pancake Rocks Trail
Horsethief Falls Trail

Gold rush wagons emblazoned with the slogan "Pikes Peak or Bust" were actually headed to the diggings around Cripple Creek and Victor on the backside of Pikes Peak. This colorful area has some very scenic trails, as you'll see.

ROAD DIRECTIONS: Starting at the community of Divide on Hwy. 24, turn south on 67 toward Cripple Creek. The turnoff for the Crags trail system is located 4.2 miles from that intersection. Watch for a bridge on your left . A sign mentions Rocky Mountain Camp. Another 1.5 miles past the camp, you reach a National Forest auto campground with restroom facilities and potable water. The trailhead for the twin

Crags Trails is located at the backside of the campground itself.
Banana Rock Trail follows another tributary. Find it by taking the path
between campsites #9 and #10.

To find the Horsethief Park trail system, stay on paved 67 until you
pass the closed railroad tunnel. Park on the other side of the tunnel.
The new trailhead is on the left. The approach to all Horsethief Park
trails leaves from here. You must return this way because the Oil
Creek trailhead farther up the road is closed.

These are not the Crags but a rock formation alongside the Crags Trail.

*THE CRAGS TRAIL, Forest Service #664, 1.5 miles one way (either way),
elevation gain 700 ft., rated easy to moderate. Features gentle valley route
to rocky overlook.*

Heavy use has created a number of paths in this scenic region, so the old Crags
Trail is really two trails following the same creek, forking at a tributary higher up,
but ending at the same high lookout. Here you have a 3/4 panorama that is limited
only by Pikes Peak on one side. From the top of these eroded granite formations,
you can see distant mountains to the north and west and the flatlands with the City
of Colorado Springs to the east, as well as nearer features such as the North Slope
reservoirs.

Because of its high altitude (above 10,000 ft.), the Crags gets and holds snow
better than other areas popular for cross-country skiing. However, the access road
is not often plowed and creates a lot of business for tow trucks, so be careful. In
summer, the Crags is very popular among hikers, bikers and horse riders, so avoid
weekends if you want more solitude.

Leaving the trailhead, the twin trail soon follows both sides of the stream. Ahead, the valley opens up. Near the head of the valley, an unofficial trail takes off to the right, but keep following the stream. As we mentioned, the creek forks and both tributaries lead to the Crags lookout. Taking the right fork, you go through a shady ravine and then climb steeply among jumbled boulders. As soon as you reach the ridge saddle the lakes of the North Slope Recreation area come into view. The vista is even better from higher up among the big crags, but if you have small children along, this would be a good place to quit, for this impressive overlook of lakes and forest and flatlands is a rewarding sight, but does require scrambling around on rocks where children might fall.

BANANA ROCK TRAIL, Forest Service #664A, currently one mile one way, rated easy to moderate. Features snow-holding cross-country ski route up tributary.

Plans call for extending this trail clear through Devil's Playground on the Pikes Peak Toll Road to the summit of Pikes Peak, but at present it fades near timberline, and that is where the Forest Service wants you to stop until that extension is built. Tragically, people are damaging the tundra by seeking their own routes above timberline, creating a lacework of trails with so many cairns that it looks like a pinball machine. Even careful walking damages tundra, and it takes many years, even generations, to regrow, so do what you can to persuade others not to hike beyond the trail.

That said, the existing first mile below timberline is a charming route that follows another tributary of Fourmile Creek. It is a favorite among cross-country skiers because it gets less sun and holds snow better than the others. A number of small paths within the campground lead to this trail, but skiers can avoid a stream crossing by taking the path near campsite #9, which begins below the confluence of Fourmile Creek and this trail's tributary. Your trail stays to the right of the tributary, passing Banana Rock, before fading near timberline.

HORSETHIEF PARK TRAIL, Forest Service #704, 1.5 miles one way, elevation gain 700 ft., rated easy. Features scenic meadow trail suitable for cross-country skiing.

Once the hideout of horse thieves, this beautiful area has become a favorite among bikers and cross-country skiers, as well as hikers and equestrians.

Trouble with the Little Ike Tunnel led to a greatly improved trailhead with a gentler approach to this easy trail. Your first 3/4 mile is an old roadway that tun-

Pancake Rocks above Horsethief Park.

nels up through dense timber. As soon as the valley opens up, turn left and cross the boggy stream to pick up the old road on the other side. Beaver workings may change this crossing, so look for it in the brush.

Your double track heads north, skirting the edge of a wide meadow lined with aspens, glorious in fall. It passes some old log ruins and forks at the head of the valley. This fork will form the basis of a triangular loop planned by the Teller County Trails Committee, but at present the right fork is especially faint as it climbs into the trees, frequently blocked by fallen timber and marked only with an occasional cairn. The planned loop will climb to the ridge top, then turn left, following the ridge to pick up the other fork, returning to the meadow.

Bikers note: Although a local guide describes a ride between Horsethief Park and The Crags, there is no such trail. There are pieces of trail in that direction, but the American Biking Association and the Forest Service oppose bushwhacking with bikes because of damage to delicate flora and soggy meadows. There is also a large parcel of private land in Putney Gulch, as shown on the Pikes Peak Atlas and on the Forest Service Visitor's Map. Please do not trespass.

HORSETHIEF PARK TO PANCAKE ROCKS, Forest Service #704A, 2.75 miles one way from tunnel, elevation gain 1,400 ft., rated moderate to difficult. Features spectacular lookout.

Hwy. 9,700   2.75 miles   11,060 Rocks

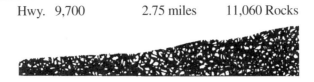

Start up from the tunnel as just explained, but do not cross the stream where the valley opens up. Instead, continue straight ahead (east) and find the intersection marked for the Falls (straight ahead) and Pancake Rocks marked two miles to the right. From here you have a steep climb up through mossy ever-greens High up, the trail seems to start downhill, and some pancake-looking rocks stand high above on the left, but this is not your destination. Keep going and the trail rises again, suddenly depositing you on a high table surrounded by rocks in the shape of stacked pancakes. The view is so grand it even seemed to impress our horses.

Remember, you must return the way you came. The old trailhead down at the southern end is closed by private property.

HORSETHIEF FALLS TRAIL, Forest Service 704B, l.75 miles one way from the tunnel, elevation gain 900 ft., rated moderate. Features forest trail to waterfall.

Hwy. 9,700   2.75 miles   10,700 Falls

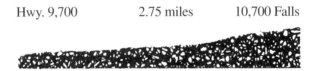

Starting back at the intersection with the trail to Pancake Rocks, head east and then south, following the stream up to the falls. This is actually a long cascade tumbling down the granite, with a seven-foot fall at the bottom. Near the base is a small bathtub worn in the rock, which must be tempting on a hot day.

WOODLAND PARK AREA

Lovell Gulch Trail
Centennial Trail (Formerly Manitou Park Bike Trail)
Painted Rocks Bike Trail
FRONT DOOR TO SCHUBARTH SYSTEM:
Schubarth Trail #721
Deadman's Creek #313
Deadman's—Hell Creek Loop
Deadman's—Schubarth Loop
Upper Stanley #707
Hell Creek #311
Schubarth—Lake Shore Loop
RAMPART RESERVOIR TRAILS:
Backdoor Trail to Schubarth System
Boatman's Loop
Stanley Rim—Schubarth Loop
Rainbow Gulch Trail
Rampart Reservoir Trail
Nichols Trail
BPW Nature Trail
Devil's Kitchen—Ormes Peak Loop

Located where Hwy. 24 intersects with 67 to Deckers, Woodland Park is headquarters for the Teller County Trail Committee, whose volunteers build and improve trails throughout the county. It is also the Front Door (vehicle access) to the fabulous National Forest Schubarth Trail system, now reopened. The non-motorized Backdoor access to Schubarth also begins at nearby Rampart Reservoir.

Because Schubarth road directions are so extensive, we're going to handle other short trails first and then present Schubarth separately in this chapter.

Note: Manitou Lake at Manitou Park is nowhere near Manitou Springs, but is owned by the city of Woodland Park and is located north of town on 67. The names are merely a coincidence.

ROAD DIRECTIONS: From I-25 at Colorado Springs, take the Cimarron Exit marked for Manitou-Pikes Peak #141. Drive 17 miles on Hwy. 24 to Woodland Park. To find the LOVELL GULCH trailhead, take the turnoff between Team Telecycle and McDonald's just as you enter Woodland Park. Go 2.2 miles north to the Dog Pound next to the Woodland Park Maintenance Center. The LOVELL GULCH parking lot is located at the Pound.

The new trailhead for CENTENNIAL TRAIL will be at the corner of Midland and Walnut next to the Pikes Peak Credit Union in downtown Woodland Park. We still like to use the old trailhead at the South Meadows Campground, 5.9 miles north of Woodland Park on County 67 or park at Manitou Lake 8 miles north on 67

To find the trailhead PAINTED ROCKS BIKE TRAIL, stay on Hwy 24 to the center of town and turn right on 67 marked for Deckers. Park at Manitou Lake or near the Painted Rocks Campground.

PAINTED ROCKS BIKE TRAIL is a short branch located just north at the Painted Rocks Campground, near Manitou Lake itself.

LOVELL GULCH TRAIL, Forest Service Trail, 5.5-mile balloon-shaped loop, elevation gain-loss 640 ft., rated easy to moderate. Features forest walk with scenic views.

Wildflowers decorate most trails, but Lovell Gulch may be the perfect habitat. Not just the meadows, but even the forest is crowded with flowers after a rain. Gentle rolling hills capture rainfall, minimizing runoff (which allows soil depth to build), and the widely spaced evergreens provide the right mix of sun and shade (energy and moisture protection). Please remember that

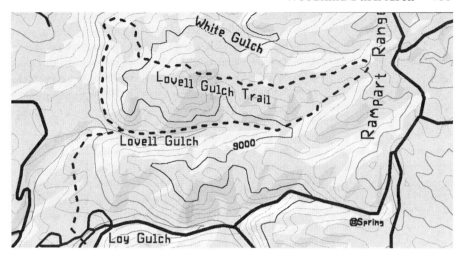

it is a federal violation to disturb wildflowers in the National Forest.

This trail is very popular with local equestrians--but locals became aware that a growing lacework of trails was trampling the area. So volunteers from the Teller County Trails Committee worked in cooperation with the Forest Service to establish the trailhead, post signs, clean up and block off many extra paths with sticks. So please take the hint and stay on the posted trail. It was designated as an official FS trail in 1990.

The first mile (the string of the balloon) is nearly level, leading north out of Woodland Park along the edge of timber. Then it crosses a stream and forks where a sign describes the loop ahead as being 3 3/4 miles. Cross-country skiers will probably want to ski this one counter-clockwise in order to gain altitude more gradually. So turn right and travel upstream along a narrow meadow for about 1.5 miles. Climbing to the top of a ridge, it loops back to the west along the ridge, offering spectacular views of Pikes Peak and Ute Pass. The descent from this ridge is the steepest section. Turn right at the fork and you're on your way back along the string.

Note: Very heavy animal traffic here makes it necessary to ask animal owners not to leave feces on the trail. Dog feces should be buried like human waste; horse manure should only be moved, not buried, because of the hole size necessary.

CENTENNIAL TRAIL (formerly MANITOU PARK BICYCLE TRAIL), Forest Service #669.2, now 7.2 miles one way, elevation gain about 100 ft., rated easy. Features wheelchair-suitable link between campgrounds and Manitou Lake, now extended all the way into Woodland Park.

Our guide doesn't cover urban trails, but this one has always had a Forest Service trail number and pretty mountain scenery all around! Years ago it was called the Manitou Park Bicycle Trail and it served as a 2.1-mile link

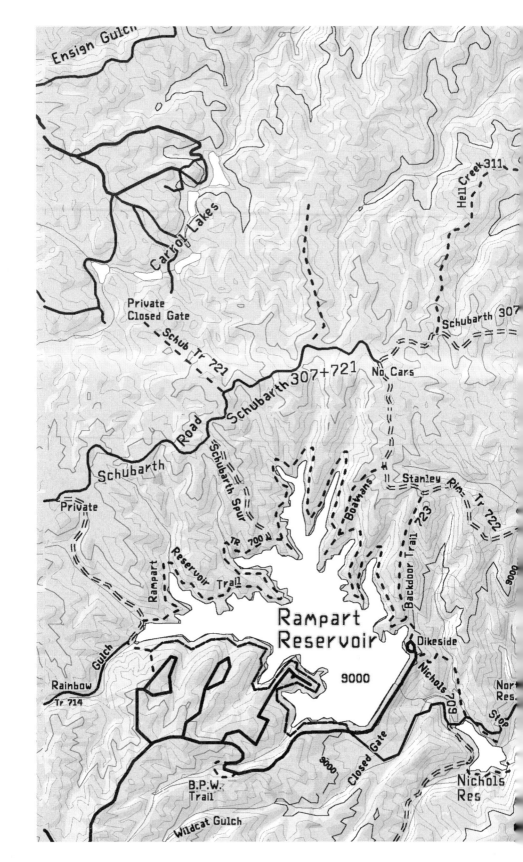

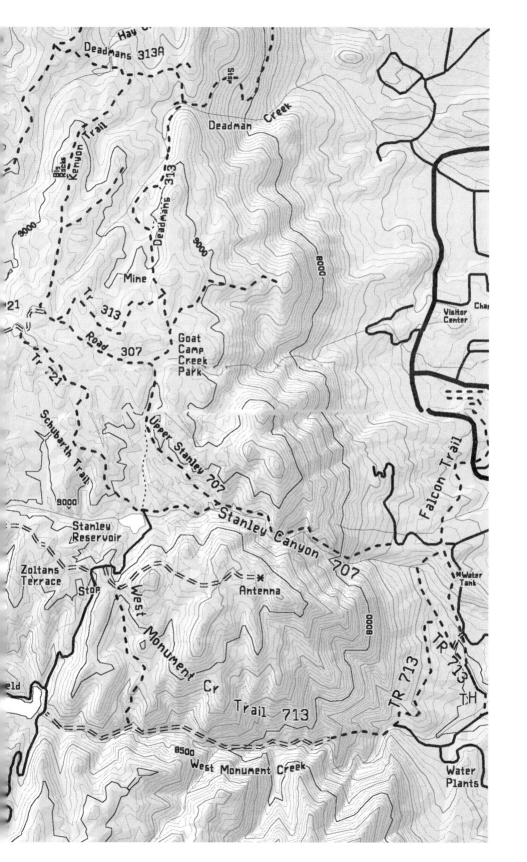

between three Forest Service pay campgrounds and the fishing lake at Manitou Park. Eight feet wide and paved, it runs like a (nearly) flat sidewalk beside County 67, perfect for wheelchairs, baby strollers and families with toddlers. Roller blading is technically permitted, but is not recommended because some of the more rolling sections tend to make the going too fast.

Today it has been renamed for the Centennial celebration and it runs all the way to Woodland Park, lacking only one half mile of reaching its eventual new trailhead downtown. As mountain folk, we still enjoy the old northern end the most. It is still very rural, the scenery hasn't changed, but we no longer have to remind you not to let the cows out.

Manitou Park itself has a boardwalk and more hard-surface trail to allow wheelchair visitors to fish in this scenic area. The park is a day-use area open from 6 a.m. to 10 p.m. The lake is stocked with catchable size rainbows by the Division of Wildlife.

PAINTED ROCKS BIKE TRAIL, Forest Service #669.1, 0.3 miles one way, elevation gain nil, rated easy. Features link between Painted Rocks Campground and Centennial Trail.

This is just a short spur off the Centennial Trail with the same hard surface and flat design, making it suitable for wheelchairs, baby strollers and toddlers. This area boasts strange red sandstone columns, some shaped like mushrooms. These were formed because softer sandstone was capped with a patch of harder rock that preserved the column while everything else weathered away around it.

FRONT DOOR TO THE FABULOUS SCHUBARTH TRAIL SYSTEM

For many years we yearned to tell you about Schubarth—a whole system of beautiful old logging routes in a little-visited area of the National Forest. Its trails aren't flat by any means, but they are gentler than most. Yet we kept Schubarth secret for a reason.

The Forest Service asked us not to mention this gem for fear that publicity might close its vehicle access. You see, that access starts off from the Rampart Range Road by crossing a neck of private land. Yet in 1993 other writers (who don't work as closely with the FS) spilled the beans, visitorship increased and on July 27, 1993, homeowners locked the gates to all traffic. Period. Many square miles of National Forest were suddenly locked away!

That sent us and the Forest Service and the Division of Wildlife searching the forest for another way in. I had the honor of suggesting, naming and mapping for the first time our Backdoor Trail, which now carries official FS designation, but that's not for vehicles. We began to feel like we were searching for the fabled Northwest Passage because the vehicle links we heard about no longer seem to exist anymore.

Meanwhile, Attorney and former Judge George Gibson discovered evidence that Schubarth is a federal road that predates private property. The District Attorney's office demanded that the home owner's association show cause for closure, and the Division of Wildlife physically removed the lock and chain.

The situation blew up when an armed homeowner tried to keep away visitors. This resulted in a felony conviction and a suspended sentence, which means serious jail time if there is another such incident. We cannot assure you that there will be no further problem, but visitors have been using this access without incident sofar. Use good judgement.

So here's how it stands for now. Although the decision is being appealed, authorities have ruled that Schubarth is like the Old Stage Road, a federal access across private property. Unless the decision is overturned, you and your grandchildren own the road itself forever. **If you find a gate closed, please reclose it behind you and fasten it just as you found it, but no one can lock you out. Otherwise, please stay in your car and stay on the road until you reach National Forest. Always respect private property, gates and livestock.**

Also be careful not to play lawyer and generalize this situation to other locations: Access law is very complex.

Finally, we can guide everyone to the many square miles of biking and hiking, horseback riding, camping and fishing available on your federal lands. Schubarth also offers access to Stanley Reservoir, the latest of the Colorado Springs forbidden lakes to be opened to public fishing.

ROAD DIRECTIONS: At present, you need a vehicle with high ground clearance to do Schubarth. Drive to Woodland Park, as described at the first of this chapter and turn right between Team Telecycle and McDonald's. Go 2.9 miles to where the pavement forks. Go right, marked Loy Creek Road. When you reach the gravel Rampart Range Road, go straight across it. This is SCHUBARTH ROAD #307 (not yet SCHUBARTH TRAIL #721).

You are now on a through access across private property, so please stay the road, respect owner's rights, reclose all gates and refasten. Cross the first cattleguard about 0.3 of a mile later in a grassy valley. Just a few yards ahead, the road T-junctions below a hill. GO RIGHT HERE and skirt the hill 0.3 miles to enter the second cattleguard. Reclose the gate.

Soon you cross the third cattleguard, entering AF Academy land called Farish, but Farish is NOT a public recreation area! Stay on the roadway. Farish is one mile across, but there is more private land beyond that last cattleguard and gate.

PLEASE RESET ODOMETER at the second farish gate-cattleguard. The Pike National Forest begins 0.7 miles beyond this last Farish gate. Horse trailers park along the roadside within the National Forest. All roads to your right (south) are closed to motorized vehicles, camping and fires because this is the boundary of the Rampart Reservoir Recreation Area.

At mile 1.1 from Farish, a sign on your right saying, "Closed to Motorized Vehicles, Camping and Fires," marks a trail that has recently been named SCHUBARTH SPUR 721A, as our map shows. That leads to Rampart Reservoir. Eight tenths of a mile deep in the National Forest (1.6 from Farish), the main track makes a sharp right turn and a fainter doubletrack goes straight ahead out onto a grassy knoll. A post to your left marks both routes at #721, which is SCHUBARTH TRAIL. That's because SCHUBARTH TRAIL #721 is a zig-zag that shares its middle portion with SCHUBARTH ROAD #307. The route ahead, the leftish fork, is where Trail #721 comes up from the Farish lakes to join our road.

To do SCHUBARTH TRAIL #721's northern leg, enter the doubletrack and immediately park off the road. (The doubletrack ahead is closed to motorized vehicles, but the entrance is a natural parking area.) To continue on SCHUBARTH ROAD to find more trails, take the prominent right fork now called both SCHUBARTH TRAIL #721 AND SCHUBARTH ROAD #307. A prominent-looking left turn at mile 2.2 leads to a system of dead-ends. Bear right here and stay on main road.

At mile 3.3, stay right, (left is officially called HELL CREEK #311, but has been called Hay Creek in the past because it skirts Hay Creek). Eight tenths of a mile farther (at mile 4.1 from Farish) watch for another old iron sign on your right, this one set back in the trees, guarding a double track to the south. That is where SCHUBARTH TRAIL #721 leaves SCHUBARTH ROAD #307 and goes down to Stanley Reservoir. Park in the trees. Not much room.

To find UPPER STANLEY TRAIL #707, continue east on SCHUBARTH ROAD another third of a mile (mile 4.4) and turn left onto DEADMAN'S #313. This is our Deadman's-Schubarth Loop, but going straight instead of left takes you down a very nasty piece of road, so go left on #313 to avoid that. DEADMAN'S #313 has always been dramatically mismapped, even by us. But GPS satellite navigation has made our new map very accurate.

One mile down DEADMAN'S, turn right at the arrowhead-shaped fork. About two-tenths farther, you arrive at a broad valley where you park. More Trails mistakenly identified this spot as Deadman's, which is what we always called it because of the road leading here, but this is, of course, the headwaters of Goat Camp Creek. Sorry. (You reach Deadman's Creek by going left at the arrowhead, past the mine and so on, which we call the DEADMAN'S-HELL CREEK LOOP.)

Okay, now that you know the name of the place where we've always parked at Goat Camp Creek meadow, notice that you can go left or right from the meadow. Left takes you to an overlook. To find UPPER STANLEY TRAIL #707 or to do the DEADMAN'S-SCHUBATH LOOP, go right along the Goat Camp meadow, following the loop-road up the aspen draw. This road is so tilted that some vehicles want to roll over, but it's a beautiful bike loop. Only 0.2 from your car, look for a crease in the grass beneath the aspen to your left. This is the trailhead for UPPER STANLEY.

SCHUBARTH TRAIL, Forest Service #721, entire route 5.1 miles, northern leg rated easy, middle motorized leg moderate, lower leg more difficult. Features access to Stanley Reservoir.

9,200   5.1 miles   8,940

Schubarth Trail is all double track and a great place for mountain biking. Indeed, it was the first place I ever tried one. Our road directions try to explain that Schubarth Trail #721 and Schubarth Road #307 are not the same, except in the middle east-west portion, where they share the same route. So we're going to park here and follow the closed-to-motorized-vehicles trail to its northern terminus, then backtrack to the car and follow the rest of the trail east, along the road, to the trail's southern leg, which leads to the lovely Stanley Reservoir.

You're in for a treat. Heading north on this doubletrack, you'll find that Schubarth Trail winds through sparse timber with big ponderosa and fir spaced among smaller aspen. It's a fairly gradual downhill, following the crest of a ridge guarded by roundish granite boulders. The only steep place is at the very end, where the trail dips to a fence and gate at the edge of Farish. Distance: 0.9 miles.

The sign at the gate reads, "Warning: U.S. Air Force Installation. It is unlawful to enter this area without permission of the installation commander. While on this installation, all personnel and the property under their control are subject to search." Beyond the gate you can see the grassy meadows of Farish and the edge of a lake. Never mind, Stanley is your lake and that's where we going. Return to your vehicle the way you came.

Reset your odometer at the car. Now we head east on the combined Schubarth Trail-Road. The timber is much thicker here, generally dominated by evergreens. The tread is firm, but heavily rutted and more difficult because the ups and downs are steeper. Great fat-tire fun.

At mile 1.2, we find a gate on the right with an iron sign saying, "Closed to Motorized Vehicles, Camping and Fires." At present, there is a confusing number of numbers around, but that's Boatman's Trail, leading down to the Boatman Picnic Ground on Rampart Reservoir, described in this chapter as the **Stanley-Schubarth Loop.**

Going on, ignore side trails until you reach mile 1.7, where the major branch to your left is **Hell Creek #311**. This is a very long and rugged route, described later.

Eight tenths of a mile farther along Schubarth at mile 2.5, watch for another old iron closed-to-motorized vehicles sign on your right, this one set back in the trees, guarding a doubletrack to the south. A marker there confirms that it is #721. **This is where Schubarth Trail leaves Schubarth Road and trundles down to Stanley Reservoir, a distance of 1.7 miles.**

This was actually the first place we ever rode mountain bikes, and it's a thrilling downhill, full of big ruts and roots and such. But it is also much steeper than the rest of Schubarth, so you'll earn your lake visit with a tough 1.7-mile climb back to this point. It is well worth the journey!

The lower leg takes you right to Stanley's dam. In our neighborly way we lobbied for the opening of this beautiful lake for over 15 years, and in the summer of 1995 that effort finally bore fruit. Stanley is now open to everyone (with a valid Colorado fishing license) who can hike, mountain bike or ride horseback to this remote lake. Five different trails lead you there and we describe them all in this book, three in this chapter, and two more in the Air Force Academy chapter. We hope that showing you so many ways to reach Stanley will help keep from crowding cadets out of the popular (but small) parking lot at the foot of Stanley Canyon Trail. Please try our other routes.

For details about the lake, see Stanley Rim--Schubarth Loop in this chapter. NOTE: Due to a temporary scarcity of whirling disease-free fish, Stanley will not be up to full fishing potential until the year 2001.

An aspen grove at the upper end of the lake is the most popular camping spot, but please do not camp within 100 feet of the water.

DEADMAN'S CREEK FS #313, first segment to arrowhead intersection measures 0.9 miles, Goat Camp parking is 0.2 miles right, backtrack that 0.2 to arrowhead, then begin major segment including #313A to Hell Creek Trail, about three more miles one way, rated easy and moderate., with a few more difficult climbs. Leads to meadow valley, long aspen glen, sidetrails to overlooks.

If you *don't* take the Schubarth Trail turnoff, but continue east on Schubarth Road through dark evergreens hanging with dwarf mistletoe, you'll come to another major fork at mile 2.9 from the Boy Scout post marked #721 both ways. See, we told you to reset your odometer there. To your left at that fork is Deadman's Creek #313. Like the number?

If you don't take **Deadman's**, but continue straight ahead here on Schubarth Road, the track gets very nasty and much, much steeper. Not for passenger cars. One government vehicle got stuck. That forms part of our **Deadman's Schubarth Loop**, but believe me, if you're still driving, take Deadman's to the left and don't dream of going straight. Besides, the best parking is down Deadman's and then right to Goat Camp.

Now on to **Deadman's.**

The beginning of this route is gentle and in good condition for being so little traveled and has only one trick. At mile 0.9 you come to a T-junction that is almost arrowhead-shaped because the forks cut backward.

The left fork is actually more of **Deadman's #313**, which once confused us, and that forms part of our **Deadman's-Hell Creek Loop**. The right goes to a clearing at the headwaters of Goat Camp Creek, a good place to park.

Going right, it's only another two tenths of a mile down through an aspen draw to Goat Camp meadow, a wide marshy place with space for a number of cars at the edge. Except in the wettest times, you have to go just downstream to find anything flowing.

We're here for a reason. Whether you want to do the Deadman's-Hell Creek Loop, or the Deadman's-Schubarth loop, or just want to find Upper Stanley Trailhead, this is the only convenient place to park more than one car.

At the meadow, there is a triangular intersection where two other paths climb away to your left and right. The right one forms our **Deadman's-Schubarth Loop**. The left one becomes a rocky singletrack that leads a third of a mile to an overlook of the Academy.

But since we're supposed to be describing **Deadman's Trail** itself, it only makes sense to follow the whole Deadman's Trail by describing next its loop with **Hell Creek.Trail**. Just remember, Deadman's goes to Hell.

So, if you park at Goat Camp meadow, you simply backtrack 0.2 to the arrowhead fork and take the other fork of the arrowhead down to find Deadman's Creek itself.

DEADMAN'S-HELL CREEK LOOP, 7.5 miles, rated more difficult. Features long loop through varied terrain with fabulous aspen glen, lookouts, camping, etc. Also access to Kenyon's Trail, which links to Schubarth.

Hell Creek is the proper name for trail #311 because that's where it eventually goes. We once called it Hay Creek because it follows the ridge above Hay Creek. Still, a trail by any name is just as beautiful, and this one takes a prize!

Okay, we parked at Goat Camp and backtrack 0.2 miles to the arrowhead-shaped fork on the ridge. Cross the ridge and take the other downhill fork. Here **Deadman's Trail #313** dives down to skirt a moist aspen draw. Within a quarter of a mile, watch for quartz tailings sparkling high on your left. That's a small quarry where someone mined several loads of feldspar and quartz. The road that served it is now just a fading greenroad that switchbacks up and hooks back a third of a mile to join Deadman's higher up.

Continuing down our aspen draw, we cross a spring (the headwaters of Deadman's Creek) and come to a poorly designed place where our track shoots up a treeless hillside, very, very steep and eroded. Struggle up that.

Or not. We have a suggestion!

After exploring this area many times, we found two ways to go here. The official trail skyrockets up that hill and dives down again later because the lumberjack vehicles that originally made this route would have bogged down following the stream. There is no obvious trail downstream, but a narrow singletrack soon shows itself, if you look. And, despite the fallen logs chewed by mountain bike sprockets, it's far nicer to follow the stream than to claw your way up that barren hill, but let me explain the hard way first just because it is, after all, the official old trail.

Okay, shoulder your mountain bike and start climbing. Finally, the trail gets more gentle as it nears the top of a long ridge. Your path follows

A spectacular overlook near Deadman's.

the crest of the ridge and comes to a place where the route ahead has been blocked with stumps. Here your trail angles hard to the left and dives down to Deadman's Creek. Do it once and you'll never do it again.

Or you can bushwhack through high brush, staying to the left of the trickling spring, and soon you find the singletrack we mentioned. Beautiful route, and it only gets better! Lately, however, many more trees have fallen across it.

Now you are wandering down the biggest and most spectacular aspen glade in the entire Schubarth area. Deadman's Creek becomes drop dead gorgeous. Watch for bear claw marks high on some of these trees. Bears do that to mark their territory and to show off their size by demonstrating how high they can reach.

Years ago a friend and I cleared this path of fallen timbers, but many others have fallen since, some quite large. Somebody needs to bring a saw.

When you cross the stream in a clearing you are about 1.7 miles from Goat Camp. Soon after that you climb to an intersection short of the ridge crest. The route to your right wraps around the base of the hill, which is worth exploring briefly because of its wide view of the Academy and the plains. But we say briefly because that path leads way-way down-down to the shooting range that is almost constantly in use at the Academy, and we are told you can't get permission to exit that way, even if you survive it.

Our route climbs out of the valley, steep and washed. When you get to the ridge crest, you'll T-junction against a doubletrack, which is FS #313A, a long spur of Deadman's #313 that we might call Son-of-Deadman's. If you turn right and climb again very steeply for a tenth of a mile, you'll top the hill marked 8933 feet on the map. The clearing up there is a blanket of wildflowers in mid June, but it always boasts a near panoramic view of plains and mountains. Breathtaking spot. Bring plenty of film.

Back down at the intersection, take #313A west along the ridge. It, too, will lead you through aspen and grassy clearings, but #313A is not recommended for passenger cars coming from the other end.

Special Note: Two tenths of a mile later notice the singletrack to your left. That's a little-traveled ridge tour that we're naming Kenyon Trail. Gary Kenyon helped us find this trail and Upper Stanley, then tragically died mountain biking nearby. At the request of his family, we're honoring Kenyon by unofficially naming this otherwise nameless route after him. From this direction, Kenyon Trail takes you 0.8 miles to the top of the biggest rock formation that you see from #311, plus a peak view a third of a mile past that. It links to Schubarth Road between Deadman's and the #721 turnoff for Stanley, but has been hidden at that end. Schubarth, however, is the logical trailhead for this little-known route, and we hope it can be opened up and signed properly. We sincerely mean no disrespect by showing you Kenyon's Trail from the wrong side, from the side coincidentally called Deadman's. It's just so hard to show you the other way. We have taken conflicting measurements, but think it is about 1.75 miles one way. Thanks, Gary. Hope your trail is officially designated someday. You really opened up this area for a lot of us.

Continuing on our **Deadman's-Hell Creek Loop**, keep going west on #313A. After crossing a stream (Yes, that's Hay Creek) at mile 2.5 from Goat Camp, your track becomes steep and rocky as it climbs up almost half a mile to T-junction against **Hell Creek Trail #311** at mile three.. To complete our loop, turn left on Hell Creek Trail, go another 2.2 miles and turn left on Schubarth at mile 5.2. After another 1.2 miles, take the left down **Deadman's #313** to return to your car at Goat Camp. Total loop about 7.5 miles.

DEADMAN'S-SCHUBARTH LOOP, 1.9 miles, rated moderate. Features scenic aspen and evergreen loop.

8,860   1.9 miles   8,860

Park in the clearing at Goat Camp and take the right fork, heading south. This green-middled doubletrack has considerable camber sometimes (one track higher than another), so much so that some vehicles might roll over. But it has no other tricks, just a rolling path that snakes along beside brushy valleys with lots of grass and wildflowers and aspen. We liked it so much the first time, we turned around and did it again in the opposite direction. Here's the difference:

Doing this loop clockwise presents you with only one tough uphill, an extremely steep and washed-out section that takes you up to the intersection of **Deadman's** and **Schubarth**. Going the other way, we had a long climb along Deadman's darker forest, then we still had to walk our bikes down that nasty bit (for safety). We liked the clockwise better. See it in aspen season.

UPPER STANLEY TRAIL, FS# 707, 1.7 miles each way, rated very easy. Features easy access to Stanley Reservoir through meadow and aspen groves.

Want to take children or a flat-land guest fishing at Stanley Reservoir? Here's the way. Of the five different trails to Stanley, this is the *only easy way,* but it's tricky to find. You'll love it.

This trail was only a legend until Gary Kenyon told us how it really works. Kenyon solved the mystery for us, and tragically he died of a heart attack while mountain biking nearby. We couldn't name this trail after him because it always had a name and number, even when we couldn't find it, so we have unofficially named another trail after him, one that he also helped us find and never had a name at all. Thanks to Gary, people will visit Stanley who could never have managed the other trails.

Old maps have always shown **Stanley Trail #707** climbing a ridge and continuing north past the lake, but a generation ago we could find no real trace of it and, thus, we took it off our own maps. Nature takes back unused trails.

Perhaps cadets created the lower part of this trail by simply wandering up the gentle valley that slopes toward Stanley. Obviously they have used this valley for camping and bonfire parties. There is little sign that the lower path was ever "built."

Only the uppermost part of the trail works as shown on old maps, and we're embarrassed that we failed to find that obscure trailhead years ago. We're urging the Forest Service to install a sign. You really have to look for it.

To find it, go to Goat Camp meadow, turn right as we described for the **Deadman's-Schubarth Loop** and go 0.2 miles from Goat Camp. Watch for a crease in the grass amid the aspens to your left. That crease crosses the trickle of Goat Camp's headwaters. See why we missed it?

Just a few yards later hook a right over a tiny saddle, and I mean tiny. This saddle has a gain of only six or ten feet, but that's enough to separate the headwaters of Goat Camp Creek from the headwaters of the unnamed drainage to Stanley Creek. Your path soon crosses the meadow amid very tall grass.

This is a wonderfully easy trail down through sunny meadows and aspen groves, a breeze on bikes going either way! There is no sign that it ever hooked right and climbed the ridge as shown on the old maps. Water starts to flow only a short distance from where this path joins main **Stanley Trail** at a triangular intersection. Turn right there, cross the trickling tributary, and you're on your way to the lake on the easiest portion of **Stanley Trail.** The only steep bit is climbing up to the dam itself. For more on the lake, see **Stanley Rim-Schubarth Loop**. Enjoy!

HELL CREEK FS #311, segment measures 4 miles one way, rated moderate. Features ridge tour beside Hay Creek to overlook, ending at headwaters of Hell Creek.

| 9,300 | 4 miles | 8,140 |

Prettier than some of Schubarth Road, Hell Creek Trail #311 is passable to cars with high ground clearance. It's an undulating tour tracing a ridge with mixed aspen forest. We picnicked near the rocks at the clearing at mile 0.7 and gawked at the peak view at mile 1.15. We're pointing out the tall granite formation that you see across the valley at mile 1.5 because there's an unnamed side trail off FS #313A on the Deadman's-Hell Creek Loop that takes you there. The turnoff for #313A is at mile 2.2. We're calling that unnamed trail Kenyon Trail.

Weaving through an unusual set of big granite boulders at mile 3.2, Hell Creek Trail takes you past a timber lean-to that looks like a caveman's clubhouse, not an effective shelter but interesting. Just a little farther on, there's a fork where the main track switchbacks down to a moist draw with aspen and some tall grass. From there it becomes a singletrack that fades away in its climb toward the Pipeline Road beneath Mt. Herman Road.

We suggest you take the other fork on top, the one that leads more faintly straight forward. That takes you out to an overlook of the plains. This hilltop clearing has been used as a campsite, but remember what a lightning rod you would be up here!

SCHUBARTH-LAKE SHORE LOOP, 6.1-mile loop, rated moderate. Features scenic tour of mixed forest and lake shore, via Schubarth Spur FS# 721A. NO VEHICLES.

Because there are so many side trails in the Schubarth area, the most common question is, "Where does that go?" This one has a beautiful answer! Even its parking area gives you a taste: big boulder, big ponderosas, glimpses of Pikes Peak. But the lake awaits! The route ahead is now designated as Schubarth Spur FS#721A.

Park near the sign that says, "No Motorized Vehicles, Camping or Fires." This ridge trail is fairly gentle for a ways, then gradually steepens as it rolls down toward Rampart Reservoir with a number of peak views on the way. Because you're going out on a point, the lake appears on both sides of your trail. This is prettiest early in the season, when Pikes Peak is still snowy, and during aspen season. We ran out of film and wished for more.

At the intersection with the **Rampart Reservoir Trail #700**, also known as Lake Shore Trail, we went down to the grassy point. Beaver that live under the bank had been chewing some aspen. From there you can see the peak, the dam and several arms of the lake with picturesque rock formations. Near the rocks straight across from you is a picnic table. That's the little-known Boatman's Picnic Ground.

You've come 1.1 miles. Hang a left onto the Lake Shore Trail, much of which is breezy-easy but has some very technical spots. At mile 3.3 from the car, you reach the four-way intersection with Boatman's Trail, at present marked only with a reddish post. Boatman's is described in the Rampart Reservoir chapter. Turn left and take the rolling double track north to Schubarth Road-Trail, a fairly gentle climb, then turn left to follow Schubarth 1.6 miles west to where you parked.

RAMPART RESERVOIR TRAILS

Backdoor Trail
Boatman's Loop
Stanley Rim-Schubarth Loop
Rainbow Gulch Trail
Rampart Reservoir Trail (Lake Shore Trail)
Nichols Reservoir Trail
BPW Nature Trail
Devil's Kitchen—Ormes Peak Loop

When Colorado Springs wanted to build more reservoirs on federal land, the Forest Service made one demand: No more closed reservoirs: No public recreation, no lakes. As a result, Rampart and Nichols Reservoirs became the first open reservoirs in the CS system and the Division of Wildlife kicked in to build restrooms and more. The result is a recreation area to make everyone proud. And its trails feed off into more adventures in the National Forest. Only the final lake in the system, Northfield, was closed as a compromise.

There is no substantial stream feeding Rampart (not to be confused with Aurora's Rampart Reservoir). Instead, the CS Rampart stores water piped over the Continental Divide from the Western Slope, then passes it down through Nichols and Northfield to a Colorado Springs treatment plant located below the mouth of West Monument Canyon at the Air Force Academy.

Rampart is stocked by the Division of Wildlife with rainbow and lake trout. The old restriction on lakers has vanished, due to the success of the breed in this lake. Rampart also has some brown and brook trout. Boating is permitted, but no water skiing or swimming are allowed.

Rampart boasts beautiful picnic facilities and pay campgrounds. A parking fee per 24-hour-day is required at Rampart Reservoir's dam area, but there is no charge for parking at Rainbow Gulch Trailhead or along Schubarth in the National Forest. The Schubarth system's vehicle access is described earlier in this chapter.

Back-country camping and motorized vehicles are not permitted in the Rampart Recreation Area, which extends north to Schubarth. Indeed, Schubarth is the dividing line between camping (north of it) and no camping (south of it).

Because we've been describing the Schubarth area in the previous section, we're going to continue by starting our trail descriptions with Backdoor Trail, which is just what it says: The backdoor into the Schubarth system.

ROAD DIRECTIONS: Although the Rampart Range Road extends from near Denver to the Garden of the Gods in Colorado Springs, most folks prefer some pavement, approaching the Rampart via Woodland Park. From I-25 in CS, take the Cimarron exit marked for Manitou-Pikes Peak #141. Go 17 miles on Hwy 24 to Woodland Park and turn right between Team Telecycle and McDonald's.

To find RAMPART RESERVOIR ITSELF, go 2.9 miles to Loy Creek Road, turn right and follow Loy to its intersection with the Rampart Range Road. SET ODOMETER AND TURN RIGHT HERE. RAINBOW GULCH TRAILHEAD will be on your left about 2.4 miles from the Loy-Rampart intersection.

At mile 4 you find the turnoff for Rampart Reservoir. Go 1.6 miles and look for the trailhead for the BPW NATURE TRAIL on your right. Continue across the Rampart Reservoir Dam and park on the far side at Dikeside Overlook. You can see NICHOLS lake from the dam. It's trailhead is at that end of the parking lot. The trailhead for RAMPART RESERVOIR TRAIL and BACKDOOR is near the boat ramp at the far end of the parking lot.

BACKDOOR TRAIL, FS s#723, segment measures 0.9 miles one way, rated steep at first but then easy; provides bike, foot and horse access to Schubarth system from paved parking lot.

This trail was never a great secret, but it never appeared on any map that we know of. So we mapped it and popularized it as a "backdoor" to the then-closed Schubarth system. Later, when Stanley Reservoir opened, a handful of government agencies invited me to lead them on a hike via this route to see if Backdoor would be a more practical way to direct the public to Stanley. Paved road and a paved parking lot made this a tempting route.

That hike convinced the City that **Backdoor** and **Stanley Rim** were the best route to suggest to people inquiring about Stanley, and the Forest Service agreed to adopt our names for these trails and to give them official FS numbers, making them part of the permanent system.

Good thing: This is a great little trail! Somehow it had escaped mapping because when it was built (before the lake was built), it was just an unimportant little spur on a finger ridge meant to allow loggers to drag trees up. The FS once considered making it a road to Rampart, had that north shore been developed with

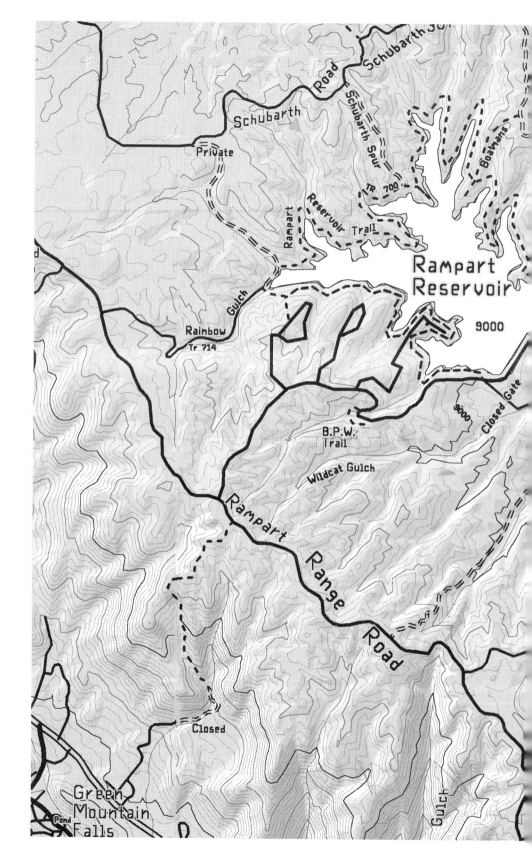

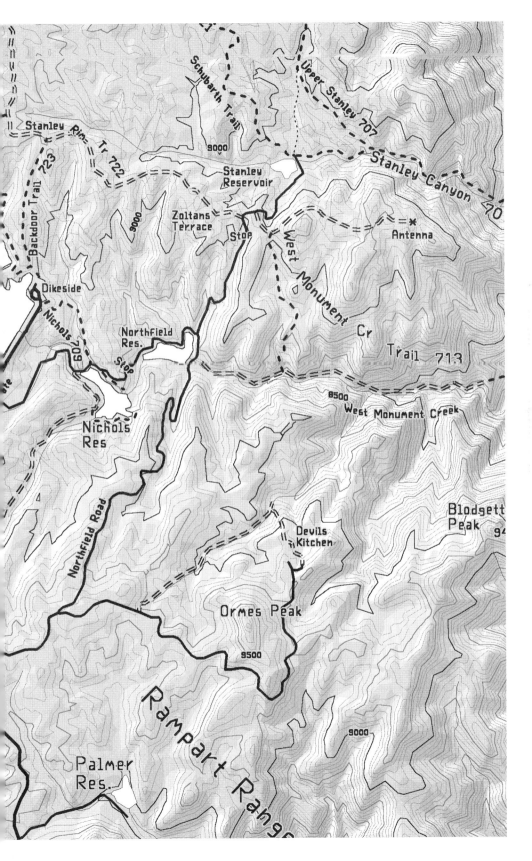

campgrounds and such. All we did was sort of rediscover it, map it, name it and popularize it until it got designated, which is a whole lot less sweat than building trail the way Volunteers for Outdoor Colorado do. We admire those folks.

Backdoor Trail begins at the far corner of the Rampart Reservoir dam's parking lot near the boat ramp, absolutely hidden in plain sight! Most people never notice it, even though it starts right where they take off on the long **Rampart Reservoir Trail**. A signless post marks the spot. The trail looks more like a watermark (right now), for it shoots right up the finger ridge there. Its first few yards are by far the steepest, and we urge you to walk your bikes both up and down that steep portion to prevent erosion.

But higher up, Backdoor soon becomes easy and downright beautiful, changing to a singletrack that snakes between big round boulders, with glimpses of the lake through the aspen and evergreens.

On top Backdoor shows its doubletrack history, but loses no charm. It's just under a mile (0.9) to the T-junction in the aspens with another doubletrack, Stanley Rim FS# 722. **From here you can do two loops: the shorter Boatman's Loop to the left or the Stanley-Schubarth Loop to your right.**

NOTE: These routes are still unmarked at present, so **please do them the way we describe them** and you'll have much less trouble finding your way. Here's why: If you're traveling a major route, looking for an unmarked side trail, it's easy to breeze on by and miss that side trail. But if you're coming up the side trail and T-junction against a plainer route, it's hard to miss that!

BOATMAN'S LOOP: 4.2 miles round trip, including Backdoor Trail access, rated moderate with one steep place .

9,000   4.2 miles   9,000

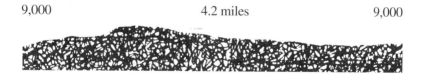

Okay, we're at the TOP of Backdoor Trail at it's intersection with Stanley Rim Trail where your odometer should read about 0.9. Stop and take a good look at this intersection because you'll have to find this spot from the reverse direction when you do the Stanley-Schubarth loop. This one is easy to miss!

Turn left onto Stanley Rim and go another 0.4 miles through aspen until you T-junction against a doubletrack. Stop again and take an even better look around because this junction was purposely hidden and blocked with ditches to keep renegade motorists from finding the **Stanley Rim Trail**. Again, you'll need

A view from Stanley Rim Trail east of its intersection with Backdoor Trail

to recognize this spot when you find it in reverse when doing the **Stanley-Schubarth Loop.**

You're now turning left onto a clear doubletrack that the Forest Service uses to service the little-known Boatman's Picnic Ground at the lake's shore. We're calling it **Boatman's Trail** because it has no other name. (Going right here would take you to Schubarth Trail-Road, an easy climb of 0.7 miles.)

The route ahead leads down a ridge through sparse timber, much of it aspen and very pretty in the fall. The trail has a firm surface and is cut by earthen waterbars that make wonderful whoop-tee-dos. **But don't get carried away because we're only going a half mile before intersecting the popular Rampart Reservoir Trail. You'll come upon it very suddenly, so don't run over anybody.** A signless post there marks the spot, but since the **Rampart Reservoir Trail** is only a singletrack, you could easily miss it by going too fast. Your odometer should read about 1.8 here. **From here we go straight ahead to find the picnic ground.**

A word about Boatman's Picnic Grounds: Many people have circled Rampart Reservoir many times without knowing about this little-used picnic ground. From our intersection, it's about 0.4 miles down to the point where there are picnic tables, an outhouse and special fire gratings among the trees and rocks at the lake shore. As it's name suggests, only boatmen generally use this beautiful spot. If you're looking for a scenic place to eat lunch, this is highly recommended!

Backtrack to the intersection of **Boatman Trail** and **Rampart**, turn right and follow the singletrack that snakes around the edge of the lake. **(If you don't visit the picnic grounds, you turn left onto Rampart Reservoir Trail.)** This picturesque path is one of the toughest sections of the shoreline trail. The sharp narrow turns, the rocks where you have to step up and down, etc., all add up to some very technical riding, though there are lovely stretches of easy stuff in between. Keep your speed down. This was never designed for bikes.

The hardest spot is ahead is at mile 3.0 where the trail drops steeply to a rock notch that is almost narrow enough to kiss your handlebars. You have to lift the bike and shove it up ahead of you as you climb out. Above you there is a short bypass that is incredibly steep and treacherous—and worse in our opinion. But the lap marks on the lake shore prove why the bypass exists. When the lake is high, the lower trail is under water!

At mile 4.4 you roll into the parking lot. If you memorized the looks of those tricky turnoffs, you're ready to do the **Stanley-Schubarth Loop,** which takes you across the dam of Stanley Reservoir.

STANLEY-SCHUBARTH LOOP, 8.3-mile balloon loop using Boatman's Trail as access. Features a tour to Zoltan's Terrace overlook and Stanley Reservoir.

9,000   8.3 miles   9,000

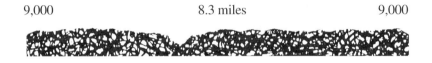

Okay, we're standing amid the aspens at the TOP of Backdoor Trail at it's T-junction with Stanley Rim Trial FS#722. Take a good look at this spot: You want to recognize it on the way back! We'll be turning right and following Stanley Rim to the east, but notice the fainter right turn just a few yards away. That's a short spur that dead-ends on a ridge, but it's a good place for a picnic.

Here your odometer should read about 0.9 miles from the Dikeside parking lot.

Now we begin the big roller coaster of **Stanley Rim**, a rutted old track through aspen and conifers with occasional glimpses of Rampart Reservoir. **Watch your odometer: There's a surprise ahead.**

Most overlooks are located at the top of a rise, but you'll still be traveling uphill through dense timber at mile 1.65 from the lake. Watch for a couple of boulders to your right immediately beside the road. They're about as big as tiny sports cars standing on end and they lean together to form a little triangular window at the bottom. Stop there, face the rocks and enter the trees, inclining to your right. Within just a few yards you step out onto a granite terrace, very broad and flat and hidden from the road, where ponderosa grow up through cracks in the terrace.

What a view! A vast rolling forest seems to stretch without interruption

all the long way to Pikes Peak. **The cone on your left is Ormes Peak,** named after the father of Robert Ormes, Manly Ormes, who founded the Pikes Peak Atlas. The late Robert Ormes served on the committee that I chaired to open Penrose-Rosemont Reservoir to public fishing a generation ago, the first such victory since 1913. He was a scrappy old gentleman who didn't like being told that he couldn't recreate on his own real estate. I've worn out many many of his maps. So with Ormes Peak and Pikes Peak side by side in this view, you can imagine how much this vista means to me, besides being darned, droolin' delicious, way too big to photograph. (You can visit Ormes Peak by doing the last trail in this chapter.)

Dolores and I cherish this Stanley Rim overlook. I found it while I was exploring alone and have never been able to find anyone else who has ever been there without our showing them, so this overlook feels like it belongs to me. I can't help wondering if Bob Ormes ever saw it.

To me, it's sort of like this: All the government officials I deal with feel emotionally that their own office is their own private space, even though it legally belongs to the public as a whole. Any such official would take personal exception to your trashing "his" office just because you happen to own it, too. And that's how I feel about my terrace.

The friends that we've taken here all voted to keep it out of the book because nobody wants to see it trashed. **Thousands of visitors could roll on by without ever discovering it. (We've watched many of them do just that!)** But having spent so many years battling the comfortable notion that the public's lands should be reserved for a privileged few, we had to tell you about it, too, because it belongs to all of us. So go and gape, as we do, but **don't let us catch you messing it up. This one has my name on the door.**

Now here's a kick: For all the climbing we seemed to do getting here, this overlook is only about a hundred feet higher than Rampart Reservoir's Dam! That's part of the reason why you see no lakes. We're lower than you think.

This glorious spot makes up for Stanley Rim's one failing: Though it traces the rim of a very pretty canyon, this rim trail has no view of Stanley Canyon itself! Too many trees in the way. Still, there's a lake view ahead.

Continue east. Old maps show the trail ahead to be blocked, but it isn't any more, and they also show a couple of side trails leading down from your right and and then joining to go back to Rampart Reservoir, which would make a nice loop. But we urge you to stay on the route we recommend because we've searched repeatedly for those side trails and can't find them. We found traces from the bottom, but they're pretty much history.

At mile 2.8 you climb up to a hilltop T-junction against a well-maintained gravel road. This is FS Road #303, linking Northfield Reservoir and Stanley Reservoir, both owned by the City of Colorado Springs. (The blocked side road to your right that you just passed on the way up here only goes to the same Northfield Road, so ignore it.)

DO NOT GO RIGHT OR SOUTH ON NORTHFIELD ROAD #303. It leads to a locked gate, where you would trespass on a closed watershed, but the Watershed Committee has gained permission for you to TURN LEFT HERE and switchback down through the pretty forest to Stanley, one of the jewels of the Rampart, now open to public fishing (with valid license). At mile 3.1 you should find Stanley's gate open.

Many years ago Stanley's fishing rights were leased to the Air Force Academy. That meant that city folks could go there to picnic and camp and watch cadets fish, but ordinary citizens were not allowed to fish for their own fish in their own lake! A bitter situation, indeed.

Even worse, banning public fishing also meant banning the Division of Wildlife's generous fish stocking program, and private stocking meant never enough fish for all the cadets who bought permits. A bitter lose-lose situation!

Now that Stanley is open to all, the DOW can stock it far more often, insuring that everyone—including the cadets—can have a better chance of catching fish. There is one temporary problem, however. This spring-fed lake is free of Whirling Disease, which is explained in our introduction. No joke, this disease is no health hazard to humans, but the disease spread to hatcheries before it was detected. For that reason, Stanley can only be stocked with fish free of the disease, and those are hard to come by right now. Stocking continues, but the truth is, Stanley will not come up to its full potential until the year 2001, when disease-free fish will be in good supply again.

This is a unique spot. Park County boasts a number of remote, stocked lakes that can only be reached by hiking, biking or riding horseback, but Stanley is El Paso County's first. (Nichols and Penrose-Rosemont are not remote, being located fairly close to parking lots. Camping is forbidden at those lakes.) The Utility road leading to Stanley will remain closed.

The little path that you see beside the lake goes all the way around, but having tried, we can assure you that it's entirely unsuitable for bikes and horses to the point of being no fun at all. It's a fisherman's trail. Indeed, the trail sometimes squeezes narrowly between barbed wire and the lake shore, but there is a gateway in the barbed wire at the first cove back to your left where a side trail leads outside of city property into a lovely aspen draw where people camp in the National Forest. Someday we hope volunteers can remove all this useless barbed wire.

Staying on the roadway, you'll cross the dam itself. The spillway at the other side is no problem. A steep little path leads down around it, but unless water is pouring over the spillway, which is rare, we generally go to the left and cross the bottom of the spillway, tiptoeing around the edge of the water.

Immediately on the other side you'll find the top of **Stanley Canyon Trail #707**, which leads down to the Academy. See AF Academy Area. You'll also find a washed out logging road next to the dam that shoots straight up the ridge. That is **Schubarth Trail #721**, which leads steeply uphill to join **Schubarth Road #307**.

It's a scenic grunt with lots of roots and ruts, but there are also gentler portions, taking you up through the woods to an iron sign that marks **Schubarth Trail** as closed to motorized vehicles. Just beyond that sign, the trail T-junctions against Schubarth Road, which is open to motor vehicles. We are now four miles above Backdoor or 4.9 miles from the Dikeside parking lot.

The route to our right is an extension of Schubarth Road. THE ROUTE TO YOUR LEFT IS BOTH SCHUBARTH TRAIL #721 AND SCHUBARTH ROAD #307. They split again farther along, but that's not part of our loop today. See Front Door to Schubarth.

TURN LEFT HERE and take off on another ridgetop roller coaster through dense timber studded with granite boulders. Eight tenths of a mile later, you'll pass a turnoff on your right for Hell Creek. Watch your odometer. It should read about 5.7 at Hell Creek. Don't turn there: Stay on the main track.

Go 0.6 miles farther (mile 6.3 from parking). At the top of a rise you'll find an iron gate to your left with an iron sign that says "Closed to Motor Vehicles, Camping and Fires." At this time there are a number of numbers here that we found confusing, but that might change. Just know that your way home is through that gate on a trail that we call **Boatman.**

Boatman's Trail ahead is much gentler and has waterbars that make whoop-tee-dos. It is so much fun that we have missed the next turnoff ourselves more than once, so watch the odometer and we'll try to show you how to go back the way you came. If you miss the next one, however, don't worry. You will intersect the popular Rampart Reservoir Shoreline Trail a half mile later (with the picnic ground straight ahead). Turn left at that intersection and you'll get back to your car by following the shore trail.

But let's find Stanley Rim. Ignore the dead-end greenroad that you see to your left about two tenths of a mile from Schubarth. The entrance to **Stanley Rim** is 0.7 miles from Schubarth and a total of seven miles from the parking lot on our loop. **It is purposely hidden!** You glimpse Pikes Peak, then lose it as you climb a rise, and atop a rise you find a number of deep ditches and downed wood on your left that hide the trail at mile 0.7. But if you go around this vehicle blockade, you'll find a clear doubletrack just beyond. That is **Stanley Rim.**

(Please do Boatman Loop first and you'll know this turnoff.)

Go just 0.4 miles on **Stanley Rim**, very gentle, and as you make a left-hand bend amid small aspen, l**ook for Backdoor on your right.** Your odometer should read about 7.4. Take that right onto **Backdoor** and then it's a breezy 0.9 miles down to the parking lot for a total balloon-loop distance of 8.3 miles.

See why this is one of our favorite rides?

RAINBOW GULCH TRAIL, Forest Service #714, 1.4 miles one way, elevation loss 120 ft., rated easy. Features gentle ski and bike trail to lake.

The access road to Rampart Reservoir's dam is closed in winter, but trails may be used by those who wish to hike or ski into the area, and Rainbow Gulch is the most popular access.

After leaving the Rampart Range Road, **Rainbow Gulch** slopes gently downhill to join the big trail that skirts the lake. Thus, it is the string on a balloon loop. It adds 2.8 miles to the journey, but is very easy. Good place to take folks who want a mountain hike without switchbacks.

Your path soon leaves the ponderosa pine forest and follows a grassy meadow and the artificial tributary to the lake. This is a great a ski trail, but is most popular with mountain bikers, hikers and equestrians. In winter, stay to the north side of the tributary where sun keeps that side free of ice.

RAMPART RESERVOIR TRAIL, Forest Service #700, officially a 12-mile loop but may be shorter, elevation gain-loss nil, rated easy for hiking and skiing, but has technical spots for bikes. Features lovely views and access to remote shores of Rampart Reservoir.

Rolling around the edge of Rampart Reservoir, this trail looks easy on the map and *is easy, but only for those who are hiking*! For mountain bikers, however, there are many challenging and technical spots! Long easy stretches tempt bikers to go too fast, then sudden, tight, narrow turns and technical surprises lead to spectacular diggers. The trail also has a lot of muddy spots where drainages come down to the lake, and bikes get messy, but this is definitely a premier ride! So slow down, be careful and enjoy the wonderful views. One hint, the southern edge of the lake is considered easier.

Team Telecycle in Woodland Park recommends that bikers ride clockwise for safety and other reasons. Be sure to pick up one of their free maps. It is much more detailed than anything we can do. We simply cannot improve on it.

Boats and fishing are permitted, but dogs must be on a leash and no overnight camping is allowed except at the pay campgrounds. No firearms, no fireworks, no open fires (grates only).

NICHOLS TRAIL, Forest Service #709, about 2.3 mile as a Y, elevation loss 280 ft., rated moderate. Features lake shore walk at Nichols Reservoir (fishing permitted).

9,000   2.3 miles   8,700

Nichols Reservoir finally free of its winter ice.

Nichols Trail begins at the Dikeside Overlook on the north end of the Rampart Reservoir Dam Parking Area, and provides access to the shores of Nichols Reservoir. It goes down through a ponderosa pine forest and follows a small drainage toward the lake. The trail forks at the reservoir to follow the lake shore. It generally stays about 30 feet above the water, following contours to stay level. Some of this work was done by the Youth Conservation Corps. The trail now goes all the way around the lake, except for the dam itself, which is closed to the public.

Nichols is stocked by the DOW with catchable rainbow trout and Snake River cutthroats, but this drinking water reservoir has many special rules to help protect the resource: no horses, no mountain bikes, no camping, no ice fishing, no boats or floatation devices of any kind, no swimming, wading or other body contact. Bait fishing is permitted. Dogs must be on a leash not longer than six feet and must stay 50 yards back from the water. You must stay off the dam. And please do not explore or fish around Northfield, located downstream to the east, until it is officially open to the public. A caretaker lives there and patrols the area.

By the way, you'll see various distances estimated for this trail, but that's because it's so hard to explain a Y-shaped trail. The lake shore is very close to the trailhead, but you must backtrack on either side of the lake because you cannot cross the dam.

BPW NATURE TRAIL, Forest Service #712, half-mile loop, elevation gain-loss 40 ft., rated easy. Features easy nature trail designed to serve everyone, including the blind and persons confined to wheelchairs.

The BPW Nature Trail is sponsored by the Colorado Federation of Business and Professional Women's Clubs and offers a wilderness experience with special facilities for blind and wheelchair visitors. The trail itself leads through three different kinds of ecosystems, including a willow bottomland, a ponderosa pine and a spruce-fir area. It has bridges, benches, and a wooden observation deck that overlooks Castaway Gulch. The path is about four feet wide and has a firm but natural tread.

This is a self-guiding nature trail with 14 stations along it. The station signs are also translated into Braille. Restrooms suitable for use by the physically handicapped are also provided.

DEVIL'S KITCHEN—ORMES PEAK LOOP, 3.8 miles, rated easy and moderate. Part-road and part trail ride.

9,280   3.8 miles   9,280

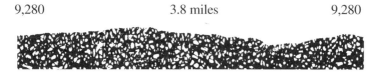

This little-used trail is fun and scenic and sorely needs more visitation to keep it in existence! One short section has deteriorated to resemble a game trail, but you should be able find it and follow it, if you follow our directions carefully.

Since this is a loop, you can start almost anywhere you find parking, but we're going to start at your first opportunity and go counter-clockwise. We strongly warn against trying this loop clockwise because you could easily miss the key turnoff and wander off toward a dead end at West Monument Canyon. When you see it for yourself, you'll understand.

Ormes Peak was named by the USGS after Manly Ormes, founder of the Pikes Peak Atlas and father of Robert Ormes, who continued to update his father's work.

ROAD DIRECTIONS: Follow our directions to Woodland Park and take the right fork (Loy Creek Road) to the intersection of Rampart Range Road. Turn right and go four miles to the entrance to Rampart Reservoir, but INSTEAD OF TAKING THAT PAVED ROUTE TO THE LAKE, RESET YOUR ODOMETER AND CONTINUE DOWN THE

RAMPART RANGE ROAD TOWARD COLORADO SPRINGS. At mile 2.1 from that intersection, turn left onto FS Road #303 marked for the Northfield Treatment Plant. One mile later at 3.1, turn right onto FS Road #302. You'll pass two left-hand turnoffs not marked on maps, one at 3.4 and another at 3.5, but stop and park to the left at the third at 3.8. Here you'll find the primitive route by which you'll return. It joins the Ormes Peak Road at a little triangle junction that leaves room for about four cars without blocking the primitive route.

Our journey begins by climbing the Ormes Peak Road, which is quite drivable by passenger car. It's a narrow roadway, very firm and not too steep, with occasional views of Pikes Peak, a very enjoyable ride. When it turns north, the downhill begins.

At mile 1.8 there is a fork. Turn right because the left fork soon dead-ends. Now our route grows rougher as it hooks down through a grassy-sloped area with large and widely spaced spruce, finally ending at a group of rounded granite boulders called the **Devil's Kitchen.** The name looks exotic, but it reminds us more of a kid's fort than anything devilish, a granite version of the forts we used to make out of huge rolled snowballs. In fact, it **looks more like the kitchen of the Pillsbury Doughboy!**

You can walk to the top without any scrambling. On top there is a weathered snag and a very small and level gravel area surrounded by boulders only about waist high. This is a lovely spot for a picnic, and on windy days you can hunker down here and still enjoy the view with some protection. The view gives glimpses of distant mountains, probably the Collegiates, plus Black Forest and even the shoulder of Pikes Peak past Ormes Peak, which from here looks like a green breast. Stretched below you is the wooded drainage that is your next destination, but there's a trick getting there.

Almost any downhill route would take you to that drainage, but we trust you don't want to get tangled up bushwhacking, which is considered most unecological for mountain bikes. Returning to the cul-de-sac below, you'll see a very plain side road. As you face the rocks, it's immediately to your left.

Don't take it!

That leads the right direction, but dead-ends above some very gnarly rocks and timber. Instead, look to the little draw between that side-road and the rocks themselves. There you'll see a faint track that looks very much like some old wash, not a trail at all. Actually, that used to be a primitive road, now just a single track, more like a game trail as it angles down toward the drainage. Increased traffic will doubtless make it plainer, but at this time, it is more like a trampled grass path down below. You can tell it was once a road because of the large stumps along its route. One big one on your left, more than waist high, was cut down by an ax, but since the log is missing, you know it was hauled out by road long ago.

You'll have to duck beneath a huge fir, still living, but toppled across the trail, then cross over a flattened dead one, go around another. Let's just say this trail needs work. Ignore a true game trail that joins from your right. **Continue down about a quarter of a mile, through a trampled campsite amid dark timber, and cross the tiny creek on a set of rotting logs. Just on the other side, you'll find a green double-track leading along the creek. Of course, we'll be turning left to climb up this creek toward our vehicle.**

But look at this intersection. If you were breezing down this double-track, doing the loop clockwise, this junction

Claw marks from a small bear that climbed this aspen to investigate a squirrel's hole

would be very very easy to miss, which would send you off down creek toward a dead end above West Monument Canyon. That's why we're having you do it counter-clockwise because this way you can't miss your turn.

As you start up the creek, your revegetating doubletrack is fairly easy until you cross the stream at mile 3.1 and then it gets steeper and more eroded. At mile 3.3 a tributary is actually running down the trail itself amid a mossy forest. Lots of aspen. **At mile 3.4, you encounter a false fork where both routes simply rejoin higher up, but at that point, look to your right at the big aspen with a woodpecker-squirrel hole high on its trunk. That trunk is clearly scarred by the claws of a black bear that climbed up and scratched at the hole!**

From here on there are no more surprises as the old double track switchbacks up to our parking spot on Ormes Peak Road.

MORE RAMPART RANGE AREA TRAILS

The Devil's Head formation as seen from the south.

Devil's Head and Devil's Head Trail
Zinn Trail at Devil's Head
Balanced Rock—Mt. Herman Loop
Ice Cave—Winding Stairs Loop
Hotel Gulch

We title this chapter More Rampart Range Trails because the Woodland Park chapter contains many others. It's a big place.

The Rampart Range is a beautiful—but confusing!—high mountain shelf that extends from the outskirts of Denver to Ute Pass. Even orienteers get lost on the Rampart because there are so many unmapped routes left over from the days when this forest was systematically logged. Every ridge seems to have an ancient rutted doubletrack and every finger ridge seems to have a spur that dead-ends. Names, numbers and signs are not very common and some are flat wrong. This is the most mismapped region we know of.

Which brings up a point. People who get lost in the woods are generally well advised to head downhill to find water, because all streams lead to civilization. But there are two notable exceptions in this book: the Lost Creek Wilderness, where streams keep vanishing into box canyons, and the entire Rampart Area, where streams lead down wild and wooly and dangerous gulches that drop off the shelf. If you should get lost, never take a chance on getting hurt as well. In the Rampart, look for trails or old double-tracks on ridgetops. By following one for a ways, you'll know if you're headed toward civilization or not by changes in the track's quality. Old logging roads are like bull-whips, wide, smooth and nice toward the civilized end, but increasingly narrow and nasty on the other end. **If your route keeps improving, you're headed out.**

Frankly, if it weren't for hunters and four-wheelers and motorcyclists, many of these old routes would have vanished long ago, but now mountain bicyclists, horse-riders and hikers are discovering that a doubletrack can be just as much fun and just as scenic as a singletrack. In some places, my wife and I can ride along together instead of one following the other.

Our future books will detail more of this wilderness, but here are some of our favorite haunts, beginning with one that may disappear:

DEVIL'S HEAD AREA

Devil's Head Trail
Zinn Trail

Devil's Head is the last forest fire lookout post in the Pike National Forest, but it's major attraction is the view. On a clear day, you can spot landmarks for a hundred miles around. Denver and Cherry Creek Reservoir almost look close by. Long's Peak stands in the distance to the north, and to the west you can see the Collegiate Peaks— Princeton, Yale, etc.— beyond Buena Vista. To the south you can see beyond Pikes Peak to the Sangre de Cristo Range, west of Pueblo.

For now at least, Devil's Head still operates as a fire spotting lookout, but the other six like it have given way to more modern methods: radar, aircraft and the many radio and phone-linked personnel who populate the region. Fire prevention seems to be working. On average, people account for slightly less than half the forest fires in the Pike National Forest. Lightning causes the majority. (Colorado also ranks second in lightning deaths, just behind Florida, so be careful.)

Unfortunately, it is lightning danger that may close the Devil's Head facility. When lightning strikes Devil's Head, it's no act of God. Just the opposite. Given it's lofty location, it would take an act of God to keep lightning from striking it. **The ranger who lives there has always sat on a stool that has big glass insulators on each leg, the kind you see on power poles!**

The Forest Service needs to outfit Devil's Head with modern lightning protection. Cost is not so much the problem as bureaucracy. You see, the FS has to put such a job out for competitive bids, and because the spot is so remote, the bidders refuse to go up there unless they know they've got the job, and nobody gets the job if bidders don't go.

We believe the solution lies with an individual benefactor who might

sidestep the bureaucratic red tape by simply donating the job so that government funds aren't involved. **Know anybody with $20,000 for a good cause?**

End of solicitation. Now about the trail!

COME EQUIPPED FOR A HIKE! The trail leading to the lookout may be only 1.37 miles, but it climbs almost 1,000 feet, and if you add in Zinn Trail, the total round trip is 3.75 miles. **Unfortunately, many of its 10,000 visitors per season come unprepared,** not bringing water or proper footgear for this steep hike. There is a faucet at the trailhead, but no water at the top, so bring plenty.

Dogs must be on a leash. Bikes and horses are allowed, but are not really appropriate because of the heavy foot traffic. Camping is banned along trails, but three large pay campgrounds have been provided along the road leading to the parking lot.

The name Devil's Head refers to one of the mountain's granite outcrops, which some think looks like a devil's profile. This can only be seen from the Rampart Range Road just to the north, but even with a FS sketch to go by, it takes a large dose of imagination and a little squinting.

The lookout opens about Memorial Day and closes in mid to late September.

ROAD DIRECTIONS: DEVIL'S HEAD is located one mile east of the scenic Rampart Range Road, 42 miles from Denver and 52 miles north of Colorado Springs. From Denver, take Santa Fe Drive (Hwy. 85) south to Sedalia, then 67 southwest to pick up the Rampart Range Road at Indian Creek Campground.

From Colorado Springs, you can try the main entrance to the Rampart Range Road in the southern part of the Garden of the Gods. Or you can bypass a lot of gravel by taking 67 north of Woodland Park for 10 miles to the gravel road marked for Rainbow Falls, a pay fishing area. From here to the Rampart is 10 miles, but after only a quarter of a mile be sure to turn right onto FS-348, then right again at the next prominent fork (unmarked). When you reach the Rampart, you are seven miles from the DEVIL'S HEAD turnoff.

DEVIL'S HEAD TRAIL, FS #611, 1.37 miles one way, elevation gain 948 ft., rated moderately difficult. Features steep climb to fire lookout post with panoramic view.

This well-developed trail has some tables and benches along its climb, as well as informative plaques sponsored by the Colorado Federation of Business and Professional Women's Clubs. The forest is dense, but has occasional lookouts. Read our introduction for special information.

Near the top, your trail T-junctions, with **Zinn Trail** to the left and **Devil's**

Head Trail continuing to the right. Soon you pass through a narrow slot in the granite and curve past some restrooms before finding the clearing where the ranger's cabin lies. **At the far edge of the clearing is a long stairway (143 steps) that jogs up huge boulders to the lookout post on top. If you think this looks high from the bottom of the steps, wait until you see the drop off on the other side! No place for acrophobics.**

You are welcome to enter the lookout post and visit with the ranger (buy a FS T-shirt: The ranger carried them up on his back along with the rest of his groceries and supplies), but your stay must be limited by the press of other visitors.

ZINN TRAIL, FS #615, 0.5 miles one way, elevation loss 400 ft., rated moderate. Features spur to overlook of Pikes Peak.

Leaving the Devil's Head Trail, Zinn Trail winds down through a cool glade, ending at a cliff-edge overlook where Pikes Peak is framed in a notch of granite. This is well worth the side-trip, but is ignored by many. A nearby bronze plaque dedicates the trail to Commander Ralph Theodore Zinn, a conservationist.

MORE RAMPART RANGE TRAILS

ROAD DIRECTIONS: Because it is so very long—and gravel—many adventurers drive the Rampart Range Road end-to-end only once: Then they start looking for ways to use paved roads to cut down their gravel driving. The following three adventures are closer to Woodland Park than to Sedalia, so many Denverites prefer to take the Interstate down to Colorado Springs, then west to Woodland Park, or they take 285 to 126 at Pine Junction and go down through Deckers to 67 north of Woodland Park, very scenic either way. Besides, these turnoffs on the Rampart can be tricky to find without watching your odometer, and odometer readings are more accurate in short distances. If you start your odometer at the northern entrance to the Rampart Range Road, your readings are unlikely to match ours.

So let's begin at Hwy. 24 in Woodland Park. Turn off Hwy 24 between Team Telecycle and McDonald's. Go 2.9 miles to the Loy Fork. Both forks lead to the gravel Rampart Range Road, but take the left fork.

To find BALANCED ROCK—MT. HERMAN LOOP and ICE CAVE— WINDING STAIR LOOP, go left at the Loy Fork and left again (north)

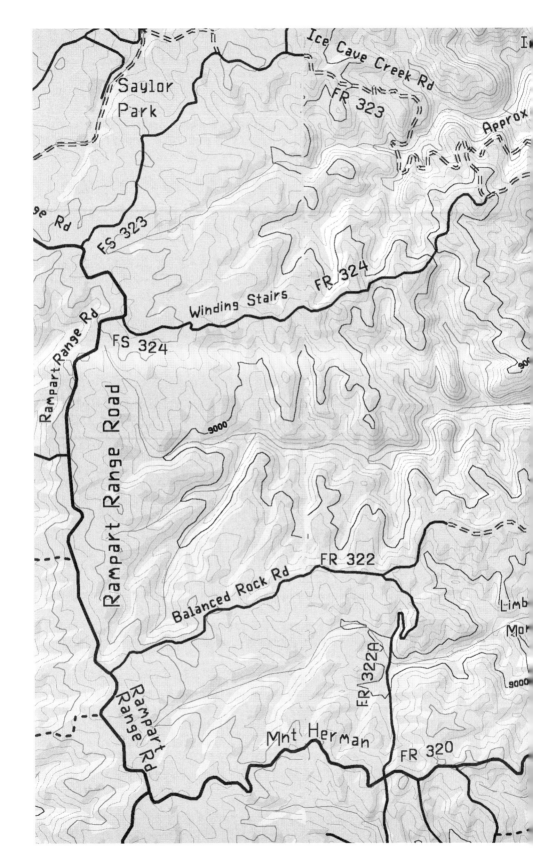

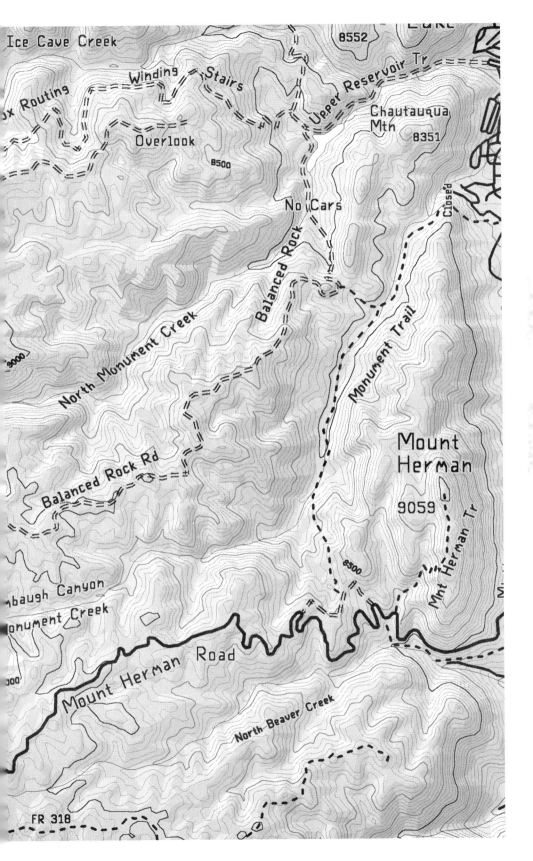

Long-lost Balanced Rock in 1912,
courtesy of Colorado Mountain Club
Archives, finally rediscovered today..

onto the Rampart Range Road. Watch your odometer because signs may be missing. Go 2.5 miles and find MT. HERMAN ROAD #320 on your right. Go one mile farther and find BALANCE ROCK ROAD #322 on your right.

Go 2.3 miles farther to mile 5.8 and WINDING STAIR #323 is on your right (this one can be recognized by its view of Pikes Peak which pops immediately into view just as you start up it). Good parking here. ICE CAVE CREEK ROAD #324 is next on your right 0.7 of a mile later. Then HOTEL GULCH #346 is another third of a mile farther, but we do not recommend doing Hotel Gulch from this end. More directions will follow.

BALANCED ROCK-MOUNT HERMAN LOOP, about 7.5 miles, rated moderate with one tough climb. Features easy side trail (about 3.5 miles up and back) with beaver ponds. NOTE: The rest of Balanced Rock down to Palmer Lake is not included in this mileage and is very gnarly and difficult.

9,360   7.5 miles   9,360

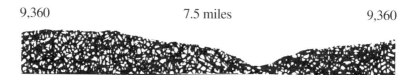

It takes a very wild wilderness to swallow up a famous landmark this huge, but our Mystery Challenge is solved! Out of thousands of readers, only Mike Henry, intrepid author of our CD-ROM companion, *Trails Guide 2001*, managed to locate the long-lost Balanced Rock, now known to be two miles east of 322A. (Randy Jacob, author of *Colorado Trail*, found and relost it and gave us clues.) Mike's new-and-dazzling-improved CD has a color photo framed just like the 1912 one. From the road, it looks like any other boulder, obscured by trees, yet those aspens do not hide it at all in the photo, which is taken from the rock's south side looking north toward the road. Compare!

A view from Balanced Rock Road

And by the way, Balanced Rock Road was not a logging road like almost all the rest in the region. It was actually a stagecoach route built in the 1890s to connect Palmer Lake with the mining areas in the mountains.

Our loop involves a piece of the Rampart Range Road, which is pretty but can also be busy and dusty, so we like to ride that portion first while we're still fresh and alert. The best parking is along **Balanced Rock Road #322** about one quarter mile from its intersection with Rampart Range Road.

From here we go south on Rampart Range Road #300 one mile and turn left on Mount Herman Road #320. (more parking on your left). This is a fairly major access, but has less traffic and much better views of Pikes Peak and rock formations. It's a winding downhill route through mostly conifer forest, with some aspen.

Watch for a four-way intersection 2.2 miles from the intersection with Rampart Range Road. To the right is #314 to Ensign Gulch, but **we'll be turning left onto #322A here.** Someone keeps taking down its carsonite, but there is an iron pipe-post that looks like it used to hinge a gate on the right of #322A about 18 feet down from the road. Maybe vandals will leave that.

Right away there is brush to your left, marking a tributary that crosses your path a half mile later. In spring this makes a puddle deep and muddy enough to trap passenger cars. At the bottom the valley opens up with grassy clearings in several directions. At its center is a tall granite formation that technical climbers enjoy.

This three-fingered valley is by far the most beautiful place we have ever seen trashed so badly, not by campers but by hearty party folks whose idea of cleanup is to heap all their glass and trash into huge fire pits. Some of the litter has military commissary markings and almost all has bullet holes, so we cringe to recommend this spot for family camping, but it could certainly benefit from better care! Please pack out some trash.

The trail downstream quickly becomes a singletrack and descends into willows. **There's a better side trail just upstream. This is not part of our main loop but worth doing if you have time.**

Cross the culvert, going north, and you'll see another abused party ground at the base of Rattlesnake Hill to your left. The steep track that goes up there is closed to motorized vehicles and goes up to join #322A. At its base, between a rock and the stream, there is a tiny singletrack. Robert Houdek of the Pikes Peak Atlas writes that, "A visit here is required of all Colorado Springs residents."

It is pretty nice, though the trail starts out badly, faint and boggy. There are several soggy places within the first third of a mile where oozing tributaries cross and where motorcycles have cut up the mud, so we gave up there and hid our bikes in the willows, only to discover that the entire rest of the trail would be great on bikes! Slog it out, folks.

The trail is a distinct, hard gravel singletrack that gently follows the valley's edge, always staying to the north of the stream. It is surprisingly easy for most of its 1.7 mile length (approximate). To your right the hillside is generally grassy with widely spaced trees, lots of them aspen. The stream soon becomes a long string of active beaver ponds, the first of which has a stick lodge in the middle. We saw ducks and frogs and lots of wildlife sign.

Back to the main track #322A, we continue our loop by going north past a high rock that comes closer to being balanced than anything we have discovered anywhere near the Balanced Rock Road, which is up ahead. But first you have to push up some steep switchbacks.

A mile above the valley floor, there is a strange intersection, where the Rattlesnake Hill route joins from your left. Keep to your right and shortly you come to **Balanced Rock Road #322**. Turn left and you'll go 2.3 miles to your car for a total loop of approximately 7.5 miles (not counting the 3.5-mile up-and-back Monument Valley side trail).

But while we're here, we're going to show you a long side-trip to see Palmer Lake's Upper Reservoir! (See Monument/Palmer Lake/Black Forest) At the intersection of #322A and Balanced Rock Road is a sign warning "Palmer Lake Watershed. Road Closed Ahead." Which is true, but the road is open to hard-core four-wheelers almost all the way to the open lake, a distance of about six miles! And even when you reach the gate near the lake, it's only closed to motorized vehicles, not boots and bikes and fishermen.

This route is very scenic with wonderful views of rock formations, at first to your left. There are a couple of false forks where side trails simply rejoin the main track. After several miles, the view switches sides showing off the formations along Monument Creek. Don't' miss the spur to your left about three miles from 322A's intersection. It leads up shortly to a grand overlook of the North Monument Creek area. Great place for lunch.

After about five miles you'll see part of Palmer Reservoir in the distance. The trail gets steep as it snakes down to end at a steel gate in an aspen draw. The lake is just out of sight around the corner.

Pikes Peak from Ice Cave Road.

ICE CAVE CREEK—WINDING STAIRS LOOP, 8.7 miles, rated easy to start, then more difficult, then easy on return. Scenic ridge tour including quartz quarry.

9,317   8.7miles   9,317

Logging at the Winding Stairs entrance off the Rampart Range Road has resulted in much better parking there, so we're going to start at there and go counter-clockwise.

As soon as you turn onto **Winding Stairs Road #324**, Pikes Peak suddenly looms, dominating the view. We set our odometers here and began the roller-coaster ride along the double track that traces the high ground to the east. You soon leave the logged area and begin a high forest ride. At mile 2.6 you come to an intersection with a carsonite marker in front of a round boulder. To the left is **FS# 323 (Ice Cave)** and straight ahead is **FS# 324, which is called Winding Stairs on maps but simply ain't.** Here's the story:

You've been on Winding Stairs all right, but Winding Stairs should end at

another arm of Palmer Lake's upper reservoir. FS#324 simply doesn't go there. Go and see. It's a very scenic ridgetop tour with spectacular views both left and right. But after about 1.6 miles of awesome scenery, #324 dead-ends amid huge rocks on a ridge from which there was never any way down.

Now go back to the intersection with #323 for the answer.

Turning north onto #323, we actually climb a little before the path starts down toward the creek bottom. Within half a mile, however, there is an extremely washed out side trail to your right. That's the historic Winding Stair that climbs down about three miles to the lake! We hiked down to make sure.

Apparently it parallels #324, but lower on the ridge. We were shown this route by Leaning Larry Leaveck of the Colorado Four-Wheelers, but it's too far gone even for his customized tree-climber. The last half mile is like a perilous washed out ski jump, mercifully ending in a glade at the lake's first arm. If you look for it from the bottom, walk up the glade in the first cove. When you see a house-sized boulder in the middle of the valley ahead, look back to the left for **Winding Stairs,** almost hidden in the trees.

If this route can be improved, properly mapped and marked, it would form about an 18-mile loop involving a tour of the lake and Balanced Rock on the return. Only advanced hikers should try it at this time, and then clockwise. As Palmer Lake Marshal Dale T. Smith put it, "On a bike, it's more than your life is worth."

Back to our descent into Ice Cave Canyon, continuing our Ice Cave—Winding Stairs Loop.

As you enter the canyon, dense evergreens give you only the most fleeting blinks of majestic rock formations downstream. At mile 4.3 from the Rampart, you arrive at the crossing of Ice Cave Creek, a brushy hollow where again trees block any distant view. Dr. Jerry Parsons, retired business manager for Lewis-Palmer School Dist., confirmed what we had been told that the the "ice caves" are like the false cave at Florissant Fossil Beds, formed by huge boulders that toppled together. Although the flash flood of 1965 must have rearranged some of those boulders, the Ice Caves are still there, but very dangerous to explore: "My son has explored some of those caves. If you don't have ropes and special equipment and know exactly what you're doing, you're not going to make it back out of there."

There are lots of raspberries and more aspen along the section that climbs steeply out of the canyon. You see more and more quartz in the road until at mile 5.7 there is a mine to your left with a short access road that cul-de-sacs around a large quartz deposit. Soon after (5.8) you find #324B taking off to your right. Stay on the main track and enjoy a gentler climb through mixed forest. At mile 6.3 take the left fork. The right fork is unmarked, but leads down to private property in Saylor Park. At mile 8.0 you reach the Rampart Range Road. Turn left and watch for traffic. Another seventh of a mile takes you back to your vehicle at the Winding Stairs turnoff.

HOTEL GULCH,10 miles up and back, rated more difficult.   Tour beside stream and beaver ponds.

7,829   5 miles   7,829

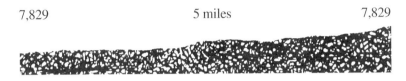

On the map, Hotel Gulch looks like a major gravel access to the Rampart Range Road, but it's not that at all! Instead, it is a narrow and rough double-track far better suited to mountain bikes than to passenger cars. Cars with high ground clearance can drive this route, but there are very few places where cars can pass each other. Indeed, it is so small that you can easily mistake side roads (not on maps) for the main route, so pay attention. Most side roads are, in fact, driveways on private property. Yet all this makes Hotel Gulch a lovely ride for fat tire fans, a charming forest route.

WARNING: A local bicycle guide suggests that you ride Hotel Gulch as a loop, using the next road south to return, but that road is closed to the public!

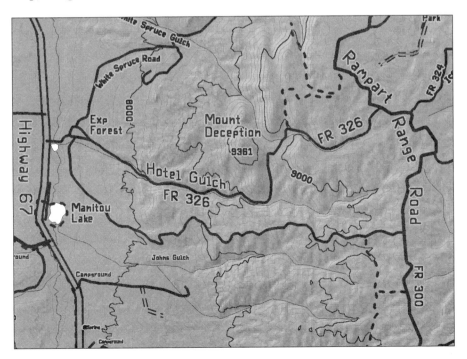

That road, usually marked #346 on maps, is closed by private property gates in the middle. Indeed, the FS has recently changed its number at the top in order to discourage the notion that it is one through road.

ROAD DIRECTIONS TO HOTEL GULCH: DO NOT take the the Rampart Range Road turnoff at Woodland Park! Instead, turn right onto 67 at the Woodland Park intersection marked for Deckers. Go 8.2 miles north and just past Manitou Lake look for a big sign marked Rocky Mountain Forest and Range Experiment Station. Turn right onto a major gravel road, then park on the right near the creek. As you look east across this little valley, you'll see the main road curve northeast and two small turnoffs to the right. Take the second right turnoff. As you enter the trees, you'll find the handsome stone buildings of the Experiment Station.

We set our odometers in front of the Experiment Station. Built during the depression, these lovely stone buildings show how the government liked to get long-lasting and artful quality for some of its public works money. They are still in use today.

As you head east on the tiny double-track, you go through a gate with a stream on your left. At only 0.8 from the station, you find a good-looking road joining from the left, but don't take it.

This is just the first of many unmarked side routes. Most of them will come from the left, so generally bear right and always follow the creek. You'll go through a fence with a sign saying **"Bramblewood, Carter Residence." You are now on a federal road through private property for awhile, so stay on track and respect private property.**

Next you come to a three-way intersection. Keep to the right and follow the creek. We have suggested that the Forest Service mark this route better to avoid confusion, but they are spread thin. On maps this is known as FS #346, but we saw no such signs.

At mile 3.1 you cross a cattle guard. Your route is through mixed aspen and ponderosa, in June graced with Columbines, and at mile 3.6 you join another creek called Spruce. **Here you'll see a a grassy slope on your left and a series of beaver ponds along the creek to your right. We enjoyed fishing those. Notice how the tall evergreens died, soaked to death, when beaver built the largest pond among them. This was our favorite part of the route,** but if you want a real workout, keep grunting up through the woods to mile 4.7 where you find the Rampart Range Road (marked only as #300 at the intersection). Going back is a fun downhill. Adding the little distance between the Experiment Station and your car makes this almost a 10-mile up-and-back and all of it legal, done this way.

FLORISSANT FOSSIL BEDS NATIONAL MONUMENT

Approaching Twin Rocks in winter along Twin Rocks Trail

Twin Rocks Trail
A Walk Through Time Trail
Petrified Forest Loop
Sawmill Trail
Boulder Creek Trail
Hornbek Wildlife Loop
Shootin' Star Trail

This is Colorado's Pompeii, an area smothered by volcanic ash and mud flows millions of years ago, preserving everything from insects to animals in deadly detail. Even the hairs on the insects' legs can be seen in these fossils. Many thousands of Florissant specimens have been collected by museums around the world. The private quarry nearby recently yielded two bird fossils with clearly defined feathers. That shop deserves a visit, too.

Nothing in Arizona's famed Petrified Forest can match the fossils at Florissant for sheer size. Eighty to ninety stumps of giant Sequoia redwoods stand in the Florissant Fossil Beds National Monument, but most remain buried to preserve them. **The largest stump is 13 feet in diameter and 41.9 feet around!** When alive, this redwood probably stood 300 feet high and was at least 700 years old.

It is a serious offense to take any fossil, not even the smallest piece, and you are urged to quickly report anyone who does! This is our national treasure. Visitors themselves have proven to be the most effective and zealous guardians of it all. Besides, you can buy legal specimens collected from outside the park at a shop nearby or you can pay to hunt your own at a deposit near Forissant itself.

Since its trail system is so gentle, you would think that this would be one of the finest cross-country ski areas along the Front Range. However, its high park terrain (meadows with scattered ponderosa) is so sunny that snow melts off faster than it would in dense forest. The Visitors Center remains open and staffed all winter, offering information, book sales and warm restrooms. All trails are gentle enough for skiing, but those on the east side of the highway are more challenging.

The Monument charges a small entrance fee year-round. This fee is required for all activiities and areas of the Monument. **This is a day-use area and hours of operation are under review at this printing, so please call 719-748-3253 for information.**

The Monument is home to elk and ground-nesting birds, so no dogs are allowed. Department of Interior rules forbid mountain bikes. At this time, horses still use the backcountry, but horses are prohibited on all trails and in all developed public use areas. Check with Rangers before coming. Snowmobiles are also banned. No camping, no hunting, no firearms, no fireworks, no open fires (grills only), no collecting of fossils, flowers, or other souvenirs. Absolutely none.

ROAD DIRECTIONS: The community of Florissant is located on Highway 24 between Divide and Lake George, 39 miles west of Colorado Springs. At Florissant take Teller County 1 south for 2.5 miles and turn right to the Visitors Center. To find Shootin' Star trailhead, continue on Teller 1 and turn left on Lower Twin Rock Road. Go 1.6 miles and park at the Barksdale Picnic Area on your left

TWIN ROCK TRAIL, 2.2 miles one way from Shootin' Star, rated easy. Features aspen draw tour past pond to rock formations.

The most scenic trail at the Fossil Beds is also the newest. It can be accessed two ways. You can start from the Visitor Center, as our map shows, or you can save 0.4 miles by going via the **Hornbek Wildlife Loop** with parking at

Pond along Twin Rocks Trail

the Hornbek Homestead (well worth seeing in itself). Either way, you begin by hiking across meadow to an intersection with **Shootin' Star** just inside the trees. The first part of the trail was borrowed from Shootin' Star, and skirts the edge of the ponderosa forest. You cross a small drainage on an old dam, then go over a little ridge to cross a more active stream on a fine bridge.

Here's where the rock formations begin, but they grow larger as you make your way up the left side of this tiny stream. You pass a big pond lined with aspen on the far side, negotiate a soggy patch using a U-shaped boardwalk and keep heading up. As you reach the edge of a big valley, you can see Twin Rocks ahead. Crossing the valley, you eventually arrive at the foot of one of the Twin Rocks. When your trail starts going uphill more steeply, you are near the park boundary, which is well marked. Go back the way you came.

PONDEROSA LOOP TRAIL, 0.5 mile loop, elevation gain nil, rated easy. Features short self-guided nature tour.

This gentle loop provides a quick but excellent introduction to the ancient environment of the area, the geologic events leading to fossil preservation and the sharp contrast between ancient Florissant and the modern montane ecosystem.

The path features giant petrified sequoia redwood stumps and an outcropping of fossil bearing shale. Numbered posts along the way point out features explained

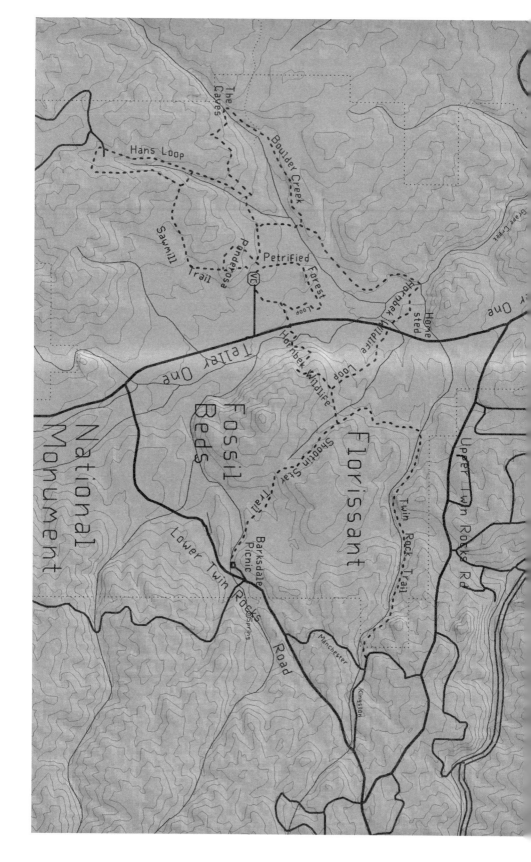

in the pamphlet. The tour only takes about twenty minutes.

PETRIFIED FOREST LOOP one mile loop, elevation gain nil, rated easy. Features geological time line interpretive trail with more giant fossilized stumps.

This trail covers part of the bank and bed of prehistoric Lake Florissant. Big Stump, one of the largest of the silica giants, was supposed to be cut into sections for shipment to the Columbian Exposition in Chicago, but the saw blades broke and can still be seen sticking out of the stump. The last portion of the trail is set up as a time line, with every two inches of the trail representing the passage of a million years. Another pamphlet is provided.

SAWMILL TRAIL, 2.2 mile loop, elevation gain-loss 200 feet, rated easy to moderate. Features scenic and varied terrain with sawmill ruins.

Starting behind the Visitors Center, Sawmill comes off the Ponderosa Loop and winds around a meadowy area, eventually climbing a ridge with a view of Pikes Peak. Then it comes down a drainage, skirting meadow and ponderosa forest to the Visitor Center.

HANS LOOP, 1.2-mile loop, elevation gain-loss 80 ft., rated moderate. Features homestead ruins.

This is an extension of Sawmill Trail, leading down from the ridge to a meadow valley with a wetlands habitat. It passes the ruins of a rustic homestead, then follows the stream down to Sawmill.

BOULDER CREEK TRAIL, 1.75-mile loop, elevation gain 120 ft., rated easy. Features unusual rock formation.

Boulder Creek Trail is a long branch off the Hornbek Wildlife Trail, leading up a sunny meadow with a stream and ponds. At the park boundary, you find The Caves, actually huge boulders that have tipped together to form a cave-like place where the stream flows through. A new route leads over the ridge to Sawmill, but is not included in our figures. Boulder Creek Trail was once known as Cave Trail.

HORNBEK WILDLIFE LOOP, 4-mile loop, elevation gain-loss 120 ft., rated easy to moderate. Features stroll to Hornbek homestead.

Beginning at Sawmill Trail near the Visitor Center, **Hornbek Wildlife Loop** leads through scattered trees and long broad meadows that were once the bed of prehistoric Lake Florissant. As the trail nears the road, you find the Hornbek homestead, faithfully recreated using old techniques, complete with bunkhouse, carriage shed, barn and root cellar. Be sure to pick up the free brochure at the Hornbek gate. It tells the story of a hard and plucky frontier woman who raised kids and cattle with admirable success.

Then your path crosses the road, arching up through the east meadow to link with **Shootin' Star** before returning to the Visitors Center. By the way, what looks like dog poop on the trail is actually coyote. Very dry specimens show this scat to be chuck full of hair because coyotes thrive on small varmints such as mice. They eat more mice than most cats ever see.

SHOOTIN' STAR TRAIL, 2 miles one way, elevation gain 80 ft., loss 120 ft., rated easy to moderate. Features scenic link with Hornbek.

Shootin' Star Trail is named after the nearby ranch, which was named after the wildflower so common here in early summer. Its highest elevation is at the southern trailhead at Barksdale Picnic Area. From here, the trail crosses a meadow, goes over a wooded ridge and then becomes **Twin Rock Trail** just inside the trees above a grassy slope leading to **Hornbek.** Cross-country skiers may want to start from the Hornbek homestead parking lot instead, because this would make the return trip downhill.

The Hornbek Homestead was lovingly recreated using old methods.

MUELLER STATE PARK and DOME ROCK WILDLIFE AREA

Dome Rock Wildlife Area is no longer part of Mueller State Park, a great disappointment to mountain bikers, but intended to better protect the bighorn.

Once the haunt of outlaws, rustlers and moonshiners, Mueller State Park and Dome Rock Wildlife Area is still a very wild land, a place of grassy meadows and lofty overlooks, of granite cliffs and aspen groves, with elk and deer and bighorn sheep, with a tumbling trout steam and a total of 12.000 acres (about 19 square miles) of forest laced with 80 miles of non-motorized trails.

Located between Cripple Creek and Divide, this popular area is now divided between two State authorities: Both offer hiking, horseback riding, cross-country skiing, snowshoeing and limited fishing. But only the northern State Park offers mountain biking and campground camping. By design, it's high-use development area is limited to only one corner of the Park. The rest—the vast backcountry—simply cannot be seen by car! (See Dome Rock)

Warning: It's a big place, unified by a trail system that is a genuine maze, and since overnight camping is not allowed in backcountry, you have to find your way back before nightfall. We describe some Wildlife Area trails as traditionally accessed through the northern Park entrance. Be careful.

ONLY THE TRAIL SYSTEM UNIFIES TWO 'PARKS'

This area is like two "parks" in one—a full service State Park in the north (where you pay to enter), plus a primitive DOW Wildlife Area in the south (with no entrance fee). Hunting is banned in the northern Park, but **seasonal hunting is allowed in the Wildlife Area to control animal numbers. Dates for hunting season change, so always wear orange reflective cap or vest in the fall.**

In the northern State Park, vehicle campers can reserve pull-out, back-in or drive-through campsites with electricity, picnic tables and fire grills. Conveniently located nearby are potable water, sanitary sewage dump, restrooms, showers, vending machines and laundry facilities. Twenty-two walk-in tent camping sites are also available near the parking lots, and **bear-proof food storage boxes have been installed. Campers who do not use them may be cited.**

PLEASE RESERVE YOUR CAMPSITE WELL IN ADVANCE. Visitors without reservations are often turned away. CALL 1-800-678-2267.

SPECIAL RESTRICTIONS ON DOGS

DOGS ARE NOT PERMITTED IN BACKCOUNTRY IN EITHER AREA, though they are allowed at the State Park's campsites, so long as they remain strictly on a leash. Since your dog may not relish being tied up at camp all day, it might be a good idea to consider leaving your pets at home.

Even the best-behaved dogs cannot help but leave a chemical message in their urine, which marks territory as belonging to them and warns wildlife to stay away. Wildlife-watching is a special feature here, largely because the area has not been scent-marked. Trips can also be ruined by run-ins with skunks, porcupines or bears, so you owe it to your family and to your pet to consider leaving your dog at home.

A-MAZING TRAILS

No kidding, you have to watch where you're going because the trail system is truly a maze! That's because the Mueller Ranch was patched together from smaller ranches, each of which developed its crude roads. Faced with many confusing routes, rangers tried to close off some tracks and eliminated them from maps, but you'll still find them in the woods, so beware. These old homestead and logging roads are wide double tracks, sometimes washed and rutted, sometimes steep, lots of fun without lots of danger. You'll have a blast. There are no dare-devil single-tracks at Mueller, but we enjoy biking everything open to mountain bicycles and our descriptions reflect that perspective.

Don't use older maps (or our older editions) because trail names and numbers have changed. Our guide is the first ever published with detailed topography. The Division of Wildlife plans to continue using the same trail names.

Most trails begin with a metal gate and look at first like service roads. In a way, they still are because rangers patrol with trucks and all terrain vehicles, as well as on foot. We have encountered rangers in the woods at Mueller far more than anywhere else in our area, so behave yourself. The rules are meant to protect the resource—and you.

Almost all of these trails lead downhill from the trailhead, which means you can breeze a long ways into the woods and have a real grunt getting back. Know your limitations and turn back in plenty of time to return to your car. If you're going to ski or snowshoe here (see special rules for the Wildlife Area), it's best to learn your way around before snow covers the trails. Make sure that someone knows where you went and, of course, don't go alone. If you do venture out alone into the State Park, let Park rangers know so they can watch for your return.

In the past, ranch buildings scattered around the Park have saved lives by serving as emergency shelters for stranded skiers, but **overnighters are strictly forbidden. Most buildings are boarded up to help prevent vandalism and are posted "Danger, Keep Out" because their rodents can transmit disease to people. Just know that rangers are wise to the ploy of phony emergencies.**

HORSEBACKING MUELLER STATE PARK

If you bring horses, either unload at the State Park's Livery parking (use Elk Meadow #18 or Livery #20) or unload at the Dome Rock Wildlife Area Trailhead. See Dome Rock. NOT ALL TRAILS ARE OPEN TO HORSES, SO FOLLOW OUR INSTRUCTIONS CLOSELY. Park authorities want you to park your trailer at the stables and then camp overnight at the campgrounds—away from your horses!—which naturally worries a lot of horse owners.

WINTER FUN AT MUELLER

Open all year long, Mueller State Park offers a number of winter adventures for the whole family, including animal tracking, cross-country skiing, snowshoeing, even tubing, sledding and snowboarding in some designated areas. See Dome Rock Wildlife Area for some winter restrictions.

Many families enjoy bringing children after a light snow to look for animal tracks. The State Park Visitor Center has displays that will help you identify the many tracks you'll see, and it's fun guessing what animals were doing at the time. We noticed a squirrel's track venturing out onto open ground, then a swirling spot where it suddenly changed direction and ran back at greater speed, probably because it saw a predator. And did you know that you can tell a doe from a buck just from their tracks? Does have a very high-stepping, mincing walk, but bucks with a load of antlers always drag their feet.

Our trail symbols indicate which trails are considered skiable by average folks, but rangers request that you always sign in and out on trail registers, let someone at home know where you're going and when you expect to return and take the usual emergency precautions. Our mountain weather changes quickly, so go prepared, carrying extra food, water and fire starter. If you ski or snowshoe alone, be sure to leave a note on your windshield with your name, destination, approximate time of return and the phone number of an emergency contact.

Tubing, sledding and snowboarding are permitted in the following designated areas in Mueller State Park, but only when there is sufficient snow cover to prevent resource damage: Preacher's Hollow picnic area, Outlook Ridge picnic area, Elk Meadow Trail area and the campground at Peak View. All other areas are closed to tubing, sledding and snowboarding.

ROAD DIRECTIONS: From I-25 in Colorado Springs, take the Cimarron Exit #141 marked for Manitou and Pikes Peak. Drive west on Hwy 24 to the community of Divide, west of Woodland Park. Turn left at Divide on Hwy 67. Go four miles and find the entrance for the northern State Park on your right. To find the southern entrance, see Dome Rock Wildlife Area at the end of this chapter.

ELK MEADOW and PEAK VIEW TRAILHEADS

Elk Meadow Trail #18
Peak View Trail #19
Peak View Loop: #18-#19

GUIDE'S NOTE: Elk Meadow is not the first trailhead you find upon entering the park (it's 1.9 miles from the entrance), but having tried it several ways, we discovered this to be the best place to begin a systematic exploration. So we start here, hemmed in by pavement, and then go around the park counter-clockwise before switching to the southern Dome Rock entrance.

Casual hikers who want to stay fairly close to pavement will enjoy the park's color-coded loops. Just select a color at the trailhead and follow the same color on Carsonite markers to return. But markers deeper in backcountry never have colors or trail names, so you must remember trail numbers and follow a map. That's why we repeat the numbers so often here and supply so many detailed topo maps.

ELK MEADOW TRAIL #18, segment measures 2.3 miles, rated easy to moderate, open to foot, bikes and horses. Part of Peak View Hiker Loop, returning via 3/4 mile footpath (easy loop for beginning cross-country skiers). Sledding, tubing and snowboarding permitted when sufficient snow cover prevents resource damage. PARTIALLY CLOSED JUNE 1-20.

Looking like an access road with a metal gate, your trail starts downhill through widely scattered aspen and evergreens. At 0.4 miles the forest grows thicker and you find a fork where your trail turns left. Ignore the access road that inclines right. At mile 0.7 the trail breaks out of the woods and curves to the north. You'll see picnic tables and a pavilion, but those are on private land beyond a fence. Now you parallel the fence and drop down into a treed drainage that is generally muddy even in fall. Cross that, follow it uphill and then start up another crease, always with a grassy slope to your right and trees to your left.

At mile 1.2 you reach the intersection with **Peak View Trail #19** on your left, which we describe next. From here on, #18 is closed June 1-120 for elk calving in the northern area. You can complete the Peak View Loop by taking #19 and then returning via the 3/4 mile footpath to the Elk Meadow Trailhead, but we're staying on Elk Meadow #18 to complete our description.

Now you wind down steeply through dense evergreens, then break out into the open for a very short climb. Ignore the access road in the trees at mile 1.3. Coming in and out of the trees, bikers get a great downhill run, finally leading to a

West side of Pikes Peak as seen from Peak View in Mueller State Park

huge meadow where your trail is atop an old railroad bed with marsh on either side. **Elk Meadow #18 ends at the intersection with Cheesman Ranch #17.**

PEAK VIEW #19, segment measures 0.3 miles, rated easy to moderate. Part of 1.5-mile Peak View loop with Elk Meadow #18, Peak View itself is open to foot only.

With its view of Pikes Peak and a charming pond, this short little trail boasts the prettiest trailhead in the park! That's why Peak View's campsites are among the most popular.

Starting at the steel gate, this track takes you down through trees, following a ridge crest to T-junction with Elk Meadow #18. Complete the 1.5-mile Peak View loop by turning right and following #18 back to its trailhead. Return along the road.

GROUSE MOUNTAIN AREA

Grouse Mountain Overlook #16
Cheesman Ranch #17
Lost Still #35 (described with Cheesman Ranch)
Moonshine #36
Dynamite Cabin#32
Cahill Pond #34
Buffalo Rock #33

GROUSE MOUNTAIN OVERLOOK #16, 0.6 miles up-and-back to summit, rated moderate; features short climb to summit overlook, open to foot only. CLOSED JUNE 1-20 FOR ELK CALVING.

Grouse Mountain Trail #16 used to be the initial access to trails in the northernmost portion of the park, but now it's only a spur off the very beginning of Cheesman Ranch #17. This spur leads hikers to the summit of Grouse Mountain itself for a grand view. But we thought we'd handle it first or otherwise you might pass it by. *It deserves a visit.*

Heading north away from the northernmost campground in the park, **Cheesman Ranch #17** is such a long trail that many people breeze by the easily-ignored turnoff that takes you up to Grouse Mountain. Cheesman begins by leading down into a dip, then up again to a place where the main track swerves right. That's where **Grouse Mountain Overlook #16** branches away to your left, much fainter and steeper at first. Watch for the Carsonite marker.

Grouse Mountain Overlook #16 is foot only. No bikes or horse are allowed up there. Higher up it is much more distinct and less steep as it curves up through the trees to the left. At the highest point you'll find a clearing, but trees on three sides limit the view to a shot of Pikes Peak. We dare guess that a lot of visitors will turn back here, but don't go back yet!

Instead, look for a carsonite arrow to the south. There you'll find a gnarly single-track trail that leads through rocks and fallen timbers, going downhill! It seems to be going nowhere, and you can't see any view developing, but just keep following it. Suddenly, it breaks out of the trees at a point of jagged rock topped by a dead and twisted bristlecone pine.

Carefully make your way out onto those jagged rocks at the foot of that tree and you'll see why this trail exists. You have a 180-degree vista, including Pikes Peak to the west, the Sangre de Cristo Range to the south and the Collegiate Range to the east. Gorgeous anytime, in late September the intervening hills are a rolling blanket of gold and green. It's no place for small kids, but it's a fabulous spot well worth the climb.

CHEESMAN RANCH #17, loop trail measuring 5.4 miles, rated part easy—part difficult, open to foot, bike and horse. CLOSED JUNE 1-20.

9,680   5.1 miles   9,680

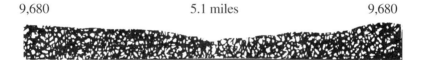

Cheesman Ranch #17 takes off from northernmost end of the campground and forms a big loop (6.3 miles) around the northern portion of the park. Here's your choice: The left (west) side of the loop is very steep, rocky and soft in places. The right (east) side is gentle and open and generally firmer. So if bikers go around clockwise, they have a gonzo downhill followed by a long steady climb back.

We think it's far better to go around counter-clockwise because then you have a long breezy downhill through the prettiest scenery and then you simply take your bike for a hike back up through the dense forest. Besides, it's safer. We don't like to spend our sunny morning in the dark forest and then wind up as lightning bait in the meadows during an afternoon thunderstorm!

Your loop begins at a strange intersection that resulted from the combining of different ranches. At that point #17 meets #17 at right angles. Since we're doing the loop counter-clockwise, we're heading straight ahead (east toward Pikes Peak).

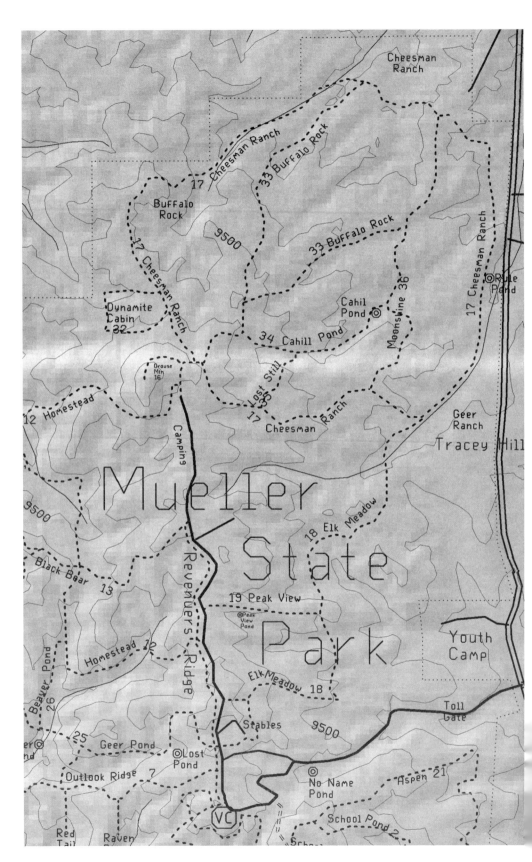

Just a few yards later, you see **Cahill Pond Trail #34 on your left**, which we'll describe later. We're headed eastward, down through forest and then out into the open, where the aspen forest is to your left and a grassy slope extends down the right side.

At mile 0.3 we find **Lost Still #35** plunging down a tunnel in the forest to your left. NOTE: **Lost Still Trail #35** is just a short connection to **Cahill Pond #34,** leading down through forest that grows dark and mossy. It's only 0.3 miles long, so that's about all we can say about it.

We're staying on #17 along the edge of the aspens.

Now we're traveling one of the places where rangers take visitors to look for elk. You can see elk-chewed aspens many places in Colorado, but here every single tree seems to be blackened with scars to a height of about six feet. Your best chance of seeing elk is early morning or late afternoon or evening, when they come out of the woods on the ridges and go to graze in the open. You'll have to be very quiet, of course, and the wind must not be carrying your scent toward them.

The terrain ahead is more and more grassy with Pikes Peak dominating the horizon. Soon your trail curves to the right through some woods to the next grassy meadow. It goes in and out of aspen groves, and now you can see curving ridges out in the grassy areas; these were terraces designed to retain moisture and prevent erosion back when this area was agricultural.

At mile 0.7 **Moonshine #36** takes off to the left. Our trail continues east across the grassland, following the crest of a finger ridge with grass on both sides. Ahead, **Elk Meadow #18** comes across the meadow from your right on an old railroad grade to join our trail.

We're now headed toward the Geer Ranch, which you can see from the highway coming in but can't see from this trail. No one lives there now.

Your meadow trail rolls on toward Rule Creek Pond, then on past a corral before veering away from the highway. Now you start climbing toward the woods again, where you find **Buffalo Rock #33** coming in from the left (south). At this intersection there is a dug-out barn with sheet metal roof and a potato sorter inside. Here we saw one of the rats that the Heath Dept. warns visitors about. Often their fleas carry disease. **Poking around in these old buildings is not recommended.**

Entering the woods, the trail steepens as it winds down to the ranch. Bikers, slow down. There is deep sand at the curve at the bottom of that last steep descent! We took a digger on that curve.

Here we find the little ranch this trail is named after, very neat and well preserved. The log cabin has white chinking and a green shingle roof. Its outhouse has a white toilet seat. Back behind the main barn and corrals there is another log house and smaller barn that were actually part of another ranch. If it weren't for the tall grass growing in the corrals, you might imagine it was still in use. Photographers will find a good view from the crest of the next hill as we leave the ranch.

At the bottom of the next little valley, **Buffalo Rock Trail #33** splits away to the left. We follow the main track that goes in a similar direction, following the ridge up. From here you can just see Buffalo Rock up ahead, but it is not impressive.

Here's where you pay for that lovely downhill tour because it's all up from here. You keep to the right of a wetland and start tracing the top of a forest ridge, leading up toward the rock. Often the track is soft and studded with rocks, steep in some places and very steep in others. We had to really push!

Cheesman takes you right up to Buffalo Rock itself at 9,540 ft. If this rock were anywhere else, it wouldn't have a name, but it happens to be the only feature in an area obscured by dark forest. You'll only know you've arrived when the trail reaches a high point with flat looking rocks visible through the trees to your left. Trees all around prevent much of a view.

You'll lose and gain some altitude through this thick forest, three times passing fire access routes that lead off toward private property. Then you'll come to the intersection where **Dynamite Cabin #32** takes off to your right (west). This trail is closed to bikes and horses and returns to your trail at a separate place only a few yards beyond. We'll describe it later.

From here on it's downhill another 0.3 miles to the intersection near Grouse Mountain, completing the loop.

MOONSHINE TRAIL #36, segment measures 0.9 miles, rated easy. Open to foot, bikes and horses. CLOSED JUNE 1-20 FOR ELK CALVING.

Moonshine #36 is a link between the Cheesman Ranch Trail #17 and Buffalo Rock #33. It skirts the edge of a beautiful aspen forest next to a huge meadow. The meadow is ridged with terraces left over from the agricultural days. This section makes great cross-country skiing, but its sunny exposure means snow won't last long.

Moonshine skirts the edge of Cahill Pond, where it intersects with the trail of that name, then climbs over a sparsely timbered ridge and crosses another grassy valley to join **Buffalo Rock #33** at the corner of a fence. Here we saw mountain blue birds, several one day and five the next.

By the way, most people associate moonshine liquor with Prohibition, but that was only its most profitable heyday. Ever since the Whisky Rebellion of 1794, country folk have made a tradition of distilling moonshine in defiance of federal tax revenuers.

DYNAMITE CABIN #32, side loop measuring 0.7 miles, rated moderately difficult. Open to hikers only. CLOSED JUNE 1-20 FOR ELK CALVING.

This is a great side trip off the Cheesman loop because it leads to an area far prettier than the forest tunnel that it leaves. Dynamite Cabin #32 forms a loop with the help of a few yards of **Cheesman Trail #17.** You can just see one "trailhead" from the other on Cheesman. Dynamite Cabin is closed to bikes and horses, so we hid our bikes and hiked it clockwise.

Your trail dives off through timber. The southern half of this old track goes through dark forest and has a lot of moss growing right in the steep trail, so I suppose bikes and horses would soon beat that up.

The cabin is in the trees on the west side of the trail, and there isn't much left of it. The roof is gone, with only a few pole rafters remaining. All the chinking is gone. But peeking inside, we could see an ornate wood stove made by the Detroit Stove Works, surely the best feature this old cabin ever had. Mr. Mueller found a couple of cases of dynamite stored in this cabin and that's where it got its name.

There's a spring-fed giardia ranch out back, but I don't think I'll have to warn you against drinking that stuff raw.

Going on up through the timber on a very overgrown track, you come to a meadow area with rock formations at the northwest corner of the trail. Here you'll find a pretty place for a picnic beneath aspen that are almost two feet in diameter. This spot makes you wonder why the cabin wasn't built here instead.

From here you go up the meadow and climb through trees to find **Cheesman #17** again.

CAHILL POND #34, segment measures 1.0 miles, rated easy. Eastern part of trail open to foot only. CLOSED JUNE 1-20 FOR ELK CALVING.

It sounds like something out of the old West, but it was only 1941 when the Cahill brothers were arrested for horse theft and murder. When they went to jail, they left behind a great mystery.

The story began when their neighbor, Sumner Osborn, shotgunned one of three men who had sneaked into the fish hatchery now known as Rainbow Valley, where Sumner was the watchman. The other two got away. According to the Gazette Telegraph, those two were John and Lester Cahill. Sumner was tried and acquitted of murder, but the Cahills never forgot.

Years later, after feuding over some disputed land between their ranches, the Cahills stole four of Sumner's horses and sold them to the Cheyenne Mountain Zoo for lion and tiger meat. Zoo officials recognized the Osborn brand, however, and sent the check to Osborn via his mother in Colorado Springs. Not to be outdone, the Cahills sent their henchman, George M. Betts, to fetch Sumner's mail from the mother's house and they forged Osborn's name to cash the check.

Sumner was furious. Then he disappeared. Some say he left his heavy sheep-skin coat hanging on a nail inside his cabin (later used as the temporary Park

Headquarters). The Sheriff mounted a huge search, even calling in the Boy Scouts to help, but they found no trace.

"We have uncovered horse-stealing, cattle-stealing and forgery in this investigation," Sheriff Markley told the newspapers. "There is no theory to follow than that Osborn is missing because there has been foul play."

Some say his body was dumped down the shaft of the Little Annie Mine. Others wondered if the Jack Rabbit Lodge hadn't been torched to destroy his body. But without a body, the Cahills could not be convicted of murder. After spending some time in prison for the livestock thefts, they were released.

The western end of the **Cahill Pond #34** begins off **Cheesman Ranch #17** just east of that strange right-angle junction of #17 and #17. Your track leads downhill through evergreen forest for 0.3 miles to an intersection where **Buffalo Rock #33** is ahead to the left and **Cahill Pond #17** turns downhill to the right.

From here on, #34 is foot only. You can see the cabin from the intersection. It sits at the edge of a meadow valley with a gorgeous view of the peak. The roof has fallen in and the floors are turning to kindling, but peeking in from outside, you can still see bits of wallpaper made out of pages from magazines like the Saturday Evening Post and National Farm.

Ahead, you have a meadow walk down toward the pond. **Lost Still #35**, a 0.3-mile shortcut to **Cheesman#17**, soon joins you from the right. Cahill Pond Trail ends at the pond itself where it intersects with **Moonshine Trail #36.**

BUFFALO ROCK #33, 3.2-mile balloon loop, rated part easy and part difficult, open to foot, bike and horses. CLOSED JUNE 1-20 FOR ELK CALVING.

9,560   3.2 miles   9,560

How this trail got its name is something of a mystery because it doesn't go to Buffalo Rock (Cheesman Ranch Trail does that) and it doesn't even have much of a view of Buffalo Rock. In fact, Buffalo Rock itself is not the sort of monument that usually earns a name. I can't imagine that it would have a name, if it weren't the only rock around.

The string of our balloon loop begins near the western end of **Cahill Pond Trail #34 amid dense forest (no bikes or horses on part of Cahill Pond).** You can see Cahill's old cabin from this intersection. Our trail climbs a bit to a right-angle intersection marked #33 in both directions. Now you begin the loop.

Like Cheesman Ranch, the left (western) half of the loop is forest and the right (eastern) half is more open. We took advantage of the morning sun by heading to the right, doing the loop counter-clockwise. That way, any afternoon lightning storms would catch us in the forest instead of out in the open.

That right track starts down through dense woods, then comes out on the brow of a ridge with a view of Pikes Peak. The aspen forest is dense to your left, but to your right the aspen are scattered through a lovely grassy park with lots of wild-flowers. Every aspen in sight has been elk-chewed.

Farther down the trees thin out and at mile 0.8, you find **Moonshine #36** joining you from the right at a fence corner. Watch for bluebirds here. Now the trail meanders north along the edge of aspen forest, very level. There are some ever-greens here twice as tall as the aspen. A half mile later, there are picnic tables among the aspen just before you T-junction with **Cheesman Ranch #17**. There is a dug-out barn with metal roof at this intersection.

Turn left. Now **Buffalo Rock #33 and #17 are the same route until after we pass the ranch itself, already described.** Once you climb out of the ranch valley and cross over into the next valley, **Buffalo Rock #33** leaves #17 at the valley floor near a couple of outbuildings. It's much less distinct than #17 here, just mashed grass, then becomes a washed-out rut going to the top of a ridge and following the ridge up.

Entering timber, you follow a fence up, then jog through a gate in the fence and grunt up a very steep section in heavy timber. At the top of a knoll, cross a grassy saddle and grunt up another ridge in the trees again. Here you'll find an artificial burn area where dead timber was cleared to simulate the way a small fire would have opened up the forest. Up through more dense timber, find the intersection where **Buffalo Rock#33** meets itself again, completing the loop.

Continuing around the park counterclockwise, we're going to describe the Werley Area Trailhead next because Homestead's Trailhead comes later, farther south.

BLACK BEAR TRAILHEAD

Black Bear Trail #13 (Formerly Werley Ranch Trail #13)
Golden Eagle Trail #14 (old Werley Ponds/Hay Cr #29)
Crazy Woman #37
Mountain Logger #31
Nobel Cabin #30
Osborn Homestead #27

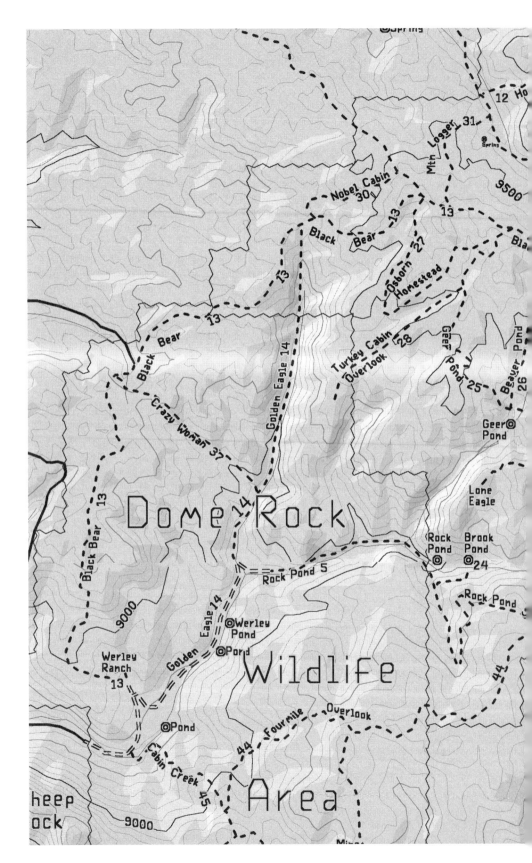

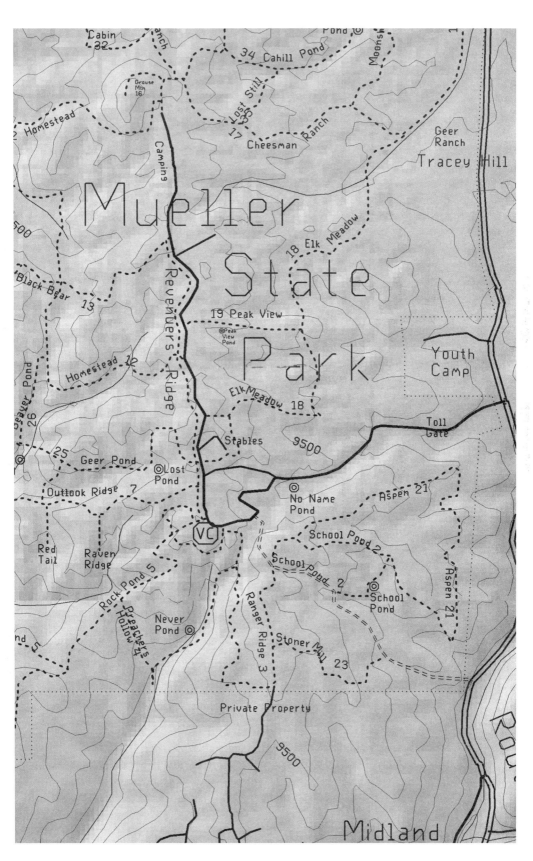

Black Bear #13, 4.5 miles one way, rated moderate. Starts out open to bike and foot only, then changes to horse and foot only in the Wildlife Area. But its other connections make it work just fine.

9,690   4.5 miles   8,800

Black Bear #13 is a major route connecting many branches and side loops, but its southern leg is now horse-and-foot country as part of Dome Rock Wildlife Area. Horses are banned from the start of this trail, but they access it via the Lost Ponds Trailhead, beginning with the Geer Ponds Trail #25. Mountain bikers enjoy most of Black Bear #13 and are only banned from its southernmost leg where it enters the Wildlife Area, yet it still serves as a major link. Consider this long ride: Lost Ponds Trailhead, beginning with Geer Ponds #25 to Black Bear #13 to Mountain Logger #31 to Homestead #12 to Cheesman Ranch #17 and then on around the northernmost areas.

Black Bear #13 begins at a "service road" gate at the west end of Mount Pisgah Point Campground. (Mt. Pisgah is the cone-shaped mountain due south.) This trail takes out on a gentle ridge, then snakes down more steeply, but it always stays on the rolling crest of ridges until it finally drops down to the ranch itself.

Within the first half mile, our trail dips down to a grassy saddle where **Homestead #12** crosses, then our main track rises again through fairly sparse forest. At mile 0.6 **Geer Pond #25** joins from the left. About a mile from the trailhead, you'll see a tumbled down cabin in a valley to your left, and just beyond this point **Mountain Logger #31** takes off to your right through very thick timber. We'll describe these branches later.

Next you come to a fence with a metal gate where **Osborn Homestead #27** (foot only) climbs away through mossy woods to your left. Just a few yards beyond, you'll find the first leg of the **Nobel Cabin #30** loop to your right (foot only). From here we climb a little, then lose 200 ft., tracing the high ground amid thinning trees down to a saddle where the **Nobel Cabin** side loop rejoins us from the right (mile 1.7).

Nearby you'll find another side trail, **Golden Eagle #14**, striking left down a draw called Hay Creek. Once again our main trail climbs up the saddle and follow the ridge crest west along the edge of the Park. After entering the Wildlife Area, you find **Crazy Woman #37**, leading down a draw to your left.

Black Bear #13 winds down to the old Werley Ranch, which is well worth seeing, very well preserved in a pleasant setting. You enter the back way, past the outbuildings, barn and corrals, which face out toward a wide and open valley. The ranch house probably saved the lives of some cross-country skiers trapped here by a storm in years past, so let's hope it stays in good condition. Our trail ends out front, where it joins **Golden Eagle #14** (left) and **Cabin Creek #45** (right).

Golden Eagle #14, segment measures 2.2 miles, rated moderate, half is in DOW Wildlife Area. No bikes.

The best of the three Werley Ponds is located right in front of the ranch. It is clearer, deeper and probably holds small brookies. The other two are located higher up this wide and open valley. Golden Eagle Trail #14 tours past them all, heading north

Just looking at the map, you might imagine that a valley tour like this would be flat and easy, but apparently the ground was too soft in the valley floor, so ranchers built their road just a little uphill. And that means your trail humps and bumps over a series of finger ridges within yards of that flat meadow!

It's a pretty route, however, and leads up the valley to a fork. The right fork is **Rock Pond #5,** but we're heading straight to a flatter valley.

From this point, you can make one of two loops returning to **Black Bear #13,** either by continuing on **Golden Eagle #14** or by chosing **Crazy Woman #37**, which appears to your left 0.3 miles from the intersection with **Rock Pond #5**. Both are very pretty, but our favorite lies ahead along the waters of North Hay Creek. Now our trail pleasantly traces the valley floor beside a trickling stream, amid aspen glades and grassy clearings graced with beautiful rocks and cliffs. The slanted rock wall to your right, studded with hardy trees, is the same ridge where **Turkey Cabin Overlook #28** dead-ends on top.

Eventually the stream peters out as you wander up through clearings with tall grass growing right in the trail. The only really steep part lies ahead where the trail jogs right to cross the drainage and launches upward along a steep and rocky portion to join **Black Bear #13** at a saddle. You are now 1.7 miles from the Black Bear Trailhead at Pisgah Point Campground.

CRAZY WOMAN #37, segment measures 0.8 miles, rated moderate, entirely located within Dome Rock Wildlife Area. No bikes.

The story goes that one night neighbors thought they heard a strange noise mingling with the howl of a blizzard. The next morning they found the hermit called "Crazy Woman" entangled in a barbed wire fence, frozen to death.

The cabin ruins beside this trail belonged to the "Crazy Woman," but you wouldn't have to be crazy to build a home on this site, for its a very nice location with a lovely view and a spring nearby.

From the bottom, you find #37 as a moist aspen draw branching left from **Golden Eagle #14.** The ruins are among the trees to your left. A little higher up, you'll find abandoned beaver works in the springflow. Even in late fall we found the trail wet where the spring crosses it. From here on it's all a steady climb through aspen and evergreens to T-junction against **Black Bear #13.**

But let's say you're coming the other way, from the top down. Suppose you're cross-country skiing or got a late start along **Black Bear #13** and you're afraid you may not be able to make it to the ranch and back before dark. Crazy Woman #37 provides a shortcut so you can do a scenic loop, returning to Black Bear #13 via Golden Eagle #14. In any season, this is a very pretty loop.

MOUNTAIN LOGGER #31, segment measures 0.6 miles, rated moderate. Open to horse, foot and bikes, providing links to northern trails. CLOSED JUNE 1-20 FOR ELK CALVING.

Mountain Logger #31 is important as a link, allowing bikes and horses to access the entire northernmost portion of the park in a roundabout sort of way. It starts off at Black Bear Trail #13, one mile from #13's trailhead and heads down through dense woods, following a finger ridge that leads to a open valley with a little puddle-pond. After crossing the valley, it T-junctions against **Homestead #12.** Bikes and horses must go left here, the right fork being foot only.

NOBEL CABIN #30, 0.8-mile side loop, rated moderate. Open to foot only.

Locals tell us that Mr. Nobel was a family man famous for his fiddling. He played at the Jack Rabbit Lodge and at most local parties. This trail leads to his homestead, though you could easily miss it without direction.

Cut into the side of a wooded ridge, **Nobel Cabin #30** goes down through a long aspen glade and then turns left in a meadow and crosses a boggy portion before entering deep forest again. As the trail starts to curve uphill again, watch for an old path on your right that leads through a marshy patch to the cabins. The three buildings there still have some walls standing. It was interesting to find a rusted lid marked "Perfectly Made Dr. Price's Phosphate Baking Powder." We hope you leave it there to charm others.

From here the main trail heads back up to a saddle clearing where **Black Bear #13** forms an intersection with **Golden Eagle Trail #14.** At that point, you are 1.7 miles from the pavement.

OSBORN HOMESTEAD #27, 1.2-mile side loop, rated moderate. Open to foot only.

This side loop takes you down to a valley where you'll find the original Osborn Homestead—not Sumner Osborn, mind you, but his brother Earl,

who came earlier. **It was Sumner who disappeared amid a feud with the Cahills. Earl had moved away by then.**

Only one end (the far west end) of this trail touches #13, so that's where we're going to start our description, but if you want to do the loop the other way around, you can find the near end by taking the turnoff for **Geer Pond #25,** as the map shows, then quickly taking a right onto **Osborn Homestead #27.**

Okay, we're starting at the metal gate on **Black Bear #13** (1.1 miles from the trailhead), turning left onto **Osborn Homestead #27** and starting up along the fence through dark and mossy forest. Then our trail rolls gently and goes out on a finger ridge where it forks. Ignore the right fork (fire access) and take the left track sharply down through aspen to the valley. Now your trail is just a faint trace in the grass and makes a sharp left to round the end of a finger ridge before taking you up the next draw. Very overgrown here. You go through a fence and through more grass and aspen with big rocks. Soon you see the remains of buildings both ahead and to your right across a marshy area, and our trail crosses the marsh to the main buildings.

From here the trail goes up steeply through woods to join **Geer Pond #25,** where you turn left to return to #13. For a description of **Geer Pond #25** and **Turkey Cabin Overlook #28,** see **Lost Pond Trailhead.**

HOMESTEAD TRAILHEAD

Homestead Trail #12
Beaver Ponds #26
Revenuer's Ridge #1
Homestead Loop #12, #26, #25, #11

HOMESTEAD TRAIL #12, segment measures 2.8 miles or part of 3.8-mile Homestead Loop; rated more difficult. Foot only, except for northernmost leg which is open to foot, bike and horse. Partially closed 6/1-20.

Homestead #12 begins near a pump house, then goes out on a ridge before diving off. Because of some utility work beneath it, much of this early section is as wide as a two-lane road. **Now Homestead is really a very nice trail, but you'll be surprised how steep that first bit is! Farther along, it is much more gentle as it breaks out of the big aspens above a meadow valley.** As you start down to cross this drainage, look up to your right to see the tumbled down logs of the homestead that gave this trail it name. Down valley, you'll see the remains of abandoned beaver dams. If you want to see beaver, go to Dome Rock Trail!

Cross the boggy valley and start down the opposite side. The trail ahead whoop-tee-does, but watch your speed on the downhill. Now you climb over a finger ridge that separates two drainages, but as you top this ridge, go out on its tip for a view of Geer Pond to the south. Now you head steeply down through the trees into the valley where you find **Beaver Ponds Trail #26** to your left, which leads to Geer Pond.

We're headed up this valley, away from Geer Pond, up through an aspen grove to a grassy saddle where our trail crosses **Black Bear #13** and then dives off through dense timber. Soon it breaks out into a grassy valley again where Mountain Logger joins from the left. Lots of aspen here. Ahead, you pass a cabin and climb through very dense evergreen forest toward Grouse Mountain. Now your trail heads downhill and eventually becomes more grassy on the southern side of Grouse Mountain. We've seen wild turkeys here. Eventually you climb up to tie into **Cheesman #17** right near its trailhead. Most people hike the road for one mile south to get back to their starting point.

BEAVER PONDS #26, segment measures 0.4 miles, rated easy. Open to bike and foot only.

This route earned its name many years ago, but beaver move away when food gets scarce, so they all moved down to Dome Rock Trail. Indeed, old dams are far more visible along Homestead Trail #12 than they are here!

This valley is very gentle, grassy on the west and edged with aspen on the east. Our trail begins on this northern end at a culvert, then roller coasters amid rocks

Hand-feeding birds is NO LONGER LEGAL in Mueller State Park.

along the west side of the valley, finally returning to the valley floor where it meets Geer Pond Trail #25 (open to bikes, horses and foot) just above the pond. See Geer Pond Trailhead.

REVENUER'S RIDGE #1, segment measures 2 miles or more, rated easy.

Revenuer's Ridge #1 skirts the paved road and is essentially designed to let visitors avoid walking on the road. It extends between Black Bear and School Pond Trailheads.

By the way, a "revenuer" is a federal officer who looks for illegal moonshine stills. A common way of detecting stills was to spot their smoke from a high ridge.

LOST POND TRAILHEAD

Lost Pond Trail #11
Geer Pond Trail #25
Turkey Cabin Overlook #28
Lost Pond Loop: #11-#25-#7

LOST POND TRAIL #11, segment measures 0.4 miles; part of Lost Pond Loop with Geer Pond and Outlook Ridge totaling 2.6 miles, rated moderate. Bike and foot, then horses join. Horses come via Livery #20 then #25.

At the trailhead, bikers and hikers take a singletrack that leads only a few yards before T-junctioning against the usual service-road-trail that begins to the south as #25. Horses come from Livery #20 and join #11 via #25 (next).

Turn right onto this road-trail and follow it down along a wooded ridge. From there it dives down a steep crease and breaks out into an aspen forest. At 0.4 you see Lost Pond on your left, just a watering hole. From here on **Geer Pond #25 strikes out alone, a major horse access to the Park and Wildlife Area beyond.**

GEER POND #25, segment measures 1.5 miles, rated moderate. Open to bikes, horses and foot. Major horse access from stables and Livery #20.

9,480   1.4 miles   9,540

Geer Pond #25 sort of shares the Lost Pond Trailhead. It begins as a road immediately south of the Lost Pond singletrack, across from Livery #20, which brings horses from the stables. From there it soon joins and shares trail with #11 as far as Lost Pond itself. Geer Pond #25 follows the trickle downstream, then keeps to the edge of the ridge. There is one steep and loose section where it goes down to the water again. At that point (0.8 miles from the parking lot) you find Outlook Ridge #7 (foot only), which comes down off the opposite ridge and through the mossy woods to join our trail from the south.

Continue following the water down to Geer Pond itself, which is much larger and prettier than Lost Pond. You're now a mile from the parking lot. Look for an eight-foot water slide/cascade amid boulders just below the dam. Cross the creek on a culvert above the pond and turn right, following the valley upstream a very short distance to the next intersection.

Here the valley track becomes known as **Beaver Ponds #26** (foot only) and **Geer Pond #25** strikes uphill to your left, climbing steeply past a granite formation and switchbacking up the ridge   At the top, you find **Turkey Cabin #28** (no bikes), branching off to your left and following the ridge out to a point of rocks, where it dead-ends at an overlook. From this intersection with #28, **Geer Pond #25** goes right and climbs along the ridge. **Osborn Homestead #27** (foot only) joins from the left a short way before Geer Pond ends at a T-junction with **Black Bear #13** (open to bikes, horses and foot at that junction, an important link).

TURKEY CABIN OVERLOOK TRAIL #28, segment measures 0.9 one way, 1.8 up and back, rated moderate. Open to foot and horse only.

Leaving Geer Pond Trail #25, this trail goes out on a ridge above Hay Creek to dead-end at a set of rocks near an old mine. From there you have a view of forested hills and open meadows, including the Werley Valley and a couple of its ponds.

OUTLOOK RIDGE TRAILHEAD

Outlook Ridge #7
Wapiti Self-Guided Nature Trail #6

OUTLOOK RIDGE #7, segment measures 1.0 miles not counting spurs, which all measure 0.3 each. Foot only. Also part of Lost Pond Loop (2.6 miles) with Geer Pond, Lost Pond and Revenuer's Ridge, rated more difficult. Loop is foot only.

9,680   1.0 miles   9,360

Well named, Outlook Ridge #7 offers a triple helping of lofty scenery. Wide and gentle at first, the trail angles down slowly from the trailhead through mixed forest. Soon you glimpse the first of many views through breaks in the trees, but that's just a taste. Then the trail rises slightly and a spur to your left leads out to the first overlook, which is really a double set of rocky perches called Raven Ridge Overlook.

This side trail forms a Y to visit both sets of rocks, angling downhill to reach them. From these cliff tops you can see Pikes Peak, Mount Pisgah, the Sangre de Cristos and the Collegiate Range. An informal single track shortcuts between the two outlooks, turning the Y into a triangular loop. **Only this first section is recommended for beginning cross-country skiers.** From here on it is more difficult.

Climb back up to the main trail and head west again, now descending sharply through thicker timber before climbing to the next intersection on a wooded shoulder. Here on your left you find the next side trail, this one leading to Red Tail Overlook, which has steps at the end to make your return easier.

This one starts out as a flat doubletrack, but quickly changes to singletrack as it dips steeply through aspen and down approximately 60 steps, finally arriving at a massive area of fairly smooth granite, a beautiful place to sit in the sun and eat your lunch. You might guess this view would be much the same as Raven Ridge, but Red Tail's vantage point is lower, so instead of offering views of Pikes Peak and Pisgah, you find a valley view graced by cliffs and aspen and Brook Pond below. Highly recommended when fall gilds the aspen!

Return to the main trail and head west again, winding down sharply and crossing a saddle where you find an intersection. Here the main trail doubles back along a fence, heading down through thick timber to end at **Geer Ponds #25. But wait!**

There's one more overlook, but not as good as the others. To find Lone Eagle Overlook, go west up the side trail leading out of the saddle. It soon grows fairly level and there are a couple of places where you can step out onto rocks to the left of the trail for abbreviated views of Pikes Peak and Red Tail. Indeed, this overlook is unusual because there is no one spot where you can say "This is it!" Viewed from some other angle, you are perched atop high rocks, but when you're up there, it feels more like being on top of a large hill because you can't see much directly below and trees edit your views. If you keep going, you can work your way down rocky terrain beside a fence, but that only lowers and does not improve the vista.

WAPITI SELF-GUIDED NATURE TRAIL #6, 0.8-mile loop, rated easy to moderate. Open to foot only.

The so-called American elk is not really an elk at all, but a different kind of animal properly called by an Indian name, wapiti. The trail that bears its name is designed to educate visitors through a series of numbered signs that correspond to information in the pamphlet published for this trail.

Completed in 1993 by park staff and the Volunteers for Outdoor Colorado, **Wapati Nature Trail #6** is a short loop that points out natural features.

ROCK POND TRAILHEAD

Rock Pond Trail #5
Fourmile Overlook Trail #44

ROCK POND TRAIL #5, segment measures 4.2 miles, rated moderate with some steeper places. Features scenic ponds. Starts as bike and foot only, then changes to bike, horse and foot as link, then changes to horse and foot only as it leaves Rock Pond going west into the Wildlife Area to #29.

9,660   2.3 miles   9,000

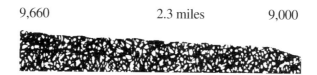

Starting at the Rock Pond trailhead, we take a shady double-track out and down the edge of a ridge. Preacher's Hollow Trail #4 joins from the left. Soon you come to a fork where Rock Pond Trail splits off to the right and Four-Mile Overlook Trail #44 goes left.

Our fork winds steeply downhill through some large aspens. Just a short distance (0.1 mile) before reaching Rock Pond itself, you'll see a marker pointing uphill to the right. That spur goes only 0.2 miles to Brook Pond (#24) , so if you have the time, go and see it. It's a pretty spot and has a lot of small brook trout.

Backtrack to the main trail (#5) to find the pond called Rock Pond just downstream. The far side of the pond is one huge slanting granite face. You can reach the top of that cliff by taking **Outlook Ridge Trail** to Lone Eagle Overlook.

Below the dam of Rock Pond our path follows the meadow valley into the northeastern part of the Dome Rock Wildlife Area and down past Nate Snare's cabin, which is on your right. Nate's place is also called Turkey Cabin because Mueller kept wild turkeys in it while stocking the ranch.

Farther down this grassy valley, you'll T-junction at a clear track that's called Golden Eagle #14, this section within the Wildlife Area.

FOURMILE OVERLOOK TRAIL #44, segment measures 3.5 miles one way, but as an out and back via Rock Pond #5 measures 8.1 miles, rated difficult; mostly located within Dome Rock Wildlife Area. No bikes.

9,420   2.9 miles   9,120

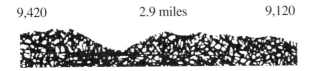

     This view is well worth the difficult journey, no matter how you get there. The overlook can also be reached via Dome Rock and Cabin Creek Trails, but that route cuts off most of the trail we need to describe, so it only makes sense for us to start from the north, which is just as popular and has the advantage of starting from a higher altitude. Judging from the map, the northern route should be easier, but it is such a roller coaster that it loses and gains more elevation than calculations can show!

     Our trail begins at 9,420 feet on the left fork where **Rock Pond Trail #5** goes right. The roller coaster ahead runs mainly through dense timber. Watch for **Hammer Homestead Trail #42** joining from your left (see Dome Rock). From here our trail loses more than 400 feet before joining **Cabin Creek Trail #45. Turn left there because our trail and #45 are the same for a short but steep climb to another T-junction where our trail goes right and Cabin Creek Trail goes left.**

     Our track rolls along the top of a ridge, climbing to its highest point before reaching the overlook. As you top this knob at 9,305 ft., you can see Wright's Reservoir to your right. This lake is hidden by Dome Rock itself when you reach the overlook beyond.

     Now our track dips down and climbs again and suddenly makes a little cul-de-sac loop on top of the ridge with no great view in any direction—just a place for ranch vehicles to turn around.

     So where's the overlook? Just leave the trail and climb the rocks ahead, inclining to the left of the loop. It's easy. And suddenly you come out on a promontory with southern Colorado laid at your feet.

     If you're afraid of heights, let us assure you that the top of this rock is a wide and long bench, so you don't have to stand at the edge to enjoy the view. Of course, you overlook Fourmile Creek, which entwines with Dome Rock Trail 700 feet below. Pikes Peak is to your left (north) and ahead lies the Sangre de Cristo Range with the Collegiates in the distance to your right. Also to your right are three bald plutons of granite. Dome Rock is the left one, identifiable by the little square rock on top that looks like a house from this distance (Surely a pretty big rock, if you were up there). The one on the right is Sheep Rock (not Sheep Nose) at 9,410.

If you have time and don't want to return the way you came, you can enjoy entirely different scenery by taking a side loop. Just follow Cabin Creek Trail #45 down to Golden Eagle #14, then up Rock Pond #5.

PREACHER'S HOLLOW TRAILHEAD

Preacher's Hollow Trail #4
Ranger Ridge Trail #3
Preacher's Hollow Loop #4-#5.

PREACHER'S HOLLOW #4, segment measures 1.3 miles, part of 1.9-mile loop, rated moderate. Open to foot only near trailhead, but open to horse and foot on southern half (accessed from Ranger Ridge) to serve as connection for other horse trails. No bikes.

9,600   1.9 miles   9,600

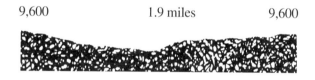

This area used to belong to a preacher named Cargil and features meadow walks amid aspens. Because of differing rules along the route, the only way to do the entire loop is on foot. Horses access the lower part via Rock Pond #5 and use Preacher's Hollow to link to the southeast part of the Park.

Starting from the Preacher's Hollow trailhead, we're going to do this loop clockwise. Your path heads down to join an old ranch double-track that takes you into an aspen draw. Ranger Ridge Trail #3 comes down to join from the left. You walk beneath widely-spaced, very tall aspen along a narrow valley. You'll pass a round water trough that used to be filled by a pipe sunk into a spring.

Soon you come to Cargil's old pond, just a tiny watering hole. On our second visit, it had just been muddied by game. This is now called Never Never Pond because it never fills and never empties. It leaks at a rate that matches the spring feeding it. The same spring-trickle continues farther down valley.

As you walk this section, watch for a big rock outcropping to your right that looks like the head of a prize-fighter with a broken nose. Just before you reach the edge of the park, you find a green and almost level grassy area where three finger valleys converge. Here your trail turns right, heading up the third valley. Your path is just mashed-grass single-track here, and once again climbs through aspen to follow the draw. Great in aspen season!

Near the top of the ridge your trail gets much steeper as it climbs up a badly washed section to end at a T-junction against Rock Pond #5, which seems like a major road. This is where horse-riders coming up from the Wildlife Area enter to explore the southeastern parts of the Park: Horses cannot continue on #5 to pavement, however, because the eastern leg of Rock Pond #5 is closed to horses. Hikers can take Rock Pond #5 and then Revenuer's Ridge #1 back to the trailhead.

RANGER RIDGE #3, segment measures 1.3 miles, rated difficult. No bikes.

9,440   1.3 miles   9,620

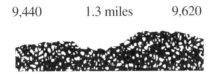

This is a convenient link, but not a favorite for scenery because much of this trail is in dark timber. Start at the Preacher's Hollow Trailhead and hike around Preacher's Hollow #4 to the left, clockwise, until you find Ranger Ridge #3 branching away to your left. Here you leave the aspen gulch and tunnel up through thick timber.

Heading south, you'll find the most difficult part of Ranger Ridge ahead. The track humps and bumps steeply along the side of a dark and mossy timber hillside. When you come to the boundary fence and turn left, it's still the same, for this route was meant only to patrol the fence. That created a trail that goes up and down like a sewing machine needle as it follows the fence.

Ahead lies a junction where the boundary track continues straight east toward Stoner Mill #23, but is not marked on the map and is no longer considered part of the official system. So here we leave the fence, turning left and following the marker for #3 northward. It's a climb.

As the trail flattens a little along the ridge, you come to a junction where Stoner Mill #23 takes off downhill to your right. Our path continues straight toward School Pond #2. A break in the trees gives you a view of Pikes Peak's back shoulder, but you're too close and too low to see the summit. The high cone that dominates the horizon is Sentinel Point, 12,527 feet.

Soon you bore down through the timber to a clearing where you T-junction against School Pond #2. Aspen-ogler's note: All of the trails in this corner of the park are great for aspen-looking, except for Ranger Ridge.

SCHOOL POND TRAILHEAD

School Pond Trail #2
Aspen Trail #21
Stoner Mill Trail #23
School Pond Loop: #2

SCHOOL POND TRAIL #2, l.5-mile loop, rated moderate, features scenic aspen and meadow trail. No bikes.

This is the first trailhead that you see on your left when entering the park, but every attempt to begin our tour here made the park seem even more confusing. One of the best features of this trail is only a few hundred yards from the trailhead, a grassy knoll to your left (or east) at the trail's first big intersection. From that knoll you have a two-way view, a big one of Pikes Peak to the east and smaller glimpses of the the Collegiate Range to the west. .

This is a pretty trail that might have been named something else because the pond itself is not a really notable feature. School Pond is more of a puddle than a pond. There never was a school here.

The name comes from the same law that lends its name to the Section 16 County Park (Penrose-Red Rock Loop) at Colorado Springs. This old law gave some parcels of public lands to the State School Board, and since school boards have little use for patches of forest, such lands have been leased out and traded through the years. This piece of the ranch, with its tiny watering hole, was once covered under that law.

School Pond area near the loop intersection

We recommend that you hike this one counter-clockwise because it's harder to go wrong that way. If you went the other way, you could miss a turn and wind up on Aspen #21 instead.

Beginning at the parking lot, School Pond starts out going uphill through the woods, then contours around a ridge, breaking out of the timber near the top of a grassy valley. Here you'll find a four-way intersection with the knoll we mentioned immediately on your left. The trail on your left is the way we'll come back.

The tunnel through the trees on your right is **Ranger Ridge #3** and connects to two others, Stoner Mill #23 and Preacher's Hollow #4. Our path lies straight ahead, a direct route to the pond.

As you start downhill, following the crease in the valley. Soon a trickling stream begins beside the trail. The hillside to your left is grassy and sunny. The draw to your right is shady, with evergreens and big aspen. Its trickle of water feeds the pond which lies below where two drainages meet. Notice the clover growing in the trail.

Our trail turns left at the pond and heads up the other drainage, which is much drier, a kind of slanting meadow. Just as you reach the edge of the trees on top, you find a T-junction with School Pond #2 heading to your left and Aspen #21 to your right.

Heading left, your trail rolls along the ridge amid widely scattered timber. It gradually curves around to complete the loop at the four-way intersection. Turn right at the marker and you're on the roadway-trail leading back to the parking lot.

ASPEN TRAIL #21, segment measures 2.5 miles, rated part moderate— part difficult. No bikes.

9,720	2.5 miles	9,720

Two sides of this triangular trail roll along ridgetops, but the difficult rating stems from that third side along the Park boundary. That easterly leg has some radical ups and downs.

Someday **Aspen #21** may be an important access to this corner of the Park for horse riders, but Livery Trail #20 does not go this far south yet. If it did (still planned) **Aspen #21** would lead riders to **School Pond#2** or **Stoner Mill #23, Ranger Ridge #3, Preacher's Hollow #4** and connect with the Wilderness Area via **Rock Pond #5. For now, Livery Trail #20 only goes to Lost Pond Th.**

Most people access **Aspen #21** from School Pond, but a new trailhead is planned at the dam of Entrance Pond, the one you pass as you drive in. The parking lot is ready (across the road) and all it lacks is a sign. Cross the dam and head up into the trees.   Soon your path T-junctions against an old double-track. If you're heading west or south, turn right and you will soon intersect with **School Pond #2.**

But we're going to take the long way around, heading left toward the park boundary. The roadway ahead was originally designed to let ranchers inspect the fence by driving more or less alongside it, and this made some steep grades. The roadway leaves the fence only when absolutely necessary. Near the corner of the park, you find a moist valley, but our path turns right and climbs back up a ridge, heading for **School Pond Trail #2.** You complete the triangle using a piece of **School Pond, up on the ridge top where the trees are widely spaced. Then** Aspen #21 doubles back east again, climbing to intersect with the trailhead path.

STONER MILL #23, 2-mile balloon loop, using part of School Pond, rated moderate, open to horse and foot only.

9,640   2 miles   9,640

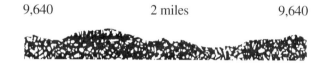

You reach Stoner Mill #23 by starting out on School Pond #2, taking a right at the four-way intersection onto Ranger Ridge #3 and then you'll find Stoner Mill #23 as a fork in that trail on top of the ridge. From there #23 dives off downhill to your left, following a lower ridge down to T-junction against a locked gate and fence at the park boundary.

Because you came down a ridge, you reach the boundary fence at a high point. The road alongside the fence dives away in both directions. From here, **Stoner Mill #23** officially goes left (east) along this fence-line road, but the same road also extends downhill along the fence in the other direction. That section is no longer officially part of the system, but it leads due west to Ranger Ridge, just in case you're curious.

Heading left (east) along the fence, we go down into a little valley, where the trail takes a hard left and then T-junctions against an old road cut into the side of the hill. The route to your right is no longer part of the system and leads to the corner of the park.

We're heading left on this roadway, climbing to a grassy spot where you have a splendid view of the peak and the valley below. Beyond this point, the trail tunnels down through deep forest (so folks coming the other way have quite a thrill when this picture window opens up at the top.) Finally we cross a ravine and T-junction against **School Pond Trail #2**. Turn left to return to the School Pond Trailhead.

DOW'S DOME ROCK WILDLIFE AREA
(NO LONGER PART OF MUELLER STATE PARK)

Dome Rock Trail #46
Cabin Creek Trail #45
Hammer Homestead #42
Hammer Overlook #39
Willow Creek/Dome View Trail #40
Sand Creek Trail #41
Spring Creek Trail #43

ROAD DIRECTIONS: The Dome Rock Trailhead is located south of the State Park. From Divide turn south on 67 toward Cripple Creek. The State Park entrance is only four miles away on your right, but GO PAST THAT and go another 1.8 miles to where 67 splits. Take the right fork, which soon becomes gravel. Two miles down this fork you'll find Dome Rock Trailhead on your right with parking for both cars and horse trailers. HORSEMEN NOTE: One driver with faulty trailer brakes rolled a rig entering here. You make a right turn into the trailhead area and then make a sharp left turn, so go slow and watch it.

DOME ROCK #46, entire segment measures 4.9 miles one way (July 16-Nov 30) but 2.4 miles to Lodge Chimney where trail closes to all users Dec 1-July 15 for bighorn lambing; traditionally rated easy, except you must ford a considerable stream 9 times! Open to horse and foot. NO MOUNTAIN BIKES, NO FIRES, NO CAMPING.

No entrance fees, but no bikes either. Fat Tire fans are deflated by the closure of this premier mountain bike ride. You see, Wildlife Areas owned by the Division of Wildlife are primitive places devoted to—well—wildlife, and no vehicular recreation is permitted. The DOW receives no tax revenues except for a federal sales tax on hunting and fishing gear, and federal auditors criticized Dome Rock for turning into more of a recreation area. The DOW was forced to cancel its lease with State Parks, who had managed this area, and revert to wildlife rules that prohibit bicycles as vehicles. And, as our guidebook previously warned, increased visitorship also forced seasonal closures of trails in the bighorn lambing grounds around the Dome Rock itself.

Traditionally, this has always been one of the most unusual, majestic and downright grin-fixing trails in Colorado. But get ready to get wet! For this trail fords Fourmile Creek nine times without any bridges and only those on

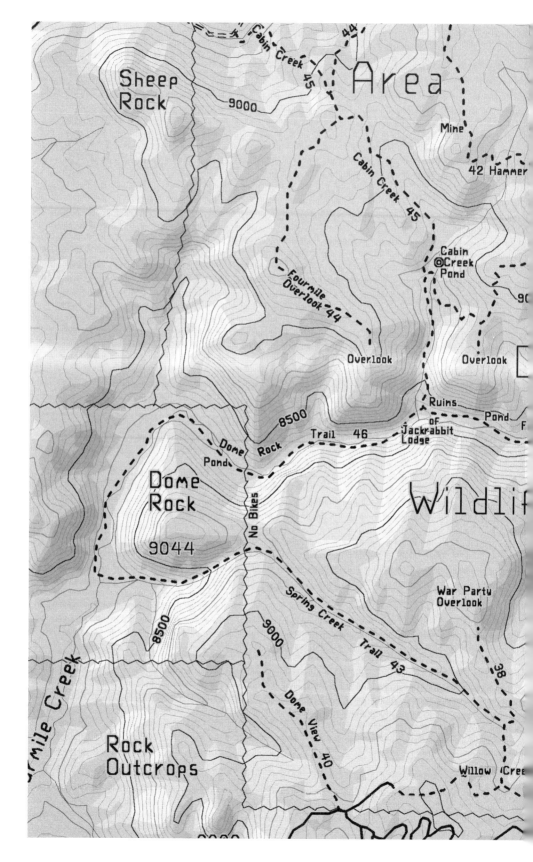

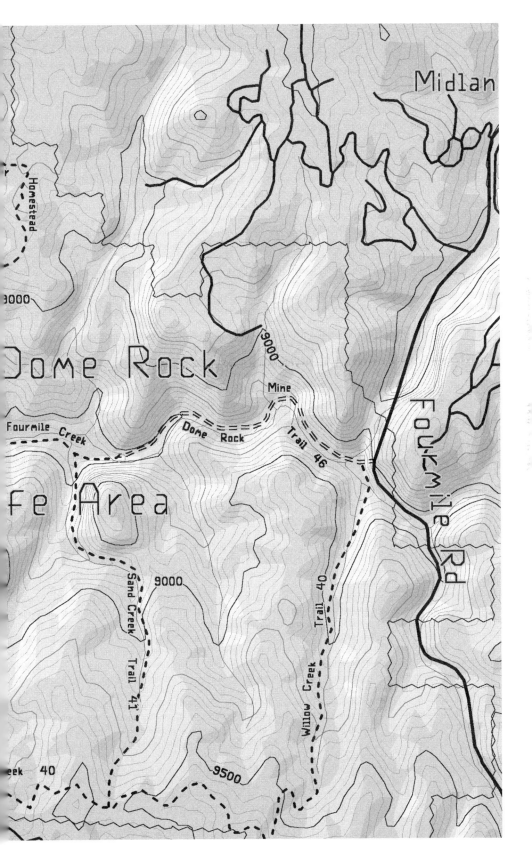

horseback ever stay dry. The Beaver Corps of Engineers have expanded dams that have swamped the trail with some big ponds. One crossing is now about 70 feet wide, but shallow. That makes it more difficult than before, but former plans to reroute the entire trail have been scrapped by the DOW, so the traditional route—and its beaver—will remain.

Because of its overall gentle grade, Dome Rock is also a favorite among cross-country skiers, but remember that the trail is closed beyond the Lodge Chimney Dec 1-July 15. Spring Creek and Dome View Trails are also closed for the lambing season.

Dome Rock Trail has a history as colorful as its scenery. After the turn of the century, coaches rolled along this trail, splashing across fords in the creek, hauling Eastern investors to the Crescent Cattle Company's private resort called Jack Rabbit Lodge. There, investors enjoyed fishing, hunting and other sports, including sporting ladies! These weren't mining camp followers, mind you, but high-class professionals from Denver, yet the ladies weren't allowed to work inside the lodge. Their profession was confined to some tent-cribs out back.

The lodge burned down in 1941, leaving only chimney ruins beside the trail. The Division of Wildlife stocks Fourmile Creek (which flows from the Crags) with Pikes Peak cutthroat, but pressure keeps them pretty small. No dogs, fires or overnighters are allowed, of course, but this southern area is open to hunting in the fall, so be sure to wear orange reflective clothing if you explore here during hunting season. Dates vary from year to year, so check.

Actually, spring is the most dangerous time to wade this trail because its

Fourmile Creek is a very considerable stream. Notice that three tributaries converge at this trailhead. Spring thaws make it swift and deep (indeed, the first ford can be thigh deep).

In such times, users have created an unofficial single track by climbing along the north side of the creek, a path far more difficult than the main trail. This social trail is not up to standards, but the DOW plans no changes. Just remember that you are very much on your own in backcountry and you are expected to make prudent decisions about your own safety. **If the situation looks dangerous, turn back.**

If we haven't scared you away, let's go! Starting at the Dome Rock Trailhead, cross the creek on a set of logs, your last "bridge." The track is rocky and rolling for half a mile to the ruins of the Sand Burr Mine, where the shaft has been closed. At mile 0.6 you swerve left to ford the stream for the first time. The alternative route, the single track social trail we mentioned, is somewhat hidden behind a large rock beside this ford.

When the creek is low, stepping stones appear just a few yards upstream, but they are always slick. The next ford is less than a tenth of a mile downstream, so you can decide for yourself whether to skip these two fords by keeping to the north side of the stream on the steep and narrow social trail. (Besides, that first ford is generally the deepest.)

Note: If you try both routes, you will be surprised at the difference. From this point on, the main trail is very flat, while the social trail goes up and down like a sewing machine needle. Even when you return uphill on the main trail, it is very easy compared to the social trail. For that reason, most repeat visitors wind up avoiding the social trail when they can. Bring tennies or a horse.

At mile 1.4 we come to the third crossing, which is more shallow. The main trail is wide and nice as goes through willows. Soon you cross again and again, so you wind up in a clearing on the south side where **Sand Creek #41** comes down to join our track at mile 1.6. Sand "Creek" is hardly more than a trickle in wet times and is generally dry in fall. The big rock formation across to the north is Sheep Nose Rock, not to be confused with Sheep Rock farther down. Big granite adds a lot of grandeur to the entire route.

Beginning here, you'll see beaver works in the creek that extend downstream quite a ways. By the way, local lore holds that one old trickster lived near Sheep Nose with a dog that was trained to fetch supper by stealing chickens from neighboring ranches!

Cross again here and continue downstream on the north side to find the chimney ruins of the Jack Rabbit Lodge at the mouth of Cabin Creek (mile 2.4).

Sheep Nose Rock towers above Dome Rock Trail.

Of course, **Cabin Creek Trail #45** climbs the tributary to the north, but our trail crosses that tributary on a culvert near the chimney and continues down Fourmile Creek.

At the base of Dome Rock (mile 3.1), you'll come to the boundary of the Dome Rock Natural Area. Ahead the creek and its trail swerve south around the rock, leading through a valley (just a bent grass path here) where bighorn sheep are often seen. Then the trail leaves the creek and angles up and along the ridge to the west for a short distance to a place where you have a good view of Dome Rock. Although the trail continues a short way to a gate at the park boundary, that view point is called the end of Dome Rock Trail.

CABIN CREEK #45, segment measures 2.6 miles, rated moderate to difficult. Open to horses and foot only. THIS OLD LINK TRAIL IS NOW CLOSED TO BIKES.

8,340   2 miles   8,800

Starting at the chimney, Cabin Creek #45 is extremely steep, rocky and loose as it struggles northward, crossing and climbing beside the tributary. Higher up, the trail grows gentler as you enter a little valley with cabin ruins

at mile 0.4. Across from the cabin ruins, Hammer Homestead Trail #42 sky-rockets up the opposite hill, somewhat obscure here and very very steep. But we stay to the west side of the creek and immediately ahead we find Cabin Creek Pond. This is a pretty pond, triangular, fairly clear, grassy-banked, a lovely setting for your picnic.

They way we heard it, this lovely spot was the scene of a lynching in the outlaw days. These cabins belonged to the White Brothers, one of which was hanged as a horsethief right here in the valley.

From here the trail skirts the pond and follows the stream up through a narrow canyon for a short ways. The canyon opens to reveal a slanting valley, wide and grassy and rimmed with trees. Here our trail leaves the stream to angle northwest up a side drainage with trees to your left and a grassy slope to your right.

Entering trees ahead, #45 climbs up to join **Fourmile Overlook #44** on a ridge top. The overlook is to your left, a good distance away but highly recommended. (See Rock Pond Trailhead). Our trail #45 turns right at this juncture. Indeed, #45 and **Fourmile Overlook #44** are the same route for a short distance, then #45 forks left and heads down very steeply through a muddy forest crease.

As we continue down the soggy draw on **Cabin Creek Trail #45**, however, we finally arrive at the big valley where you'll see the first of the Werley Ponds and the trail that bears that name. Cross the dam of that pond and incline to the left, crossing the valley and finally joining **North Hay Creek/Werley Ponds Trail #29** near a gate that leads out of the Dome Rock Wildlife Area to private property.

HAMMER HOMESTEAD #42, segment measures about 2 miles, rated difficult. Open to horse and foot only. No bikes. Leads to Hammer Overlook #39 and Fourmile Overlook #44.

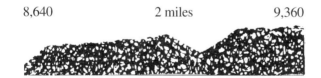

8,640   2 miles   9,360

Leaving the cabin ruins at Cabin Creek, the lower leg of this trail is one of the steepest in the park. Indeed, it should switchback right away, but seems to have been designed for rockets! The switchbacks come later.

At the top, #42 enters the trees at a saddle where it T-junctions against a ridge road that climbs in both directions. Turning right takes you to **Hammer Overlook #39**, a short spur which is well worth seeing, but not as good as Fourmile Overlook because you don't get the same broad, unobstructed sweep. Instead, Hammer Overlook is 150 feet lower, has more trees in your way, and has a number of rock outcroppings with a different view from each. From one you see Pikes Peak, and from another you see Dome Rock with the square-looking boulder on top.

From this ridge the main trial goes north, bumping along the ridge crest, climbing 400 feet to the edge of the park before turning west and dropping down into the headwaters of Cabin Creek.

From there it struggles up a very steep section for another 300-foot altitude gain to a cliff-edge overlook at 9,403 feet. Quite a spot! And historic, too, for the Little Annie Mine is only yards away, perhaps concealing the body of poor Mr. Osborn. Rumors to that effect caused two official searches of the shaft, but nothing was ever found.

The mine is very secluded, so here's how to find it. As you stand gazing at the view from the overlook, the mine is located to your right and downhill. There is no path. Just work your way down through the rocks and look for a small fence enclosure that guards the shaft. There is no shaft house or any other debris, just wire around a well-like hole in the rock near the cliff's edge.

Notice that the shaft goes straight down, following a "dike," a place where the surrounding rock spit and different rock squished up through the crack. This shaft is reputed to have been several hundred feet deep, though a stone tossed into doesn't seem to drop far, perhaps because the lower part slants or perhaps because of rocks thrown in. (Still, if you threw a body down a shaft, wouldn't you throw a lot of rocks in to bury it?) You can see a sample of the ore at the Visitor Center.

Go back to the overlook and follow the trail north along the ridge to T-junction against **Fourmile Overlook #44.**

WILLOW CREEK/DOME VIEW TRAIL #40, segment measures 4.9 miles one way to Dome View Overlook, rated moderate to difficult. No bikes.

Even if you see this trail described in mountain bike publications, it is definitely closed to bikes. Yet for those willing to hoof it on two legs or four, this long trail provides important links and beautiful views well worth the journey.

Willow Creek/Dome View #40 begins along the stream that bears its name. A gate keeps it locked away from public vehicles at the horse trailer parking area at the park's southern entrance. Go left from the trailhead sign.

Willow Creek itself is one of those trickling streams that just about stops in the fall. Your track starts up beside it, crosses it to the west side, and then leaves the water, gradually gaining altitude along the ridge beside it. You pass through lovely stands of aspen, and at mile 1.3 your track makes a right turn away from the creek and winds up steeply through more aspen to a high place where Pikes Peak pops into view.

The route ahead wanders near the park boundary, which is all fenced and has a number of fire access gates leading in from private property. At mile 2.5 you find the turnoff to **Sand Creek #41** on your right. You can also see Mount Pisgah from this juncture.

At mile 3.1 our trail forks. The right fork is a side trail that leads past **Spring Creek Trail #43** to **War Party Overlook #38**, which is only half a mile away, so we'll check out now. Your trail goes down steeply through very large aspen and crosses a tiny stream, which is Spring Creek itself. **Its trail #43 is a singletrack on the north side of the water. Watch for it among the trees.**

Passing Spring Creek Trail for now, we climb steeply out of this drainage and hook a left at a saddle on top. Then we continue up through mixed trees to arrive at the top of a grassy ridge studded with limber pine. Now you walk out on a single track toward some giant rocks that cap the ridge: This is War Party Overlook. That rock formation, one of the prettiest in the park, actually blocks your view to the north and would be dangerous to climb without technical gear, but from its base you have distant views to the east and west.

Going back to the fork on **Willow Creek/Dome View #40**, we now take the other fork toward Dome View Overlook, which is at mile 4.7 from the trailhead. Go out on a grassy ridge amid scattered limber pine and small ponderosa and climb around on the big boulders. Unlike Fourmile Overlook across canyon, this one is not a single viewing spot but an area with a number of places where you can find vistas in different directions. Dome Rock, of course, is actually 56 feet below you from this perch and is just one of several granite plutons in view. Of course, you can always identify Dome Rock by the little squarish boulder on top.

This is the end of our trail #40. Return the way you came.

SAND CREEK #41, 1.7 miles one way or 5.6 miles as a loop with Dome Rock and Willow Creek/Dome View Trails, rated easy downhill and steeply difficult uphill. No bikes.

How else can we rate a trail like this? Going down is easy and going up is tough because it's all one steep slant following a crease in the forest. Sand Creek itself is more sand than creek, barely seeping by fall. You find the top, of course, at mile 2.5 along **Willow Creek Trail/Dome View #51**. There is one narrow grassy meadow with a stock tank along this route, but the rest is all in deep timber, lovely aspen, ponderosa and such, with no views. It breaks out of the trees at a meadow beside **Dome Rock Trail #46**. From here it is 1.6 miles to the Dome Rock Trailhead, so your loop will measure 5.6 miles.

SPRING CREEK TRAIL #43, segment measures 2 miles one way, forming nearly 10-mile loop with Dome Rock and Willow Creek/Dome View Trails, rated difficult. Open to foot and horse. No bikes. Closed Dec 1-July 15.

This trail almost didn't make it. Years ago, when it was decided that Spring Creek Trail would be closed to bikes, there was some question as to whether or not many hikers could use it and still get back by nightfall. That's because it is off to itself, hard to reach, and the natural loop that it forms with Willow Creek/Dome View Trail and Dome Rock Trail measures about ten miles! In rough terrain, that's a very long day, so use good boots and double socks and get an early start.

The top of this trail is located about 0.2 miles off **Willow Creek/Dome View Trail #40** along the side trail that leads to War Party Overlook. That side trail meets **Willow Creek/Dome View** at mile 3.1 from the trailhead. It appears as a single track in the trees just across Spring Creek.

From there on down, #43 stays to the north of the creek. There is a meadow with a cabin en route. Later on it gets very steep and rough as it goes down to the base of Dome Rock itself.

Once reaching the grassy valley in the Dome Rock Natural Area, **Spring Creek Trail #43** fords Fourmile Creek just upstream from its confluence with Spring Creek. From there you climb up the opposite side a short distance to hook into **Dome Rock Trail #46. As you can see, this one is not for beginners.**

DECKERS/CHEESMAN AREA

Gill Trail
Shoreline Trail
Cheesman Dam Trail

Glistening water flowing beside the highway near Deckers lures many people to pull over and fly fish those sections of the South Platte River open to the public. Yet often visitors don't realize that local trails open up miles of better fishing upstream! Gill Trail offers Gold Medal catch-and-release fishing along the Platte, and Cheesman Reservoir features a variety of lake fishing.

Cheesman is a mountain jewel. As Denver's major water source, this lake was closed to all recreation for many years. Now Denver Water welcomes limited recreation, including fishing, hiking and bird watching on a day-use basis. There are many special rules, of course, and the public's cooperation is needed to protect the resource.

In the fall, many people explore Cheesman just to watch our nation's symbol. There are fewer bald eagles at Cheesman these days, due to a shortage of stocker salmon, but you can still see a few. Young ones look much like goldens, all brown, but goldens don't fish. Bald eagles attain their white plumage

Many people learn to fly fish on the Platte.

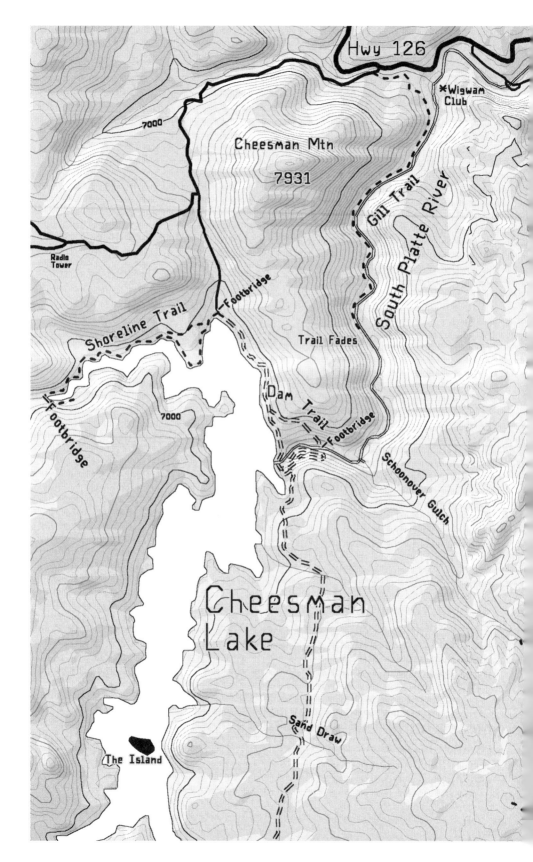

with maturity and they live mostly on fish. We've seen as many as three circling in the sky at the same time.

The Division of Wildlife stocks Cheesman with lake trout, smallmouth bass, etc..There are also brown trout, pike and yellow perch. Only one of the lake's 18 miles of shoreline is closed to fishing, that being the first mile from the gate leading east to the far side of the dam. You must stay off the dam, but may walk any other section of road in the area.

The problem with fishing Cheesman is access. This is a deep lake amid rocky timber with steep banks. In fall, lower levels create stretches of sandy gravel beach, but even these are interrupted by rock formations. No boats or floatation devices are allowed, so this means scrambling treacherous terrain. For that reason, Denver Water and the Colorado Division of Wildlife have been building trails to help you access more shoreline.

Unlike **Gill Trail, Cheesman** trails are closed in winter (Jan 1- April 30), but fishermen who want to access the river just below the dam are allowed to enter the gate and walk roads to the footbridge. See **Cheesman Dam Trail** for directions. Dogs must be on a leash (strictly enforced). No swimming or wading (no water-body contact at all), no hunting, firearms or fireworks, no fires, no camping, horses or bikes. Pack your trash. Caretakers vigorously patrol in boats and with trained security dogs to make sure that backpackers don't try to camp along remote shore-lines. Remember, you must return to your car within one half hour after sunset. Flies and artificial lures only.

ROAD DIRECTION: From Denver take Hwy. 285 south to Pine Junction, then head south on 126 toward Deckers. From Colorado Springs, take Hwy. 24 west to Woodland Park, then right on 67 to Deckers. The trail-head for GILL is 2.6 miles west of Deckers on 126. The other Gill trail-head is located a tenth of a mile farther west where 211 branches off toward Cheesman. Don't park at that Intersection; instead, park at Wigwam Campground another third of a mile west on 126. Wigwam Campground is now a pay campground.

To find SHORELINE and the CHEESMAN DAM TRAIL, take the Cheesman turnoff (211) 2.7 miles west of Deckers and follow the signs 3.2 miles to the lake. Park outside the fence. As you enter the gate, Shoreline is immediately on your right. CHEESMAN DAM TRAIL is straight ahead, but you must walk roads to reach it. See its trail description for directions.

GILL TRAIL, Forest Service #610, over 2 miles one way, elevation gain measures about 300 ft. but is actually larger; rated moderate at first, then very difficult scrambling high in the canyon. Features Gold Medal wild trout fishing, catch-and-release only.

Gold Medal Fishing means that it's just about as good as fishing can be. If you've ever envied the Wigwam Club's private stretch of the river along 126, take heart: You own an even longer stretch of the same water just upstream. This is a "wild trout" stream, not stocked, but it is also a catch-and-release area, so fish must be returned immediately to the water.

That also means the trout are big and plentiful and highly educated. TV's Curt Gowdy called this one of the finest trout streams in the world, and biologists believe that even the Indians never saw better. This marvelous habitat also happens to be set in one of the most beautiful canyons you'll ever see.

Get an early start because the two parking areas serving the two trailheads both fill up quickly. And bring a flashlight. Often the fish start biting at dusk, and without a flashlight, you might have to leave just when things get lively.

Topo maps show **Gill** going all the way to the lake, but it doesn't. It starts out well, but braids and fades and finally vanishes in the cliffs well short of the dam. DOW officers routinely clamber the entire distance to enforce the law, but even though they know all the tricks of the route, they still call it extremely difficult at the far end. Also dangerous. It's an easy place to break a leg, but a hard place to get help. Still, if you want to get away from the crowd, all you have to do is explore a little farther upstream.

Gill also looks flat on maps, rising only a few hundred feet in several miles, but actually it jumps up and down so sharply that its real elevation gain is surely more than a thousand feet.

Because there are two parking areas, two trailheads have developed, but both trails soon join up before starting the climb up and over a wooded ridge. Once you see the river, the trail forks. The left fork goes directly down to the water, and from there you can work your way upstream. Those who want to fish farther up take the right fork, which is a good trail, staying high and offering many scenic views. Trouble is, when waters are clearest, you can see fish from the upper trail, tempting some to shortcut, which always causes erosion damage, if not skin damage.

You'll also notice trails across river, but those are only pieces, not a continuous route, made by fishermen who wade across. The only public footbridge is just below the dam. Just upstream from the footbridge is a cable marking the no-fishing boundary 1,000 feet below the base of the dam. Another trail from the footbridge leads up to the east side of Cheesman Lake. See **Cheesman Dam Trail**.

Remember, the fish along **Gill** are professional entertainers who must be returned to work immediately. Only artificial flies and lures may be used. Spectacular rainbows and browns prove this system works. Report any violators.

Gill is a FS trail, technically open to many activities that are not truly appropriate. It is meant to be a rugged experience, especially upstream. Horsemen, hunters and mountain bikers should consider going elsewhere, and backpackers will have a tough time finding a good place to pitch a tent.

If you want to camp nearby, you have your choice of three FS campgrounds.

Wigwam is a pay campground with a well, but please ignore the emergency bin and haul your trash away. Lone Rock, nearer Deckers on the same road, is a pay reservation campground. Kelsey is another pay campground eight miles northwest of Deckers on 126.

SHORELINE TRAIL, Denver Water Dept., 2 miles one-way; elevation gain nil, rated easy. Features fishing access to beautiful lake.

As you enter the gate, **Shoreline Trail** is immediately on your right. It soon forks. Going left allows you to follow the shoreline around the point. Going right, you find a shortcut over a low ridge. Both meet up beyond the point and then continue along the north shore, leading west toward the Goose Creek inlet. (Goose Creek is known as Lost Creek where it repeatedly dives underground in the Lost Creek Wilderness.)

So far, two miles of this trail have been built, as far as the inlet. But the DOW has completed a footbridge spanning the inlet and has built more trail to access some of the lake's west shore.

CHEESMAN DAM TRAIL, Division of Wildlife, less than half mile one way, but access road adds more than a mile to this; elevation gain about 300 feet, rated moderate. Features access to lake's east shore with spectacular view of dam.

This is a short but steep trail, allowing you to reach the east side of the lake without crossing the dam (a major no-no). Since it is only a link, your real hike will be on the access roads leading to and beyond this trail.

Beginning at the gate, walk the road straight ahead toward the dam. This mile is the only shore section closed to fishing. Just before you reach the dam, take the road that branches to your left, climbing uphill. Higher up the road forks, but keep to the left. The right fork leads to another caretaker's residence called the Cliff Dwellers, which you'll see later. Then the road pitches downhill and ends at a footbridge that crosses the river just below the dam.

Downstream you'll see a bit of trail used by fishermen, but this does not really connect to **Gill,** as explained. Hardy souls can scramble the route, just as officers do, but it is dangerous and difficult. During winter, when Cheesman trails are closed, you can still come this way to fish this portion of the river, but you may not climb the **Cheesman Dam Trail** beyond the bridge and you must return to the gate by sunset.

Upstream you will see a cable marking the no-fishing boundary. 1,000 feet below the base of the dam. Your trail begins across the bridge.

It's all up from here, a series of four switchbacks that climb through timber to a road at the top of the canyon. Every switchback gives you a better view of the dam. For us, this was a charming surprise. Instead of being the usual slab of concrete, this dam looks like something the Incas might have built.

Man's first attempt to plug the gorge was rejected by the river itself. An earthen dam, lined with boiler plate, was swept away in the 1800s. So engineers took a lesson from the cliffs forming the gorge and built a dam made of the same granite. Large blocks were cut and artfully pieced together to form a graceful monument that blends in with the surrounding cliffs. Finished in 1905, it has an historical designation.

When you reach the road, notice the Cliff Dwellers cabin perched on the cliffs across canyon. Turn to the left and hike the road until it joins the road coming from the dam. Again turn left and you will be hiking along the east shoreline. Have fun!

TARRYALL AREA

Brookside-McCurdy Trail
Ute Creek Trail
Lizard Rock Trail

The mining town of Tarryall was called Puma City back in 1896. It seems that an unsociable prospector named Rocky Mountain Jim moved to this scenic valley to get away from the hectic life in Cripple Creek, but his dream of solitude ended when his gold discovery brought a population of a thousand!

ROAD DIRECTIONS: From I-25 in Colorado Springs take the Cimarron Exit #141 and go west on Hwy 24, past Woodland Park and Divide. The Tarryall Road turnoff is located only 1.2 miles beyond Lake George. Travel about 13 miles on Tarryall Road and find Spruce Grove Campground and the trailhead for LIZARD ROCK. At mile 14.7 find Twin Eagles Campground with the southern trailhead for BROOKSIDE-

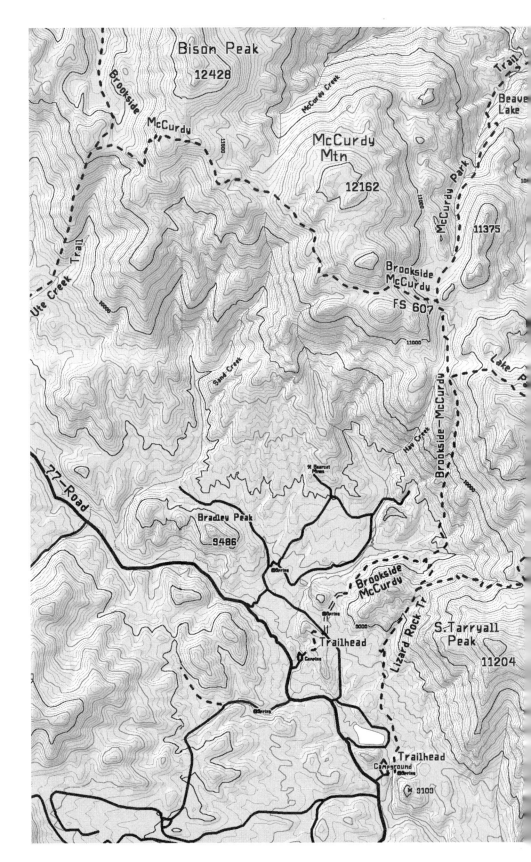

MCCURDY. This is an approach to Hankins Pass in the Lost Creek Wilderness. Restroom facilities, a horse loading chute and ample parking are available at the trailhead. For directions to the BROOKSIDE-MCCURDY northern trailhead, see DEER CREEK/BAILEY AREA. For directions to the middle of BROOKSIDE-MCCURDY, see KENOSHA PASS AREA. To find the trailhead for UTE CREEK, travel another 5.5 miles past Twin Eagles and look for parking and a foot-bridge on your right. Note: You must pay to park at Twin Eagles Campground, but not at Spruce Grove nearby.

BROOKSIDE McCURDY, Forest Service #607, about 38 miles one way, elevation gain 5,750 ft., loss 4,180 ft.; rated difficult. Features spectacular and varied scenery.

8,640 from Tarryall　　　about 5.0 miles　　　to McCurdy Pk 10,900

Just pretend you're eating an elephant, one bite at a time. This is a 38-mile giant. Aside from Colorado Trail 1776, Brookside-McCurdy is the longest trail in the Pike National Forest, snaking all the way from Bailey on Highway 285 from Denver to Tarryall Road, near the old mining town. Indeed, the Colorado Trail *is* Brookside-McCurdy for a ways. Like the CT 1776, it is generally done in pieces, being accessed from many points. We could describe it either direction, but Tarryall won the coin toss.

Beginning at Twin Eagles Campground on Tarryall Road, the path climbs up to an old road, turns left onto the road and soon changes into a path once more that winds through evergreens and aspens. A ranch meadow is spread below. Soon you pass the sign where **Hankins Pass Trail** branches away to the right. You cross tiny tributaries of Hay Creek and then begin the grueling switchbacks that take you up through red granite crags similar to those in the Lost Creek Wilderness ahead. Two of the crags have window holes through them. Each switchback offers a loftier view of Pikes Peak and the Tarryall Valley.

Near 10,720 feet you find the junction where **Lake Park Trail** heads uphill to your right. Climb a meadow valley and follow its stream up to the saddle ridge above its headwaters. From here you overlook the broad valley of McCurdy Park, with the beginning of **McCurdy Park Trail** going right, but **Brookside-McCurdy** turns left and climbs up past McCurdy Mountain toward Bison Pass.

Here you climb through a ghost forest created by a fire around 1868 or 1869. The trees died upright and many remain that way, now weathered to look like driftwood. Erosion of soil after the fire prevented new trees from

growing, so you find a grassy timberline environment just below the altitude where timberline usually begins. Your trail continues to climb toward the real timberline into bighorn sheep country. Indeed, the Pikes Peak herd was reestablished with bighorns captured here.

Near Bison Pass you arrive at a grassy knoll at 11,900 feet where you can see across South Park to Antero Reservoir and the mountain ranges beyond. Your trail dives off that western slope, switchbacking down through loose gravel and through bristlecone pines that have reestablished themselves in this part of the forest. You arrive at a ridge saddle where

Ute Creek Trail heads south-west toward Tarryall River. Your trail turns north and follows a gentle path through spruce and fir and past long meadows, following Indian creek down to Lost Park Campground.

From here you follow the meadow of the North Fork of Lost Creek north for two miles. Your path curves northwest and finds the remains of an 1890s sawmill. **Your trail crosses the creek and joins Colorado Trail #1776. The two trails are one for another two miles as you travel northwest up another meadow valley.**

A sign marks the point where **Brookside-McCurdy** heads north again beside a tributary that is hidden in the trees. This steep and rocky path leads up to a ridge saddle, then down the other side to Craig Park, which is similar to the brushy and boggy valley that you just left. After a short stretch going upstream, your trail turns to the right at its junction with **Craig Park Trail.** See DEER CREEK/BAILEY AREA.

From Craig Park your trail rises gradually for half a mile, leading north, then takes a long series of switchbacks down from a saddle to the top of a ridge dividing MacArthur and Brookside Gulches at about 10,000 ft. Here we find a trail rediscovered by Ranger Ralph Bradt a few years ago. A shot-up sign led him to this overgrown path that never appeared on maps and never had a number. It's now being called **"Brookside AG" Trail #719** and joins the reroute of **Ben Tyler.**

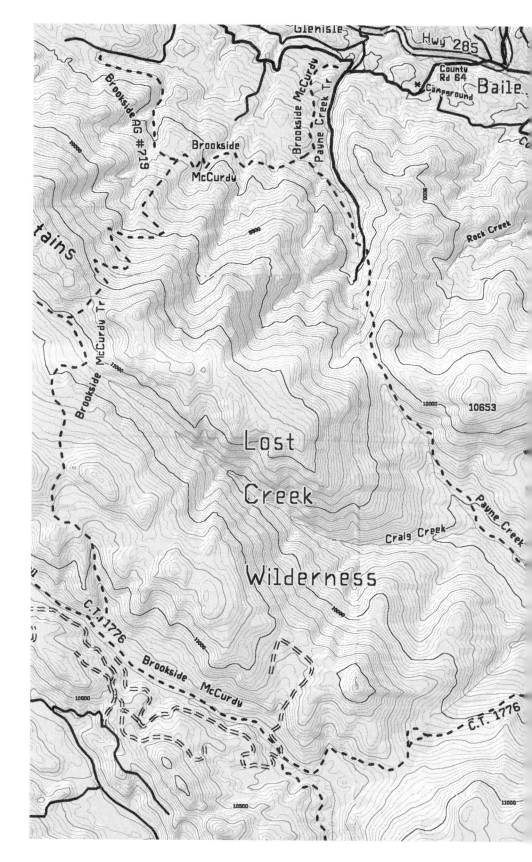

Brookside-McCurdy continues down the ridge, then veers east just below the wilderness boundary to join Payne Creek Trail. Together the two continue another mile to the **Payne Creek-Brookside Trailhead.** See DEER CREEK/BAILEY AREA for directions. **Hey, what's 38 miles when you're having fun?**

UTE CREEK TRAIL Forest Service #629, about 3 miles one way, elevation gain 2,620 ft., rated difficult. Features forest climb to Brookside-McCurdy.

8,680   3.0 miles   11,300

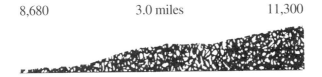

This is sometimes used to form a loop with Brookside-McCurdy, for it joins that longer trail at the top of Bison Pass. Both trails end at Tarryall Road, but 5.5 miles apart, so that much of your 20.5-mile loop is road travel.

Ute Creek Trail begins at a footbridge crossing Tarryall River, skirts private property where a beaver pond lies then begins climbing beside Ute Creek. It is a long sustained climb with no relief. This area boasts very large ponderosa pines, as well as aspen and blue spruce. After crossing near the fork of tributaries, the trail leaves the creekside and rises steeply on a wooded hillside.

The trail ends on a saddle ridge at nearly 11,300 feet, with a grand vista of the

A view of Tarryall's Spring Grove Campground

You don't have to squint too hard to see "the lizard" in profile, crawling from right to left with his tail extending down to the right.

Tarryall Valley below. Signs mark its juncture with **Brookside-McCurdy.** The total distance of the **Ute Creek/Brookside-McCurdy Loop,** including road travel, is estimated at 20.5 miles. But again, what's that if you're having fun?

LIZARD ROCK TRAIL, Forest Service #658, 2.5 miles one way, rated easy, then moderate. Features easy climb past Lizard Rock to Hankins Pass.

8,500   2.5 miles   9,280

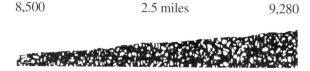

   Some rock formations have very imaginative names, but Lizard Rock really looks like an iguana crouching atop a mountain. The trailhead is located at a pay campground, but you can also access it by parking outside the campground. The trail skirts private property, then wanders up a drainage before climbing up toward Lizard Rock, which will be on your left, elevation 9,526. The trail does not climb to the rock itself, but goes past it to link with the newer switchbacks of **Hankins Pass.** The old **Hankins Pass** route is closed.

   Bikers note: Mountain bikes are discouraged on Lizard Rock Trail only because the top of the trail leads right into the Lost Creek Wilderness, where bicycles are not permitted.

LOST CREEK WILDERNESS

Beaver dammed a gorge to create this deep lake on McCurdy Park Trail

Hankins Pass Trail
Lake Park Trail
McCurdy Park Trail
Goose Creek Trail

The Lost Creek region has been set aside as a Wilderness Area to protect its primitive nature. Mountain bikes are prohibited, so you can only see this wonderland by hiking or riding horseback, a hard journey either way. This was the last refuge of Colorado's wild bison. The last four were killed off by poachers here in 1901.

Robert Leisure offered this description of Lost Creek's strange geology in his novel, *Black Mountain*: "Jim, I took only a quart of whiskey to help out my breakfast coffee, but I saw whales, teakettles, cowled monks, ships and sheep, frogs, dragons, Indians, colonial squires, kings, clowns, and goblins. It seemed like a city in the sky, its ornaments both noble and grotesque, a strange, secret place where silence in those tortuous corridors and nibbled granite avenues is broken only by the monotone of a crazy river. I call the river 'crazy' because it seems to hate the sunlight. It forms nine separate box canyons and flows as often under the ground as above."

This "lost creek," disappearing under cliffs and reappearing from caves beyond, makes this wilderness an especially dangerous place to get lost in, so beware. If you want a very long expedition, you can approach the Lost Creek area by two long trails, but the most popular route is the shortest one, which is still a staggering 24-mile loop that begins and ends near Goose Creek Campground. Many parts of this loop are difficult and most hikers take two to four days to complete it. Even on horseback, it's a very long ride. (We'll show you a box canyon often used by horseriders.) Just make sure that you take along everything you need. You will be a long way from help.

The loop can be hiked in either direction, of course, but we will describe it clockwise, beginning with Hankins Pass and ending with Goose Creek Trail. **Our CD-Rom topos make what we think is an important correction ignored by the USGS in their last update of their topos. So far as we know, we offer the only field-corrected map of this area.**

ROAD DIRECTIONS: From Denver, take Hwy 285 to Pine Junction, then south on I26. From Colorado Springs, take Hwy 24 west to Woodland Park, then 67 north to Deckers; cross the bridge onto 126. To find the Goose Creek Trailhead, take the gravel road (FS 211) that joins Highway 126 just three miles west of Deckers. Follow the signs to Goose Creek, a distance of 11 miles, then keep heading south another 3.5 miles, taking Trailhead Road to your right. Horses unload at a special parking area along this road. Both Hankins Pass and Goose Creek Trails share a common trailhead at the auto parking lot.

Log bridge on Hankins Pass Trail

HANKINS PASS TRAIL, Forest Service #630, 5.9 miles one way, elevation gain 1,820 ft., loss

1,070 ft., rated moderate to difficult.   Features access to Lake Park and Brookside-McCurdy Trails.

8,200 Goose Cr TH   5.9 miles   Hankins TH at Tarryall 8,940

Leaving the trailhead shared with Goose Creek, your path dips into Hankins Gulch, crosses a stream at the bottom, then forks. The left fork leads to Hankins Pass and the right fork to Goose Creek. Now you begin following the stream uphill through spruce and large aspens. There are no confusing side trails. About halfway to the pass itself, you find an aspen meadow with active beaver ponds, a nice place to camp and fish for brookies. Above this point, the path crosses the stream and follows the hillside above it. The trail eventually leads above the headwaters to a saddle ridge, and there you find an intersection with **Lake Park Trail.**

If you continue on Hankins, you will go down a set of switchbacks on the other side of the ridge and join first with **Lizard Rock** and then with **Brookside-McCurdy Trail.** Hankins ends there at the intersection with **Brookside-McCurdy.** From there you can take **Brookside-McCurdy** north to McCurdy Park, then **McCurdy Park Trail** and **Goose Creek Trail,** making a circuit, but that route is longer and the more difficult because you lose more than 1,000 feet of altitude and must make up that loss by climbing killer switchbacks.

The more popular route is still pretty difficult: Turn right off **Hankins Pass** onto **Lake Park Trail** at the saddle ridge. This eventually leads you to **Brookside-McCurdy** below McCurdy Park.

LAKE PARK,   Forest Service #639 3 miles from Hankins Pass to Brookside-McCurdy Trails, 1.25 miles to Lake Park itself; elevation gain 1,480 ft., loss 720 ft.; rated difficult. Features grand vistas and camping at Lake Park.

10,000 Hankins   3.0 miles   McCurdy 10,720

As you stand atop Hankins Pass itself, the sign says "Lake Park Three Miles" and points uphill. Be sure to fill your canteens (boil or treat) because the Lake Park Trail is a long, dry march over high country. It begins at 10,000 feet and climbs to almost 11,000 feet before descending to join Brookside-McCurdy.

Lake Park is a high meadow surrounded by majestic rock formations and the silvery snags of a ghost forest, created by fire. All lakes eventually silt up, but the process is quickened if a forest fire denudes the mountainside and increases erosion. Today, the lakes are only shallow puddles in the midst of bog. Campers will find good places on the south side of the meadow, but to reach flowing water, you must bushwhack carefully across the bogs to the streams that come down creases in the north slope. **Test the ground with care because some of these bogs are very deep!**

The trail climbs out of the park on the west side, very rocky and steep. As you cross the highest portion, watch for alpine columbine, a high-altitude miniature of the State Flower. From here the trail dives down to join **Brookside-McCurdy.** (Our map doesn't show all the switchbacks you descend there.) At this T-junction, Lake Park is about two miles behind, Tarryall Creek is about 4 3/4 miles to the south and McCurdy Park is about one mile north. That last mile to McCurdy Park climbs to the headwaters of a creek and up to a saddle ridge that overlooks the park.

McCURDY PARK TRAIL, Forest Service #628, 5.3 miles one way, elevation gain about 820 ft., loss over 2,000 ft.; rated moderate. Features camping at McCurdy Park, lake fishing north of park.

10,900   5.3 miles   9.420

McCurdy Park is a high valley with a flowing stream. Many of the most beautiful rock formations in the Lost Creek area are located along this trail.

Since we are describing the circuit from clockwise, we assume that you will be approaching McCurdy Park from the south, along **Brookside-McCurdy Trail**. **Brookside-McCurdy** is a very long trail (38 miles) that leads to McCurdy Park and then branches away to the west. **McCurdy Park Trail** begins at this intersection on a ridge overlooking McCurdy Park itself.

From this point you travel through the long grassy valley, following a stream north. Then you leave the creek and take a long series of steep switchbacks down the side of a canyon. At the bottom you find a deep lake that was built by beaver at a narrow part of the gorge. There are only a couple of campsites, so if you wish to stay here, try to arrive early. Although Lost Creek contains many brookies, the Forest Service reports they have never heard of anyone catching fish in this beautiful lake! We never caught any either, but mountain lakes are always boom or bust and we have no explanation. If you have luck, let us know.

From here the trail climbs up and over ridges and crosses a stream. **The USGS** topographic map still shows this stream to be the one draining from the

Lost Creek becomes Goose Creek when it stops being lost.

beaver lake, which would mean that the water comes from your right as you cross it, but the **map is mistaken**. The water comes from your left and is another lost piece of Lost Creek. See our CD-Rom map. A few campsites are available here, and many sections of Lost Creek have nice brookies.

Up and over more steep ridges and you find another stream crossing at Refrigerator Gulch. The USGS map shows you crossing at beaver ponds, but these have now turned to swamp so you would hardly know you were in the right place. Keep track of your drainages: They are your best navigation, even here.

As soon as you cross this stream, you find that the trail branches left and right. The right branch looks very distinct because it leads to a box canyon used by horse riders as a campsite and natural corral. Another piece of Lost Creek emerges in the box canyon, so horses have water but limited forage.

The left branch leads up to a saddle ridge where **McCurdy Park Trail** ends at a junction with **Goose Creek Trail.** From this point **Goose Creek Trail** follows the ridge north toward Wigwam Park or descends the ridge to complete the circuit by winding up at Goose Creek Campground. A sign marks the intersection.

GOOSE CREEK TRAIL, Forest Service #612, 11.8 miles one way; elevation gain 2,090 ft., loss 780 ft.; rated difficult. Features fishing, camping and majestic rock formations.

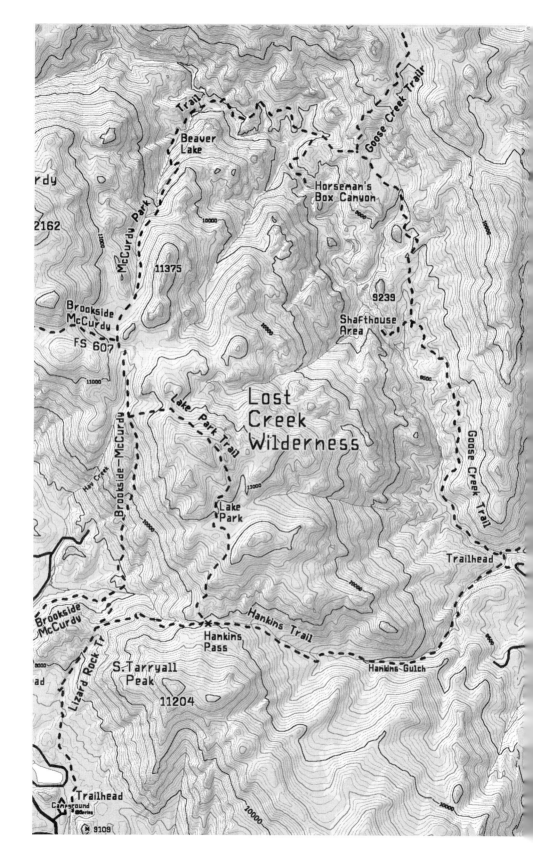

The Forest Service would like to remind you that Goose Creek Trail is one of Colorado's most overly-popular trails. So if you're looking for a place to get away from it all, this is not it. One of the purposes of this guide is to give you choices between such overly-popular trails and others that are little-visited at all. Still, Goose Creek is so far from front range cities that only its beauty can account for its popularity.

If you hike the Lost Creek circuit clockwise, you will join Goose Creek Trail at a ridgetop east of Refrigerator Gulch. But there is no use beginning our description in the middle, so let's start back at the main Goose Creek-Hankins trailhead.

The early part of this trail is popular among fishermen who are after the rainbows and brookies, so it is wide and easy and has a fine bridge. (**Lost Creek becomes Goose Creek when it stops being lost.**)

As you leave the auto parking lot, you descend a trail and cross a fairly small stream that flows from Hankins Gulch. These signs direct you to the left for **Hankins Pass Trail** or to the right for **Goose Creek Trail.**

Goose Creek is wide and active, occasionally interrupted by the beaver corps of engineers. The campsites are in the meadow across the stream, so campers can be away from the day traffic. Farther upstream the trail grows narrower and steeper. As you descend a ridge well away from Goose Creek itself, you find a trickle of water crossing your path and a clear trail branching away to the left. This leads to a fascinating and scenic area called the Shafthouse.

Follow this path and you will find several log cabins, but the State Health Dept. warns that sleeping in old cabins is dangerous because their vermin spread disease. They should be used only in emergencies. There is very little firewood close by. At the cabins, the trail goes left and right, left to dead-end at Goose Creek itself and right to the Shafthouse area.

Many years ago engineers tried to dam Reservoir Gulch by sinking a shaft and pumping concrete underground in an attempt to stop the flow of Lost Creek. Yet the creek only found new channels underground. You will not find a shaft or a house at the "Shafthouse," but you will find some rusting equipment on a concrete slab and some very pretty scenery. Just a few yards before you reach the machinery, there is an opening in the rock on the left side of the trail where giant boulders have tumbled together to form a cave-like room. Yet the room has a concrete floor! Fred Flintstone would love it.

Return to the main trail and follow it north to find another charming area, the upper end of Reservoir Gulch. This area offers more campsites with a convenient stream. It's a steep climb out of this area to the saddle ridge where **Goose Creek Trail** joins **McCurdy Park Trail,** and from there **Goose Creek Trail** leads north, crossing over into another watershed and following a stream downhill past a balanced rock pinnacle toward **Wigwam Trail**. That's where **Goose Creek Trail** ends.

WELLINGTON LAKE AREA

Wigwam Trail leads to Lost Park, but road access is from Kenosha Pass

Rolling Creek Trail
Wigwam Trail

Wellington Lake is located on a gravel road between Bailey and Buffalo Creek. The lake itself is private, but since all the small roads in this area have signs pointing toward Wellington Lake, that's a good place to start our directions to this remote and little-visited area. Because the trails described here enter the Lost Creek Wilderness, mountain bikes are prohibited.

ROAD DIRECTIONS: From Denver, take Hwy 285 about 39 miles to Bailey. Go left on County 68 in Bailey, which becomes FS 543 (called 560 on the FS Visitor's Map, but marked 543 on the road). At mile 5.2, take the right fork (now FS 560) marked for Wellington Lake. About 8 miles from Bailey the Colorado Trail #1776 crosses from your left and continues up a little dirt road on your right that leads back 0.3 miles to the trailhead for both CT 1776 and ROLLING CREEK TRAILS. If you pass the Jefferson County School's Windy Peak Outdoor Lab, you missed the turnoff. Go back 0.7 miles to find it.

From Colorado Springs, take Hwy 24 to Woodland Park, 67 north to Deckers, cross the bridge onto I26. From Deckers follow 126 11.3 miles to FS-550. Turn left and follow 550 (5.1 mile), which then becomes FS-543. When you reach Wellington Lake, turn right. Only 0.7 miles past Jeffco School's Windy Peak Outdoor Lab, find parking for ROLLING CREEK TRAIL and the CT on a little dirt road leading back 0.3 miles to your left.

To find WIGWAM TRAILHEAD, go south from Wellington Lake five miles. The trailhead turnoff will be on your right after you cross Stoney Pass. Since this can be a rather round-about way of getting there from Colorado Springs, however, we will describe a shorter but more complex route from Deckers: Take Hwy 126 west of Deckers for three miles and turn left onto the gravel road marked for Lost Valley Ranch, Cheesman Lake, etc (FS 211). Travel 1.1 miles and turn right at the fork marked JVL and Lost Valley Ranch. Travel another 1.1 miles and turn right at the fork marked Wellington Lake (FS 560). Two and one-half miles later you will turn right again following a sign toward Wellington Lake. Only 2.6 miles later you find the WIGWAM TRAIL road marked on your left. This is a dirt road that gets worse as you travel the 1.4 miles to the parking area. The last section may be very poor, so explore ahead on foot before attempting it.

ROLLING CREEK, Forest Service #663, 9 miles one way, elevation gain 2,782 ft., loss 1,412 ft.; rated moderate to difficult. Features forest trail, then steep climb through canyon.

| 8,280 | 9.0 miles | 9,650 |

This trail begins with a pleasant forest walk with no exceptionally steep parts. You cross small ridges and intermittent streams, heading toward the rock formation known as The Castle, where you cross Rolling Creek itself. At first you leave the creek and hike up into the woods to a place where the old route from Bancroft Ranch has been closed off. Turn right and climb a little farther and you return to the creek once more.

Now you begin the most beautiful part of the climb, a steep section that takes you up through a place where boulders have tumbled together in interesting ways. The forest is cool and mossy here, a charming place. (Some brookies, but small.) There are a tremendous number of dead trees here, causing a continuous problem of deadfall across the trail.

Finally, you leave the creek as you start up the ridge that separates this water-

shed from the Wigwam watershed beyond. Then you go up and over the ridge and down to Wigwam Park, where a sign marks the southern intersection with **Wigwam Trail.** Beautiful valley.

WIGWAM TRAIL, Forest Service #609, 13.3 miles one way; elevation gain 2,220 ft.,loss 500ft.:rated moderate. Features meadows and forest with fishing at creeks and beaver ponds.

8,200   13.3 miles   9120

Wigwam is a long and varied trail with only a few steep sections. Much of the trail skirts long valleys rich in wildlife such as grouse, beaver and deer. The DOW rates Wigwam's brook trout fishing as "good, but needs fishing" to improve size. Eat 'em!

Beginning at the eastern trailhead, start down a washed out four-wheel track to a glade where you find Wigwam Creek and a small pond. Follow Wigwam upstream, crossing and recrossing on log bridges. You pass through a rolling forest, then climb more steeply. The creek beside you forms small waterfalls.

At Wigwam Park itself, the creek meanders through a grassland, often interrupted by beaver dams. Your trail stays on the northern edge of this valley, finally coming to a sign indicating that **Goose Creek Trail** is to your left, across the valley. **From there you can see the tributary ravine that Goose Creek Trail follows, and framed within this notch is a rock formation with a thumb like projection that has a balanced rock on its tip!**

The largest beaver pond marked on old topographic maps is now a flat field of grass that makes comfortable camping. There used to be a huge dam here, about six feet tall and over 200 feel long. This kind of beaver activity built much of the flatland seen in Wigwam Park and elsewhere in Colorado.

As you follow the valley higher, you find a sign for **Rolling Creek Trail** on your right. Farther up the valley, you find a place where the original trail becomes faint and where a newer trail crosses Wigwam Creek. Take the new trail, cross the creek, and follow it up through the woods to a higher park.

At the entrance of this park, your trail is covered with water from a spring that flows from beneath a huge rock. That is the clearest source of water in this park, but it still needs boiling because the pool itself may be contaminated.

The trail grows more more faint as you climb up to the low saddle ridge (only 10,150 feet) that separates Wigwam from the East Lost Creek watershed. **Wigwam Trail** continues down into East Lost Park, across Lost Creek and along an even wider valley to end at Lost Park Campground. (See **Kenosha Pass Area**.).

BAILEY/DEER CREEK AREA

Only part of Rosalie leads through this ghost forest left by a very old burn.

Meridian Trail
Rosalie Trail (see Guanella Pass for map)
Tanglewood Trail
Payne Creek Trail (Craig Meadow)
Ben Tyler Trail
Craig Park Trail

This scenic area in the northeast corner of Park County is a jumping off point for some long and lovely pack trails. We say "pack trails" because—unfortunately—only one of them, Meridian Trail, is actually open to mountain bikes, and even the last 10th of a mile of Meridian is closed to bikes where it enters a Wilderness Area at a saddle.

Indeed, the Bailey/Deer Creek region lies between two Wilderness Areas, Mount Evans and Lost Creek. Now that mountain bikes have become so popular, fewer people attempt extra long trails on foot, but there's a hint in that statement. Here's a place fewer people go. And that's the kind of place I like best.

Aside from the Colorado Trail 1776, Brookside-McCurdy is the longest trail in the Pike National Forest (38 miles!) and was rerouted at this end a few years back, making it a little longer. Like 1776, most people do Brookside-McCurdy in pieces, for it has many access points. Indeed, 1776 borrowed part of it. We actually describe Brookside-McCurdy from the Tarryall end just to keep Lizard Rock and Ute Indian from getting lonely in that chapter, but next edition we may turn that around. It deserves more detail.

Craig Park is another long trail made even longer by the fact that it has no road access and can only be reached via Brookside-McCurdy or Ben Tyler. You won't meet many people in Craig Park.

ROAD DIRECTIONS: From Denver take Highway 285 into the mountains. From Colorado Springs, take Hwy 24 to Woodland Park, go north on 67, cross the bridge at Deckers onto I26 and go to Pine Junction, where you turn left at its intersection with 285. We're all Bailey bound.

To find trailheads for MERIDIAN and ROSALIE-TANGLEWOOD, watch for a prominent turnoff marked "Deer Creek" at a stoplight (indeed the first ever stoplight in Park County) after you pass Pine Junction and before you reach Bailey. This is County 43. Follow this paved road about 6.8 miles west to a fork. The right fork, marked "Camp Rosalie," leads to MERIDIAN TRAILHEAD on County 47. The left fork, a continuation of County 43, leads to the Deer Creek Trailhead for the ROSALIE-TANGLEWOOD TRAILS. Here are more details:
To find the MERIDIAN TRAILHEAD, follow County 47 for 1.4 miles. Markers mention Camp Rosalie. Pass the turnoff to Meridian Campground; the trail does NOT begin there. When you reach Prospector Way, turn left onto Prospector Way and wind back one mile, passing Camp Rosalie, to the MERIDIAN TRAILHEAD. Your road now dead-ends at MERIDIAN TRAILHEAD.

To find the ROSALIE-TANGLEWOOD TRAILHEAD, take the left fork on Deer Creek Road marked "Deer Creek Campground," a continuation of County 43. The pavement ends a mile later and the road becomes gravel. Then you come to a Y with the Deer Creek Campground on the left. Take the right fork, which leads shortly to the ROSALIE-TANGLEWOOD TRAILHEAD. Only one path leaves the parking area: Rosalie and TANGLEWOOD divide higher up, but here's another change. Years ago they used to divide only a short distance from the trailhead, but ROSALIE now leaves TANGLEWOOD about a mile up.

To find the trailhead for PAYNE CREEK and BROOKSIDE MCCURDY, proceed to Bailey, which is located beside the North Fork of the South Platte River on Hwy. 285 about 39 miles from Denver. Turn south off Hwy. 285 at Moore Lumber and Hardware in Bailey and follow a paved

road (County Rd 64) until it curves back toward the highway. At the beginning of this curve is a gravel road that leads straight ahead. Proceed 1.5 miles on gravel to PAYNE CREEK/BROOKSIDE TRAILHEAD. CRAIG PARK TRAIL can only be accessed via BROOKSIDE-MCCURDY or BEN TYLER. For directions to the southern trailhead for BROOKSIDE-MCCURDY, see TARRYALL AREA. For directions to the middle, see KENOSHA PASS AREA.

The trailhead for BEN TYLER is located off Hwy. 285, almost six miles west of Bailey. A new trailhead is still being planned off the highway at Gibbs Gulch nearby. Watch for signs.

MERIDIAN TRAIL, Forest Service #604, 3 miles one way, elevation gain 1,710 ft., rated moderate. Features forest climb to a junction with other trails leading out of the Pike National Forest

9,030   3.0 miles   10,740

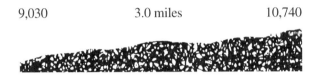

Meridian Trail connects to a larger system of trails in Arapahoe National Forest. It is a very clear and well-marked route, but there are two points of confusion: It does not leave from Meridian Campground and its destination, called Meridian Trail Campground on old maps, has been erased. There never was much of a campground there anyhow, just a spring and an out-house. Even its signs have changed.

Of the three trails in the Deer Creek Area, **Meridian** is still the best choice for inexperienced trail horses. It begins on a gentle gravel path, growing rocky only at the top.

From the trailhead bridge, **Meridian Trail** climbs a long ridge high above Elk Creek. There are no real creeks along this route, but small springs that cross the path higher up provide water. As you angle northeast, you travel through a grove of aspen that are unusually tall and straight. Must be beautiful in the fall.

At the top there used to be a pair of signs on the northern edge of the saddle. The sign pointing northwest said, "Lost Creek 4, Truesdell Creek 6, Beartrack Lakes 7," and the one pointing northeast said "Lost Creek 6, Indian Creek Park 7, Brook Forest 12," but in keeping with the Wilderness philosophy, Wilderness signs no longer give distances, only trail names. Still, we thought the old distances worth mentioning (even if they were only estimates) in case you want to wander that far. Those other trails are not in our area (every guide has to have a limit somewhere) and, of course, that Lost Creek is no relation to the Lost Creek and its Wilderness Area in our region.

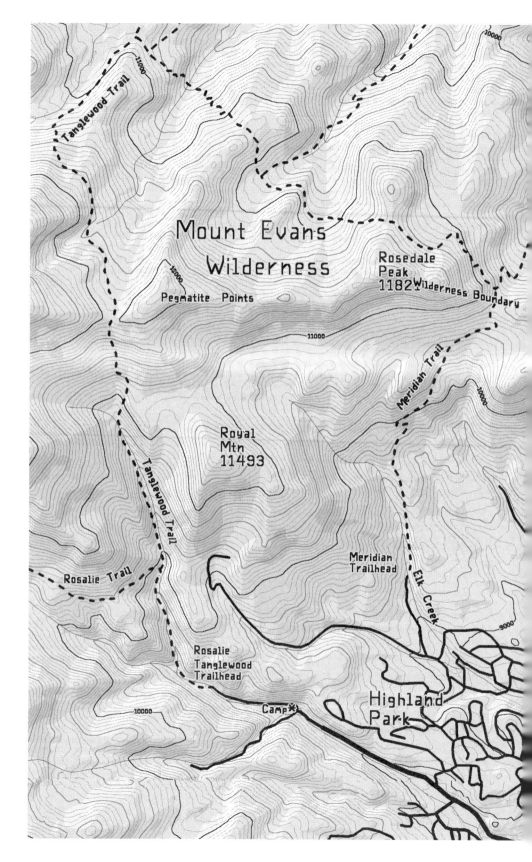

As mentioned earlier, almost all of **Meridian** is open to bikes clear up to the Wilderness boundary at the saddle. Stop there.

And by the way, we personally wish that all trails in any proposed Wilderness be measured with a trail wheel before designation because even trail wheels are banned from Wilderness Areas. Okay, no distances on signs, but I still like to know how far I'm going so I can plan my food better. No food, no fun.

ROSALIE TRAIL, Forest Service #603, 12 miles one way; elevation gain 3,560 ft., loss 1,120 ft.; rated difficult. Features high altitude trek to Guanella Pass. SEE GUANELLA PASS FOR REST OF MAP.

9,248   about 7.5 miles   to Abyss Tr 10,760

Rosalie is a long and rugged trail that twice climbs to timberline, yet even at its highest points, you find yourself surrounded by bald giants, including Mount Evans. Our description begins at the bottom because the lower section is the most popular.

Trailriders will find convenient corrals at the parking area, but **Rosalie** is so rugged that it can only be recommended for more experienced trail horses. About a mile from the trailhead, the **Rosalie-Tanglewood** path splits and **Rosalie** goes to the left to climb along and across Deer Creek. This path snakes up through forest and clearings where grouse, deer and beaver are often seen.

As you can see by the map, you take the left or southern fork at the headwaters of Deer Creek, but since the right fork is by far the larger stream, the left may appear as only a minor tributary or marshy ravine in late summer. The right fork swerves hard to the north at this point, so a compass can help make sure that you have found the right place.

Keep heading west up the green ravine. You are headed for a bald saddle ridge between two bald peaks known as Tahana on the north and Kataka on the south. Just short of the saddle there is another trail coming from Kataka Mountain and joining your own. This is the destination of **Threemile Creek Trail.** (SEE GUANELLA PASS AREA.)

The ridge saddle is that kind of timberline margin where trees grow only in scattered spots, all stunted and windswept. To the north you can see Mount Evans with its building on top and cars going up the switchbacks. Due west is Geneva Mountain, and to its right you see two green ravines where streams angle down to join Scott-Gomer Creek, which runs north-south below you at this point. **Rosalie** will follow that wide ravine on the right up to timberline and then beyond to Guanella Pass.

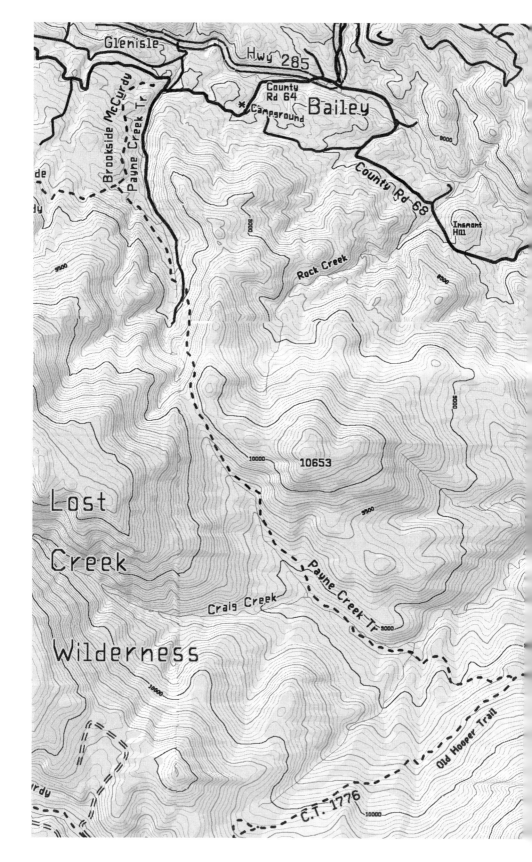

Now your path starts switchbacking down the moraine toward **Abyss Lake Trail** at Scott-Gomer Creek (Scott-Gomer used to be the name of Abyss Lake Trail). On the way, our path angles down through a ghost forest created by a fire long ago, a place where the trees look like weathered driftwood planted upright, and here's a forestry lesson:

The media has trouble with complex issues. For years forest fires were considered all bad, so when the Yellowstone fire proved to be renewing, media felt tricked and switched to the bumper-sticker simplification that forest fires are always blessings in disguise, which can be downright TRUE. Fires really are part of the natural cycle, but then again, **fires can only renew a forest if the soils remain intact. If the fire is too hot, the terrain too steep, then the unprotected soil, so ancient, so fragile, hanging by the threads of living roots, can simply wash away after a hot fire, filling valleys, making flat ground out of beaver ponds—and leaving slopes such as this so poor in soil that new trees cannot regrow.**

At the bottom you cross a fork of Scott-Gomer Creek, then cross **Abyss Lake Trail** in the manner shown on the map. This creek area is a popular campground, but has no fish, as we explain in the GUANELLA PASS AREA chapter.

Now your trail begins to make up the altitude lost in descending to Scott-Gomer. It's a long and steady climb to timberline and above, eventually intersecting a path that used to be a road. A post marks this intersection so that explorers coming downhill won't miss Rosalie and wind up going south along the wrong route. This closed road leads to a dead-end on the shoulder of Geneva Mountain at 12,179 feet.

Rosalie itself climbs to 11,800 feet before winding down to the trailhead at Guanella Pass. To find the upper trailhead by road, see GUANELLA PASS AREA.

TANGLEWOOD TRAIL, Forest Service #636, 5 miles one way; elevation gain 2,494 ft., rated difficult. Features charming streamside hike, rugged climb above timberline to lakes.

| 9,248 | 5.0 miles | 11,742 |

If you want to fish Roosevelt Lakes, you'll certainly have to earn the opportunity, for Tanglewood is a high and rocky route. The lower section is gentle and popular among dayhikers, but the higher you go, the rougher and rockier it gets.

There are convenient horse corrals at the trailhead, but trailriders are warned

Vegetarian horse snears at steak frying on campfire.

that Tanglewood is not suitable for training horses unaccustomed to climbing in the rocks. (Meridian Trail would be better.)

As you leave the trailhead, **Tanglewood** shares its route with **Rosalie,** but the two divide a mile up. For **Tanglewood** take the right fork, cross the creek above the old culvert that washed out, then follow up along a path that used to be a road. You cross and recross this tumbling creek, ascending through forest and small clearings. High up, the trail leaves the creek and climbs up above timberline. Here the trail fades somewhat in the rocks, so head toward a wooden post erected on the ridge saddle. There's not much of a trail there, either, but this marks the place where you're supposed to cross over.

From here you have a spectacular view and can see for miles, but oddly enough, you cannot see Roosevelt Lakes which lie directly below. The lakes are in the bottom of a glacial depression, and you must go some distance on this gentle incline before you see them.

A trail from Beartrack Lakes connects with **Tanglewood** at Roosevelt Lakes, but that's out of our area.

PAYNE CREEK TRAIL (CRAIG MEADOW), Forest Service #637, about 6 miles one way; elevation gain 1,030 ft., loss 1200 ft. Rated moderate. Features scenic meadow with beaver ponds and good fishing.

8,440 from Brookside   About 6.0 miles   to CT 1776 9,315

Craig Meadow is a grassy park with beaver ponds, a great place to catch brookies up to eight inches long. The trail leading there is called PAYNE CREEK TRAIL, but it does not really follow Payne Creek very far. Still, this name helps keep it from being confused with Craig Park Trail.

Starting at the trailhead, you climb the ridge between Brookside Gulch and Payne Creek, going up through the woods to the T-junction where Brookside-McCurdy heads west and Payne Creek Trail heads southeast along the ridge above Payne Creek. Eventually, it picks up a tributary of Craig Creek and follows that down to the meadow. Your trail makes a bog crossing at Craig Creek and follows the stream where the beavers are at work. Large blue spruce grow widely spaced in the meadow.

Beyond the meadow, the trail crosses Bluestem Creek and then you will find an old road known as Pine Ridge joining the trail from the right. This is now closed to vehicles.

From here you begin climbing a trail uphill through the trees to join do Trail #1776 two miles from the meadow. This is where Payne Creek Trail ends.

One warning: There is no trail between Craig Meadow and Craig Park upstream because this creek plunges through a treacherous rock gorge called Black Canyon where hikers have become lost and injured.

BEN TYLER TRAIL, Forest Service #606, 9 miles one way, elevation gain 2,920 ft., loss 2,040 ft., rated moderate to difficult. Features streamside and high mountain hiking and horseriding now within Wilderness.

8,720 Gibbs Gulch   About 9.0 miles   to CT 1776 9,600

The way we heard it, Ben Tyler lived with is family near the mouth of the gulch that bears his name and there he had a lumber operation in the early days. He sawed up timber and shipped it by rail to mining towns. As you hike or horseback this spectacular trail, you can thank Ben for showing the way.

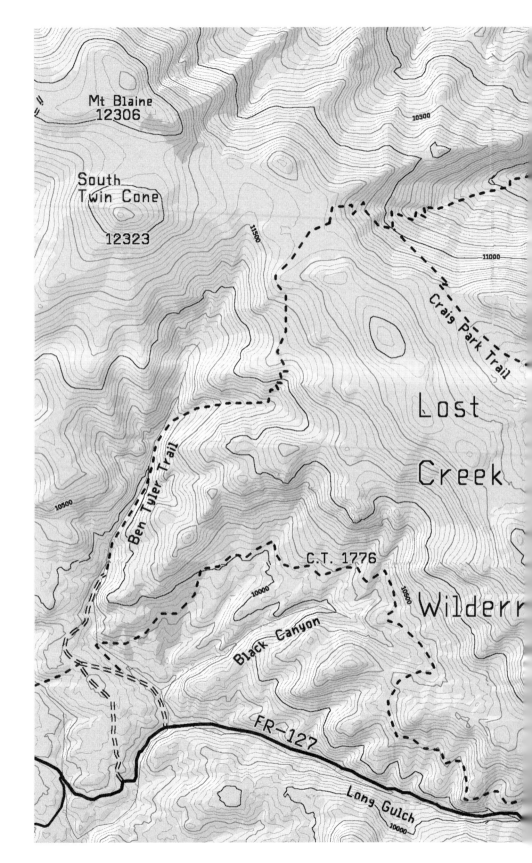

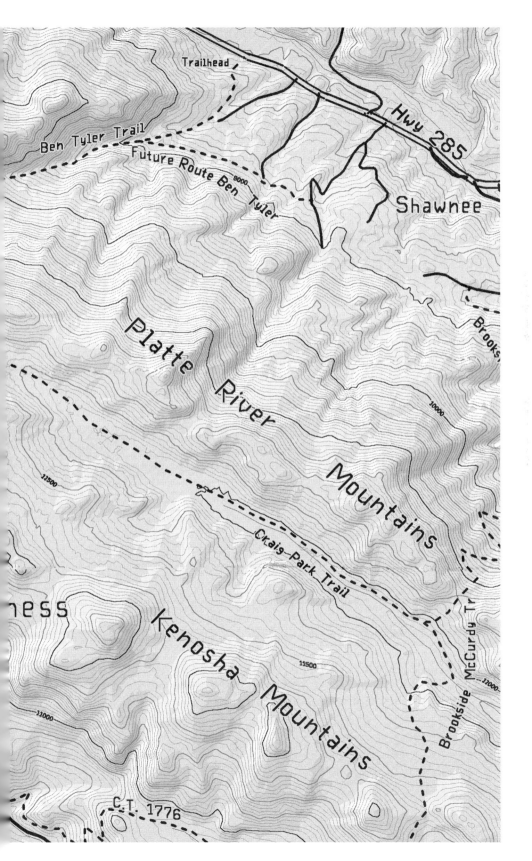

Starting at the highway or at the new trailhead still being planned at Gibbs Gulch, climb steadily toward Ben Tyler Creek. Your trail quickly enters the Lost Creek Wilderness and follows the creek up through the woods, crosses the stream and continues to follow it past ancient beaver doings toward the place where loggers' cabins used to be. Only the foundation and some trash remain now. They are located on the west side of the creek.

Your trail continues up the east side, leaves the water and then begins rising very steeply. A short side path returns to the creek higher up, and from there you have a view of the gulch laid out below. The hillsides are practically nothing but aspens, a golden vista in late September. Brook trout fishing along the creek is rated above average by the Division of Wildlife.

Now your path becomes a little less distinct (and less popular) because it switchbacks up past its junction with Craig Park Trail and on up to a high ridge. Then it angles down the other side, where you'll find an outstanding view of distant mountain ranges. Heading down, your trail joins **Rock Creek** and follows that down to a road access off East Lost Park Road (see KENOSHA PASS AREA).

CRAIG PARK TRAIL, Forest Service #608, 7 miles one way; elevation gain 660 ft., loss 630 ft., rated moderately easy, but hard to get to! Features long meadow with brook trout fishing

Few trails in our area are so little traveled as this one. That's because Craig Park has no road access of its own. As we mentioned, you cannot reach it except by hiking or horsebacking to it from Ben Tyler or Brookside-McCurdy, which adds many miles to the trail length given above.

But once you get there, you find a long grassy meadow area surrounded by wooded hills and rock outcroppings. The lower part of the trail is very easy going and is interrupted only by several bogs that you must get around. The only steep section is at the west end, where the trail climbs up above the headwaters of Craig Creek to a high ridge, where it joins Ben Tyler.

Craig Park is normally explored as part of a long excursion, but if your purpose is to reach Craig Park itself, the most popular route seems to be from the north end of Brookside-McCurdy, a distance of 5.5 miles. Brook trout fishing is rated excellent.

Repeat Warning: No trail links Craig Park with Craig Meadow downstream because Craig Creek plunges through a steep and dangerous gorge where hikers have become lost and injured.

GUANELLA PASS AREA

Threemile Trail
Burning Bear Trail
Abyss Lake Trail (old Scott-Gomer)
Shelf Lake Trail
South Park Trail to Square Tops Lakes

For those coming from I-70 at Georgetown, west of Denver, Guanella Pass is a gateway to the Pike National Forest and its Mount Evans Wilderness. Six major Pike National Forest trailheads are also located along this pass. At its foot on the southern side lies the small town of Grant, 10.5 miles west of Bailey on Hwy. 285. Since many Denverites come by the scenic Hwy 285 and because long odometer readings get inaccurate, Grant is the best place to set our odometer and begin our road directions.

Bikers Note: Threemile and Abyss Lake Trails lie within the Mount Evans Wilderness, where no mountain bicycles are permitted. Yet Burning Bear, Shelf Lake and South Park Trails all lie *outside* the Wilderness boundary, so bikes are okay on those trails.!

ROAD DIRECTIONS: The trailhead for THREEMILE is exactly three miles up this road from Grant. Watch for it on your right. Drive another 2.1 miles and you find BURNING BEAR on your left. ABYSS LAKE is

Threemile Creek on Guanella Pass

located on your right just beyond. Drive another two miles and watch for a pair of gravel roads that cut away to the left. Take the second of those two roads and travel 3.2 miles to SHELF LAKE TRAILHEAD, which is on your right.

Going higher on the Guanella Pass road, you find a pair of trail-heads at the very top. SOUTH PARK strikes out to the west and ROSALIE heads east. For ROSALIE, see BAILEY/DEER CREEK AREA.

THREEMILE CREEK, Forest Service #635, 6 miles one way; elevation gain 2,600 ft., loss 200 ft., rated moderate. Features streamside link to timberline and intersection with Rosalie.

9,000	6.0 miles	11,670

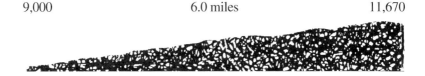

Threemile Creek Trail is six miles long, and even Threemile Creek is longer than three miles. It just happens to be the creek you find three miles up from Highway 285.

This trail is a popular link to the very middle of two other long trails, **Rosalie** and **Abyss Lake**, making the whole system more complex. As the path leaves the parking lot, it climbs steadily to avoid private property where Threemile Creek crosses the road. The creek is somewhat hidden from view and your trail won't find it for half a mile.

Then you join and cross the creek and begin weaving up it as it passes through small grassy areas and cool forest with rock formations on either side. It's a steady and somewhat rocky climb. The brook trout fishing is rated above average on this section of the creek. Steeper sections high up are not as good, being scoured.

Old maps show **Threemile Trail** looping southeast around Spearhead Mountain, but instead it climbs steeply up the ridge between the two branches of Threemile Creek. At timberline, it rises gradually along the east side of the valley until it crosses the east side of the saddle, then drops down to join the **Rosalie Trail** at about 11,600 feet.

There on the saddle, **Threemile Trail** ends at a junction with **Rosalie**. A sign marks the spot. (For description of **Rosalie**, see BAILEY/DEER CREEK AREA.)

BURNING BEAR, Forest Service #601, 5 miles one way; elevation gain 1,160 ft., loss 1,120 ft. Features popular stroll beside valley and through forest, excellent for cross-country skiing.

9,600 Geneva Cr	5.0 miles	Park County 60 9,540

This is a good trail for easy strolling or cross-country skiing because it is very gentle for a long way. The trailhead is located beside Geneva Creek. Here, Geneva Creek winds through a long valley where cattle graze. Enter the fence near the stream and follow Geneva upstream to a wooden bridge. After crossing the bridge, continue upstream on a trail that stays just inside the trees. This area is used for judging snowpack depth, so please stay on the trail when snow is on the ground.

Eventually your trail turns up the tributary that flows from Burning Bear Gulch, a stream too small for fishing. Even here the trail is fairly gentle as it climbs slowly through the forest. You pass the remains of a log cabin, and finally cross to the south (or left) side of the stream, where you find a mild set of switchbacks that lead up and over a wooded ridge into another watershed.

From here it is downhill all the way. You follow a tributary to Lamping Creek, then down Lamping Creek itself to a rough gravel road. This is Park County 60, which joins Hwy. 285 at Webster, about 14 miles west of Bailey.

ABYSS LAKE TRAIL, (formerly Scott-Gomer), Forest Service #602, 8 miles one-way; elevation gain 3,050 ft. Features high mountain scenery and link to other long trails.

9,620   3.0 miles   12,650

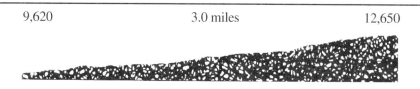

First of all, we have to warn you about the apparent shortcut shown on old maps. From one of the switchbacks on the side of Mount Evans you can actually see Abyss Lake and old maps show a route leading down from that overlook, but the route is actually a rockslide area for a long way. This is extremely dangerous because the rocks are loose and you may easily start a slide toward one of your companions below, or you may be struck by rocks dislodged (or thrown) by visitors on the overlook above.

So our description will begin at the main trailhead on the Guanella Pass road. You climb up through the forest on a trail that resembles an old road. The forest is young and you don't find the creek for quite a ways.

When you do, you may be surprised at how little you see of Scott-Gomer Creek, for the trail gives only a glimpse of it through the brush and only crosses in two places. After the first stream crossing, the real scenery begins with high mountains crowning the trees ahead.

This is a wide stream where we see fly fishermen wading up its middle, but DOW **researchers discovered an amazing problem: No fish!** The place is so beautiful, so full of other wildlife, that no one ever guessed it could have an environmental problem. There are a few fish near the very bottom, where tributaries dilute water from higher up, but there are no fish beyond that because of heavy metals naturally occurring in the geology. This is not a man-made problem, and the levels are quite low, but trout are especially sensitive and have a hard time during the winter, when there is no runoff to dilute the spring water. It's just barely bad enough to keep them from breeding. Summer water is much better.

After the second crossing, you begin climbing an old road again through aspen. Eventually you cross a tributary that joins the creek from the left and just beyond you cross **Rosalie Trail.**

Your trail stays to the left of the main creek, climbing in the trees to avoid bogs in the grassy areas above. We saw fresh bear tracks there. The higher you go, the more faint the trail becomes, yet the ground is very open at this altitude and is surrounded by high landmarks such as Mount Evans ahead.

There used to be no trail at all once you are near either Frozen Lake or Abyss Lake, but use has established a path now. Simply follow their drainage.

SHELF LAKE, Forest Service #634, 3.5 miles one way: elevation gain 1,852 ft. Features high fishing lake.

10,138   3.5miles   11,990

The State of Colorado uses airplanes to stock this lake with cutthroat trout, but the only way you can get there is by climbing a very steep and rocky trail to the 12,000 foot level. The trail begins next to a large heap of smelter's slag that looks like coal, and it climbs through aspens, heading up Smelter Gulch. Some of the toughest going is in the first half mile.

Your trail becomes a little less rugged as you bike or hike a meadow area there, but most of your trail stays just inside the trees.

Finally you cross the creek near some beaver workings. All the fishing is above at the lake; the creek is poor, and the large pond shown on old topo maps has become a marsh. Follow the water as it curves to the left above timberline and find the big green bowl. Here the trail becomes fainter, but to your left the main stream tumbles down a steep ridge. Shelf Lake is up above that ridge, surrounded by tundra and vistas, so get ready for some steep climbing.

If you sit quietly near the shore, pika may come out and feed on the grass. These high altitude members of the rabbit family look something like guinea pigs with round ears. They store grass by making little haystacks under the protection of rocks. There are quite a few at Shelf Lake.

SOUTH PARK TRAIL TO SQUARE TOP LAKES, Forest Service #600, 2 miles one-way; elevation gain 377 ft. Features tundra trek to high fishing lakes.

11,669   2.0 miles   12.046

South Park Trail is very old and used to be about 26 miles long, but after decades of neglect, most of it faded away. Many years ago we stumbled onto the Youth Conservation Corps. in the woods; we were both searching for South Park Trail. We wanted to explore it and they wanted to repair it, but we both failed. Today, the FS is no longer interested in restoring most it because of DOW concerns about the elk calving area around upper Kirby and Bruno Gulches. Get the hint? Let's cooperate with their conservation effort.

The top two miles of this forgotten trail still exist in slow growing tundra. Actually you are following the ruts made by trucks that were once used to stock the lakes with fish. The DOW has used airplanes now for years to stock the lakes with cutthroat trout, but ruts made on tundra last for generations. Please stay on trail.

The trailhead is located at the very top of Guanella Pass, well above timberline. Park on the west side of the road and proceed west downhill to the boggy region that feeds Duck Lake below. Duck Lake is private property and can be seen from the road.

After crossing the boggy stream, you climb again and incline to the left. It's a strange hike, in that you can go for a long ways and still look back to see your car! At last you climb up to the far pocket where the lower lake hides. A small glacier on the far side feeds the lake, and the water is deepest over there. The other lake is located just above.

The altitude of the lower lake is 12,046 feet, so take it easy. Please stay on the trail to avoid damaging delicate tundra.

KENOSHA PASS AREA

Jefferson Lake in early spring, before the crowds arrive.

Gibson Lake Trail
Jefferson Lake Trail
West Jefferson Creek Trail
Wilderness On Wheels Model Mountain Access Facility

Closer to Denver than to Colorado Springs (only 58 miles west on 285) Kenosha Pass sees a lot of visitors, especially now that Colorado Trail 1776 crosses Hwy. 285 at the top of the pass. This gentle place is especially beautiful when the aspens are in their glory, for Kenosha Pass is covered with them.

ROAD DIRECTIONS: From Denver, take Hwy 285 southwest for 58 miles. Kenosha Pass is 20 miles past Bailey. From Colorado Springs, take Hwy 24 west just past Hartsel, then Hwy 9 to Fairplay and turn north on 285. Kenosha Pass is about 21.5 miles from Fairplay.

The turnoff toward GIBSON LAKE and the lower trailhead for BURNING BEAR is located 13.7 miles west of Bailey on Highway 285 and is called

Park County 60. Signs warn that the road is not suitable for passenger cars, but passenger cars can reach BURNING BEAR TRAILHEAD, which is now located three miles from the highway. It was rerouted a few years ago to avoid private property and is now well marked.

The road grows worse as you travel toward GIBSON LAKE TRAILHEAD, which is located 6.4 miles from the highway, just past Hall Valley Campground. You need high ground clearance and four-wheel drive to try this road.

The turnoff for JEFFERSON LAKE is located at Jefferson on Highway 285 and is well marked all the way. The road is good. Distance: 8 miles. On the way, you'll pass the Lodgepole and Jefferson Campgrounds, trailheads for WEST JEFFERSON CREEK TRAIL. Park outside the Jefferson Campground.

Slightly more than a mile north of Jefferson is a turnoff for Lost Park Road, Travel southeast for 7.3 miles and you will see a turnoff to Ben Tyler's southern trailhead, which is also an approach to Craig Park Trail #608, and Colorado Trail -1776. The Lost Park Campground, with its western trailhead for Wigwam and access to the center of Brookside-McCurdy, is located 19.1 miles from Hwy. 285. Horse trailers often park along the road near the campground.

To find the Wilderness on Wheels Model Mountain Access Facility from Denver, take Hwy. 285 south for 60 miles. The W.O.W. facility is on your left 3.8 miles west of Grant. From Colorado Springs, take Hwy, 24 west to Woodland Park, then 67 to Deckers, 126 to Pine Junction, then Hwy. 285 past Bailey and Grant.

GIBSON LAKE, Forest Service #633, 2.5 miles one way; elevation gain 1,530 ft., rated difficult. Features alpine fishing lake.

2.5 miles   10,320   11,850

This may seem like one of the longest 2.5-mile hikes in our area because Gibson Lake Trail is a constant climb over rocky ground at high altitude. The actual length of this trail depends on the kind of vehicle you bring. If you have a passenger car, you won't be able to get near the actual trailhead, so you'll have to walk extra miles. If you drive a vehicle with high ground clearance 4x4, you may be able to drive to the trailhead.

Beyond the trailhead, you cross the North Fork of the South Platte on a fine wooden bridge, and there the improvements end. You're in backcountry.

The trail itself is wide and rocky, a ghost of an old mining road. It follows the Lake Fork closely, so you have frequent glimpses of the noisy waterfalls and fast water. Indeed, the water is fast enough to discourage fish in the creek. Fast water scours the creek bottom, wiping out the stuff fish need to eat.

Follow this water up above timberline toward a pocket at the base of granite walls. The trail

grows more faint above timberline, but stacked rocks mark the way. The creek splits up at this high level, but you curve to the left. You cannot see the lake until you are very close. One day we saw a mountain lion scampered away from a ledge overlooking the lake.

Gibson Lake has a self-sustaining brook trout population. If you've never seen a really good-sized brook trout, this is a good place. The only larger ones we've ever seen are from the North Slope Lakes on Pikes Peak. We dined on a 19-incher on the evening of its opening, the best we've ever tasted.

JEFFERSON LAKE, Forest Service #642, 1.5 mile loop; elevation gain 40 ft. Features access to shores of stocked fishing lake.

The State of Colorado stocks Jefferson Lake with rainbow, cutthroat and lake trout and the road extends all the way to the lake, so this is a very popular spot with picnic tables and restrooms and quite a bit of parking. Because of this heavy use, no camping is allowed near the lake itself, but you will pass auto campgrounds on the way to the lake.

This lake is surrounded by scenic mountains, and the only way to see this scenery from every angle is to hike the 1.5 mile trail that circles the lake. A stream and a smaller brook enter the lake on the far side. The trail is best on the eastern shore and makes a nice stroll for persons who do not ordinarily hike.

We cannot exclude Jefferson Lake because of mere popularity, but this area is already considered over-used by the Forest Service and cannot be recommended as a place to "get away from it all."

WEST JEFFERSON TRAIL, Forest Service #643, about five miles one way, elevation gain 1,530 ft., rated moderate. Features fishing access to West Jefferson Creek and forms loop with Colorado Trail 1776.

10,100   5.0 miles   11,690

The Forest Service does not consider this trail suitable for horses or mountain bicycles because of a tough stream crossing and stepping stones across high boggy ground, but its easy grades make it a great hike. Sometimes called the Jefferson Creek Loop Trail, it can be used to form a loop with Colorado Trail 1776.

You may start at either the Lodgepole or Jefferson Campgrounds, which are both pay campgrounds, but there is a free parking lot just outside of Jefferson Campground. When hiked as a loop, people often start up the Colorado Trail from where it crosses the Jefferson Lake Road just south of Beaver Ponds Picnic Ground (no place to park there). Go 5.3 miles northwest on the CT and look for West Jefferson Creek Trail when you reach timberline. It takes off through the tundra to your right (northeast), descending into a bowl below the Continental Divide. Snow drifts beside the trail often last until mid-summer here, so it is best to explore this trail later in the season. There are stepping stones across the soggy ground formed by the drifts, so this is not an appropriate area for mountain bikes.

Then your trail enters the trees 0.6 miles after leaving the CT and makes at least 14 switchbacks down to the headwaters of Jefferson Creek. Now you travel

Bears brag by showing how high they can reach, slashing aspen to mark territory.

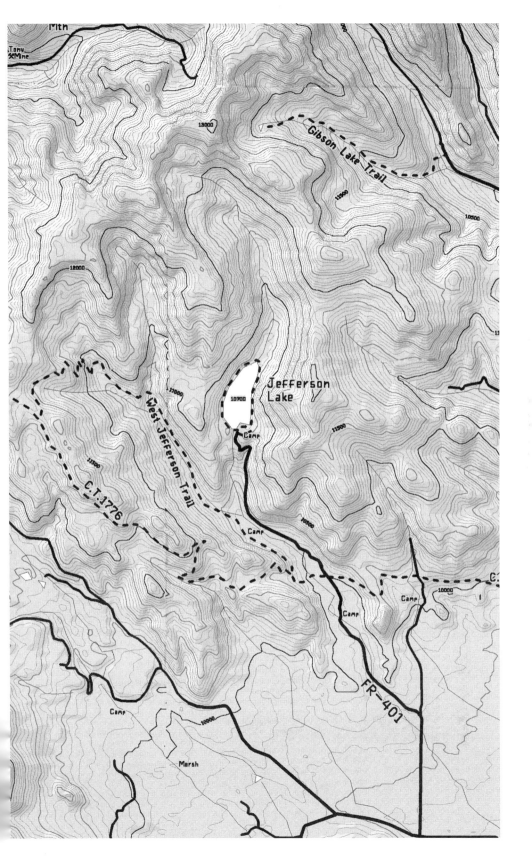

southeast for several miles, staying just above the marshy creek bottom. Jefferson Creek and its beaver ponds have a lot of brook trout, and there are primitive camp-sites along some to of its tributaries. Finally you cross the creek and continue down an old road to the Jefferson Creek Campground.

WILDERNESS ON WHEELS
MODEL MOUNTAIN ACCESS FACILITY

Working with a special permit from the Pike National Forest, the Wilderness on Wheels Foundation has built a model disabled- accessible facility near Kenosha Pass. This area features a boardwalk that meanders through one of Colorado's lush forests. It offers both stream and pond fishing and accessible sites for camping out.

W.O.W. BOARDWALK TRAIL, eventually 7 miles, elevation gain eventually 3,300 ft., rated very easy at streamside, easy climbing mountain. (Rise ratio: 1 ft. up for 12 ft. out.)

Under volunteer construction, this boardwalk is eight feet wide and is planned to reach the summit of North Twin Cone Peak (12,300 ft.). There are level rest areas every 50 to 80 feet and picnic sites along the way. With over one mile completed, the elevation gain on the first mile is 200 feet.

The trail begins in an area featuring elevated tent decks, fire rings, boardwalks built around trees and wheelchair accessible restrooms. It follows Kenosha Creek for 1,000 feet of accessible brook-trout fishing. The Colorado Division of Wildlife stocks an adjacent pond with catchable size rainbow trout.

Work on the summit has been delayed by the decision to develop the lower area first. A 600-foot spur has been constructed with gazebos to shelter visitors from the weather. The largest of these has a roof that is a scale model of the Great Pyramid oriented true north. It was designed by engineering students from the Colorado School of Mines and built with support from the Housing & Building Association of Colorado Springs/Pikes Peak Region, the Metro Denver Homebuilders Association and the Department of Veteran Affairs.

No pets are allowed. As in any wilderness environment, all trash must be packed out. Potable water is available. The facility is open from mid April through mid October. **There is no fee, but donations are requested. For reservations and information call 303-751-3959 or www.coloradopros.com/wow.**

BUFFALO PEAKS WILDERNESS

Rich Creek Trail
Rough and Tumble Creek Trail
Salt Creek
McQuaid Trail (NOT INSIDE WILDERNESS: BIKES OKAY)

Rich and Rough and Tumble Creek Trails share a common trailhead, so they can be hiked as a circuit. They both offer good brook trout fishing and better scenery, and now Salt Creek Trail makes another huge loop possible with Tumble Creek Trail (25.7 miles)!

Bikers note: Rich Creek and Rough and Tumble Trails are closed to mountain bikes because of the Buffalo Peaks Wilderness Area. Some of the Salt Creek Trail is outside the Wilderness, but farther south it weaves in and out of the Wilderness boundary, so please obey signs. Wilderness rules are vigorously enforced.

ROAD DIRECTIONS, From Denver, take Hwy. 285 past Fairplay. From Colorado Springs, find the same spot by taking Hwy 24 West 79 miles to Antero Junction, then turn right on Hwy 285. Between Fairplay and Antero Junction, two county roads lead away from this highway toward Weston Pass: Take either one, depending on which direction

you are coming from. Both Park County 22 and Park County 5 head
west for about 7 miles, then join. Three miles west of this union, look
for a parking area beside the stream. The USGS topo marks this spot
as Rich Creek Campground, but there is no campground. There is the
RICH CREEK TRAILHEAD. The loop begins and ends here.

ROUGH AND TUMBLE and SALT CREEK TRAILS can also be
approached from the Buffalo Peaks Road (FS-431), which leaves Hwy.
285 about 13 miles south of Fairplay. To find SALT CREEK
TRAILHEAD go about five miles to a big sagebrush park and watch for
a road on your left (FS-431.2D), which leads less than a quarter mile to
a closure. Walk up the closed road to hit SALT CREEK TRAIL.

To find ROUGH AND TUMBLE another way, stay on FS-431. Just over
8.5 miles from the highway, the road enters a clearing where a sawmill
once stood. The road then becomes primitive. Passenger cars may
proceed about 1/2 mile farther to park at the road closure above Lynch
Creek. After crossing Lynch Creek, the road leads about 3/4 mile down
to a point where a southwestern tributary joins Tumble Creek and the
main trail. Turn left to climb the main trail toward Buffalo Meadows.

To access other parts of SALT CREEK TRAIL, take Salt Creek Road
(FS-435) off Hwy. 285 less than two miles north of Antero Junction.
About five miles from the highway, the road forks. To the left is FS-
436, a rough road requiring power and high ground clearance. To the
right is Salt Creek Road #435, suitable for passenger cars. Both
access the trail.

To find MCQUAID TRAIL, to ease confusion, let's start over. From
Denver take Hwy 285 West. About 19 miles past Fairplay, find Salt
Creek Road. From Colorado Springs, find the same spot by taking
Hwy 24 West 79 miles to Antero Junction, then turn right on Hwy 285
for 1.6 miles to find Salt Creek Road #435. SET YOUR ODOMETER
HERE. At mile 3.15 look for a MCQUAID TRAILHEAD sign on your right
that is (at present) angled so oddly that you see it better if you pass it
and look back! You may park along the side of the road. Horse trailers
use the camping spot near the creek to the south below the road.

*RICH CREEK, Forest Service #616, 6.5 miles one way, but can be hiked
as an 11.5 mile circuit with Tumble Creek; elevation gain 1,890 ft., loss
520 ft. Features mountain meadow fishing with grand vista of South Park
region. Makes 11.3-mile loop with Tumble Trail.*

9,948   About 6.5 miles   11,160

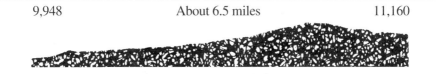

Cross Rich Creek on a footbridge constructed by South Park High School students, follow the path upstream for a few yards and you come to a fork marked "Tumble Creek" to the left and "Rich Creek" to the right. Turning right, the trail crosses and recrosses Rich Creek, then grows steeper before breaking out of the timber into a high valley. From the edge of the valley you can see the mountains and flats of the South Park region. A weathered snag has toppled beside the trail, adding itself to the vista.

Ahead lies a long, curving valley, wide open and grassy, with Rich Creek often hidden in the boggy brush at the valley center. DOW research shows that brook trout fishing is very good here, but your trail turns into a cattle path, for this valley is grazed under permit from the Forest Service. See our advice in the introduction about meeting cattle. It could save you some hassle.

As you start up the headwaters basin, the trail used to be nothing but a cattle path that faded into brush, but now the trail is better defined. The beaver corps of engineers is constantly shifting their works, however, so be aware that the stream crossing might be flooded. Also be aware that mysterious side-trails are generally nothing more than dead-end paths worn by cattle that are grazing into brush, then backing out again.

You are headed for the low wooded saddle that separates the Rich Creek headwaters from the watershed beyond. To complete the circuit, climb over this wooded saddle and follow the trail down to Tumble Creek, another good brookie stream.

ROUGH AND TUMBLE CREEK, Forest Service #617, 5.3 miles one way to the junction that links Rough and Tumble with Rich Creek, 11.3 miles overall to the Fourmile Trailhead in the San Isabel National Forest; elevation gain 1,670 ft. Features many beaver ponds and stream fishing.

9,948 Rich Cr TH   5.3 miles   Junction Rich Tr 11,160

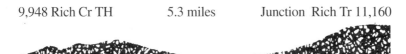

The National Forest Visitor Map shows this trail to be very long and it is, extending over a saddle and down the Fourmile Creek watershed into the San Isabel National Forest. There it often called Fourmile Trail, since it follows a

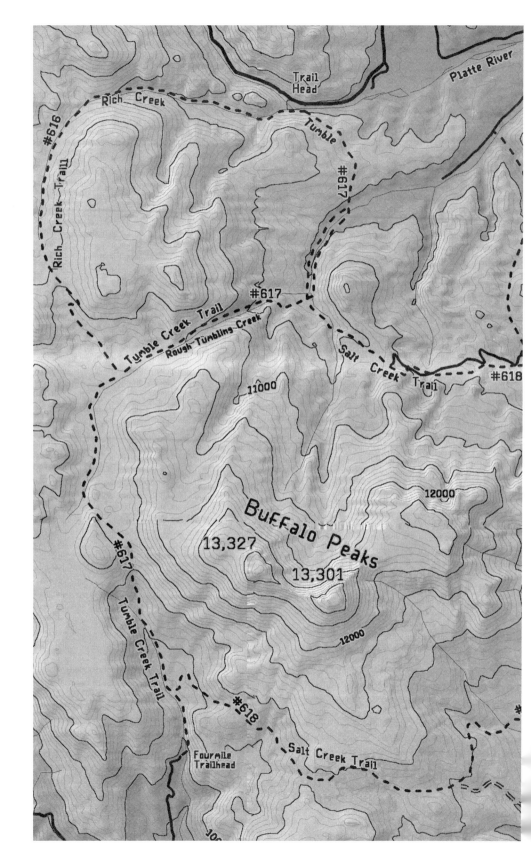

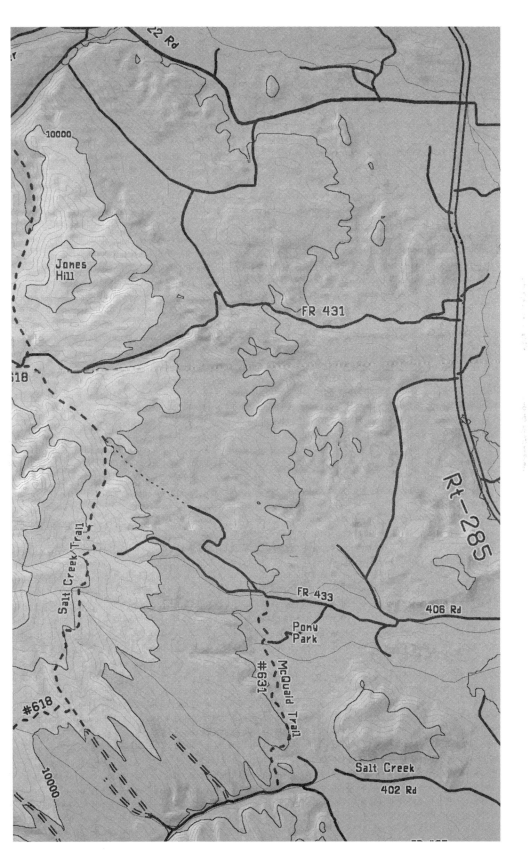

creek by that name, with a trailhead by that name at the end of a road by that name, but its #617 shows that it's all **Rough and Tumble Creek Trail.**

We have told you how to use Rich Creek to join this trail high up to make a long circuit, but we will describe Rough and Tumble Creek from the bottom trailhead for the benefit of those not making the circuit.

Cross the footbridge at the Rich Creek Trailhead and take the left fork that is marked "Tumble Creek, 2 miles." That means it is two miles to the creek itself. Hike up and over a high ridge, then drop down into the watershed known on old topo maps as Rough and Tumbling Creek. As soon as you arrive, you will see beaver ponds extending up and down the valley. Some will be abandoned, others active, a good brook trout area.

Your trail has been rerouted in this area, now staying on the northwest side of Tumble Creek until it crosses just above the junction with Lynch Creek. Cross on a large timber at a popular campsite above the mouth of Lynch Creek. Horses cross nearby.

A few yards farther up, another tributary enters Rough and Tumble Creek from the southwest. At this point the trail veers away from Tumble and follows the tributary a short distance before continuing up the ridge that separates the two streams. For awhile you are away from both creeks, then the path takes you to a log crossing Rough and Tumble. **Here the creek earns its name, tumbling down rocks in a narrow gorge. And here you start up switchbacks beside that stream. This is the most difficult part of the trail, but perhaps the most beautiful.**

Above lies a wide-open valley where Rough and Tumble Creek snakes along, growing slower as you follow it up. Soon the trail is only a cattle path that may wander anywhere, so you simply follow the valley as far as you please. Theoretically, **Tumble Creek Trail** extends up the valley to its head, then changes its name (but not its number) to **Fourmile Creek Trail** as it slides into the San Isabel National Forest and joins **Salt Creek Trail** farther down (mile 10.1).

If you want to travel the **Rich Creek** circuit, the third tributary on your right is the one that leads to the saddle ridge connecting to **Rich Creek**, but the number of active tributaries may change in wet or dry times, so watch for a signpost that marks the route. If something happens to that signpost, you could miss the turnoff. **For that reason, we believe the circuit is best hiked or horsebacked counterclockwise (Rich then Tumble) because the saddle you take from Rich Creek is very obvious and T-junctions against this long trail.**

SALT CREEK TRAIL,   Forest Service #618, 15.6 miles one way or 25.7 miles as a loop with Tumble, elevation gain 2,270 ft., loss 2,230 ft.; rated easy to moderate. Features scenic tour of Buffalo Peaks Wilderness Area.

Over and and over over again, we planned to do this trail on horseback, only to have our trip spoiled by breakdowns and then snow. Our next edition should have this trail in more detail.

This long trail begins in the Pike National Forest, then wanders into the San Isabel National Forest, where it finally joins an extension of **Tumble Trail,** which is still sometimes called **Fourmile Trail** in that area.

Salt Creek Trail is a mixture of single track and primitive. It skirts the lower slopes of Buffalo Peak, with views to the east and southeast across South Park. This is bighorn country, though the terrain is gentle aspen and evergreen forest with only a few steep spots. Eventually your trail hits Salt Creek Road (FS-435), a passenger car access. From here the trail drops down to cross Brush Park and a branch of Salt Creek, then goes up over a ridge crowned with bristlecone pines. At the Middle Fork of Salt Creek the trail crosses FS-436, a rough road. About a quarter of a mile farther, you'll find the remains of an old sawmill.

From here the trail wanders up between the Middle and South forks of Salt Creek, up through country that still shows the effects of heavy logging in the early part of the century. Eventually your path finds a flat area where trees are sparse, then crosses a saddle, dropping down into the San Isabel National Forest to join Fourmile Creek and its trail.

This the route is more distinct now but still very remote. Climb the **Fourmile (Tumble) Trail #617,** following Fourmile Creek to a saddle and over into Buffalo Meadows, which leads across the long grassy valley down to Tumble Creek.

McQUAID TRAIL, FS #631, 3.0 miles one way, rated easy to moderate, features forest trip culminating with vista of Buffalo Peaks and Antero Reservoir from meadow. NOT INSIDE WILDERNESS: BIKES OKAY!

"Finished" in 1994, this trail was not so much built as simply marked out without disturbing the ground, a novel and inexpensive approach that we applaud. When we first visited we were still able to see flecks of blue paint that were dripped on the ground like fairy tale breadcrumbs to mark the route. Then trail builders simply lined the route with old logs, sticks, rocks, anything to indicate the way, trusting that use by hikers, mountain bikers and horses would create the path. Seems to work, but it made for some bumpy mountain biking on our maiden voyage.

At present, the steepest place on this whole trail is right where it leaves the road and shoots up to the sign that marks it. Strange! But from there it climbs more gently up the crest of a grassy ridge and into the woods. Looking east, you see Pikes Peak and Hwy 285.

At mile 0.4 you cross a spring, then an old pack trail that has been closed off in both directions before going through a gate in a fence (0.9). Less than a quarter of a mile later you pass through another gate.

McQuaid Trail—outside the Wilderness—ends in the midst of this meadow.

Your next vista is at 1.6 where you break out of the dark timber to glimpse South Park to the east. At mile 1.8 you go through another fence and see Buffalo Peaks in the distance. Now it's downhill through the woods to cross a nice little brook on a wide and thick plank at mile 2.2. Just beyond, break out of the trees to cross a small valley where a primitive road (#433) goes up to Pony Park. Good campsite here. Signs at both sides of the valley help keep you on track, for McQuaid is still very faint here.

Now you head up into widely spaced ponderosa. Your forest journey ends at a long and wide meadow framing a view of Buffalo Peaks to the left and Antero Reservoir to the right. Here in the midst of the meadow is a sign marking this as the end of McQuaid Trail at mile 2.95. On bikes this took (us) just over one hour with the easiest riding on the northern half. Going back was easier.

JEFFERSON COUNTY OPEN SPACE PARKS

Blasting down a trail in Jeffco's Mount Falcon Open Space Park.

What hath a sales tax wrought? Not much of a sales tax, mind you. Just 1/2 of one per cent, but drool at the results, neighbors. Welcome to Jeffco.

Jefferson County voted in a 1/2 of one per cent sales tax to pay for Open Space Parks. The result is the most beautiful, the most impressive, the best planned, the best mapped, the best patrolled and best maintained parks program we've ever seen, and we've been watching for many years now! Everything is high-tech, high-quality, and there are no entrance fees.

Did I say no entrance fees? I mean, no entrance fees!

The bathrooms don't stink unless something goes wrong, and if anything goes wrong, it's fixed in a hurry. The parking lots are great. Signs are well done. No litter, no hassles, no problem. After years and years, we only see the program expanding and improving, buying up more precious open space, the ranches and private estates of empire-builders, and in so doing, Jefferson County is building an empire of Open Space. And just in time, just as open space is disappearing.

Notice how FAR I'm driving to spend my money in Jeffco, and thereby actually pay the tax that brought me! Hint to visitors: Buy gas in Jeffco. Eat there. Buy something. Tip the waitress: She'll pass it on. Spend in Jeffco. Then add up that 1/2 per cent and you'll see that it comes nowhere near what you pay to enter other parks. Jeffco is doing something right here.

Other park managers won't mind me bragging about Jeffco because they all admire and envy what Jeffco has accomplished. They can't help it.

Note that our Chapter 3 had to be a Jeffco Open Space Park, Pine Valley Ranch Park, the paved access to the superb Buffalo Creek Mountain Bike Area. That park had been the private estate of a millionaire, and it is now the playground for all of us. Let's take a look at some others, south of I-70 west of Denver, and we'll start with another huge private estate that now belongs to all of us:

But first the rules: no hunting, no firearms, no fireworks, no open fires (grills only), no camping and no collecting of wild-flowers, rocks or any other souvenirs. Hours are from one hour before sunrise to one hour after sunset. But the one rule that may surprise you is this: **Dogs must absolutely be on a leash at all times anywhere in Jefferson County, not just in the parks. The the first offense fine is $30, but can go as high as $300 or more for habitual offenders.**

Truth is, we've had so much fun at Jeffco parks that we never bothered to take many pictures there. Next edition will fix that.

MOUNT FALCON PARK

Surely a millionaire conservationist would select a majestic spot for his dream castle in the mountains—and that's exactly what John Brisben Walker did. Unfortunately, the castle was struck by lightning and burned in 1918, but all the natural wonders still remain

If you start at the lower trailhead on Hwy. 8, just south of Red Rocks Park, you have a long climb up through grasslands, then through brush, then forest along the hiker-only Turkey Trot Trail. But we'll start at the top, where the scenery is best and the grades are easiest. This is where you'll want to go cross-country skiing or take the family for leisurely outings. The high trailhead boasts a beautiful picnic area, potable water, clean restrooms and even a pay phone to report fires or other emergencies. Yet all trails lead downhill from here, so save a little energy for the return trip. Horses can be rented just outside the park's high entrance.

The usual rules apply: no hunting, no firearms, no fireworks, no camping, no open fires (grills only), no collecting of wildflowers, rocks or Other souvenirs.

Dogs must be on a leash. Park hours are one our before sunrise to one hour after sunset.

ROAD DIRECTIONS: To reach the upper trails, take the Parmalee Gulch Road exit off Hwy. 285 (also marked Indian Hills). This exit is located 2.5 miles west of the Evergreen-Hwy. 8 exit off 285 or northwest of Conifer. Go three miles to Indian Hills and turn right at the Mount Falcon Park sign. Follow this winding road past the stables to the trailhead. The lower trailhead can be reached from Hwy. 8, which connects Morrison with 285. From Hwy. 8 turn west onto Forest St., about a mile from Morrison, then right onto Vine, which leads to the parking area. Picnic and restroom facilities are available at this area also.

PARMALEE TRAIL, 1.7 miles, elevation gain 700 ft., loss 820; rated moderate to difficult. Features fun bike and equestrian route.

This is one of the more difficult and less traveled trails, diving downhill and washboarding over two drainages before climbing back up to Meadow Trail. Parmalee is a favorite among equestrians because there is less traffic and because there is some water available at stream crossings-at least, early in the year. Fine views to the south.

CASTLE TRAIL, 3.9 miles, elevation loss 1,750 ft. from high trail-head, rated easy at the top, difficult below. Features fabulous scenery, castle ruins, great cross-country skiing.

6,000   3.9 miles   7,500

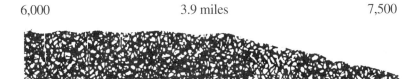

Described from the top or bottom, this would sound like two entirely different trails because the top is so easy and the bottom is so steep. This the park's longest trail, tracing the top of the ridge, and it is the spine to which four other trails connect. Many people use it as a one-way downhill adventure by leaving another car at the bottom. Clever fencing around the castle ruins allows you to see it all without the danger of climbing around among the crumbling walls and chimneys.

WALKER'S DREAM, 0.3 miles one way, elevation gain 240 ft., loss 120; rated moderate. Features scenic lookout.

Walker dreamed of having the President of the United Slates as a next door neighbor, so he began to build a presidential summer home near his castle. Thousands of Colorado school children contributed dimes to the project, but construction never went beyond the foundation and laying of a cornerstone carved from Colorado marble. No President ever visited Mt. Falcon, but from this perch you can see another of Walker's dreams that did come true, Red Rocks Park Amphitheater.

TWO DOG TRAIL, 0.3 miles one way, altitude gain 100 ft, loss 40 feet, rated easy. Features another scenic lookout.

Every promontory in the park offers another fabulous view, so that is the purpose of this short side trail. It leads up a forest path to a meadow overlook with vistas to the north, east and south.

MEADOW TRAIL, 0.8 mile, elevation gain 160 ft., loss 240 ft., ruled easy. Features great cross-country skiing, hiking.

A favorite with cross-country skiers and bikers. Meadow Trail takes off south from Castle Trail and rounds a lovely meadow, forming connections with three other trails. Described from the top or bottom, this would sound like two entirely different trails because the top is so easy and the bottom so steep. This is the park's longest trail, tracing the top of the ridge, and is the spine to which four other trails connect. Many people use it as a one-way downhill adventure by leaving another car at the bottom. The top also ranks as one of the area's most spectacular cross-country ski trails. The views must be seen to be believed. Clever fencing around the castle ruins allows you to see it all without the danger of climbing around among the crumbling walls and chimneys.

TOWER TRAIL, 0.6 miles one way, elevation gain 140 feet, loss 240 feet; ruled moderate. Features wonderful views.

This shorty features two remarkable lookout points, a wooden tower reminiscent of fire watch lowers and a large pavilion called Eagle Eye Shelter, which can be reserved for group activities. Just keep an eagle eye on small children, however, for the pavilion is a high perch, with views of Pikes Peak and Hwy. 285.

OLD UTE TRAIL, 0.6 miles as a balloon loop, elevation gain 180 ft., loss 180 ft.; rated moderate. Features technical biking.

If it weren't so short, this trail might have to be rated more difficult because of many steep bumps and rocks that don't map out for elevation gain. Bikers will find it far more narrow and technical than most other trails. More great views.

DEVIL'S ELBOW, 1.1 miles as a loop, elevation gain-loss 150 ft.; rated moderate. Features loop trail with southern views.

The Devil's Elbow starts down a steep grassy saddle, then circles a ridge that is thinly forested on the south and thickly forested on the north. Your path dips into land owned by Denver Mountain Parks before returning to Mount Falcon. Combined with Old Ute, you can make a 3.4-mile loop from the upper parking lot.

Flying kites at Elk Meadow Park

ELK MEADOW PARK

The best time to see elk at Elk Meadow Park is just after sunrise or just before sunset, with your best chance in fall and winter. In the spring, the herds calve in a state wildlife area next door. Then the herds break up, one herd summering in Genesee and the other on Mount Evans. In daylight hours, elk are pretty crafty at hiding from you, but often you'll find where they bedded down in the grass at night.

Some Elk Meadow Trails are great for cross-country skiing after winter storms. Park rangers sometimes groom the trails with snowmobiles. Nearly two square miles in itself, this park seems even larger because its trail system wanders into adjacent areas owned by the Denver Mountain Parks and the Division of Wildlife. You can help encourage such inter-governmental cooperation by obeying all rules. For example, keeping your dog on a leash is a very serious matter. Aside from elk, there are also ground-nesting birds to protect..

ROAD DIRECTIONS: Easy access to the park is at Lewis Ridge Road off Hwy. 74. A second parking lot and trailhead, with its scenic picnic area, is located 1.25 miles west of Hwy. 74 on Stagecoach Blvd.

PAINTER'S PAUSE, one mile one way, elevation gain 200 ft.; rated easy. Features easy strolling, cross-country skiing, jogging, etc.

Paralleling the highway, this trail is used by joggers and cross-country skiers because it is so flat. Rubber flap erosion barriers that fold down when a tire hits them. This trail is most important as a link to other areas of the park.

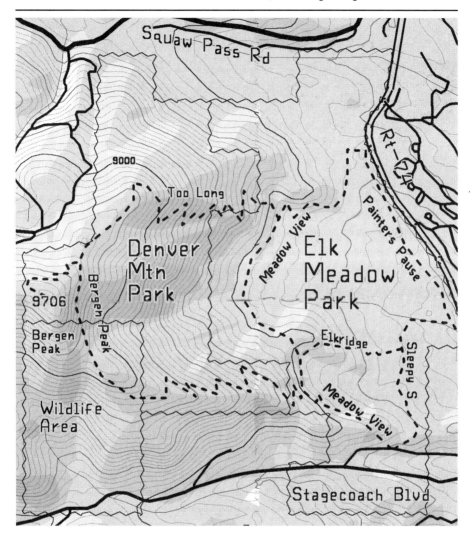

MEADOW VIEW, Three miles one way, elevation gain-toss 350 ft.; rated easy. Features easy meadow link to higher trails and picnic area.

Leaving the highway behind, this lovely trail circles the back edge of the meadow, dodging in and out of the woods. If you're looking for elk, this is your route. Cross-country skiers and bikers will enjoy its gentle roll. Both ends are at the same elevation, but if you start at the north, your climb is more gradual.

ELK RIDGE TRAIL, 0.5 miles one way, elevation gain 240 ft., rated moderate. Features link with other trails to form loops.

This ridge walk allows you to make two different loops, using Meadow View and Sleepy "S" (2.6 miles) or those trails plus Painter's Pause for a loop of four miles.

SLEEPY 'S' TRAIL, 1.1 miles one way, elevation gain 160 ft., rated easy. Features more cross-country skiing amid scattered ponderosa.

Named for its shape, this trail snakes through scattered ponderosa, a marvelous wildflower area. Cross-country skiers and families with small children enjoy this easy route. Ignore the side trail at the northern end: it only leads to the park manager's residence.

TOO LONG TRAIL, 2.4 miles one way, elevation gain 1,120 ft., rated moderate to difficult. Features scenic forest climb to Bergen Peak Trail.

8,080   2.4 miles   9,200

Don't let the name and all the switchbacks worry you. If it weren't so long, this trail would be pretty steep, but all those switchbacks are designed to make it easier. If you're looking for a shorter adventure, try for the scenic overlook about a mile up the trail: Combined with your approach via Meadow View, that will make a four-mile round trip. Farther up. Too Long crosses a stream and eventually leads to the Bergen Peak Trail.

BERGEN PEAK TRAIL, 2.7 miles one way, elevation gain 1,708 ft., rated more difficult. Features climb to mountain summit.

8,000   2.7 miles   9,708

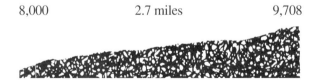

Even horses will want a rest on these switchbacks, and if you can pedal a bike up this route, you're doing very well. Most of the trail climbs through dense ponderosa forest, but there are occasional views of distant mountains. The trail fades on a rocky ridge before reaching the very top, but it is fairly easy to work your way up to the summit. Just watch your back trail to make sure that you can find your way back the same way.

ALDERFER/THREE SISTERS PARK

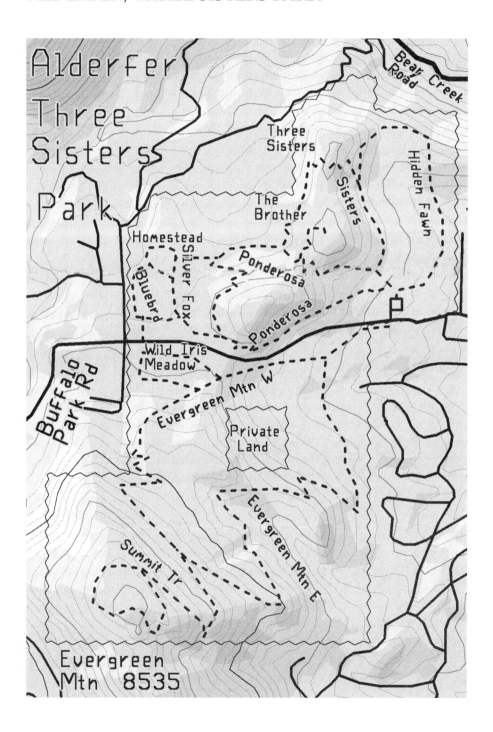

Ever since Evergreen was settled, four rock formations called The Three Sisters and The Brother have been landmarks. Now more than a thousand acres of this beautiful area have become a Jefferson County Open Space Park. This is a popular area for mountain biking, horseback riding and cross-country skiing.

ROAD DIRECTIONS, Only 0.6 miles south of downtown Evergreen on Hwy. 73, take Buffalo Park Road west for 1.4 miles.

HIDDEN FAWN TRAIL, One mile one way, elevation gain-loss 160 ft., rated easy. Features cross-country skiing and easy riding and hiking.

Arching through ponderosa forest, this is a very pretty trail enjoyed by cross-country skiers and anyone else looking for a gentle journey. It also connects to an easy portion of Three Sisters and to a fairly easy piece of 'Ponderosa Trail, forming a loop 0.39 miles longer.

PONDEROSA TRAIL, 1.76 mile loop, elevation gain-loss 400 ft., rated easy to moderate. Features more challenging cross-country skiing.

Our description of this loop begins at its intersection with Hidden Fawn. Skiers will want to turn left and go clockwise because this is the gentlest climb. The trail repeatedly contours, then switchbacks to follow the next contour. On the west side it loses elevation, going down to skirt the edge of a meadow before climbing toward The Brother Trail. Skiers often avoid that area by taking Three Sisters instead.

THREE SISTERS TRAIL, one mile one way, elevation gain 80 ft., loss 260, if done clockwise; rated easy to moderate. Features more skiing and access to landmark rock formations.

Going clockwise, Three Sisters starts out rolling gently through the pines for over a third of a mile before switchbacking up to the saddle between the big rocks. There is no easy way to the top of the rocks themselves, and we urge you not to try. (Do The Brother instead.) Then it switchbacks down to another easy stretch leading to Ponderosa Trail.

THE BROTHERS TRAIL, 0.18 miles one way, elevation gain 80 ft., rated moderate. Features fabulous panorama.

Once you see this view, you'll understand why you needn't bother trying to scale The Sisters. The Brother is actually much taller and bigger than its siblings. The path leads to within a few feet of the top and from there it's easy to Find a way up. Best of all, the top is quite broad, so you don't have to stand near an edge to enjoy the panorama, which includes Mount Evans, the Alderfer Ranch, Evergreen and a lot more.

SILVER FOX, BLUEBIRD MEADOW and HOMESTEAD TRAILS, short trails totaling 1.1 miles, rated easy. Feature easy loops in north west comer of park with restrooms and picnic facilities.

James T. Hester homesteaded this area in 1873, but his barn and house burned down in 1894. The remains of the ice house and potato cellar were visible until recently, but now this charming area has been laced with three short trails, only one of which (Homestead) has any altitude gain. Because they are next to the parking lot (which was sorely needed), these trails see a lot of use.

WILD IRIS MEADOW LOOP, 0.7 miles, rated easy. Features easy loop near parking, restrooms and picnic facilities.

Wild iris are a delicate blue miniature of the ones grown in gardens. You'll see them blooming here in June. Along with the loops just to the north, this one is great for cross-country skiing.

RANCH VIEW, EVERGREEN MOUNTAIN TRAILS EAST AND WEST, totalling 4.2 miles as balloon loop, rated easy to moderate. Feature varied terrain with link to Summit Trail.

Starting out as a "string" across gentle ground, the balloon portion of our balloon loop quickly starts switchbacking up the slopes of Evergreen Mountain. Be sure to check out the view from the overlook on Evergreen Mountain. East.

By the way, most of the evergreens that gave this mountain its name are lodgepole pine, the slender straight trees so prized by Indians as tepee poles. They were extensively traded across the plains, where no suitable trees grew. Dragging poles behind horses wore down their length, so Indians near the mountains used the longest poles, then traded them off to more eastern tribes when the poles got shorter.

SUMMIT TRAIL, 1.4 miles, rated moderate, then easy. Features balloon loop trek to summit of Evergreen Mountain.

Branching off the Evergreen Mountain Trail, Summit Trail climbs another 376 feet through lodgepole forest, looping to the crest of Evergreen Mountain at 8,536 feet. Views to the west and south (including Pikes Peak) are well worth the climb.

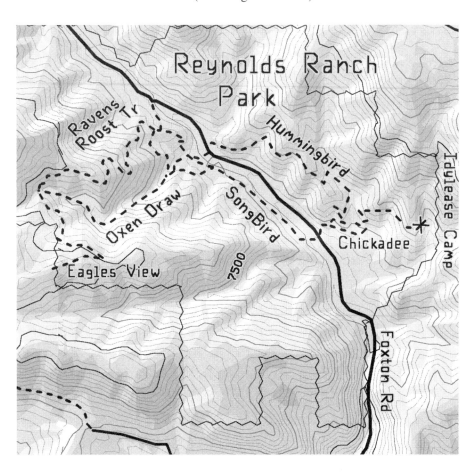

REYNOLDS PARK

This was one of the first areas settled in pioneer days. The Reynolds Ranch house, now the park manager's home, once served as a Pony Express station and as a stop for pack trains trekking between Denver and Leadville. Between 1913 and 1942, the park was a dude ranch called Idylease. At one time there were 14 cabins for guests who came from as far away as the East

Coast. Later, the Reynolds family switched to cattle ranching. The park is named in memory of John A. Reynolds, whose family gave a large portion of the ranch to Jefferson County.

The main parking area is beside a stream where picnic tables are arranged among the shade trees. There are clean restrooms and potable water. Camping is allowed by permit only. Contact the Open Space Administration at 303-291-5925. See Chickadee Trail. Dogs must be on a leash. No hunting, no firearms, no fireworks, no open fires (grills only), no collecting of wildflowers, rocks or other souvenirs. Park hours are one hour before sunrise to one hour after sunset.

ROAD DIRECTIONS, Just 6.6 miles north of Pine Junction or immediately south of Conifer on Hwy. 285, take the turnoff marked Foxton Road (County 97). Five miles later the pavement ends, and the road cuts through Reynolds Park. Parking is on the right for most trails, but another lot farther down serves Idylease campground.

SONGBIRD TRAIL, 0.5 miles one way, elevation toss 160 ft., rated easy. Features easy hiking or cross-country skiing.

This gentle streamside trail does attract a lot of songbirds, but in winter it attracts cross-country skiers. It connects with Elkhorn, next.

ELKHORN INTERPRETIVE TRAIL, 0.9 mile loop, elevation gain 240 ft., rated easy. Features easy nature study.

This easy nature trail is marked with a series of numbered signposts. Look for the interpretive guide pamphlet available at the trailhead near the restrooms, then follow the numbers. Great place to teach the kids about plants and animals. Gentle enough for cross-country skiing.

OXEN DRAW, 0.6 miles one way, elevation gain 440 ft., rated moderate. Features forest hike to higher trail.

In snowless times. **Oxen Draw** is the best route up the mountain, easier than Raven's Roost. It climbs through a heavily timbered ravine, but should be avoided in winter or early spring because it can gather up to a foot of ice.

EAGLE'S VIEW TRAIL, 0.7 miles one way, elevation gain 300 ft., rated moderate. Features fine lookout.

Our favorite, this short trail takes off from the intersection of Oxen Draw and Raven's Roost. It climbs up through dense limber to a grassy ridge guarded by ponderosa. From the overlook, you can see Pikes Peak and a lot more. Great picnic spot. No tables.

RAVEN'S ROOST, 0.9 miles one way, elevation gain 240 ft., rated moderate. Features ridge hike to higher trail.

When ice fills Oxen Draw, this is your best route to Eagle's View. It begins as road, then changes to single track as it follows a rocky ridge with a sunny southern exposure. Pretty steep, but short.

HUMMINGBIRD TRAIL, 1.3 miles one way, elevation gain 160 ft., loss 200; rated moderate. Features sunny hillside hike.

This is a good winter trail because its southern exposure helps keep it free of snow and ice. Good for winter conditioning. Bikers watch out for cactus. Good views of the rest of the park.

CHICKADEE, less than a mile one way, elevation gain 160 ft., rated moderate. Features access to campground.

Like Hummingbird, Chickadee climbs a high dry ridge. After crossing a grassy slope, it leads to Idylease Campground, which is just inside the trees. Clean restrooms, but water provided in steel drums is not for drinking. Bring your own. Each of the five sites has a table and grill. Free permits to camp here are available from the office at 18301 W. 10th Ave. in Golden.

MEYER RANCH PARK

Legend holds that the Meyer Ranch once served as the winter home for animals of the P.T. Barnum Circus for several years during the late 1880s. And in 1915 Norman Meyer discovered an old board on the ranch marked "Circus Town, 1889." In the 1940s, a portion of what is now Meyer Ranch Park was a ski hill.

The Meyers still reside in the historic Victorian home on the north side of Hwy. 285; please respect their privacy. Some 397 acres of their ranch now belong to the public as a Jeffco Open Space Park.

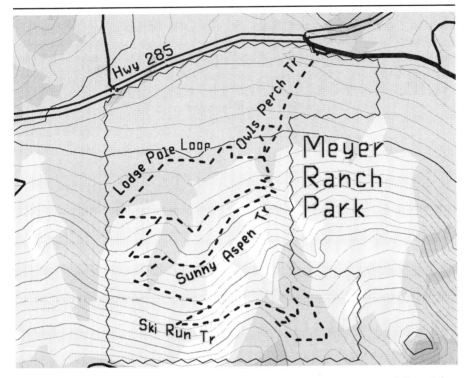

Its trail system begins with a meadow often used for crosscountry skiing. After big snowstorms, park officials sometimes use snowmobiles to make additional ski trails here. But as you move up into the trees, trails gradually become more difficult, with the steepest trail leading to the top of the mountain.

Picnic tables, grills and clean restrooms are provided, but there is no potable water in the park. Dogs on leash only. No hunting, no firearms, no fireworks, no open fires (grills only), no camping, no collecting of wildflowers, rocks or other souvenirs. Park hours are one hour before sunrise to one hour after sunset.

ROAD DIRECTIONS: The community of Aspen Park is located on Hwy. 285 between Conifer and Pine Junction. Just east of Aspen Park turn onto South Turkey Creek Rd. Meyer Ranch Park is immediately on your right.

OWL'S PERCH TRAIL, 0.4 miles, elevation gain 135 ft., loss 50 ft.; rated easy. Features cross-country skiing, easy hiking.

This is just a stroll across the old hay meadow on a wide trail that leads to the trees. Restrooms are located near the end of this trail, where it forms a little balloon loop. Lodge-pole Loop Trail takes off from the upper end of the balloon.

LODGE-POLE LOOP, 1.14 miles, elevation gain-loss 150 ft., rated easy. Features picnicking and cross-country skiing.

Like Owl's Perch, this gentle trail is used by cross-country skiers and families looking for a non-strenuous outing. It winds through scattered ponderosa pines, an area thick with wildflowers after a rain, and has picnic tables.

SUNNY ASPEN TRAIL, 0.82 miles, elevation gain 175 ft., loss 150 ft.; rated moderate. Features forest link to higher trail.

Sunny Aspen is not so sunny because it wanders through a dense forest that really doesn't contain a whole lot of aspens either. Large logs used as erosion barriers form a wide stairway that is perfect for horses, but hard on mountain bikes. Many logs have sprocket marks on them. At the top of this horseshoe loop, where Old Ski Run Trail takes off, there is a tiny clearing with sun and aspens, probably the spot trail-namers had in mind.

OLD SKI RUN TRAIL, 1.36 miles including small balloon loop at summit, elevation gain-loss 375 ft., rated moderately difficult. Features climb to mountain top.

This upper section was used as a ski trail in the 1940s, so there are no level spots. It's pretty much all uphill through dense, mixed forest. Oddly enough, the best views are not from the summit loop, but from a spot just below the loop. A wooden bench marks this overlook where you can see Aspen Park and Mount Evans. Great place to eat your lunch.

DEER CREEK CANYON PARK

Located two miles west of Chatfield Reservoir on Deer Creek Canyon Road, Deer Creek Canyon Park had its beginnings as a hunting and camping ground for Ute and Arapahoe Indians. This area was first homesteaded in 1872 by John Williamson of Plymouth, England. His Glen Plym Ranch, as well as the Couch and Clark homesteads, all lay within the current 1,721-acre park. Colorado's famous cannibal, Alfred E. Packer, spent his last years in a cabin in nearby Phillipsburg.

Diverse habitats make this park rich in wildlife. Especially important is the scrub oak habitat. These small oaks produce acorns that support grouse, turkeys, mule deer, elk, squirrels, black bears and, in turn the mountain lions and birds of

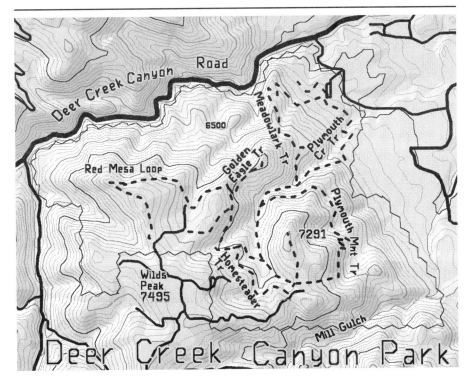

prey higher up the food chain. Development along Colorado's Front Range has cleared away much of this important food source, so Jefferson County has been wise to protect theirs.

Trails branch away from a single parking lot. Horses and bikes are welcome on all trails except for Meadowlark, Golden Eagle and Homesteader. There are 9.5 miles of trails.

The usual day-use-only park rules apply. Dogs must remain on leash unless otherwise posted and fires are permitted only in designated grills or camp stoves.

LAIR-O-THE-BEAR PARK

You don't really need a map of Lair 0' The Bear because you can actually see most of this creekside park as you drive along Hwy. 74. It's 319 acres extend for 1.5 miles along the highway and extend less than half a mile up the slope across Bear Creek. (Of course, a map is included on the free park brochure.)

This Jefferson County Open Space Park features picnicking and trout fishing (including a handicapped access fishing deck and restrooms) as well as short trails for hiking, mountain biking, horseback riding and cross-country skiing. It's longest trail is Bruin Bluff Trail that snakes for 1.3 miles up along the slope.

Bear Creek is a sizeable stream that flows from Mount Evans and down through the town of Evergreen. Its proximity to Hwy. 74 makes it very popular, so the Division of Wildlife stocks it with catchable-sized trout. The park itself boasts one and a half miles of fishing, but there are another four miles downstream along a strip of adjacent undeveloped land owned by Denver Mountain Parks.

This streamside environment is a magnet for wildlife. The park has a healthy colony of beaver, and the best time to see them is early morning and evening. Also watch for dippers, small gray wren-like birds that actually swim under water to feed.

There are ponderosa pines, juniper and yucca on the more arid slopes, but the north-facing slopes have Douglas Fir with a sparse understory of mosses and ferns.

ROAD DIRECTIONS: From Denver, drive to Morrison and take Hwy. 74 west. The entrance is about 1.5 miles west of Idledale.

From Colorado Springs, take I-70 to the outskirts of Denver, then I-470 west to Morrison and then Hwy 74 west.

DENVER MOUNTAIN PARKS

Corwina Park
O'Fallon Park

Every reference has to draw the line somewhere. If we didn't, just how big would this book be, with all this detail? We drew the line at Interstate 70, which seems to be a pretty natural way to bisect the Front Range west of Denver. Unfortunately, Denver Mountain Parks' best trails happen to fall north of this divider. So this edition south of I-70 has to be skimpy in the treatment of Denver Mountain Parks.

Denver Mountain Parks does own a patchwork of land in Jefferson County, including a beautiful parcel called O'Fallon, which we have campaigned to restore for many years. Still, those lands south of 1-70 (our area) have few trails due to lack of funding or due to the smallish size of each parcel.

Two areas adjacent to Jefferson County Open Space Parks share in those county trail systems, and we applaud this inter-governmental cooperation. For example, Bergen Peak Trail begins in Jeffco's Elk Meadow Park, then quickly climbs to DMP country to reach the summit, and there is a spur trail called Turkey Trot off Jeffco's Mount Falcon Park that also ventures across DMP land.

But the only Denver Mountain Park in our area with a mountain trail of its own is little Upper Corwina Park near O'Fallon Park. But we like O'Fallon better, and unlike other guides that gave up on O'Fallon years ago, we'll keep showing off O'Fallon until somebody finds funding and volunteer work to restore it's trail system.

ROAD DIRECTIONS: Beginning at Morrison, west of Denver, take Hwy. 74 west. At mile 6.2, pass Lower Corwina Park, with picnic areas on both sides of highway. Only 0.8 miles later, find Upper Corwina Park on your left. O'Fallon Park is another quarter of a mile west, again on the left, only half a mile from Kittredge.

UPPER CORWINA PARK TRAIL, Denver Mountain Parks, 0.8 miles one way, elevation gain 300ft., rated moderate. Features forest trail to aspen meadow.

Like Lower Corwina Park downstream, Upper Corwina is generally considered a roadside picnic area with a trout stream (stocked by the Division of Wildlife with catchable size rainbows). Yet near the restrooms there is a trail leading up the draw. This straight-forward path climbs through a timbered ravine, steep at first, then more gentle, as it finds an open meadow with aspens. For those willing to pack their picnic, this is a good choice.

O'FALLON PARK, Denver Mountain Parks, trails destroyed, but features maze of logging roads amid beautiful forest.

Though other authors have dropped O'Fallon from their guidebook, we're stubborn about appealing for volunteers and funding to restore its trail system. We admire this lovely place, but you have to be careful there.

You see, years ago, foresters cut a lacework of logging roads to remove beetle-infested trees. The cure saved the forest, but destroyed the trails, making the area so confusing that we could never map it. Still, this is a charming and beautiful area, a flourishing habitat with great potential. Then a forest fire in March of 1991 damaged about 55 acres of this 860-acre park. Talk about tough luck!

We cannot recommend O'Fallon for the average family looking for a late afternoon adventure. This is for bushwhackers. Fortunately, the park is bounded by highway on the north and west and is not a vast wilderness (860 acres), but it is no place to go for a stroll late in the day or you might have trouble finding your way back before dark!

O'Fallon does have streamside picnic areas with shade trees, a trout stream stocked with rainbows, level areas for games, and a giant four-place stone barbecue that is often mistaken for a chimney ruin when seen from the highway.

AIKEN CANYON PRESERVE

Aiken Canyon Loop

Threatened in the 1980s by mining for that most strategic of all Front Range treasures—gravel—1900 acres of this living treasure is now protected by the Nature Conservancy. With new residential development literally knocking at the gate, this preservation came just in time, and the Nature Conservancy is to be commended.

Opened to the public in 1994, Aiken Canyon Preserve features high quality foothills ecosystems toured by a six-mile trail open to foot only. This is the first place in our area where I saw scat from both bear and mountain lion only a short distance apart on the same trail, a place where young golden eagles were calling to each other after leaving their nest in the canyon. The variety and density of species of all kinds, right down to the mushrooms, was something we had been told about, but still found surprisingly impressive.

The preserve is open for hiking only from dawn to dusk year round on Saturdays, Sundays and Mondays. **Pets are strictly banned to protect the wildlife. Please stay on the trail.**

ROAD DIRECTIONS: From I-25 drive south of Colorado Springs and take the South Academy exit. Go west on South Academy and take the final exit to go south on Highway 115 (which is Nevada in downtown Colorado Springs). Drive south on Highway 115 about 12.5 miles (not the 11 so often mentioned). Just past Wild Horse Road, turn right onto Turkey Canyon Ranch Road and find the trailhead parking on your right.

The trail leading into the canyon gives you no clue as to what awaits you higher up. Don't judge it by what you find early. Those who live along the foothills may think this lower area looks more like their own backyards, shrub and grasslands marked by Gambels oak, pinon pine, one-seeded juniper, mountain mahogany, sage, needle-grass and some cactus. Our familiarity hardly breeds appreciation of this type of habitat that is quickly disappearing to residential development, but to biologists and game managers, this ecosystem is both productive in terms of food and cover and strategic as a corridor linking the mountains to the plains. Through that corridor the wild things of the Beaver Creek Wilderness communicate with remote areas of Fort Carson.

Soon your trail splits. The left fork offers the best views, but that high route is also the steepest, so we'll leave that for our return. The right fork takes the low route along washes and meadows, making it the best ascent.

Pinon gives way to large ponderosa pines and white fir (which looks something like blue spruce, only softer and with longer, blunt needles). Yet since this particular canyon was never logged, nothing you see below will compare to the huge specimens higher up that are over 250 years old! The area abounds with wild turkey, jack rabbits, mule deer, badgers, bobcats, gray fox, tuft-eared and spruce squirrels. Their tracks can be found in the sandy washes and, of course, are everywhere after a snowfall.

Yet the area is most famed for its birds, some 75 species identified by ornithologist Charles Aiken, who lived in Turkey Creek Canyon. There are hairy and downy woodpeckers, three species of nuthatches and many raptors, including prairie falcons, northern harriers, Cooper's hawks, sharp-shinned hawks and golden eagles. Mexican spotted owls, listed as threatened by the U.S. Fish and Wildlife Service, are found in the nearby Beaver Creek Wilderness and have potential habitat here among the old-growth forest.

This loop is so simple and presents so little chance for getting lost that we are providing no map.

BEAVER CREEK WILDERNESS
Wilderness Loop Trail

The parking lot amid abandoned farmland gives you no clue about the wild mountains you are about to explore. You can see the clear-water stream that flows from the canyon in the distance, but the beauties of this place await those who lace up hiking boots or climb onto a horse. You have a long drink of scenery ahead. This is a very wild place.

Now officially a Wilderness Area, the usual rules apply: no bicycles or motorized vehicles allowed, pets must be under strict control (actually, you are encouraged to leave them at home), pack out all trash and always leave everything natural. This is a living museum. Of course, you may camp overnight using low-impact techniques and build campfires, except in times of high fire danger. Nevertheless, you are encouraged to use backpacker stoves instead of campfires for a number of reasons, including fire safety. But if you do build a fire, please keep it small in order to preserve the dead wood that is part of the ecosystem and always erase your fire ring. Do it right and there should nothing but some bent grass as evidence of your camp. This is a place to whisper and tread softly.

Beaver Creek Loop Trail, Bureau of Land Management, perhaps longer than the BLM's estimate of 7 miles, rated easy, then moderate, then downright difficult, then easy again as a balloon loop.

6,120	7 miles	6,120

ROAD DIRECTIONS: On Hwy 50 between Pueblo and Canon City, there is a sign on the north side of the road that simply says "Victor-Cripple Creek." This spot is about six miles east of Canon City or 4.2 miles west of the intersection of Hwy 115 from Colorado Springs. Turn north (left) on this road and go 1.7 miles, then turn right. Take the next left only 0.3 miles later and go 10 miles to find the gate of the State Wildlife Area. Go another 0.9 miles and find the parking lot for Beaver Creek Wilderness.

The first part of your trail is in a State Wildlife Area, but once you cross the field ahead and start up into the rocks, you'll pass a Carsonite sign mark-

ing the Wilderness Area boundary. The trail fork that you pass on your left is just a fisherman's shortcut down to the stream, but doesn't follow on.

Keep to the main trail above the stream. The Division of Wildlife no longer brags about Beaver as a fishery because a flash flood filled in many of its best holes with gravel and the stream may need years to recover. Still, it is wide and scenic, on its way to healing.

One of the first things you'll notice along here is the rocks. They shine and sparkle and glisten. It's as if my childhood rock collection from all over Colorado were dumped out along this trail. The Gneiss (pronounced nice) is very nice, indeed. And there is gleaming quartz and shiny flakes of mica so large and transparent that you would think someone had torn up cellophane along the way.

Near a cliff, your trail seems to fork three ways. The right one that goes up a draw is the way we'll come back. IT IS VERY IMPORTANT YOU DO THIS LOOP CLOCKWISE, as you'll see later. To your left, the low trail only goes to the river and the high one to the left is the stairway we need to the upper canyon.

The trail ahead has views of the canyon and creek, sometimes from on high, sometimes from beside the water. The most confusing place is on a high knoll practically bald except for candelabra cactus. Sugarloaf Mountain stands guard to your south. There is a fire ring there, and the high trail ahead should be somewhat blocked by some wood, but people keep moving it. We've also found the cairn there scattered. If you step over the wood and keep going on the high trail, you'll find that it goes around a corner and then fades and narrows and disappears way up high!

Go back to the cairn on the knoll and notice the easily-ignored trail in the brush that switchbacks steeply down to the water. Follow that and scramble down, using an iron spike in the granite near the water to climb down, then cross stepping stones beside the main creek. I found it quite a stretch.

This is the spot that makes rangers say that horses should not use this half of the loop. We did find tracks that showed that a horse had apparently made it, but I've never ridden a horse that good or a horse that I was that mad at. I mean, that horse literally jumped to the streambed with a rider! It's not for children, either.

Your main trail scales the canyon wall again and then descends a number of times. There are side trails that take campers to the water, but the terrain is simply too rugged to allow any trail to follow the stream very far. Signs would help.

We call one set of switchbacks the Floxin Follies because it was there that Dolores fell victim to a later-publicized reaction to a new antibiotic. Suddenly she couldn't see, got vertigo and couldn't stand up, and then she fell asleep in the rocks on the trail!

I couldn't carry her, so I had to wait it out. And growing curious about the confluence we were looking for, I strayed down to the water's edge, only to find the biggest mountain lion print I had ever seen in the snow there. We're not usually worried about mountain lions, but a lady asleep in the trail

Scrambling like this is why our Wilderness Loop is not recommended for horses or children.

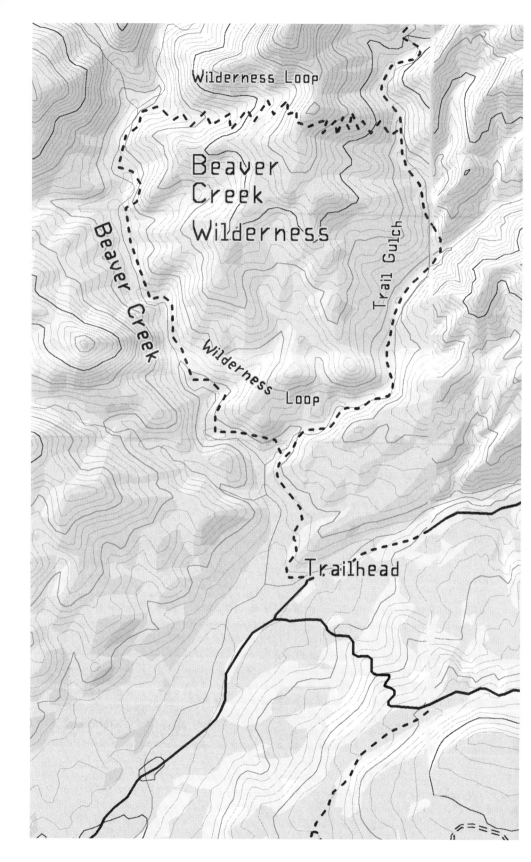

might make a very tempting meal, so I scurried back to Dolores and helped her wake up. That day we barely made it back to the car before nightfall.

This trail is so rugged that you tend to think the confluence of the two Beaver Creeks must be just around the corner, but it's a long, long way. The trick is a place marked by a cairn where the trail, now much fainter, leaves the stream and goes up a brushy hillside. From there it continues high before going down to the confluence area, which has dramatic views of rocks up both canyons. Watch for the iron stoveworks out on a promontory of rock. Now your trail starts east above a tributary and climbs through forest along an old utility route. You'll see pieces of old poles and big porcelain insulators.

There are some great views of the canyon behind you for awhile, but this trail is an unrelenting climb, growing fainter as you go. You top the ridge at 7,400 feet and immediately start down an even steeper trail on the other side. This route is so steep that we had trouble keeping our footing and landed on our bottoms several times, so make sure you have great boots and take a walking stick to help steady yourself. Tough going.

Penrose horseman Buck Ingram told us about one ride he took over this very steep section. It was such tough going that they had to stop every twenty yards to let the horses rest. They had an old dog with them who would flop in the shade of a bush every time they stopped, but the ground was so steep that when the old dog would try to relax, the action of his panting would start him scoot-scoot-scooting back down the mountain.

"We'd better hurry over this mountain, Buck," one of the riders said. "If we don't, that old dog's going to wind up making the trip twice!"

This side of the ridge is much drier and has far less scenery. You'll see more old utility poles and finally T-junction against a plain doubletrack in the valley beyond. A rock cairn marks the spot, but if you look around, you'll see how easy it would be to miss that turnoff, if you were going to do the loop the other way around. And since the main track continues up Trail Gulch for miles from here, you might not discover your mistake for a long time.

From here on down, the trail is gentle and plain, which makes Trail Gulch suitable for cross-country skiing, though its low altitude doesn't allow it to hold its snow very well. Horses also do best in Trail Gulch and keep it well trodden. In the sand of the doubletrack we saw a bear's footprint and scat from a bobcat.

You'll have little trouble finding the fork among the rocks where you return along the balloon's string to the trailhead parking area.

Note: Our one objection to the Wilderness system is the way trails fail to be measured before Wilderness designation, then become illegal to measure afterwards. Knowing how far you're going is a valuable safety consideration. Be careful out there. If I could help you more, I would.

Trails Guide 2001
ON CD-ROM
Colorado's High Tech Trailguide
Blows Away All Others—Paper or Disc!!!

Complete coverage of the entire Pike National Forest plus nearby Parks, Open Space and Wilderness Areas. Loaded with info on hundreds of trails and color photos.

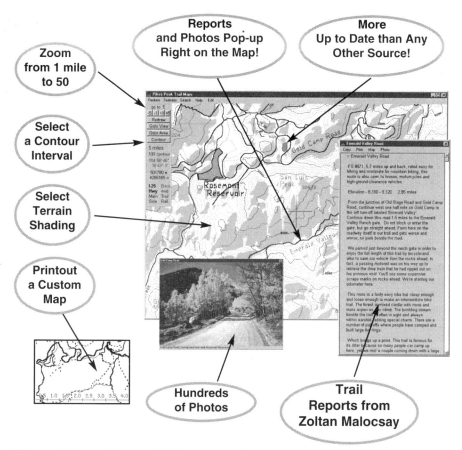

Reports and Photos Pop-up Right on the Map!

More Up to Date than Any Other Source!

Zoom from 1 mile to 50

Select a Contour Interval

Select Terrain Shading

Printout a Custom Map

Hundreds of Photos

Trail Reports from Zoltan Malocsay

From **Ghost Town Software** at Better Bookstores
Also visit our web site at **www.GhostTownSoftware.com**
for **free** trail info, photos and demos.